Feminism and Religion

Recent Titles in
Women's Psychology

Single Mother in Charge: How to Successfully Pursue Happiness
Sandy Chalkoun

Women and Mental Disorders, Four Volumes
Paula K. Lundberg-Love, Kevin L. Nadal, and Michele A. Paludi, Editors

Reproductive Justice: A Global Concern
Joan C. Chrisler, Editor

The Psychology of Love, Four Volumes
Michele A. Paludi, Editor

An Essential Handbook of Women's Sexuality, Two Volumes
Donna Castañeda, Editor

Psychological Health of Women of Color: Intersections, Challenges, and Opportunities
Lillian Comas-Díaz and Beverly Greene, Editors

Violence against Girls and Women: International Perspectives, Two Volumes
Janet A. Sigal and Florence L. Denmark, Editors

The Praeger Handbook on Women's Cancers: Personal and Psychosocial Insights
Michele A. Paludi, Editor

The Wrong Prescription for Women: How Medicine and Media Create a "Need" for Treatments, Drugs, and Surgery
Maureen C. McHugh and Joan C. Chrisler, Editors

Bullies in the Workplace: Seeing and Stopping Adults Who Abuse Their Co-Workers and Employees
Michele A. Paludi, Editor

Sexual Harassment in Education and Work Settings: Current Research and Best Practices for Prevention
Michele A. Paludi, Jennifer L. Martin, James E. Gruber, and Susan Fineran, Editors

Why Congress Needs Women: Bringing Sanity to the House and the Senate
Michele A. Paludi, Editor

Feminism and Religion

How Faiths View Women and Their Rights

Michele A. Paludi and
J. Harold Ellens, Editors

Women's Psychology
Michele A. Paludi, Series Editor

An Imprint of ABC-CLIO, LLC
Santa Barbara, California • Denver, Colorado

Library of Congress Cataloging-in-Publication Data

Names: Paludi, Michele Antoinette, editor.
Title: Feminism and religion : how faiths view women and their rights / Michele A. Paludi and J. Harold Ellens, editors.
Description: Santa Barbara : Praeger, 2016. | Series: Women's psychology | Includes index.
Identifiers: LCCN 2015043436 | ISBN 9781440838880 (hardcover: alk. paper) ISBN 978-1-4408-3889-7 (ebook)
Subjects: LCSH: Women and religion. | Women—Religious aspects. | Feminism—Religious aspects. | Women's rights—Religious aspects.
Classification: LCC BL458 .F4538 2016 | DDC 200.82—dc23
LC record available at http://lccn.loc.gov/2015043436

ISBN: 978-1-4408-3888-0
EISBN: 978-1-4408-3889-7

20 19 18 17 16 1 2 3 4 5

This book is also available on the World Wide Web as an eBook.
Visit www.abc-clio.com for details.

Praeger
An Imprint of ABC-CLIO, LLC

ABC-CLIO, LLC
130 Cremona Drive, P.O. Box 1911
Santa Barbara, California 93116-1911

This book is printed on acid-free paper ♾
Manufactured in the United States of America

Michele A. Paludi:

"To terrify children with the image of hell, to consider women an inferior creation—is that good for the world?"

—Christopher Hitchens

For Antoinette Peccichio Paludi and Michael Paludi, who taught me to think for myself and to value all people and treat them all with dignity and respect.

J. Harold Ellens:

To Brett Alexander Ellens-Hutchison, who I hope will grow up to honor and cherish women, and celebrate the fruits of such love.

Contents

Series Foreword xi
Michele A. Paludi

Foreword xv
J. Harold Ellens

Acknowledgments xvii

Introduction xix
Michele A. Paludi

PART I: VIEWS FROM THE BIBLE AND BUDDHISM TO THE QURAN AND TAOISM

1. Is Faith in the Bible and Feminism Compatible? 3
   Virginia Ingram

2. The Goddess-Worshipping Age: Feminist Egalitarianism in Prehistory and Early History 17
   Maija Jespersen

3. Feminist Perspectives from the Hebrew Bible 39
   Ilona Rashkow

4. The Church, Woman, Leadership, and the Body 59
   Silvia Geruza Fernandez Rodrigues

5. Feminism Re-frames Who Wrote Hebrew Scriptures: 10th-Century Tamar, the "Master" Storyteller 75
Adrien J. Bledstein

6. Women in the Holy Quran 95
Sayyed Mohsen Fatemi

7. Feminism in Hinduism: Female Deities and Their Influence on South Asian Culture 103
Divyaben Patel, Katherine Anne E. Scott, Paula K. Lundberg-Love, and Jeanine M. Galusha-Glasscock

8. Feminism in Buddhism 117
Linda Chiang

9. Femineity in the Gospel of John 129
Kamila Blessing

10. Feminism in the Eastern Orthodox Church 143
Maria Stoyadinova

11. The Mystical Feminine in Baha'i Scriptures 157
Paula A. Drewek

PART II: RELIGIOUS PHILOSOPHY IN FEMINISM AND FEMINIST ACTION

12. Martial Religion, Ravaging Warfare, and Rape: Polytheistic Greek and Monotheistic Israelite Views 173
Kathy L. Gaca

13. Judaism and Feminism 205
Ilona Rashkow

14. A Room Prepared: Women and the Mystic Experience 221
Anna Byrne

15. The Feminine Spiritual 235
Deborah Brock

16. Feminism and the Pro-Life/Pro-Choice Debate 249
Jennifer Elisa Veninga

17. Historical Resonances of the Feminine in the Brazilian Christian Religions 263
Patricia Nobre

18. Faith and Feminism: Resolving the Gender Issue through Mythology and Archetype 277
Deborah Brock

19. Feminist, Womanist, and *Mujerista* Theologies in Conversation 293
Suzanne M. Coyle

20. Confucianism and Feminism 303
Mary Wittbold

21. Men Are Not Yang and Women Are Not Yin: Gender Construction in the *Tao Te Ching* and the *I Ching* 321
Maija Jespersen

22. American Muslim Women and Faith-Inspired Activism 335
Asma Uddin and Firdaus Arastu

23. Special Women in the Holy Quran 359
Sayyed Mohsen Fatemi

24. Feminism and the Future of Religion 365
J. Harold Ellens

About the Editors and Contributors 371

Index 381

Series Foreword

Michele A. Paludi

Because women's work is never done and is underpaid or unpaid or boring or repetitious and we're the first to get fired and what we look like is more important than what we do and if we get raped it's our fault and if we get beaten we must have provoked it and if we raise our voices we're nagging bitches and if we enjoy sex we're nymphos and if we don't we're frigid and if we love women it's because we can't get a "real" man and if we ask our doctor too many questions we're neurotic and/or pushy and if we expect childcare we're selfish and if we stand up for our rights we're aggressive and "unfeminine" and if we don't we're typical weak females and if we want to get married we're out to trap a man and if we don't we're unnatural and because we still can't get an adequate safe contraceptive but men can walk on the moon and if we can't cope or don't want a pregnancy we're made to feel guilty about abortion and . . . for lots of other reasons we are part of the women's liberation movement.

Author unknown, quoted in The Torch, *September 14, 1987*

This sentiment underlies the major goals of Praeger's book series, "Women's Psychology":

1. Valuing women. The books in this series value women by valuing children and working for affordable child care; valuing women by respecting all physiques, not just placing value on slender women; valuing women by acknowledging older women's wisdom, beauty,

aging; valuing women who have been sexually victimized and viewing them as survivors; valuing women who work inside and outside of the home; and valuing women by respecting their choices of careers, of whom they mentor, of their reproductive rights, their spirituality and their sexuality.

2. Treating women as the norm. Thus the books in this series make up for women's issues typically being omitted, trivialized, or dismissed from other books on psychology.
3. Taking a non-Eurocentric view of women's experiences. The books in this series integrate the scholarship on race and ethnicity into women's psychology, thus providing a psychology of *all* women. Women typically have been described collectively, but we are diverse.
4. Facilitating connections between readers' experiences and psychological theories and empirical research. The books in this series offer readers opportunities to challenge their views about women, feminism, sexual victimization, gender role socialization, education, and equal rights. These texts thus encourage women readers to value themselves and others. The accounts of women's experiences as reflected through research and personal stories in the texts in this series have been included for readers to derive strength from the efforts of others who have worked for social change on the interpersonal, organizational, and societal levels.

A student in one of my courses on the psychology of women once stated:

> I learned so much about women. Women face many issues: discrimination, sexism, prejudices . . . by society. Women need to work together to change how society views us. I learned so much and talked about many of the issues brought up in class to my friends and family. My attitudes have changed toward a lot of things. I got to look at myself, my life, and what I see for the future. (Paludi, 2002)

It is my hope that readers of the books in this series also reflect on the topics and look at themselves, their own lives, and what they see for the future.

I am honored to have *Feminism and Religion: How Faiths View Women and Their Rights* included in this series on Women's Psychology. This book offers readers inspirational accounts of women and religion. All of the contributors to this book are deeply committed to ensuring women's equal rights in faiths. I am honored to have had the opportunity to work with them on this volume. A special note of appreciation to J. Harold Ellens, the co-editor of this volume, for his graciousness, caring style, and commitment to making women central, not marginal, in religions.

REFERENCE

Paludi, M. (2002). *The psychology of women.* 2nd ed. Upper Saddle River, NJ: Prentice Hall.

Foreword

J. Harold Ellens

Feminism has become a vital movement in American culture. It settled down earnestly to its task about 40 years ago. Since then it has developed in almost every possible direction, affording multiple new perspectives for every academic discipline. Feminist viewpoints have addressed and illuminated nearly every aspect of our society with critical and innovative insights. It has expanded our world of life and thought, as well as reforming our conscience and consciousness.

This has given rise to restiveness among some who have resisted it, holding on, as firmly as they have been able, to the values and traditions of Patriarchy. They have been wrong all along. There have been those, however, who readily adopted the values of the feminist project but felt that the rage and hostility of the first generation of feminists was unhelpful and even offensive. When the second generation of feminist thought began to show itself to be less angry and more thoughtful, it was welcomed though many males and females found it difficult to parse exactly how and why the language was all about power brokering. Many feminists seemed to promote the idea that for a woman to achieve her full potential it was necessary for her to become masculinized or at least to conduct herself in a manner that she was busy denigrating in a male. It is understandable that there was some considerable ambivalence in the way the second generation formulated its self-concept since no good role models for liberated women existed at that time.

The third generation of feminists in the American scholarly world, and in the society in general, seems to have brought with it a healthier and more wholistic sense of where it stands and how to function in the world. We are fortunate that the movement has continued to mature. The leaders who have brought about this salutary growth in the American society and its values system were preceded, of course, by heroic women, and men, in the long and suffering generations of womanist champions throughout history but particularly since the early nineteenth century in America and abroad.

This is not the place to develop a history of feminism but rather to introduce this surprisingly informative book, celebrating nearly thirty generative and original new views on feminism in America and, indeed, worldwide. This volume presents cross-cultural studies, interfaith reports, international assessments, and multidisciplinary perspectives. Never before has such an endeavor by so esteemed a cadre of scholars reached the marketplace of ideas in quite this ideal form.

Professors, students, and lay readers who borrow books at municipal and academic libraries or buy them at their favorite book stores are going to be very glad to encounter this extraordinary work.

Acknowledgments

Michele A. Paludi

I thank Debbie Carvalko for encouraging me to edit this volume and others that have as their main goal to bring women and women's experiences to the forefront.

I also thank my sisters, Rosalie and Lucille, for their support.

And to Rev. John Provost and Rev. Rafael Wanjohi for willingness to share conversation and meals with a feminist.

J. Harold Ellens

I thank Mary Wittbold, whose physical and spiritual support makes it possible for me to continue this work, and Frank Shiflett, who keeps my computer from eating everything I create.

Introduction

Michele A. Paludi

> Man enjoys the great advantage of having a god endorse the code he writes; and since man exercises a sovereign authority over women it is especially fortunate that this authority has been vested in him by the Supreme Being. For the Jews, Mohammedans and Christians among others, man is master by divine right; the fear of God will therefore repress any impulse towards revolt in the downtrodden female.
>
> Simone de Beauvoir

> The study of women in world religions radically alters our understanding of religion: not only our understanding of who participates in religion, but also our understanding of what constitutes religious actions and how we read religious texts.
>
> Serinity Young

RELIGION: THE "BIGGEST PROBLEM" FACING FEMINISM TODAY?

Speaking at the Makers Conference in February 2014, Gloria Steinem stated that religion is the "biggest problem" facing feminism today. According to Steinem: "What we don't talk about enough is religion. I think that spirituality is one thing. But religion is just politics in the sky. I think we really have to talk about it. Because it gains power from silence" (quoted in Calloway-Hanauer, 2014).

Steinem's assertion that religion "gains power from silence" suggests we openly address sexism in religion's treatment of women. In the name of religion women have been generally looked upon as the "other" or as second-class participants in religious ritual. For example, the creation story describes God creating man "in His own image." God then made Eve from Adam's rib. Women are thus viewed as being made from men and secondary in relation to men (Doyle & Paludi, 1998). Individuals have used this version of the creation story to justify the idea of a husband's dominance over his wife (Sapp, 1977). Eve is also portrayed as evil; she succumbs to temptation and guides Adam into sin. Eve is described as being primarily responsible for women's as well as men's expulsion from paradise. God curses Eve because of her act and foretells her sufferings and her subjugation to man: "Unto the woman he said, I will greatly multiply thy sorrow and thy conception; in sorrow thou shalt bring forth children; and thy desire shall be to thy husband, and he shall rule over thee" (Gen. 3:16).

Other examples of ways religion has been anti-woman include:

> Woman does not possess the image of God in herself but only when taken together with the male who is her head, so that the whole substance is one image. But when she is assigned the role as helpmate, a function that pertains to her alone, then she is not the image of God. But as far as the man is concerned, he is by himself alone the image of God just as fully and completely as when he and the woman are joined together into one. (Saint Augustine, Bishop of Hippo Regius, 354–430)

> Woman is a misbegotten man and has a faulty and defective nature in comparison to his. Therefore she is unsure in herself. What she cannot get, she seeks to obtain through lying and diabolical deceptions. And so, to put it briefly, one must be on one's guard with every woman, as if she were a poisonous snake and the horned devil. . . .Thus in evil and perverse doings woman is cleverer, that is, slyer, than man. Her feelings drive woman toward every evil, just as reason impels man toward all good. (Saint Albertus Magnus, Dominican theologian, 13th century)

> The Holiness of God is not evidenced in women when they are brash, brassy, boisterous, brazen, head-strong, strong-willed, loud-mouthed, overly-talkative, having to have the last word, challenging, controlling, manipulative, critical, conceited, arrogant, aggressive, assertive, strident, interruptive, undisciplined, insubordinate, disruptive, dominating, domineering, or clamoring for power. Rather, women accept God's holy order and character by being humbly and unobtrusively respectful and receptive in functional subordination to God, church leadership, and husbands. (James Fowler, *Women in the Church,* 1999)

> Blessed art Thou, O Lord our God, King of the Universe, that I was not born a woman. (Traditional Jewish prayer for men)

Furthermore, in traditional Chinese religious beliefs, the yin and yang are bipolar opposites: the yin (feminine) is believed to represent evil, ignorance, and darkness. The yang, however, which represents the masculine, is believed to represent goodness, intellect, and light (Pauwels, 1998). In Hinduism, women are defined in terms of their husbands. Thus, women who are not married or are widows do not have personal identities (Siegel, Choldin, & Orost, 1995). Buddhist monks believed women's bodies are evil, lustful, and greedy. Consequently, women cannot become spiritually realized. The following passage from "The Tale of King Udayana of Valsa" describes Buddhists' views toward women:

> Women can be the cause of great suffering.
> If desire is destroyed, there will be everlasting happiness.
> The dead snake and dog are detestable.
> But women are even more detestable than they are.

Religions advocate both a status quo view of gender roles and provide support for society's patriarchal views of gender differences, consequently endorsing gender discrimination (Zwissler, 2012). For example, while the Sri Lankan government provides male monks with housing, health care, food, and education, it provides no such assistance and opportunities to women monks, who are expected to meditate, serve as housekeepers to male monks, and sacrifice. In Saudi Arabia in 2012, a woman was beaten by her husband; she required hospitalization. His sentence was to memorize sections of the Quran and quotes from Muhammad. In 2009, a judge in Saudi Arabia ruled that a husband beating a woman is justifiable if she spent too much money on clothing.

Religion has been used to justify marrying young girls to older men who rape them. The Yogi Vasistha states: "For fear of commencement of puberty let the father give his daughter in marriage while she is still going about naked. For if she remains at home after the marriageable age sin falls upon the father." There are approximately 24 million child brides in India. Many girls are married off before the age of twelve. Girls are raped by their husbands, and many of the girls die during pregnancy because of their bodies not being physically mature to sustain a pregnancy. Dowry disputes result in in-laws murdering the young girls. The Baudhayana states: "The girls should be given while she is still immature; even from an unworthy man she should not be withheld if she has attained womanhood." And, according to the Angirasmriti, there is "no atonement" for men who have sex with a girl who began menstruating before marriage. Some texts indicate that the girl's father and husband will "fall into hell" if she is married after menarche and that their forefathers will be reincarnated as insects.

Empirical research in the social sciences has noted that religious denominations that are more traditional in their theological teachings are more likely to discriminate against women's successes in education and the workplace and at the same time support traditional roles for women (Rhodes, 1983). This theme is seen throughout the research on the psychology of women, notably gender biases in language, gender biases in how media portrays women—especially feminist women—and gender biases in psychologists' definition of a mentally healthy adult (see Kite, Deaux, & Haines, 2008). The male is perceived as normative; the female is a deviation from the norm.

CLINTON, WOODHULL, JOHNSON, AND WALLSTRÖM: TALKING ABOUT RELIGION AND BREAKING SILENCE ABOUT THE SUBJUGATION OF WOMEN

> I decided it's better to scream. Silence is the real crime against humanity.
>
> Nadezhda Mandelstam

Religion is currently being used in discussions about Hillary Clinton's presidency for the United States. For example, in a speech Clinton gave in April 2015, she noted:

> Far too many women are still denied critical access to reproductive health care and safe childbirth. All the laws we've passed don't count for much if they're not enforced. . . . Rights have to exist in practice—not just on paper. Laws have to be backed up with resources and political will. And deep-seated cultural codes, religious beliefs, and structural biases have to be changed.

Breaking silence by speaking out against the subjugation of women carries with it great risk, however. Clinton has been "condemned" by David Ripley from Idaho Chooses Life. According to Ripley:

> We have known for some time that abortion would be Hillary's primary campaign message. . . . What made this particular speech unique was Hillary's bold declaration that God needed to get His act together on this whole abortion thing. It was past time to update the Ten Commandments. . . . Now, of course, most of those "religious beliefs" are based upon clear teachings within Scripture that teach us to hold children precious, to sacrifice ourselves for others—and, above all, not to kill the innocent. What Clinton and her comrades on

> the Left do not seem to understand is that our religious beliefs are not a matter of personal opinion, but, rather, one of submission to our Creator . . . Clinton is not the first self-proclaimed leader to shake a fist at the Almighty. One can presume that He is not particularly impressed; though His heart is undoubtedly grieved. . . . And we can all be grieved that a person of such arrogance stands a chance of becoming president over this great nation.

Religion is used against Clinton as a fear tactic to divert votes from her. It is used to denigrate her. Paludi (in production) noted that this modern-day criticism of women politicians is reminiscent of what Victoria Woodhull experienced in 1872. She was the first woman candidate for the United States presidency. She campaigned on a platform that included women's suffrage, nationalization of railroads, an eight-hour workday, abolition of the death penalty, and welfare for the poor (Greenspan, 2013). On election day, the local newspaper published an article authored by Woodhull in which she criticized Henry Ward Beecher. She received backlash and was arrested for sending obscene material in the mail. She had stated that Beecher was an adulterer. She also had stated that a Wall Street trader seduced adolescent girls after giving them alcohol. Woodhull was arrested and spent election day in jail. She was eventually found to be not guilty. However, she endured severe criticism in the press for speaking out against violence against women and women's rights in general. Harriet Beecher Stowe referred to Woodhull as a "vile jailbird and impudent witch" (reported in Greenspan, 2013, p. 2). She was depicted in cartoons by Thomas Nast as "Mrs. Satan" (reported in Greenspan, 2013, p. 2).

Fast forward to August 2015, when the first Republican debate for candidates for Presidency in 2016 was held. Women's issues were again relegated to the bottom of concerns for the candidates. Chapin (2015) expressed her concern over the theme of the debate with respect to women:

> . . . all the Republican candidates were running to be president of the Republic of Gilead, with Carly Fiorina in the role of Aunt Lydia. For those unfamiliar with the reference, the Republic of Gilead is a dystopian future U.S., as envisioned by writer Margaret Atwood in her book *The Handmaid's Tale*. Society is strictly segregated by class and gender roles, and social status is assigned by fertility and sexual productivity. "Aunts" collaborate in the oppression of other women. Abortion is banned, women are chattel and men are in charge.
>
> Which is pretty much how the Republican candidates on stage see American women and reproductive rights. Florida Sen. Marco Rubio had to actually correct himself to say he opposed a rape and incest exception for abortion. Because now, in the Republican Party, forcing

> sexual assault victims to carry a resulting pregnancy to term is standard. (p. 1)

One of the Republican candidates at this first debate, Donald Trump, was asked by reporter Megyn Kelly about derogatory comments he has made toward women. In response to Ms. Kelly's question, Mr. Trump referred to her as a "bimbo." He also stated, "You could see there was blood coming out of her eyes, blood coming out of her—wherever" (Campbell, 2015, p. 1). This statement has been interpreted as being a sexist reference to Ms. Kelly menstruating. Ms. Kelly subsequently received death threats by supporters of Mr. Trump. His views on women were further addressed in an interview about abortion (see Santoro, 2011, p. 1):

> Guthrie: "Is there a right to privacy in the Constitution?"
> Trump: "I guess there is, I guess there is. And why, just out of curiosity, why do you ask that question?"
>
> When pressed to explain how his position on the right to privacy "squares" with his anti-abortion position, Trump responded: "Well, that's a pretty strange way of getting to pro-life. I mean, it's a very unique way of asking about pro-life. What does that have to do with privacy? How are you equating pro-life with privacy?"
>
> Guthrie asked, "Well, you know about the *Roe v. Wade* decision?" Trump responded, "Yes, right, sure. Look, I am pro-life. I've said it. I'm very strong there."

Pro-life? Obviously these examples suggest not pro-women's lives.

Sonia Johnson also broke silence by addressing sexism in religion as well. She openly supported the Equal Rights Amendment in 1977. Johnson was a Mormon. In 1979, Johnson delivered a speech at the annual conference of the American Psychological Association entitled "Patriarchal Panic: Sexual Politics in the Mormon Church." In her presentation, Johnson denounced the lobbying efforts in which the Church of the Latter Day Saints was engaging to prevent the passage of the Equal Rights Amendment. According to Johnson:

> I receive phone calls and letters from Mormon women all over the country and each has a story or two to tell: how two Mormon women in one meeting independently stood and spoke of their Mother in Heaven, how they met afterwards and wept together in joy at having found and named Her; how a courageous Mormon woman is preparing to make the first public demand for priesthood. The time has come . . . for women to insist upon full religious enfranchisement. This statement is the Mormon woman's equivalent of the shot heard around the world! Our patriarchy may be The Last Unmitigated but

> is no longer unchallenged. A multitude of Mormon women are through asking permission. We are waking up and growing up and in our waking and growing can be heard distinctly the death rattle of the patriarchy.

Sonia Johnson's speech led the Mormon Church to excommunicate her. During her "trial," Johnson was accused of having "publicly taught that the Church is dedicated to imposing the Prophet's moral directives upon all Americans; when it is the doctrine of the Church that all people are free to choose for themselves those moral directives dictated by their own consciences" (Benson, 2005).

In March 2015, Sweden's foreign minister, Margot Wallström, denounced the way Saudi Arabia subjugates women. Wallström was referring to how women cannot travel, cannot conduct official business, or marry without men's permission. She also referred to the practice of young girls marrying old men who rape them. As Cohen (2015) noted, Wallström was "telling no more than the truth." She has been experiencing a backlash, however, for discussing misogynist behavior. Cohen (2015) agrees with Steinem when he stated:

> . . . the rights of women always come last. To be sure, there are Twitter storms about sexist men and media feeding frenzies whenever a public figure uses "inappropriate language." But when a politician tries to campaign for the rights of women suffering under a brutally misogynistic clerical culture she isn't cheered on but met with an embarrassed and hugely revealing silence. (p. 3)

CHRIST'S TEACHINGS VS. ORGANIZATION OF RELIGIONS

In 2014, President Jimmy Carter published his book, *A Call to Action: Women, Religion, Violence, and Power.* President Carter discusses that his decision to leave the Southern Baptist Convention was a direct result of their 2012 vote that women must be subservient to their husbands, a ruling he states is contradictory to his commitment to gender equality. President Carter is still a Baptist and attends a Baptist church where his wife is a Deacon and a woman serves as Pastor.

As President Carter discusses, Jesus brought forth an entirely different view of women, one which caused great consternation among the Pharisees and also his disciples. A passage that illustrates Jesus's view of women involves Mary and Martha.

> In the course of their journey he came to a village, and a woman named Martha welcomed him into her house. She had a sister called Mary, who sat down at the Lord's feet and listened to him speaking.

> Now Martha who was distracted with all the serving said, "Lord, do you not care that my sister is leaving me to do the serving all by myself? Please tell her to help me." But the Lord answered: "Martha, Martha," he said, "you worry and fret about so many things, and yet few are needed, indeed only one. It is Mary who has chosen the better part; it is not to be taken from her." (Luke 10:38–42)

In this passage Jesus established a view of women unacceptable in Jewish society. Swidler (1971) actually referred to Jesus as the first feminist. Jesus viewed women as equal to men in terms of learning and education. He asked women to learn the message of the New Gospel and share it just as he commanded of men. According to Parvey (1974):

> The inclusion of this story about Jesus, unique to Luke's gospel, is the keystone of the changed status of women that it reflects. While previously the learning of Scriptures was limited to men, now it is opened to women. The story of Mary and Martha enabled women to choose. Mary departed from her ascribed role and was commended by Jesus for so doing. This meant that other women were encouraged to choose this new alternative: to be allowed, as were the young men, to learn the Scriptures at the feet of a rabbi. (p. 141)

Despite the fact Jesus was egalitarian in his treatment of women and men, this perspective was not shared by his disciples. The Christian church fell into a misogynous pattern. Many religious scholars have cited the teachings of St. Paul as contributing to the anti-woman approach taken by Christianity (Parvey, 1974). While St. Paul was preaching in Corinth he found that women were acting in ways that went against Jewish tradition and thus causing some rift in the congregation. To admonish these women, he wrote:

> As in all of the churches of the saints, the women should keep silence in the churches. For they are not permitted to speak, but should be subordinate, as even the law says. (1 Cor. 14:34–35)

St. Paul also asserted that man "is the image and glory of God; the woman is the glory of the man" (1 Cor. 11:7).

The masculine bias that exists in religious scholarship has omitted women from religion despite the fact that women have played prominent roles in the founding and practicing of religions (Doyle & Paludi, 1998, p. 209). Setta (1989) and Carroll (1992) noted that women have been attracted to "Mary cults." According to Setta (1989, p. 86):

> Women were allowed full participation in such cults and worshipped Mary as God. Mary cults, such as the Marinites and Collyridians, began as early as the second century and continue . . . In part, they developed in response to the absence of the feminine and female in the expression of Christianity.

Several women are mentioned in the Acts of the Apostles (e.g., Acts 13:50, 17:4). For example, Tabitha is believed to have been a disciple (Parvey, 1974). In the scriptures she is introduced as "a certain disciple named Tabitha, which by interpretation is called Dorcus" (9:36). She has been described as a model to the community; as someone who dedicated her time to producing garments for poor individuals. When she died, her body was laid out in an "upper chamber." This is significant since the "upper chamber" was the scene of the Last Supper; a quiet place that is believed to promote contact with God. Tabitha was raised from the dead by Peter, the first miracle performed by an apostle of Jesus. According to Parvey (1974):

> To be recorded by a fellow disciple, she must have been considered indispensable to the congregation. Her exact status remains unknown but that she was much more than merely one of the many followers is clear from the story about her. (p. 145)

FEMINISM AS "LIFE RAFT"

> I think feminism is about the spirit.
>
> Jane Fonda

> Listen to your heart.
> Listen to your instincts.
> Listen to inner voice.
> It is your true self.
> It will guide you to make the right choices.
>
> Lailah Gifty Akita

Our Inner Lives, a project of feminist.com, recently had a question submitted to them by Amilynn:

> My name is Amilynn and I am 16 years old. I have just recently discovered the concept of feminism although I now realize it has been present, but taken for granted, in my everyday life. I have read bits and pieces of feminist literature and feel as if I am starting to understand feminism and it excites me. . . . I do, however, have a question

> that has prevented me from moving forward with a feminist mentality. I have been raised in a very loving Christian home. My parents have instilled in me since birth a very strong sense of morals and belief in God and Jesus Christ. My issue is that Christianity is a very paternalistic religion, and emphasizes the power of the male gender. In the Bible it states that men are to be spiritual leaders over women, and that women should submit to their husbands. Also God is obviously portrayed as being a male, and no females have made as great of an impact as any male has in the Bible. . . . I do not want to submit to any man. I want to live my life to fulfill my passions and goals, and not to have to compromise any of that for men. But I also do not want to have to choose between my beliefs and feminism. Is there a way I can incorporate one into another? I do not know how to deal with the clashing of two belief systems.

Amilynn's question has been asked by many feminists who hold strong religious beliefs. There is no easy answer to this question; however, I believe we have an obligation to address the issue for the next generation of feminists. And that is why I wanted to co-edit this volume on feminism and religion. Contributors to this text share WATER's commitment to religious and spiritual practices related to feminism. WATER is the Women's Alliance for Theology, Ethics, and Ritual. This organization was founded by Mary Hunt and Diann Neu in 1983. The programs offered by WATER include spiritual counseling, teleconferences on spirituality, and resources for religious scholars. Hunt informed *Ms. Magazine* about WATER's goals (see Dove-Viebahn, 2012):

> Our common goal is to empower women to make choices about and contributions to their own spirituality as they engage in justice work. . . . Both feminism and spirituality focus on important quality of life issues . . .While postmodernity is well on the way to jettisoning patriarchal religions (albeit not fast enough), there is still a widespread hunger for spiritual nourishment, for making sense of the world's complexities. Religions do that, not by their dogmas or doctrines, but by the mere fact of connecting people who want to ask questions together and try out various answers. (Dove-Viebahn, 2012, p. 1)

It is my hope that this book will serve as a "life raft" (Klonis, Endo, Crosby, & Worell, 1997) for women and men who do not want to choose between their faith and feminism. This volume breaks the silence surrounding religion and women. We don't have to choose. And, we can value a diversity of forms of religious expressions, including spirituality in ourselves and in others. To me, that is truly feminist.

REFERENCES

Benson, S. (2005). The Sonia Johnson speech that blew the lid off Mormon Maledumb's secretly organized and dishonest efforts to defeat the Equal Rights Amendment. Retrieved on August 28, 2015, from http://www.exmormon.org/mormon/mormon415.htm

Calloway-Hanauer, J. (2014). Is religion the 'biggest problem' facing feminism today? Retrieved on August 26, 2015, from https://sojo.net/articles/religion-biggest-problem-facing-feminism-today.

Campbell, C. (2015). Donald Trump launches new scathing attack against Megyn Kelly, shares another 'bimbo' insult against her. Retrieved on August 27, 2015, from www.businessinsider.com/donald-trump-goes-after-megyn-kelly-again-2015-8

Carroll, M. (1992). *The cult of the Virgin Mary.* Princeton, NJ: Princeton University Press.

Carter, J. (2014). *A call to action: Women, religion, violence, and power*. New York: Simon & Schuster.

Chapin, L. (2015). Sexist smorgasbord. Retrieved on August 27, 2015, from http://www.usnews.com/opinion/blogs/laura-chapin/2015/08/07/the-gop-debates-sexist-stand-against-womens-rights

Cohen, N. (2015). Sweden's feminist foreign minister has dared to tell the truth about Saudi Arabia. What happens now concerns us all. Retrieved on August 20, 2015, from www.spectator.co.uk/features/9481542/swedens-feminist-foreign-minister-has-dared-to-tell-the-truth-about-saudi-arabia-what-happens-now-concerns-us-all/

Dove-Viebahn, A. (2012). Future of feminism: Shaping feminist spirituality. Retrieved on August 25, 2015, from http://msmagazine.com/blog/2012/03/25/future-of-feminism-shaping-feminist-spirituality/

Doyle, J. & Paludi, M. (1998). *Sex and gender: The human experience.* New York: McGraw-Hill.

Ertelt, S. (2015). Hillary Clinton pushes abortion in first speech as candidate: Too many women "denied" abortions. Retrieved on August 28, 2015, from http://www.lifenews.com/2015/04/24/hillary-clinton-pushes-abortion-in-first-speech-as-candidate-too-many-women-denied-abortion/

Ertelt, S. (2015). Hillary Clinton: Force Christians to change their religious views to support abortion. Retrieved on August 28, 2015, from http://www.lifenews.com/2015/04/27/hillary-clinton-force-christians-to-change-their-religious-views-to-support-abortion/

Fowler, J. (1999). Women in the church. Retrieved on November 25, 2015, from http://www.christinyou.net/pages/womeninchurch.html

Greenspan, J. (2013). 9 things you should know about Victoria Woodhull. Retrieved on May 10, 2015, from http://www.history.com/news/9-things-you-should-know-about-victoria-woodhull

Kite, M., Deaux, K., & Haines, E. (2008). Gender stereotypes. In F. Denmark & M. Paludi (Eds.), *Psychology of women: A handbook of issues and theories* (pp. 205–236). Santa Barbara, CA: Praeger.

Klonis, S., Endo, J., Crosby, F., & Worell, J. (1997). Feminism as life raft. *Psychology of Women Quarterly, 21,* 333–345.

Our Inner Lives (2015). *Blog.* Retrieved on August 20, 2015, from http://www.feminist.com/ourinnerlives/

Paludi, M. (Ed.). (in production). *Why congress needs more women.* Santa Barbara, CA: Praeger.

Parvey, C. (1974). The theology and leadership of women in the New Testament. In R. Ruether (Ed.), *Religion and sexism.* New York: Simon & Schuster.

Pauwels, A. (1998). *Women changing language.* New York: Longman.

Rhodes, A. (1983). Effects of religious domination on sex differences in occupational expectations. *Sex Roles, 9,* 93–108.

Santoro, E. (2011). Pro-lifers: Donald Trump doesn't understand how pro-life works. Retrieved on August 27, 2015, from http://talkingpointsmemo.com/dc/pro-lifers-donald-trump-doesn-t-understand-how-pro-life-works-video.

Sapp, S. (1977). *Sexuality, the Bible, and science.* Philadelphia: Fortress Press.

Setta, S. (1989). Empowering women from the sanctuary to the cosmos: Reflections on the nature of gender. In D. Kaufman (Ed.), *Public/private spheres: Women past and present.* Boston: Northeastern Custom Book Program.

Siegel, R., Choldin, S., & Orost, J. (1995). The impact of three patriarchal religions on women. In J. Chrisler & A. Hemstreet (Eds.), *Variations on a theme: Diversity and the psychology of women* (pp. 107–144). Albany, New York: State University of New York Press.

Swidler, L. (1971). Jesus was a feminist. *Catholic World, 212,* 177–183.

Zwissler, L. (2012). Feminism and religion: Intersections between western activism, theology, and theory. *Religion Compass, 6,* 354–368.

Part I

Views from the Bible and Buddhism to the Quran and Taoism

Chapter 1

Is Faith in the Bible and Feminism Compatible?

Virginia Ingram

Feminist biblical criticism is now considered to be a standard method of biblical exegesis. Few theology students make their way through theology degrees without encountering some form of feminist theory. Similarly, books on feminism and the Bible are read by people in the broader community. Most of these resources acknowledge the danger of the patriarchal historical context of the Bible. They also recognize that the Bible is an essential artifact, as it preserves the message of grace.

In order to deal with this tension, scholars have suggested that we "re-read" the Bible, subvert patriarchy where it appears, and hold the Bible up to psychological analysis. These approaches to patriarchy in the Bible are certainly necessary. However, are they enough in light of research which suggests that stereotype priming takes place beyond our awareness and out of our control?

This chapter will explain the threat of stereotype priming as it occurs in implicit associative memory and self-concept. New research suggests that feminism and faith in the Bible are compatible at a conscious level, but may not be when we speak of the unconscious mind. The intention of this chapter, therefore, is to unravel this proposition in order to determine whether or not faith in the Bible is compatible with feminism. In order to do so, research concerning subliminal stereotype priming will be discussed alongside popular methods of feminist biblical criticism. Although this discussion does not offer a clear solution to the problem, the findings of this research do challenge the immutable nature of the canon of the Bible and the lectionary.

Before discussing research in neuropsychology and how it applies to the problem of feminism and the Bible, it is necessary to briefly outline the historical position of the Bible and feminism. Nowhere is this more clearly expressed than in the words of Elizabeth Cady Stanton. Stanton was a leader in the suffragette movement. She believed that the progress of the suffragettes was being stymied by reference to the Bible. She sought to redress this by contributing to and editing *The Women's Bible. The Women's Bible* is a collection of biblical commentaries by educated women who strived to challenge biblical passages that are typically patriarchal. Stanton, a woman ahead of her time, lost her status in the movement because of this project, which was perceived to be too radical. However, the concrete problems of patriarchy in the Bible were understood by Stanton. She recognized that the Bible was not only a religious-cultural document, but that it also created culture. The culture she was familiar with was created from a divinely prescribed patriarchy, and all of its institutions were fashioned around this idea.

> The canon and civil law; church and state; priests and legislators; all political parties and religious denominations have alike taught that woman was made after man, of man, and for man, an inferior being, and subject to man. Creeds, codes, Scriptures and statutes, are all built on this idea. The fashions, forms, ceremonies and customs of society, church ordinances and discipline all grow out of this idea. (Stanton, 2003)

If this was not bad enough, women had little chance of breaking free from these oppressive structures because the instrument of oppression (patriarchy as it is expressed in the Bible) also became the mode of appeal. "When, in the early part of the Nineteenth Century, women began to protest against civil and political degradation, they were referred to the Bible for an answer. When they protested against their unequal position in the church, they were referred to the Bible for an answer" (Stanton, 2003). Church synods still suffer from this circular mode of authority.

In retrospect, we might say that Stanton's ideas were not so outrageous and that her position was moderate. Stanton (2003) argued that there are important values in the Bible, particularly the golden rule, which she credited as having had as much of an impact on the world as patriarchal ideas have. Stanton also acknowledged the aesthetic appeal of the Bible and the narratives which speak of the higher nature of individuals of both genders. Therefore, Stanton had the same partial acceptance of the Bible that is popular with feminist, liberal, or progressive scholars today. "The Bible cannot be accepted or rejected as a whole, its teachings are varied and its lessons differ widely from each other" (Stanton, 2003).

If we move forward a century, however, we discover that it is more difficult to hold this conflicted view of the Bible with credibility. We now know stereotypes are created unconsciously through associations that are beyond our awareness and control. At this implicit level, associations are drawn from external stimuli. Quite simply, the stronger associations override the weaker associations. The strong associations then influence behavior (Fine, 2010). Implicit associations in the Bible are therefore threatening to feminism, as the social ordering in the Bible, which becomes the stronger association, is patriarchal. For instance, the Bible expresses the idea that women are secondary to men, and the message of grace is spoken through the authority of men. In order to discuss the threat of subliminal priming to feminism further, it is necessary to explain the workings of associative memory.

Associative memory is a type of learning that draws from the environment unconsciously. Implicit associative learning is important as it is an efficient way to learn about the world around us without the distraction of conscious reflection and discrimination. For instance, most people can eat without the need to consciously go through all of the steps which are involved to do so. The drawback of associative memory is that it is indiscriminate with the information that it takes in.

However, although associative memory is indiscriminate in the type of material it receives, it always favors the greater influence. It is, therefore, reasonable to assume that associative memory draws its associations from cultural patterns in society and the media. These associations are reinforced beyond conscious filtering. Of particular interest to feminist biblical scholars is Cordelia Fine's remark, "What this means is that if you are a liberal, politically correct sort of a person, then chances are you won't like your implicit mind's attitudes" (Fine, 2010). By extension of this, it may be posited that a woman may be a conscious feminist but unconsciously reinforce the idea of a woman's subjugation to a man.

Before discussing the workings of associative memory any further, it will be profitable to discuss some of the methods of biblical criticism which provide a counter-narrative to patriarchy. In doing so, it is important to evaluate whether or not these methods can produce a greater influence than that of patriarchal domination, as associative learning assumes the greater influence.

Phyllis Trible echoed Stanton's sentiment that the Bible cannot be wholly accepted or wholly rejected when she wrote, "Yet I myself perceive neither war nor neutrality between biblical faith and Women's Liberation" (Trible, 1973). In league with this statement, Trible (1973) calls upon people to re-read the Bible instead of insisting that the Bible be rewritten. In doing so, Trible suggests that the reader focus attention on passages that disavow sexism. For example, although it can reasonably be assumed that the book of Hosea was written by a man, Yahweh is portrayed in the image of a woman (Hosea 11:1–11).

However, the passages in the Bible that disavow sexism are limited and the greater association is with patriarchal domination. Therefore, it might be argued that this suggestion would have little bearing on the average worshipper as far as associative implicit learning is concerned. It may, however, be greatly influential to a person who only reads passages that speak of God in feminine terms, as this would become the greater influence, or to people like Trible who have a strong association with feminism.

A feminist lens allows Trible (1973) to view the Exodus as setting the trajectory for feminism, as Exodus emphasizes the theme of freedom from oppression from slavery. However, this association requires the kind of reflection and complex thought which is unknown in implicit associative learning. Associative memory may take in the explicit message of freedom from slavery but it will not make the leap to feminism.

Another counter-narrative Trible puts forth is the idea of the corporate personality. The corporate personality is a single unit made up of individuals. As far as the corporate personality is concerned, we all bear the burdens of our fellow humans. Trible writes, "To the extent that women are enslaved, so too men are enslaved. The oppression of one individual or one group is the oppression of all individuals and all groups. Solidarity marks the sexes. In sexism we all die, victim or victor. In liberation we all live equally as human beings" (Trible, 1973). As stated above, this message will only register in the associative implicit memory if it is stated explicitly and is the stronger message. This may be the case when Paul talks of Christians as one body (1 Cor. 12:12–27), and may have indeed made its way into Christian culture as a dominant motif. However, this message is contained in a historical-cultural context which supports patriarchy, the antithesis of feminism.

As far as associative implicit memory is concerned, it would be better if the Bible was rewritten, as the greater influence is already embedded in society and thereby doubles back on itself to reinforce the patriarchal themes of the Bible. To re-read patriarchy out of the Bible is helpful at a rational level; however, it is less profitable where associative implicit memory is concerned, as the Bible was written in patriarchal times and the unconscious mind registers this without reflection.

Yet, the growth in feminist biblical criticism indicates that patriarchy, which is the greater influence of implicit memory, may at some stage be rivalled by feminist critiques. Just as Trible's exegesis "depatriarchalizes" the Bible at a rational level, so too Cheryl Exum "subverts" androcentric passages in the Bible. This she achieves by focusing on the deconstructive method of feminist biblical criticism and psychoanalytic literary theory. Exum subverts male accounts of the stories of women in the Bible and gives women the voice that they had previously been denied.

This lost voice resurfaces in feminist methodologies that expose the general difficulty with patriarchy and, in particular, the oppressive force patriarchy has been in the cultural heritage of women. Exum claims that this hermeneutic ensures that patriarchy remains exposed as an untenable form of social ordering and a dishonest representation of the world and the divine (Exum, 1993). However, the difficulty with subverting a text in order to counteract patriarchy is that the original text remains available to the associative implicit memory. Moreover, like Trible's work, Exum's methodology requires a good deal of intellectual acumen and may not be immediately accessible to some churchgoers.

One strategy for countering patriarchy in the Bible is to create teaching programs and sermons that disavow sexism and draw on the foundations created by Trible, Exum, and other feminist biblical scholars. It must be assumed that this method can be effective in creating a greater influence to the unconscious mind if the teachings are consistent and intellectually available. Yet, it cannot be ignored that despite our greatest efforts, the Bible (in its raw form, without sophisticated commentary) will always be viewed by most churchgoers as the authoritative voice or, in terms of associative implicit memory, the greater influence. The Bible does not have a book that is reasonably attributed to a female writer.

To disavow sexism in the associative implicit memory, women in the Bible need to have the same authoritative voice as men. Otherwise, feminist exegesis that is taken in with awareness is not reinforced at a subliminal level. Hence, it is important to consider adding feminine writings to the canon of the Bible or creating a companion work, written by women, which is afforded equal status as the Bible. To examine this possibility, it is profitable to compare the "male values" that David Clines discusses in *The Scandal of the Male Bible* with the feminine aspects of *The Gospel of Mary*. In doing so, we can imagine the benefits of contributing the experience of an authoritative woman to the Bible.

Clines (2015) suggests that the dominant male values in the Bible are as follows: "1. strength, 2. violence and killing, 3. size, 4. honor, 5. holiness, 6. womanlessness, 7. totalitarian thinking, and 8. binary thinking." Consider the contrast of these "male values" to the themes in *The Gospel of Mary*. Instead of strength, there is an unabashed account of weeping and distress. Violence and killing are replaced by unity and reconciliation. For example, Jesus is asked, "Will matter be utterly destroyed or not?" (Unknown author, in King, 2003). The Saviour's reply is, "Every modelled form, every creature, exists in and with each other" (Unknown author, in King, 2003). This is not necessarily a different teaching from Jesus, but a different interpretation of Jesus's teaching, through the lens of Mary.

Outward signs of honor are replaced with a focus on internal transformation. It goes without saying that the narrative is not womanless, yet it is not manless either. The narrative speaks of healthy debate and also warns against black and white or totalitarian thinking. For example, "Don't promulgate law like a lawgiver or you will be dominated by it" (Unknown author, in King, 2003). Finally, there is a warning against binary thinking and a call to inclusiveness.

Moreover, *The Gospel of Mary* is an early account of the difficulties of patriarchy in the emerging Christian movement. This narrative suggests that Jesus taught people of both genders equally. Consider the following clash between Mary, Andrew, Peter, and Levi (or the priest). When Mary tells this group what Jesus taught her, both Andrew and Peter suggest that she is lying. In binary terms, Peter remarks, "Did he, then, speak with a woman in private without our knowing it? Are we to turn around and listen to her? Did he choose her over us?" Discredited and excluded, Mary becomes upset. However, Levi responds, "Peter you have always been a wrathful person. Now I see you contending against the woman like the Adversaries. For if the Saviour made her worthy, who are you then for your part to reject her? Assuredly the Saviour's knowledge of her is completely reliable. That is why he loved her more than us" (Unknown author, in King, 2003). The male characters fight over the worthiness of Mary's testimony, and there is still evidence of patriarchal rule. However, this gospel eliminates the difficulty of divinely appointed male supremacy.

Would it be the case that the associative implicit memory would pick up on the greater influence that men and women are equal in God's eyes if documents written by women expressing this idea were given equal status and equal reading time in church? There are difficulties with this proposition when it concerns *The Gospel of Mary.* Gospels, for instance, were written of historical encounters with Christ that documented at least some of the things that Christ said and did. This cannot be proven of *The Gospel of Mary.* Indeed, there are reasons to dispute the legitimacy of this work. However, it is still profitable to have the discussion. Moreover, if not *The Gospel of Mary,* there are other valuable works written by women that could be read with the same authority as the canon of the Bible.

Of course, there are certainly women who have prominent roles in the Bible, and the Bible even hints at women in leadership positions. Yet, these associations are merely hinted at and in respect to associative memory constitute the weaker associations, which are always lost to the stronger associations. Therefore, adding a female voice to the canon of the Bible is a worthy proposition. However, unless women are given an equally authoritative voice from the lectern, the implicit associative memory will still register this as the weaker association.

The strategy of giving women equality in the church will need to be a combined approach. Women's readings, feminist exegesis, and female priests may act together to counterbalance patriarchy in the Bible. The last example has already proved to be successful, as tests show that women who are exposed to other women in leadership roles associate women and leadership easily at the implicit level (Fine, 2010). Therefore, the presence of women in leadership roles in the church is successful in itself in deconstructing patriarchy. Yet it is not enough, as women in leadership roles are not strongly supported by the Bible.

Another helpful proposition is that of subtracting harmful material from the Bible. This is not a threatening proposition when we consider the history of the books in the Bible and the canon of the Bible itself. Scholars are certain that the books in the Bible were often subject to multiple revisions. The study of this phenomenon is called redaction criticism. The thought of revising sacred texts was not an insurmountable concern for the ancient Israelites.

Moreover, it is worth noting that Jesus did not write down his teachings or create a foundation document for Christianity. He had a flexible attitude to the laws of Israel; his priority was always to the welfare of individuals and the community, not to rigid adherence to written works. Indeed, it might be argued that Jesus would not favor a superstitious response to the Bible.

Moreover, when we speak of the canon of the Bible, we tend to forget that there have been numerous canons of the Bible throughout history and there are still different canons of the Bible that are used in different Christian denominations. In more recent times, Bruce Metzger consciously altered the Bible to make the language gender inclusive. This version of the Bible (NRSV) is the Bible that is traditionally used in educational institutions, and is often the version chosen for church readings.

In order to substantiate the proposition that the Bible, or lectionary, be altered, it is helpful to return to the workings of the implicit associative memory. The following example demonstrates how powerful and subtle stereotypes can be in changing self-perception.

Measures of implicit associations tell us that men are implicitly associated with "science, math, career, hierarchy, and high authority." Women on the other hand are implicitly associated with "liberal arts, family and domesticity, egalitarianism, and low authority." These associations in turn distort our self-perception (Fine, 2010).

> Researchers asked American university students to rate their mathematical and verbal abilities, but beforehand, some students were asked to note down their gender in a short demographics section

> and others to mark their ethnicity. The simple process of ticking a box had surprising effects. European American women, for example, felt more confident about their verbal skills when gender was salient (consistent with the prevailing belief the females have the edge when it comes to language skills) and rated their math ability lower compared with when they identified themselves as European American. In contrast, European American men rated their math ability higher when they were thinking of themselves as men (rather than as European Americans), but their verbal abilities better when their ethnicity had been made salient. (Fine, 2010)

Of further concern, experiments suggest that self-perception affects performance. In the same series of tests, it was shown that women performed worse in math tests when they were told that mathematics was traditionally a male subject than they did when this idea was not reinforced. Similarly, women performed worse in the same tests when they were positioned in a classroom that was dominated by men than they did in a room with an equal number of men and women. It was suggested, in the latter case, that the women associated the disproportionate number of men in the room with the idea that women must not be very good at math (Fine, 2010).

Given the change of self-perception that comes about with the simple association of gender on a survey, how greater the risk with patriarchal themes in the Bible? Yet, if we were to remove passages of the Bible either from the Bible itself, or from the lectionary, how would we decide which passages to remove and which to preserve? Ellens's laws of psychological hermeneutics are useful for this task. At this juncture it is imperative to note that this was not the intention of these laws, which were intended rather as an interpretative lens. However, given the workings of implicit associative memory, I would suggest that there is an argument for eliminating harmful metaphors from the Bible. Ellens's laws of psychological hermeneutics will be outlined in full.

Ellens's laws of psychological biblical hermeneutics do not mention feminism; however, they are useful to feminist theologians. Indeed, Ellens has created a methodology that is compatible with Elisabeth Schüssler Fiorenza's (1996) concern that traditional feminist biblical criticism does not speak in specifics. For example, the experience of an African American woman in a lower socio-economic area is different from the experience of an Anglo-Saxon woman from a privileged background. Ellens's (2012) focus on treating a person as a Living Human Document, deserving of the same care and specificity as we put into interpreting sacred texts, treats this problem.

Ellens's first law of biblical hermeneutics suggests that it is necessary to separate the cultural-historical matrix from the essential message of grace, in order to discuss the word of God. For Ellens, the word of grace is always conceived in terms which are universal, unconditional, and radical. Ellens argues that the "golden thread of grace" that runs the entire length of the Bible must be considered the primary message of the Bible and, therefore, the key to interpretation. The benefit of applying this law is that attention is diverted from the harmful metaphors in the Bible, so that the attention of the reader is on the essential and saving message of grace (Ellens, in Ingram, 2012).

In reference to the question of the compatibility of faith in the Bible and feminism, Ellens's first law of biblical hermeneutics determines that patriarchy is historical-cultural garbage. Ellens's first law also goes towards reinforcing the message of grace as the greater influence. However, finding the essential message of grace in the Bible is still a discriminating process and, therefore, this is not an exact solution as far as implicit associative learning is concerned.

Ellens's second law of psychological hermeneutics suggests a solution for working through the ambiguity in the Bible. It reads, "That which, in the Bible, is psychospiritually destructive for the Living Human Document is not the divine word. That which is psychospiritually constructive for the Living Human Document is the divine word of God. That word will always be about grace" (Ellens, in Ingram, 2012).

Ellens's third law of psychological hermeneutics suggests that it is necessary to use psychology as the arbiter of what is psychospiritually constructive and destructive for the Living Human Document. Psychology then becomes a means of discovering what is the divine truth (Ellens, in Ingram, 2012). This methodology is profitable on a number of different fronts: (1) it avoids the circular argument of having the Bible as the critic of the Bible; (2) it accounts for advances in the social sciences; and (3) it interprets the Bible by a worldview that has more of an acceptance of the equality of women.

However, as sublime as Ellens's hermeneutics are, how do they reach the average pew-sitter, or, to be more specific, how do they reach the irregular churchgoer? Up until this stage in the argument, it may have been countered that in this enlightened age, the propositions put forth in this chapter are all a bit esoteric and that the author is offering merely pie-in-the-sky solutions. Unfortunately, we cannot afford to be so dismissive when we consider the research put forth by Steven Tracey.

Tracey (2007) recounts a study on domestic violence which sought to profile abusers. This study included a number of different groups of men, including churchgoers (of different denominations) and non-churchgoers. The study indicated that the highest incidence of domestic violence occurs in homes of men who attend conservative Protestant churches irregularly.

> What is it about periodic attendance at conservative churches that makes men more likely to abuse their wives, even more than

> non-churchgoers? Based on what we know about the dynamics of abuse and abusers, I would suggest the following: When men come into conservative Protestant churches, for the most part they are going to hear some form of patriarchal gender views, that is, male headship. For men who are significantly insecure, immature, and/or misogynistic, patriarchal teaching in any form may merely serve to confirm their views of male superiority and their right to dominate women. (Tracey, 2007)

The confusion that irregular attendees of church are confronted with can be illustrated in the book 1 Corinthians. Paul's discourse on love might be spoken of as the panacea for all ills: "Love is patient; love is kind; love is not envious or boastful or arrogant or rude. It does not insist on its own way; it is not irritable or resentful; it does not rejoice in wrongdoing, but rejoices in the truth. It bears all things, believes all things, hopes all things, endures all things. Love never ends" (1 Cor. 13:4–8).

Yet, two chapters earlier in 1 Cor. 11, Paul says to the congregation, "But I want you to understand that Christ is the head of every man, and the husband is the head of his wife . . . For a man ought not to have his head veiled, since he is the image of God; but woman is the reflection of man. Indeed, man was not made from woman, but woman was made from man. Neither was man created for the sake of woman, but woman was created for the sake of man" (1 Cor. 11:3–9).

Paul redeems himself when he remarks that men are not independent of women as men come into being through women (1 Cor. 11:11–12). However, his view is questionable again a few chapters later when he remarks, "As in all churches of the saints, women should be silent in the churches. For they are not permitted to speak, but should be subordinate, as the law also says. If there is anything they desire to know, let them ask their husbands at home. For it is shameful for a woman to speak in church. Or did the word of God originate with you? Or are you the only one it has reached?" (1 Cor. 14:33–36).

What is an irregular conservative Protestant male churchgoer to make of all of this? If his associations are already of male domination of women, then it would seem likely that he would take in the information about male supremacy and leave out the message of grace. This church attendee is not schooled in feminist biblical criticism or Ellens's laws of psychological hermeneutics.

Does this study support the importance of removing these toxic readings from the Bible or the lectionary? Might this suggestion also empower the female irregular conservative Protestant churchgoer who is primed explicitly and implicitly not to challenge her husband, but is taught instead to obey him? Is it not important to remove texts which encourage the relationship of abuser and abusee? In order to discuss this further, it is helpful to return to the associative implicit memory once more, in order to discuss the self-concept and how it relates to patriarchal material.

The stereotypes which develop in implicit associative learning not only affect the way we perceive the world at large; stereotypes also affect the way we view ourselves, as self-concept is changeable and influenced by the environment. The active-self draws on different stereotypes to engage with changing situations. For instance, it is argued that we draw on a number of different stereotypical roles to go about our daily business. These might be mother, teacher, artist, church-goer, etc. Research also suggests that self-perceptions can be shaped by the perceptions that other people have of us, and that we adapt our self-concept to live up to the perceptions of us that are held by others (Fine, 2010).

Maybe this was the behavior that Stanton observed when she noted, "So perverted is the religious element in her nature, that with faith and works she is the chief support of the church and clergy, the very powers that make her emancipation impossible" (Stanton, 2003). Is it possible that women take on the role of submissive women when they enter church? Do women take on the role that is expected of them in accordance with the Bible, the liturgy, and the perceptions that other churchgoers have of them?

On the flip side of the study into spousal abuse, it would appear that conservative Protestant men who attend church regularly have the lowest spousal abuse rates. Tracey (2007) suggests that the reason for this is that men who regularly attend church develop a balanced view of the Bible and teachings on family life, that they are exposed to loving and "non-dominating masculinity" in church, and that the support of the community gives men a greater sense of self-esteem, which makes them less liable to want to control women and children.

It may be assumed that these men are familiar with Bible study classes, spend time in prayer and personal reflection, and have an understanding of grace. These kinds of men may be aware of feminist biblical criticism and Ellens's laws of psychological hermeneutics. However, it is naïve to suggest that the answer based on this survey is to encourage men to attend church regularly. This mode of thinking sidesteps the problem that the Church and the Bible, when encountered irregularly, are more dangerous than if they are not used at all. This should be of great concern to church leaders and biblical scholars.

On a more positive note, it may be profitable to consider Jesus Christ as a model of behavior. Take, for example, students who were told to imagine themselves in different roles. These students were asked to imagine themselves as, among others things, a professor and a cheerleader. The self-perceptions in these cases were not too surprising: thinking of a professor made a person feel smarter, while thinking of a cheerleader made a person feel more attractive. What is surprising is that these students were given a test after imagining themselves in different roles, and the students who imagined themselves as professors performed better in analytical tasks than they had before they imagined themselves as professors. Similarly, the students who had imagined themselves to be cheerleaders performed poorer than they had previously (Fine, 2010).

I wonder what the findings would have been if the researchers had instead asked the participants to imagine that they were Christ. Would this mean that they would feel more charitable? In turn, would this make them more charitable? Undeniably, at the center of Christianity is a figure who can attract little criticism from feminists. Christ had women in his ministry and engaged with women as equals. Indeed, Christ's ministry to the outcasts of society and his desire to end oppression must make him appealing to any feminist.

However, Christ as the divine man may reinforce the idea of male supremacy. For example, it has been argued that the relationship between Mary and Christ is a relationship that reinforces the idea of the subordination of women to men. In this instance, Mary is the creature and Christ is divine. Mary Daly argues, "In the way this comes through to the popular mentality, the psychological implications are that the male is divine and the female is a creature" (Daly, in Maron, 1968).

Therefore, there is no easy answer to the question, Is faith in the Bible compatible with feminism? The Bible is a bane and a boon for feminists. It is a bane inasmuch as it is a foundational document that reinforces patriarchy. It is a boon because it delivers the saving message of grace. Given the strength of the negative aspect of the Bible, it is imperative that theologians and churches work to correct this deficit. On the other hand, the strength of the positive message of grace in the Bible means that the Bible must be maintained. It is not tenable to entertain a "throwing the baby out with the bathwater" approach to the problem of the historical context of the Bible.

This chapter has argued that implicit associative learning takes place beyond our awareness and control and responds to the strongest influence. Given this knowledge of the unconscious mind, it is unlikely that feminist biblical criticism can cope with the problem on its own. Instead, the problem of patriarchal views in the Bible must be approached from different angles. If churches are serious about creating a balance, it is necessary to encourage feminist interpretations of the Bible, alongside feminine testimonies of faith and the presence of women in leadership roles. Moreover, if the church is truly serious about empowering women, it is necessary to consider action to tackle disempowering readings. In a bold move, the Bible might be revised; in a softer scenario, the lectionary might be redressed.

REFERENCES

Clines, D. (2015). The scandal of a male bible. The Ethel M. Wood Lecture for 2015.

Exum, C. (1993). *Fragmented women: Feminist sub(versions) of biblical narratives.* Sheffield: Sheffield Academic Press.

Fine, C. (2010). *Delusions of gender.* London: Icon Books.

Fiorenza, E. (1996). Introduction: Feminist liberation theology as critical sophialogy. In E. Fiorenza (Ed.), *The power of naming: A concilium reader in feminist liberation theology* (pp. xiii–xxxviii). New York: Orbis Books.

Ingram, V. (2012). Satire and cognitive dissonance in the book of Jonah, in the light of Ellens' laws of psychological hermeneutics. In H. Ellens (Ed.), *A festschrift honoring Wayne G. Rollins.* New York: T & T Clark.

King, K. (Ed.). (2003). *The gospel of Mary of Magdala: Jesus and the first woman apostle.* California: Polebridge Press.

Maron, E. (1968). An interview with theologian Mary Daly. *US Catholic, 34*(5), 21–24.

Society of Biblical Literature. (1993). *The HarperCollins study Bible, NRSV.* New York: HarperCollins Publishers, Inc.

Stanton, E. (2003). Introduction. In E. Stanton (Ed.), *The women's Bible.* Retrieved from: www.gutenberg.org/cache/epub/9880/pg9880.html

Tracey, S. (2007). Patriarchy and domestic violence: Challenging common misconceptions, *JETS, 50*(3), 573–594.

Trible, P. (1973). Depatriarchalizing in Biblical interpretation. *Journal of the American Academy of Religion, 41*(1), 30–48.

Chapter 2

The Goddess-Worshipping Age: Feminist Egalitarianism in Prehistory and Early History

Maija Jespersen

INTRODUCTION

I was 25 before I learned there was a period of human history wherein female deities were powerful in their own right. I was in New Zealand, doing work trade on an organic farm, and I idly picked up my host's book, *Lost Goddesses of Early Greece*. It was about the transition in Greek myth from independent, strong Goddesses to Goddesses who were subservient, resentful, and often childish. The latter description reminded me of Eve, the main woman in Christianity—besides Mary, whose main power was to stay silent and forgive. Plus they weren't even Goddesses.

I read on. Here were women acting brave, strong, powerful, wise, and loving, without a male overlord. I had never encountered this image before. I suddenly saw with a horrified shudder the gaping abyss in the spectrum of women's role models that I had lived with all my life. For this reason alone, learning about the era of Goddess worship is invaluable.

The second reason is about power dynamics. When I ask people about feminism, I often hear phrases like "when women take over" or "when women are running things"—phrases that describe reversed power dynamics, not transformed power dynamics. Can we even imagine a society wherein one sex is not oppressing the other? Like, who would be in charge? Neolithic society can give us a clue. Burial sites show males and females were differentiated, but in status and economic power, equals (Leroi-Gourhan, 1967, p. 174; Eisler, 1995, pp. 25–26; Gimbutas, 1999, pp. 61, 114). A look at this culture helps us answer the question: what would fully realized feminism, wherein men and women treat each other as equals, look like? Some of the most intriguing artifacts display characteristics of both genders, suggesting the presence of a dyadic concept that is not even part of our current thinking.

The third reason it is important to know about Goddess-worshipping societies is the bearing it has on the question of what is natural. Some of the achievements made in the Neolithic challenge popular arguments that males naturally evolved into a position of dominance. For a society that believes male dominance to be natural, feminism can only occupy the role of a moral standard.

If, on the other hand, a culture teaches its members that men and women evolved in egalitarian societies, fully actualized feminism would be seen as perfectly compatible with human instincts and drives. Eliminating gender-based injustices would not be seen as trying to *suppress* innate drives, but as trying to *restore* them.

THE ARGUMENTS

We have perhaps all heard of "Venus figurines," small, very ancient statuettes of very fat women, minimizing the head and feet and exaggerating the breasts, vulva, and buttocks. The Venus of Willendorf (Figure 1.A, on page 23) is perhaps the most famous one. But what do they mean?

One category of arguments holds that the Venus figurines represent a pre-religious cult, and may have represented a female-dominant society. Way back in our primitive past, when people didn't understand the male's role in procreation, women's powerful status was based on the mystery of birth. This naturally gave way to male dominance as that mystery was solved, or as society otherwise progressed.

There are variations of this theory, the most basic being that as soon as males were no longer in mystical awe of females, they gained dominance because their larger size and strength made them more valuable as hunters and protectors. A variation of this theory holds that gender hierarchy developed with agriculture. The assumption here is that men wanted to become dominant earlier, but couldn't because as hunter-gatherers, they depended on the food women gathered. But handling large animals and wielding plows and scythes required much more strength than gathering nuts and berries, and that is when men took over food production and women became dependent on them (Prinz, 2012). Another branch of this theory relies not on brute strength, but on left-brained-ness. The rise in importance of left-brained technologies, including the neurological changes wrought by the development in writing (Shlain, 1998), are what led to male supremacy. These theories have in common the stance that male dominance is a natural or even essential part of developing a complex society.

A second group argues that the Venus figurines are part of a much larger body of evidence indicating a widespread, continuous Goddess-worshipping culture (Gimbutas, 1991, p. 222). This culture was well developed in the Neolithic age, with roots stretching back to the Paleolithic. In some places like Minoan Crete, this culture lasted into the historical age (Gadon, 1989, pp. 87–107). In these cultures, a female Goddess was worshipped as the supreme deity, giving life, sustaining her children, and welcoming them back at death (Eisler, 1995, p. 19).

Archaeologist Marija Gimbutas named this culture "Old Europe." According to her, the vast majority of imagery from both Paleolithic and Neolithic ages represents the female.

> The goddess is nature and earth herself, pulsating with the seasons, bringing life in spring and death in winter. She also represents continuity of life as a perpetual regenerator, protectress, and nourisher. . . . The woman's body was regarded as parthenogenetic, that is, creating life out of itself. This ability was celebrated in religion. In Neolithic times and earlier in the Upper Paleolithic, religion centered on the feminine power, as shown by the abundance of female symbolism. . . . The imagery of Neolithic art is overwhelmingly feminine: the female body, and particularly its generative parts—vulva and uterus or womb—are predominant. (Gimbutas, 1999, pp. 112–113)

At some point in the Neolithic, the religion also began to include representations of a male God, who was born and died each year and served as a son/consort to the eternal Goddess (Eisler, 1995, p. 24), but the Goddess remained the overarching deity. According to Gimbutas, only three to five percent of Neolithic art shows male imagery (Gimbutas, 1991, p. 223).

Although the religious imagery was mostly female, Neolithic society was egalitarian (Gimbutas, 1999, p. 114). Eisler explains why female-centered religious imagery would not have translated into a female-dominated society:

> [T]he primacy of the Goddess—and with this the centrality of the values symbolized by the nurturing and regenerating powers incarnated in the female body—does not justify the inference that women here dominated men. This becomes apparent if we begin by analogizing

> from the one human relationship that even in male-dominant societies is not generally conceptualized in superiority-inferiority terms. This is the relationship between mother and child. . . . [B]oth men and women were the children of the Goddess, as they were the children of the women who headed the families and clans. And while this certainly gave women a great deal of power, analogizing from our present-day mother-child relationship, it seems to have been a power that was more equated with responsibility and love than with oppression, privilege, and fear. (Eisler, 1995, pp. 27–28)

The difference is due to a fundamentally different model of relationships: the "dominator" model ranks one gender over the other, while a "partnership" model emphasizes connections rather than rank (Eisler, 1995, p. xvii). The partnership/dominator distinction allows for congruence between overwhelmingly female religious imagery and the material egalitarianism evidenced by Neolithic remains (Eisler, 1995, p. 26). It also helps us understand the description of this as a peaceful age, with the settlements lacking fortifications, and no sign of weapons except those for hunting until 4500 BCE (Gimbutas, 1991, p. 352).

The age of Goddess worship was brought to an end not by natural social evolution but by violent takeover. A horse-riding, hierarchical, and warlike people from the Russian Steppes migrated in a series of invasions between 5000 and 3000 BCE, leaving clear archaeological and linguistic traces of a different culture (Gimbutas, 1991, p. 352).

A third position is that the gender egalitarianism reflected in the grave goods *was* reflected by the religion. Representations of males exist and are even plentiful, but have been overlooked for a variety of reasons. The possibility that the male Neolithic God was worshipped outside in nature rather than in a temple that would have better preserved evidence (Gimbutas, 1991, p. 249), the classification of phallic objects as non-religious, and the contested meanings of symbols are all factors.

Some objects seem almost bisexual and defy easy interpretation. They suggest the presence of an idea that is not mentioned in the literature on either prehistoric European culture or Goddess worship: that of a *dyad*. A dyad is a way of conceiving of a pair, wherein the pair is defined as "a single entity that is made up of two similar yet distinguishable components" (Du, 2002, p. 30). Was this dyadic concept in play in the Goddess-Worshipping era? Could the supreme deity have been not a him or a her, but some kind of *them?*

THE UPPER PALEOLITHIC AGE (40,000–9600 BCE)

To answer this question, we must look way back in time to the artifacts left by early man. Several human species lived during that time, but *Homo sapiens* is the one that developed art and culture and became us now. *Homo sapiens* originated in Africa, and left some extremely ancient art there to document their artistic consciousness (Aubert et al., 2014; Prehistoric Art Timeline, ND) before migrating to Europe and the Near East and developing the fantastic artistic civilization found there. The great cave panels at Lascaux and Chauvet caves in France and the other beautiful sculptures and drawings are but a fraction of what remains of their artistic production (Leroi-Gourhan, 1967, p. 31). The Bison of le Tuc d'Audoubert, for example, are beautifully modeled relief sculptures carved in the soft clay of a cave wall 13,000 years ago. This male and female pair of buffalo, two feet tall, still stand there and sniff the air while the clay on either side of them has slid away. How delicate! What other works have been lost, we will never know.

The most highly developed murals and sculptures occurred in France and the northern (Cantabrian) region of Spain, so Leroi-Gourhan (1967) christened this culture "Franco-Cantabrian." Leroi-Gourhan (1967) points to numerous factors that indicate that Paleolithic people traveled and traded across the European sites, including consistent artistic conventions, a common set of abstracted symbols, and a carving of a sole—a distinctively shaped, ocean-dwelling fish—that was found high up in the Pyrenees (p. 79). This culture was consistent across a wide geographic region, including areas of Portugal, Italy, Germany, and even as far away as Lake Baikal in Siberia (p. 32).

But were they religious? Besides the level of art, a number of factors indicate they were. Franco-Cantabrian image making developed on two levels simultaneously. Carefully detailed images, like buffalo and horses, were carved on more durable objects, while at the same time, simplified versions were carved in greater quantities and on less durable materials (Leroi-Gourhan, 1967, p. 67). Consistent use of symbolism implies an oral tradition:

> [F]rom first to last the meaning of the signs, even the most abstract ones, was clear to all who used them. This is proved by repeated revivals of realism in every period, but especially in the last one, when fish suddenly recover their tails and fins, and the barbed sign regains its male sexual character. Clearly such facts can only find their explanations in a body of generalized oral traditions, as may occur with a body of religious traditions. (p. 80)
>
> Early people buried their dead in beds of red ochre, suggesting the reverse of birth. Humans also returned to the earth's womb at death. . . . The dead were buried in the fetal position with their arms across their chests, their bodies marked with red ochre, the pigmented earth, symbolic of life-giving blood. (Gadon, 1989, p. 6)

The concept of returning to the same place you came from deserves unpacking. If you emerge from and return back to the same place, it would suggest that place is, or is a gateway to, the source of life. A source separate from individual human lives (because this was obviously a symbolic act; nobody was trying to actually put people back into their real mothers) suggests a concept of human life as in some form continuous before birth and after death. There is recognition of, or at least belief in, the eternal. In the early part of the Upper Paleolithic, some caves had deposits of red ochre 8 inches deep, suggesting burial was not the only religious ceremony (Leroi-Gourhan 1967, p. 40).

Neurobiology also indicates that they were religious, for entirely different reasons (Lewis-Williams, 2002). As modern humans, they had the same brain structure as we do. That means they would have had dream and trance states common to people in all societies. It is the attempt to make sense of these altered states—which can include physical sensations and even symbols produced by chemicals in the optic nerve and eyeball—that constitute the origin of the shamanistic religions that are ubiquitous among hunter-gatherers across cultures and time (Lewis-Williams, 2002, p. 132). The Paleolithic symbols and even the placement of images in the caves are consistent with symbols and rituals of modern shamanistic cultures, too; all signs point to Paleolithic cave art and artifacts as indicating the presence of a full-blown shamanistic tradition (Lewis-Williams, 2002, pp. 205–227).

Upper Paleolithic Objects

French archaeologist Leroi-Gourhan assembled a massive catalog of Paleolithic artifacts in 1967 and with it his theory that cave art and artifacts show a balance of male and female representations. He made initial associations of animals with genders based on what animals occurred with or on clearly phallic or clearly feminine objects. From there, he observed patterns among these animals in the cave paintings—sophisticated pairings, always indicating a balance of male and female. "It is nevertheless surprising," he comments in the catalog, "that no one has ever noticed that the signs occur so frequently in pairs" (Leroi-Gourhan, 1967, p. 147).

Interestingly, though, in the part of his catalog dealing with objects, Leroi-Gourhan categorizes all of the female statuettes as "Objects of Religious Significance," while all of the carved phalluses were categorized as "Decorated Weapons, Tools, and Ornaments"—in other words, not of religious importance. We wonder if the later claims that there was virtually no male imagery in the Paleolithic (Gimbutas, 1991, p. 246) could be related to the fact that phallic imagery was originally categorized as non-religious? An assortment of artifacts in Figure 1 demonstrates that both female and male imagery were indeed present.

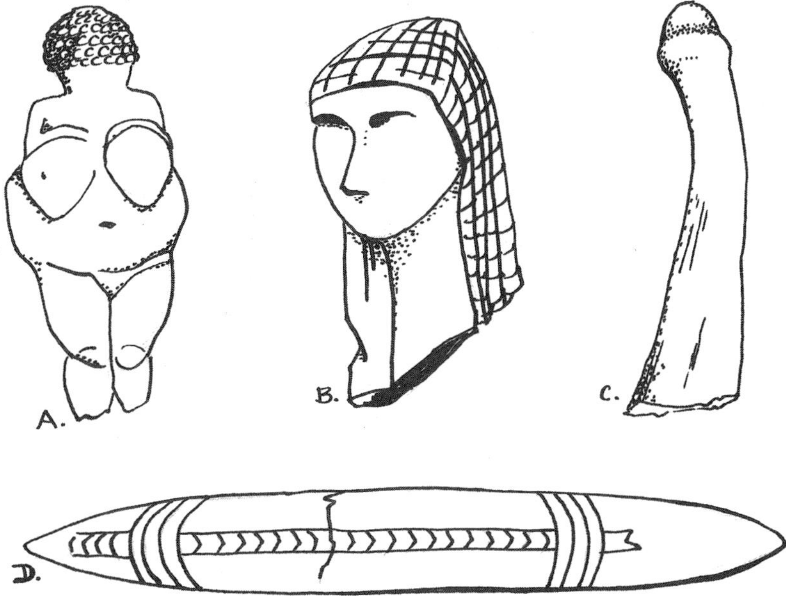

Figure 1. Possible Male and Female Objects from the Paleolithic

A. Venus of Willendorf, fig. 3 in Gadon (1989, p. 6), captioned, "The Earth Mother of Willendorf." Courtesy of Natural History Museum, Vienna.

B. Venus of Brassempouy: fig. 3 in Baring and Cashford (1991, p. 9), captioned, "Head of a Goddess." Courtesy of Musées Réunis du Louvre, Paris.

C. Decorated Half-rounded Rod, fig. 38 in Leroi-Gourhan (1967, p. 75). Original image/no credit given.

D. Handle of a Pierced Staff, fig. 180 in Leroi-Gourhan (1967, p. 396). Original image/no credit given.

Perhaps best known among the "Venus" figurines is the Venus of Willendorf (Figure 1.A). Often exemplified as a primitive fertility sculpture, it actually is not that primitive but is a remarkably accurately modeled fat woman. To list a few anatomical points, the hips are narrower than the widest part of the belly, the thighs bulge, showing the quadriceps, and emerge from the hip (as opposed to the belly, just continuing down the leg, undifferentiated), the kneecap is correctly pictured, the shin begins slightly posterior to where the upper thigh left off, the fat roll of the mons pubis is separate from the belly fat as it is on a real person, the breasts flatten against the body where they would naturally be thinner. The figure is pictured with her head reclining downwards, the face area blank, the hair indicated by a pattern.

But before thinking Paleolithic people were only interested in fertility, consider the Venus of Brassempouy (Figure 1.B), a delicate head and face of a woman with blank eyes and mouth, reminiscent of a Japanime ghost—the opposite of sexualized. The coexistence of these two pieces suggests that obese women with minimized faces and feet were a style of sculpture, not indications of the limitations of Upper Paleolithic artists.

The category "Decorated Weapons, Tools, and Ornaments" includes spears, pierced staffs, spear-throwers, spatulas (used as palettes for mixing ochre), half-rounded rods, objects to be suspended, and pendants. Numerous examples of phallic imagery appear on objects in this category, including quite graphic ones (Figure 1.C) (Leroi-Gourhan, 1967, p. 60). Some of these are decorated too elaborately for practical use (Figure 1.D) (Leroi-Gourhan, 1967, p. 70) but remain in the category of functional (non-religious) items, likely because of their resemblance to the items that did have practical purposes.

Leroi-Gourhan's assessment of Paleolithic society was one in which "the core of the system rests on the alternation, complementarity, or antagonism between male and female values" (Leroi-Gourhan, 1967, p. 74). But some objects suggest more than simple complementarity.

These combine male and female in a way that is puzzling without the concept of a dyad, and have been subject to widely varying interpretations. The abstract figure represented by drawing Figure 2.B, for example, was captioned "Ivory Rod with Breasts" by Baring and Cashford (1991, p. 11) and "Abstract Female with Breasts" by Gadon (1989, p. 7), with neither caption noting the phallic imagery that the main body suggests. Figure 2.C was captioned "Pendant bead of mammoth-ivory in the shape of an elongated neck with pierced hole and two breasts [. . .]" by Baring and Cashford (1991, p. 14), again with no suggestion of the phallic element. The idea of one image including both phallus and breasts is foreign to a hierarchical culture. We are used to one gender occupying a central position. Even if each gender is central in different areas, someone still has to be in charge. Right?

Not so in a culture familiar with dyads. A dyad, you may recall, is a whole made up of two distinguishable parts, neither of which is dominant or could even exist on its own. More on dyads at the end of the Paleolithic, though.

Figure 2.A is a combination of male and female, with the phallic carving and the drilled hole. Leroi-Gourhan (1967) notes that these pierced rods of reindeer antler were the most consistently found type of object throughout every strata of the Upper Paleolithic (p. 59). Perhaps the frequency of male and female in one object reflected a larger overall belief not just in pairing and complementarity, but an interdependence that constituted something more dyadic.

Then, in 9600 BCE, the world around primitive man literally melted. How apocalyptic it must have seemed! The ice that formed their landscape,

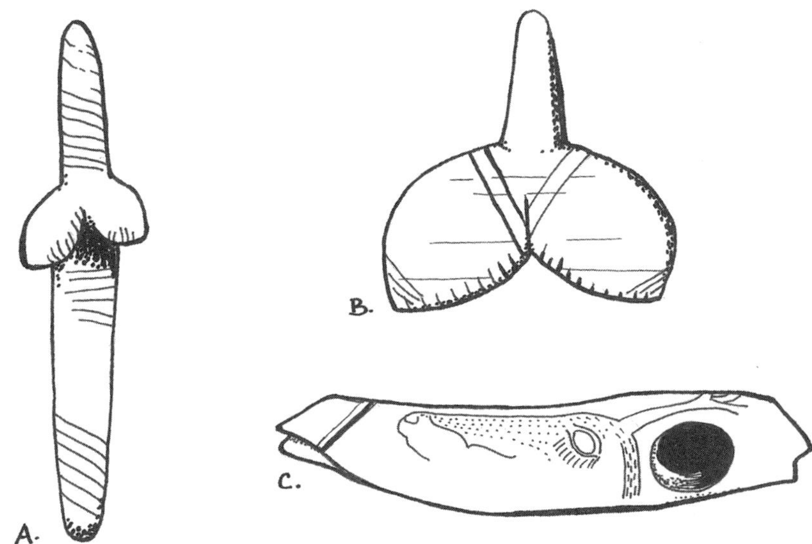

Figure 2. Possible Dyadic Objects from the Paleolithic

A. Pierced Staff: fig. 190 in Leroi-Gourhan (1967, p. 397). Original image/no credit given.

B. Fig. 6 in Baring and Cashford (1991, p. 11), captioned, "Ivory rod with breasts," Anthropos Institut, Moravske Museum, Brno. Image from J. Jelinek, by permission of Artia, Prague.

C. Fig. 12 in Baring and Cashford (1991, p. 14), captioned, "Pendant bead in the shape of an elongated neck with pierced hole and two breasts engraved as wings on the front." Image courtesy of Anthropos Institut, Moravske Museum, Brno.

across which they traveled, whose ecosystem they understood and hunted in and thrived in, melted away. The whole position of humans in the food chain changed: the wooly mammoths they used to eat died out—but on the other hand, so did the saber-tooth tigers that used to eat them. Their modes of hunting and travel, their clothing—almost every tool of survival they had developed—would have suddenly become obsolete. And, as you would expect after such a cataclysmic change, the cultural record goes dark. That record reemerges centuries—or in some places thousands of years—later, in the Neolithic.

DYADS

The division of the world into pairs of opposites seems to be a western, if not universal, tendency, and indeed the world does often seem to present itself in terms of pairs. Experienced time is divided into time in the dark and time in the light, which become our concepts of day and night. The heavenly bodies shedding light during those times are the sun and moon. The ancient Chinese observed that the universe moved according to forces that were combinations of active and yielding, and named these motions yin and yang. The humans and all of the animals display two biological genders, male and female.[1] It is as though paired-ness is an organizing principle of the universe.

There are many ways to interpret that dualism, though, including dichotomous, complementary, dialectical, and dyadic (Du, 2002, pp. 29–30). Are the members of the pair opposites? Are they struggling against each other, defined by contradiction, as in a Marxist dialectic? Or do they see each other as necessary parts of one whole, distinguishable but without independent identities? That last is the dyadic worldview. Shanshan Du's (2002) book, *Chopsticks Only Work in Pairs*, about the Lahu, a dyadic culture in southwestern China, explores this concept in depth.

> The dyadic principle focuses on the wholeness of the pair and highlights the similarities and harmony between the two components, which identify with each other through their shared membership and joint function in the whole. A dyad is comparable to an organic compound consisting of two elements in which neither element has an essential nature of its own and, therefore, no internally bounded identity. Being *one* identity that consists of *two* parts, the dyadic "pair" can be considered both "one" and "two," depending on the linguistic context. (Du, 2002, p. 30)

True gender equality is so unheard of in modern society, it is usually dismissed as a utopian fantasy (Du, 2002, pp. 2–9). And yet, based on gravesites, the Neolithic age was an age of gender equality (Gimbutas, 1991, p. 324; Eisler, 1995, p. 26). If we are to interpret the artifacts of a gender-egalitarian culture with no historical record, it makes sense to explore the concepts being used by a known gender-egalitarian culture that exists in the present. This provides a broader conceptual palette than relying solely on structures and ideologies from a patriarchal culture—like that of an all-powerful deity of one gender.

Equality among the Lahu takes the form of the husband and wife working as a team and supporting each other as much as possible—both at home and in public life. Men are involved in all stages of raising the family: in supporting women during pregnancy by doing extra work, participating in childbirth by catching the baby and cutting the umbilical cord, and fully participating in childcare by carrying a child around as they hunt or otherwise work (Du, 2002, pp. 80–97). Politically, the traditional structure of village leadership is a male/female pair, although the communist regime imposed singular village leaders in the 1950s, and only a few villages have recovered their traditional paired leadership (Du, 2002, pp. 115–118). So, although they have had to modify their ways to fit in with the outside world, the Lahu traditional way is for both genders to have equal powers and make equal contributions to the family and larger society.

Religiously, the Lahu God is a set of male-female twins, Xuel-Sha, which is both singular and plural.[2] The God and Goddess twins are individually named Xuel Yad and Sha Yad, but in stories, they always act together. For example, in the Lahu creation myth,

> There was no sun / Day was unable to divide,
> There was no moon / Night was unable to divide.
> This was not too difficult for Xuel Yad / This was not too hard for Sha Yad.
> Xuel Yad had an idea / Sha Yad had a plan,
> Xuel Yad wanted to make / a flower in the sky,
> Sha Yad intended to create / a flower on the earth.
> The sky flower of Xuel Yad / was the sun in the sky,
> The earth flower of Sha Yad / was the moon in the sky. (Du, 2002, p. 33)

This short stanza shows how the Lahu conceived of not just God, but the whole world in pairs. The initial problem is stated in terms of both day *and* night. Xuel Sha had a plan for both the earth *and* sky. They solved the problem by creating the sun *and* the moon. Their belief in dyadic pairing as an organizational principle of not just religion but all of life is evident in their common phrase, "Everything comes in pairs: aloneness does not exist" (Du, 2002, p. 40).

The cooperation and unity of intent between the two parts of the pair make Xuel Sha fundamentally different from God and Goddess pairs construed in more oppositional relationships, like Zeus and Hera. They not only have very distinct identities; they frequently act at cross-purposes. Hera goes around creating trouble with her feminine emotions, and Zeus restores order with his masculine rationality (Du, 2002, p. 35). This is a pair, but not a dyad.

THE NEOLITHIC AGE

When we left Paleolithic people, they were wandering around bewildered after the retreat of the ice that had defined their landscape and lifestyle for so long. In the warmest places first, and later going northwards, people began to plant, harvest, and store grains. It is this beginning of agriculture, the transition from being food gatherers to food producers, which defines them as Neolithic people. The advent of the Neolithic is not a single fixed date, but different dates in different places. In the Near East, it started in 9000 BCE; in southeast Europe, 7000 BCE; in central Europe, 5500 BCE; and in northern Europe, 4000 BCE. The development of agriculture in Europe gradually followed in the wake of the retreating ice.

Neolithic people developed the technology to fire pottery, so the number of relics they left increased dramatically. Instead of hundreds, they left thousands of relics. The bone animal sculptures they made are consistent with Paleolithic imagery, suggesting cultural continuity (Gimbutas, 1991, pp. 2, 222).

As nomadic lifestyles gave way to settled ones, Neolithic people built permanent dwellings and left behind entire city layouts and burial sites, including houses of several rooms and multiple-storied temples (Gimbutas, 1991, p. viii). The sites surveyed by Gimbutas (1991) in her survey of Neolithic Europe and the Near East, *Civilization of the Goddess: The World of Old Europe*, include locations all across Europe, from Greece to the Balkans to Denmark.

There are suggestions that this was a peaceful age. For example, these Neolithic towns were laid out in pleasant but indefensible ways. Houses and buildings would be in an open field near good pastures and a stream, for example, instead of on a nearby cliff.

> Hill forts in inaccessible locations are not known to Old Europe, nor are daggers, spears, and halberds. Neolithic villages were occasionally encircled by ditches but seldom by palisades or stone retaining walls. Earthen ramparts and other defensive structures occur only in later Neolithic and Copper Age settlements when measures were taken to protect villages from an influx of human intruders. These changes became visible in central Europe only toward the end of the 5th and during the 4th millennium B.C. (p. x)

This claim is corroborated by Ferguson's (2013) conclusion that widespread human-against-human violence, and specifically warfare, was not archaeologically evident until around 5000 BCE.

Based on grave sites and the items in them, this was a gender-egalitarian age with matrilineal descent. The grave goods indicate both gender differentiation and a high degree of economic equality (Gimbutas, 1991, p. 324). In the broadly spread LBK culture, for example,

> [T]he analysis of grave goods . . . indicates two distinct categories of graves: those of male traders and craftsmen, and those of prominent women in religious life. The evidence, as stated, indicates some men of status but not ruling rank, and some elder women who were obviously honored. (Gimbutas, 1991, p. 334)

Tombs in Malta, Sardinia, and in megalithic graves in western Europe from Portugal to Denmark display no distinctions in class or gender (Gimbutas, 1999, p. 65). And although in some graves there was some association of particular objects with each gender, like woodworking tools found in men's graves and grain grinding tools in women's graves, in other cemeteries the same objects, including jewelry, axes, chisels, and grain-grinding stones, appear in both graves (Gimbutas, 1999, p. 114).

Although Sumerian cuneiform and Egyptian hieroglyphs are usually considered the oldest forms of writing, Gimbutas (1991) makes a strong case that writing developed during the Neolithic, by comparing a set of symbols found in multiple sites to classical Cypriot and showing that many signs are exactly the same. A variety of symbols that had already been in use started appearing in compounds between 6000 and 5300 BCE. By 5000 BCE, these had developed into a script with 30 core signs and 100 modified signs and was being used by multiple Old European cultures, including Vinca, Karanovo, and Tisza. This language has not been deciphered and disappears on mainland Europe towards 4000 BCE, although it may have remained on Crete and Cypress, evolving into classical Cypriot (pp. 320–321).

Eisler (1995) asserts that many major advances in civilization were developed under these matrilineal, Goddess-worshipping societies, including law, government, judgeship, trade by land and sea (which were already known from the Paleolithic), education, and administration (pp. 66–67). If her claim is accurate, it would put at least a few claims of male dominance as a process of social evolution on shakier ground.

Neolithic Religion

As society became more complex and diverse, so did representations of the Goddess (Berger, 1985, p. 5). Everything still happened under the auspices of an overarching divine Mother goddess, who gave people life, gave life to everything that nurtured them and everything in nature, and accepted them back into her "cosmic womb" at death (Eisler, 1995, p. 19). But in the Neolithic, she began to be represented by a much wider diversity of forms and images.

Female Imagery

Neolithic female statues number in the thousands and are found in every level of excavation (Gimbutas, 1999, p. 4). The Goddess falls into three basic categories. The first is the life-giving and life-sustaining goddess as represented by statues emphasizing the vulva, breasts, and buttocks, by symbols of the vulva (a lozenge with a dot or line in it) or pubic triangle, by a woman holding or entwined with a snake as the snake goddess, by a woman holding or surrounded by flora and fauna as the Mistress of Animals and Plants, and as the animals bear, deer, and elk (Gimbutas, 1991, p. 223). The second is the death Goddess: stiff, white figures sometimes found in graves and represented by owls, vultures, and other birds of prey, possibly in association with excarnation practices that took place before burial (Gimbutas, 1991, p. 222). The third is the Goddess of regeneration, represented by fish, frogs, goats, hedgehogs, and a bull's head with horns (Gimbutas, 1999, p. 26).

Wait, a bull's head with horns? Also known as *bucrania*, bulls' horns were so common throughout the Neolithic that some populations, especially in the Anatolia region, were called "The People of the Bull" (Twiss and Russell, 2009). In the town of Catal Huyuk, for example, sculpted bucrania and/or paintings of bulls were found in most of the shrines; in some rooms, a row of massive bucrania stretched down a whole wall, or over doorways, and in other symbolically important places (Gimbutas, 1991, pp. 255–256).

Normally, bucrania are considered to represent the male principle in Neolithic art (Gadon, 1989, p. 30). Gimbutas (1991), however, interprets bucrania as representing a uterus and fallopian tubes, which primitive people may have noticed while the birds of prey were excarnating the dead (p. 244). As a uterus, bucrania would directly represent the regenerative powers of the Goddess (Gimbutas, 1999, p. 142). Gimbutas's characterization of bull horns as a directly female symbol helps account for her statement that males are only represented in five percent of Neolithic imagery (Gimbutas, 1991, p. 246).

Within the category of generative Goddess, one of the most popular representations throughout Neolithic Europe is the Mistress of Animals and Plants (Gimbutas, 1991, p. 223). Gimbutas (1991) separates the Mistress of Animals and Plants from the Pregnant Goddess/Goddess of Fertility, whose life corresponded with the seasonal death and renewal of plant life, and who was worshipped at bread ovens (Gimbutas, 1991, p. 342). In other interpretations, however, these two merge into one Grain Protectress, who appears from the Near East to Celtic and Germanic areas in northern Europe, and around whom seasonal dramas were enacted to promote the fertility of crops (Berger, 1985, pp. 1–9). She is also known as the Pregnant Vegetation Goddess, who represents agricultural fertility and annually mates with her consort, the Year God (Gadon, 1989, pp. 48–51).

Male Imagery

Besides the contested bucrania, there were Gods. The Neolithic Goddess had a son or partner God who presided with her over all activities of life and death (Eisler, 1995, pp. 26–27). Gimbutas (1991) describes five categories of male imagery. The first two are phases of the Vegetation

God, the consort of the Grain/Vegetation Goddess, who went through an annual life cycle in which he was born in the spring, matured in the summer, and died in the fall (p. 342). The Strong God of Vegetation is portrayed as an ithyphallic young man, expressing the potency of spring. The Dying God of Vegetation, portrayed as a serious or thoughtful-looking old man, is also seen as a consort of the Vegetation Goddess, but this time representing the maturity of the seasonal cycle before its death in winter. Eisler (1995) also describes statues of elderly men, suggesting they were venerated as well as old women (p. 26). The third category is that of Phallic God or Snake (pp. 248–250), the snake being an animal associated with both the female and the male (p. 236). The fourth category is Centaurs, which appear late in the Chalcolithic period, and the fifth is the Guardian of Wild Nature or Master of Animals, a partner figure to the Mistress of Animals (p. 251). These admittedly seem to overlap, and the last category is distinguishable from the first to the extent that the Master of Animals does not undergo annual death and renewal, like the Vegetation God.

In addition to the God or the male aspects of God, the Neolithic contains phallic imagery, either graphically as a phallus or symbolically as the snake or the tree of life (Gimbutas, 1999, p. 37). Maltese temples, for example, contain niche altars holding sculptures of double or triple phalli (Gimbutas, 1999, p. 117). Some writers argue that with the advent of agriculture, primitive people must have figured out the males' role in procreation, because phallic symbols, male statues with erect phalluses, and bull-men started appearing whereas male imagery had earlier been lacking (Gadon, 1989, p. 50). But we saw male imagery from the Paleolithic. Could it be that here again, the original categorization of male images as non-religious rears its ugly head? Could it be the appearance of phallic imagery in what may be construed as temples that makes it suddenly visible?

Bucrania are also numerous, as mentioned above, and although Gimbutas categorizes bucrania as female imagery, she is virtually alone in doing so, even among feminist writers. Eisler (1995) describes boars and bull horns as symbols of the male, central in both Neolithic shrines and in the later Minoan and Mycenaean cultures (pp. 26–27). She puts a fine point on it, declaring the bucranium to be a symbol of the male, but one that existed within a religion that worshipped an overarching Mother goddess, and therefore *indirectly* a symbol of the Goddess (p. 22). Gadon (1989), however, points out that the bull not only represented the male in the Neolithic, but continued to do so after the transition to male-dominant religions, for example, as an animal form of both Shiva and Zeus (pp. 30–31).

It is not cut and dried. Bucrania could represent the male, but still indicate a Goddess mother figure, as is suggested in the image of a female giving birth to a young bull at Catal Huyuk (Eisler, 1989, p. 22). Alternatively, representations of a female giving birth to both genders do not preclude the knowledge that males are also required to bring this birth about. It is entirely possible that males had more than just an assisting role, theologically. Whether temples like the ones at Catal Huyuk are seen as overwhelmingly female or representing both genders in a balanced way depends on the interpretation of the various images.

Dyadic Imagery

The Vegetation Goddess has a partner in the Vegetation God. The Mistress of Animals has a partner in the Master of Animals. This is starting to not seem like such an overwhelmingly female-oriented religion after all. What other partnerships exist? Probing further, we find more.

> In both the Neolithic and the historical era, the earth fertility goddess sometimes was portrayed with a male partner. The female and male deities discovered in a grave of the Hamangia culture from the early fifth millennium BCE, on the coast of the Black Sea, very likely represent a sister and brother pair rather than a married couple, since in European mythologies the female and male deities are known to be sister and brother pairs (for example, the Lithuanian earth mother, Zemyna, has a brother, Zeminikas, and the Scandinavian great-goddess, Freyja, has a brother, Freyr). (Gimbutas, 1999, p. 118)

One grave from the Hamangia culture on the Black Sea contained a male-female pair of statues, both the same size (Figure 3.A) (Gimbutas, 1991, p. 249). These sister and brother pairs sound a lot like Xuel-Sha, the brother and sister twins that together make up the Lahu God.

Neolithic representations of paired-ness went even further than couples and twins, though. The east Balkan Karanovo culture left a statue of male and female fused into one being like conjoined twins (Figure 3.B). This artifact has been interpreted as representing a sacred marriage (Gimbutas, 1999, p. 18), but we cannot help noticing how startlingly consistent it is with the concept of dyads as described above by Du (2002): a single whole made of a distinguishable, but not independent, pair. Some figures contain both male and female aspects on a single piece. Gimbutas explains,

> In the sculptural representations of the early Neolithic, the phallus as divine energy is often shown fused with the life-creating female body: for example, the goddess sometimes has a phallic neck. Clearly, in this religious system the two sexes complement each other and thus invigorate the powers of life. (Gimbutas, 1999, p. 117)

The "Figure with Phallic Neck and Breasts" shown in Figure 3.C is one such figure. Gadon (1989) describes this as a goddess with a phallic neck (p. 51),

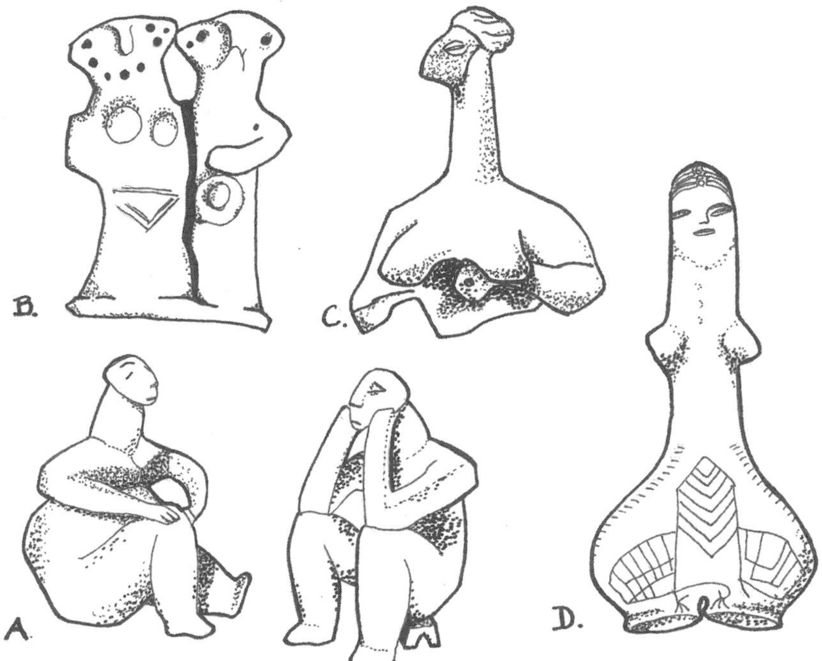

Figure 3. Possible Dyadic Objects from the Neolithic

A. Goddess and God Pair, fig. 7–42 in Gimbutas (1991, p. 249), captioned, "The masked female and male gods in thoughtful posture, found in a grave." Image copyright Marija Gimbutas, 1974.

B. Dyadic Pair, fig. 10 in Gimbutas (1999, p. 18), captioned, "'The Gumelnita Lovers,' conjoined male and female terra cotta statuette, possibly portrays a sacred marriage." Original drawing by Marija Gimbutas.

C. Figure with Phallic Neck and Breasts, fig. 39 in Gadon (1989, p. 51), captioned, "Phallic Goddess: The Self-Fertilizing Virgin Mother." Image courtesy of Marija Gimbutas.

D. Phallic/Female Figure, fig. 31 in Gimbutas (1991, p. 37), captioned, "Phallic energy intensifies the strength of the formidable goddess of regeneration." Original drawing by Marija Gimbutas.

but why is it not equally describable as a male figure with breasts? Or both? Similarly, Gimbutas (1991) describes Figure 3.D this way: "Phallic energy intensifies the strength of the formidable goddess of regeneration—her upper body resembles a phallus and her lower body resembles testicles" (p. 37). But if both the upper and lower body—in other words, the entire body except the breasts—resemble male sexual organs, why is this figure still described as primarily female? Is it because we simply don't use dyadic concepts much in the west, so in order to understand it, we need to label it as one or the other?

Even with the presence of some contested imagery, it seems possible to conclude from artifacts and burial sites that women had powerful religious representation and enjoyed status in Neolithic society equal to that of men. Although it is beyond the scope of this chapter to draw any definitive conclusions about the transition to male dominance, we have attempted to highlight some contradictions between the evidence of gender egalitarianism during the Neolithic and the claims that male dominance developed with agriculture—and likewise with writing.

THE GODDESS IN HISTORY

As the timeline proceeds and humanity enters the historical age, we have historical references of Goddess-worshipping cultures and the myths they held. To mention a few: across the Near East, people prayed to Innin, Inanna, Nana, Nut, Anat, Anahita, Astarte, Istar, Isis, Auset, Ishara, Asherah, Ashtart, Ashtoreth, Attoret, Attar, and Hathor, all goddesses (Stone, 1976, p. 9). The relatedness of the names suggests that they are regional and linguistic branches of the same religion. Ancient Sumerian records describe a very close version and likely continuation of the rituals around the Vegetation Goddess and God surmised from the Neolithic: Inanna selects the king, makes him divine, and then their copulation brings forth all of the plant life with which she nourishes humankind (Berger, 1985, p. 12). Neolithic association of the bear with regenerative powers of the Goddess (because they hibernate and reemerge from the earth in the spring) is echoed in the later myth of the Celtic bear goddess Artio (Gimbutas, 1999, p. 183), as well as the association of the Greek Goddess Artemis, who governs birth, with the bear (Gimbutas, 1999, p. 156).

Many Goddesses had attributes we currently associate with masculinity, like strength, wisdom, and left-brained pursuits. Writing, for example, was credited to Sarasvati in India and Nidaba in Sumer, while the Celtic Cerridwen was the Goddess of intelligence (Stone, 1976, pp. 3–4). These attributes of the female deity were matched by real women, like the female scholar Hypatia, professor of mathematics, astronomy, and philosophy in fourth century BCE Alexandria (Eisler, 1995, pp. 132–133).

Ashtoreth and other pagan deities are mentioned in the Bible, but the female gender of those deities is obscured by using the masculine word for God (Stone, 1976, p. xviii). This is the same kind of obfuscation we saw resulting from Leroi-Gourhan's cataloging of the phallic objects as non-religious, but in reverse. By denying the presence of either male or female in a sacred realm, you remove the possibility from people's minds of that gender being sacred. There is a clear trajectory forward through history from the strong Goddesses of the Neolithic and early historical age, to the powerful but subordinate Goddesses of the classical Greek age, to the Abrahamic present with no Goddesses at all.

Minoan Crete is one example of a culture that remained Goddess-worshipping and matrilineal (meaning name and property passed through the mother's line rather than the father's) into the historical age (Stone, 1976, p. 46). This could be partly because the proto-Indo-European invaders Gimbutas describes came on horseback, but were not initially skilled at ocean navigation (Gimbutas, 1999, p. 131). Numerous depictions of a bare-breasted Goddess figure, sometimes holding snakes, populate Minoan art (Baring and Cashford, 1991, p. 111). Murals of this civilization show women mingling freely with men, taking part in parades and civic ceremonies, and engaging in the very athletic, co-ed ceremony called bull-leaping, wherein people dance around and sometimes over a charging bull (Gimbutas, 1991, p. 345). We know from laws written on the walls of a temple at Gortyna that women who got married still retained control over their property and had access to divorce (Gimbutas, 1991, p. 346). Taken together these form a comprehensive picture of a society consistent with the Neolithic age, in which women enjoyed both high status and theological representation—especially by comparison to later ages when both were lost.

CONCLUSION

"Religion supports and perpetuates the social organization it reflects," according to Eisler (1995, p. 67), and one area of contradiction this chapter seeks to highlight is the contradiction between a gender-egalitarian society and an over-arching God or Goddess of a single gender. The hypothesis of this chapter is that a gender-egalitarian society should have a gender-egalitarian conception of God, something like the dyadic God Xuel-Sha worshipped in the egalitarian Lahu society. Multiple artifacts in the Neolithic suggest a dyadic concept was operational: the pairing of the Mistress and Master of Animals, the pairing of the Vegetation God and Goddess, statues of male and female pairs found in non-amorous positions, partially fused, or completely merged into a single figure. This dyadic concept is highly consistent with the equality found in the burial sites; more so than that of a benign but all-powerful female deity.

It is possible that the understandable feminist zeal around this discovery of Goddesses who were not subservient to male partners may have led to obfuscation of some of the male imagery. It is also possible that the strong current of dyadic symbolism has gone largely unnoticed because mainstream western and eastern cultures are organized hierarchically, largely without the concept of dyads. But I would like to close this chapter with a question: what if 35,000 years of our social evolution was not characterized by one gender dominating the other, either benignly or despotically? After all, benign fascism is still fascism. But how might our gender norms—and our whole hierarchical worldview—change, if we thought of men and women sharing power in a non-dominating, non-exclusionary way, as our most natural state?

NOTES

1. LGBT studies have identified that there are more than two genders, biologically as well as identity-wise, and we regret the need to limit the analysis to the two biological genders of male and female and the discussion to heteronormative behavior due to space restrictions.

2. This is often obscured, however, and the bulk of Chinese literature describes Xuel-Sha as a single God with unspecified gender, or male, or female with a husband; according to Du (2002), only a few researchers have explored the dyadic nature of the deity (p. 36).

REFERENCES

Aubert, M., Brumm, A., Ramil, M., Sutinka, T., Saptomo, E. W., Hakim, B., Morwood, M. J., van den Bergh, G. D., Kinsley, L., & Dosseto, A. (2014). Pleistocene cave art from Sulawesi, Indonesia. *Nature, 514*, 223–227.

Baring, A., & Cashford, J. (1991). *The myth of the goddess: Evolution of an image*. New York, NY: Penguin (Viking Arcana).

Berger, P. (1985). *The goddess obscured: Transformation of the grain protectress from goddess to saint*. Boston: Beacon Press.

Du, S. (2002). *Chopsticks only work in pairs: Gender unity and gender equality among the Lahu of southwest China*. New York, NY: Columbia University Press.

Eisler, R. (1995). *The chalice and the blade: Our history, our future*. New York, NY: HarperCollins.

Ferguson, B. (2013). The prehistory of war and peace in Europe and the Near East. In D. Fry (Ed.), *On war, peace, and human nature: The convergence of evolutionary and cultural views*. New York, NY: Oxford University Press.

Gadon, E. (1989). *The once and future goddess: A symbol for our time*. Philadelphia, PA: Harper & Row.

Gimbutas, M. (1991). The *civilization of the goddess: The world of old Europe*. San Francisco: Harper.

Gimbutas, M., & Dexter, M. R. (Eds.). (1999). *The living goddesses*. Berkeley, CA: University of California Press.

Leroi-Gourhan, A. (1967). *Treasures of prehistoric art*. New York, NY: Harry N. Abrams.

Lewis-Williams, D. (2002). *The mind in the cave*. London: Thames & Hudson, Ltd.

Prehistoric Art Timeline: Chronological List of Dates of Paleolithic, Mesolithic, & Neolithic Culture. (ND). In *Encyclopedia of Art*. Retrieved on August 27, 2015, from http://www.visual-arts-cork.com/prehistoric-art-timeline.htm

Prinz, J. (2012). Why are men so violent? *Psychology Today, Experiments in Philosophy,* Feb. 3, 2012. Retrieved from: https://www.psychologytoday.com/blog/experiments-in-philosophy/201202/why-are-men-so-violent

Shlain, L. (1998). *The alphabet versus the goddess: The conflict between word and image.* New York, NY: Penguin.

Stone, M. (1976). *When God was a woman.* New York, NY: Harcourt, Inc.

Twiss, K. C., & Russell, N. (2009). Taking the bull by the horns: Ideology, masculinity, and cattle horns at Çatalhöyük (Turkey). *Paléorient, 35*(2),19–32.

Chapter 3

Feminist Perspectives from the Hebrew Bible

Ilona Rashkow

INTRODUCTION

Feminist biblical hermeneutics have their roots in the women's movements of the nineteenth century with the publication of Elizabeth Cady Stanton's *The Woman's Bible*, a collection of essays on passages of the Hebrew Bible and New Testament dealing with women (Stanton, 1895). Her overall objective was to use textual analysis and historical criticism to dismantle the traditional male interpretation of biblical passages and replace them with a feminist perspective. The effort was a success, which may be why Stanton and *The Woman's Bible* were criticized, more for her audacity in taking on the project than in what she actually said about the Bible or its merits.

This chapter is divided into three sections: First is a discussion of the historical development of biblical hermeneutics within the academy; next are examples of various approaches; and finally, there is an application of some of the various methodologies as to the Adam and Eve narrative of Genesis 1–3.

HISTORICAL DEVELOPMENT

The Society of Biblical Literature section "Women in the Biblical World" had always included a few papers and topics in the area of feminist interpretation. The interests of the section were much broader than feminist biblical hermeneutics and included papers dealing with historical, sociological, and literary studies from the ancient world as well as biblical literature. Elsewhere in programs of the annual meetings of the Society of Biblical Literature, feminist biblical hermeneutics appeared only occasionally.

At the annual Society of Biblical Literature meeting in 1980, a Centennial Session was moderated by Phyllis Trible on "The Effects of Women's Studies on Biblical Studies." One of the results of this session was the beginning of feminist biblical hermeneutics as a major research concentration within the academy and its attendant increase in published work and scholarly interest in feminist biblical studies.

In 1987, the program for the "Women in the Biblical World" section included a panel moderated by Elisabeth Schüssler Fiorenza on issues of feminist hermeneutics, and her presidential address emphasized the importance of feminist biblical criticism.

However, feminist biblical hermeneutics, although an area of interest within the academy, did not become an actual program unit until a proposal was submitted in 1989 with plans for an ongoing section as a regular part of the Society of Biblical Literature program. The original section was co-chaired by Sharon H. Ringe and Bruce Birch with a steering committee composed of Katharine Doob Sakenfeld, Hal Taussig, and Renita J. Weems.[1]

Cheryl Exum, in answering the question, "What does 'feminist' mean with regard to biblical hermeneutics and methods?" wrote:

> "Feminist" means taking as the starting point not the biblical text but rather the issues and concerns of feminism as a world view and as a political enterprise. Feminist criticism is, for me, defined by its critical stance, its position outside the ideology of the biblical text, for only when we step outside the Bible's androcentric ideology (or, theology) can we engage genuinely critical questions about what the text says—and does not say—about women, about its underlying assumptions about gender roles, about its motivation for portraying women in a particular way, and about what the text conceals and unintentionally reveals about the fact of women's suppression. (Exum, 2010)

Of course, it could (and has been) argued that "feminist" and "Hebrew Bible" in the same sentence is oxymoronic. As Amy Kalmanofsky writes:

> The Bible, I argue, is invested in the social hierarchy because it serves the religious hierarchy. It protects and privileges masculinity in society because it wants, above all, to protect and privilege God's masculinity and authority. The social hierarchy that should exist between men and women mirrors the religious hierarchy that should exist between God and Israel. If the social hierarchy is compromised, as it is in Eve and Adam's story, the religious hierarchy is also compromised. The Bible's gender-bending stories protect the Bible's preferred hierarchies by depicting a world in which both are threatened. The Bible wants men to behave like men, and women to behave like women. Above all, it wants women to submit to men, and men to submit to God. (Kalmanofsky, 2015)

Skepticism notwithstanding, feminist Hebrew Bible criticism is now a well-established method of inquiry. There are numerous sessions devoted now to feminist criticism at the Annual Regional, National, and International Conferences of the Society of Biblical Literature. Indeed, at the 2010 Society of Biblical Literature Annual Meeting, a standing-room only session was devoted to a landmark interdisciplinary and international feminist project, *The Bible and Women: An Encyclopedia of Exegesis and Cultural History,* and interest in this area of scholarship has grown exponentially (http://www.bibleandwomen.org/EN/). In 2014, the Society of Biblical Literature published a landmark collection of essays on feminist biblical studies in the twentieth century edited by Elisabeth Schüssler Fiorenza (Fiorenza, 2014). The first section traces the evolution and development of feminist biblical studies as a "conversation" among feminists around the world. The second section introduces, reviews, and discusses the hermeneutic religious "spaces" created by feminist biblical studies. The third section discusses academic methods of reading and interpretation that dismantle androcentric language and *kyriarchal* authority, a phrase coined by Fiorenza in 1992 to describe her theory of interconnected, interacting, and self-extending systems of domination and submission, in which individuals might be oppressed in some relationships and privileged in others. The fourth and final section returns to the first with work that transgresses academic boundaries in order to explore the transforming, inspiring, and institutionalizing feminist work that has been and is being done to change religious mindsets of domination and to enable women *and* men to engage in critical readings of the Bible.

The 2015 annual meeting of the Society of Biblical Literature lists over 20 papers under the rubric "Feminist Biblical Hermeneutics," in addition to approximately 20 papers in the "Women in the Biblical World" unit; 15 papers in the unit "Recovering Female Interpreters of the Bible"; and 15 papers devoted to "Gender, Sexuality, and the Bible," among others. As of June 2015, the *Review of Biblical Literature* has published reviews of 6,012 books, of which 46 books had "feminist" in the title. Of these 46, six were published in the last five years.

VARIOUS APPROACHES TO FEMINIST BIBLICAL CRITICISM

It should be noted at the outset that most scholars differentiate between "sex," "gender," and "sexuality."

Speaking broadly, "sex" refers to a biological identity ("male" or "female") that is ordinarily, but not always, fixed.

"Gender" is a socially constructed ideology that is reflected in our culture: political, social, economic, educational, and religious institutions, and is coded in the language we use. There are many scholarly discussions about "gender": some scholars emphasize individual identity, while others stress social and cultural influences. There are also scholarly discussions over whether gender identity is fixed over time, or whether it is fluid and even mutable (see, for example, Kalmanofsky, 2015).

"Sexuality" encompasses sexual orientation, an object or objects of sexual desire, and sexual practices.

Although many scholars have argued that feminist criticism is by definition *gender* criticism because of its focus on the female gender, I am not discussing gender criticism because the relationship between feminist and gender criticism is, in fact, more complex than is within the purview of this chapter. The two approaches are not polar opposites but, rather, exist along a continuum of attitudes toward sex, sexuality, gender, and language. For example, one area of biblical scholarship is "gender-*bending*," a term associated most often with queer theory and its efforts to destabilize gender by identifying "a new identity distinct from both heterosexual and homosexual labels" or that "falls outside the boundaries defined by heterosexuality" (see Kalmanofsky, 2015; Macwilliam, 2011, p. 4).

Few readers could dispute the overwhelming orientation of the Hebrew Bible to the male world: while there are female characters, and there are even a few fragments of women's writings, the women in this text are exceptions. One example of how the Hebrew Bible focuses on men far more than on women is in the number of women mentioned by name. The text identifies a total of 1,426 people, of whom 1,315 are men. That means only 111 women are identified—about 9 percent of the total. As noted by Elizabeth Cady Stanton:

> The canons and civil law; church and state; priests and legislators; all political parties and religious denominations have alike taught that woman was made after man, of man, and for man, an inferior being, subject to man. Creeds, codes, Scriptures and statutes, are all based on this idea. The fashions, forms, ceremonies and customs of society, church ordinances and discipline, all grow out of this idea. . . . The

> Bible teaches that woman brought sin and death into the world, that she precipitated the fall of the race, that she was arraigned before the judgment seat of Heaven, tried, condemned and sentenced. . . . Here is the Bible position of woman briefly summed up. (Stanton, 1895, p. 17)

Conservative traditionalists and liberal feminists agree that for the most part, the Hebrew Bible portrays women as secondary to men. Traditional scholarship, particularly that of conservative theologians rather than biblical scholars, tends to assume that God intended this secondary role for women based, in great part, on the Genesis narrative (which I discuss below).

This perspective has a strong historical and sociological basis. The Bible is a product of ancient Near Eastern patriarchal societies where men dominated, if not monopolized, the civil and religious bureaucracies. Certainly, males have occupied a special place in biblical narratives. Beginning with the dramatic ritual of circumcision, the covenant between God, Abraham, and *male* offspring established in Genesis reflects a chain of fathers and sons and highlights their special relationship. Certainly throughout the Bible, a son has been regarded as a special blessing; indeed, sons are so important that three of the four matriarchs had sons by their handmaids when they thought they were incapable of conceiving sons. While it is not surprising that biblical narratives depict a definable family structure, what is surprising, however, is the conspicuous absence of a figure lurking beneath the text, a figure repeatedly subjected to erasure, exclusion, and transformation. The Hebrew Bible virtually ignores daughters. Narrative after narrative describes the desire for male children, the lengths to which women would go to have sons, and the great joy surrounding the birth of a boy. Indeed, of the possible structural permutations of parent-child relationships, the father and son pair is the one most frequently in focus, and the mother and son is second. Mother-daughter and father-daughter pairs receive the least narrative attention and reflect a hierarchy of value that isolates the daughter as the most absent member of the family institution. Since the daughter's presence is normal and necessary to the biological realities of family, and given the relevance of the daughter as the figure upon whose mobility the entire kinship structure rests, her lack of narrative presence is significant and calls attention to itself (see, for example, Rashkow, 2000). On the other hand, women's voices *can* be heard occasionally and biblical narratives *do* exist which portray women as strong leaders, both on the national and personal level.

Although feminist biblical hermeneutics is not monolithic, one aspect shared in common is appropriately a stance of suspicion. Feminist critics recognize that patriarchy was one of the most stable features of ancient biblical society over the thousand-plus years of the Bible's composition and redaction and the two thousand years of interpretation which followed. Thus, in studying any biblical text, feminists are alert not only for explicit patriarchal bias in the text, but also for evidence of more subtle phallocentrism in the worldview of biblical interpreters. It should be emphasized, however, that exposing phallocentric interests is not an accusation of blatant misogyny but rather a recognition of a religiously and culturally inherited and deep-rooted gender bias.

Acknowledging the patriarchy of biblical materials, feminist biblical scholars approach the text at least two different ways: looking to texts about women to counteract famous texts used against women; and looking to the Bible generally (that is, not particularly to texts about women) for a perspective offering a critique of patriarchy. Subsumed under both approaches is the larger issue of interpretation. Of course, interpretation cannot be defined in any absolute sense, as if by challenging earlier, predominantly male readings, one will be closer to the "truth" or the "real" meaning. Most theorists—biblical and otherwise—agree that reading is an activity which can never be exact since everyone brings cultural and personal contexts to the act of reading. From the ways in which one understands interpersonal relations to the meanings of specific words, assumptions and beliefs "bias" a reader; they provide a framework that obscures certain connotations/denotations and brings others to the foreground. In fact, to suggest that there is one proper way to read a text is anathema to feminist biblical scholars who instead favor a multiplicity of interpretations. Admittedly, a feminist reading is not "neutral": it involves the issue of interests, and a person's interests determine the questions asked of a text. In this quest, feminist biblical scholars are no more capable of the "authoritative" interpretation than any other reader.

As a corollary, one question which many scholars try to address is if it is even possible to make assumptions about women in the biblical world based solely on the Hebrew Bible. As Carol Myers has pointed out:

> Scholars have noted a discrepancy between information in authoritative written sources and information gleaned from other materials—including but not limited to iconography, archaeological data, epigraphic remains, direct observation (in the case of ethnography), archives, commercial records, and other nonprescriptive documents. The daily lives of ordinary women, it turns out, were rather different from the impression given by official written sources. In all these disciplines, it has become clear that attempting to draw conclusions about gendered behavior and family relationships on the basis of a limited set of texts produces flawed results. (Myers, 2014)

The most obvious feature of feminist biblical criticism is that it addresses the identity of "female." Feminist biblical criticism accords a privileged status to the experience and interests of women readers: that is, the recognition that in theories that overlook the issue of sexual differences, the appearance of universality is, in essence, the male perspective. As a result, until fairly recently, there was an exclusion of the female voice from the institutions in which Bible theory and criticism are taught. According to the Society of Biblical Literature November 2014 report, of the almost 8,500 members, only 23% are female.

Another point contributing to female readings is the relationship of the reader to biblical characters, arguably one of the most important being the deity. It has been argued, of course, that the deity in the Hebrew Bible is not male and has no sex. Some feminist scholars enumerate female images of God such as mother (e.g., Num. 11:12; Deut. 32:11; Isa. 46:3–4, 49:15–16, 66:13; Ps. 131:2; Job 38:28–29), as well as wet-nurse and midwife, and use these citations as a counterbalance to a masculine characterization of the deity (Trible, 1978, chaps. 2 and 3). In addition, recent theological literature stresses that the "Father" God and "Lord" God are not to be understood literally and naively: "God-names and properties have only symbolic significance" (Heine, 1989, p. 14). There is nothing intrinsically male about the strangest of all God's names ("I shall be who I shall be") (Exod. 3:14). But what does "only" mean? Feminist concerns for a female image of God seem a little forced, especially when the gender of a word is used as proof. To illustrate, the word "spirit" has a variety of genders depending upon the language: in German it is male, in Greek neuter, in Hebrew feminine, and in English, of course, nouns have no gender at all.

On the other hand, there is no doubt that male designations for the divine qualities and modes of action predominate in Hebrew Scriptures. Even attributes and actions that are themselves gender-neutral are read through the "filter of male language" (Plaskow, 1990, p. 123). When the issues are justice, law, anger, punishment, and power, God is portrayed using male terminology, male pronouns, and in terms of male characteristics and images. To quote Cynthia Ozick, "The hand that leads Israel out of Egypt is a male hand, whether or not it is called so explicitly" (Ozick, 1983, p. 122). God is a man of war (Exod. 15:3), a shepherd (most famously in Ps. 23:1), a king (1 Sam. 12:12; Ps. 10:16), and a father (Deut. 32:6; Isa. 1:2–4, 64:7; Ps. 68:6, 103:13; Prov. 3:12).

As many scholars have noted, one of the most distinctive features of Genesis is the frequent use of a variation on the divine epithet "God of your/his/their *father*[s]," with "Abraham" and or "Isaac" added in apposition to "father" (e.g., Gen. 24:12; 28:13; 31:5, 29; 32:10; 46:1, 3) (see, e.g., Sarna, 1989, pp. 396–397; Cross, 1983, pp. 4–43; Alt, 1967; Haran, 1965, pp. 51–52; Hyatt, 1955). This appellation is particularly appropriate in the patriarchal narratives, since they revolve around the lives of fathers. Indeed, according to Peter Miscall, the text *is* the chronicle of the fathers: "that is the core, the essential meaning" (Miscall, 1983, p. 4). Even when the epithet is not used, however, it is clear that Hebrew Scriptures describe the special, personal relationship of a particular male deity and a particular male community in terms of father and son.

Another area of feminist biblical criticism is how the Bible represents sexual differences and questions assumptions that arise in an exegetical tradition that has been almost entirely male. That is, it challenges the view that traditional readings reflect the "objective" value judgments of history and posterity and sees it instead as culture-bound. Some theorists feel that feminist biblical scholars should develop a separate "feminist canon" of interpretation, while others argue that rather than restricting efforts to construct a "female counter-canon" of hermeneutics, there should be a radical challenge to the dominant male interpretations and traditions.

Although interested in the subject of language and writing, generally speaking, feminist biblical scholars analyze biblical texts by close reading and historical scholarship rather than by abstractly discussing language, and two major schools have developed. One approach, "feminist critique," examines how women characters are portrayed, exposing the patriarchal ideology implicit in the texts, and demonstrating that attitudes and traditions reinforcing systematic masculine dominance are inscribed in the biblical canon. Examples include the stereotypical images of women as angels or monsters, the textual harassment of women in biblical narratives, and even the exclusion of certain categories of women from the text (such as daughters).

Another focus of feminist biblical hermeneutics is "gynocriticism," studies of biblical writings believed to have been written by women. Scholars examine, compare, and contrast the "female texts" to the "male texts" to help discern how women writers may have perceived themselves and imagined reality. For example, gynocriticism is concerned with identifying topics and themes that are taken to be distinctively "female" subject matter, such as the world of domesticity, or the special experiences of menstruation, gestation, delivery, nurturing, mother-daughter relationships, female bonding, lesbian relationships, goddess worship, etc. Several scholars, for example, attribute Song of Songs to a female voice (see, for example, Brenner, 1993). Again, this might be explained historically. Until recently the patriarchal values which dominate our culture couldn't help but obscure the possibility of even considering female authorship.

A third area is "female aesthetics," perhaps the most difficult to categorize. The single designation "woman reader" glosses over crucial differences, and, as a result, feminist biblical critics have been attempting to avoid a "universal" female reading, which is as false as the "generic masculine." Feminists of color, postcolonial feminists, lesbian, bisexual, and transgender feminists have stressed that women are not defined solely by the fact that they are biologically female; other attributes (such as religion, class, and sexual orientation) are important also, making the problems and goals of one group of women different from those of another. As a result, today's feminist critics, biblical and otherwise, seldom focus on "woman" as a monolithic category; rather, "women" are members of different societies with different concerns. However, some generalizations are essential to theory formation; in order to examine the implications of feminist criticism, there is an assumption of a common ground in the experiences and perspectives of different kinds of women that sets women apart from men. Of course, the same holds true if one is concerned with discussing the implications of nationality, class, or sexual orientation. Thus, every feminist theorist is faced with the challenge of devising a reading that avoids exclusions, and at the same time, avoids generalizations.

While the Bible may have an androcentric perspective on culture, women were, nevertheless, part of that culture and experienced it from a different perspective. Thus, inquiries *into* women's activities without adopting the text's perspective *on* those activities is another appropriate and necessary pursuit. The majority of feminists use at least one of two possible approaches: social-historical processes of inquiry (which describe the roles and functions of women within the contexts of the larger social world reconstructed by cultural data) and literary methods (which involve the role of metaphor, rhetorical and new criticisms, and narratology). Both methods explore the roles of women in the Bible and noncanonical literature that appear to have been overlooked or misconstrued—usually by male interpreters. This brings us back to the point about not allowing the perspective biases inherent in the text to limit and define the range of questions one can ask. Women *did* exist even in patriarchal cultures, and if we take *that* as a point of departure rather than grant the relatively limited text the authority to speak on women's behalf, then we have every reason to try to ascertain, from a *female* perspective, the realities of biblical-era female existence which lie below the surface.

AN APPLICATION OF FEMINIST BIBLICAL CRITICISM: ADAM AND EVE

The remainder of this chapter explores one of the most well-known narratives in the Western literary tradition, that of Adam and Eve, as an example of how some feminist biblical critics interpret the text.

Pre-Feminist Readings

The text with which most English-speaking readers are familiar is an English translation which portrays Adam as superior and inherently good. On the other hand, Eve is portrayed as inferior, a temptress and troublemaker, dependent upon and dominated by her husband. While the Hebrew Bible is certainly a source of these English texts, and these texts are "biblical," they do not reflect wholly the language and poetics of the biblical writer. In part, this is due to the problems of translation. In greater part, however, the differences between the Hebrew Bible and the English translations are due to conscious and unconscious interpretive practices. Feminist readings of this narrative discussed below are not presented against any "*mis*-readings" of other biblical scholars, but rather highlight the ambiguity inherent in the Hebrew narrative. The creation of Woman is a good place to start.

One of the most well-circulated documents immediately preceding the Reformation was the *Malleus Maleficarum* which devotes long passages to the perfidy of women, all of its arguments based on Christian biblical commentators and the Vulgate Old Testament ["For it is true that in the Old Testament the Scriptures have much that is evil to say about women" (Institoris, [1486] 1970, p. xliv)]. Women, according to the *Malleus Maleficarum,* are a "foe to friendship," an "unescapable punishment," a "necessary evil," a "natural temptation," a "desirable calamity," a "domestic danger," a "delectable detriment," and an "evil of nature" (Institoris, [1486] 1970, p. 2043). All wickedness is but little to the wickedness of a woman because of the first temptress, Eve, and her imitators. Women are feebler both in mind and body:

> For as regards intellect, or the understanding of spiritual things, they seem to be of a different nature from men . . . the natural reason is that she is more carnal than a man, as is clear from her many carnal abominations. And it should be noted that there was a defect in the formation of the first woman, since she was formed from a bent rib, that is, a rib of the breast, which is bent as it were in a contrary direction to a man. And since through this defect she is an imperfect animal, she always deceives . . . And all this is indicated by the etymology of the word . . .for *Femina* comes from *Fe* and *Minus*, since she is ever weaker. (Institoris, [1486] 1970, p. 44)

Although the devil tempted Eve to sin, it was Eve who seduced Adam, and as a result, Eve is the cause of death in this world:

> She is more bitter than death . . . because bodily death is an open and terrible enemy, but woman is a wheedling and secret enemy. (Institoris, [1486] 1970, p. 47)

The author of the *Ancrene Riwle*, a popular 13th-century didactic work addressed to a large community of women, puts this characterization to new uses. He begins with the familiar comparison of Eve and Mary, criticizing Eve for talking too much and praising Mary at length for her sparing use of words:

> Eve had a long talk with the serpent in Paradise; she told him the entire lesson that God had delivered to her and to Adam so that the fiend understood immediately Eve's weakness. Our Lady, Saint Mary, acted entirely different. She didn't tell the angel any stories but asked as little as possible. So, yes, my dear sisters, follow the example of Our Lady, not the chattering Eve. (Dobson, 1972, p. 54)

Based on this view of women and following the teachings of the early Christian fathers, throughout the Middle Ages and the Renaissance, men wrote didactic treatises, especially for women. A. A. Hentsch compiled a collection of 114 such treatises from the time of Jerome to the Reformation, written in Latin, French, Italian, English, Spanish, and Catalan (Hentsch, 1903).

Feminist Readings

Not surprisingly, the Adam and Eve narrative in Genesis is one of the most discussed biblical texts by feminist critics. Virtually all feminist readings question the traditional characterizations of Adam and Eve (see, for example, Trible, 1978; and the chapter in Fewell, 1999, which quotes Bal, Jobling, and others).

What are some of the questions I ask of the Genesis 1–3 account? Of course, there is a subjective and therefore broadly political component in the very *process* of question formulation since questions themselves are, after all, interpretive frameworks.

The first (obviously rhetorical question) is if we should follow Plato and ban the narrative because it *is* troublesome, or whether we should tolerate it as Aristotle tolerated tragedy. More seriously, I ask what is the "*his*tory" vs. "*her*story" of a given text. One way of teasing out these differences is to engage in critical free play. But a good deal depends on how "difference" is defined. Deconstruction, as literary theorists remind us, is more of an "undoing" than a "destruction," and manifests itself in the careful teasing out of warring forces of signification within the text—forces which cannot be controlled by one single interpretation. Insofar as feminist criticism is capable of being described, it operates by putting *everything* into question, including the normal operations *for* putting things into question. That is, feminist criticism is not simply a reversal of categories and priorities, but an attempt to undo both a given order of priorities and the system that makes that order possible. Questioning the "*his*tory" of the Bible in relation to the "*her*story" therefore also questions the priorities of a phallocratic order.

Another specific question I ask is the relationship between literary discourse and power. Discourse analysis belongs to many fields, but it seems particularly appropriate for feminist literary studies of the Bible. The literary implications of discourse have been developed recently, extending the discussion in linguistic circles about the relationship between gender, language, and social structure to the narrative. I am intrigued by the meaning of particular symbols in biblical dialogues. Who speaks? When? Under what circumstances? What are the social and dialectical aspects? Indeed, what are the implications of using speech acts as a symbolic medium at all, since individual words can mean more than they seem to mean and do more than they seem to do?

A *cautionary* question I ask is what is entailed in doing a "reading" at all? What degree of latitude is permissible in an activity which, as I said earlier, can never aspire to exactitude? Feminist criticism is certainly not a clarion call to abandon the rigorous pursuit of intellectual accuracy, and "misreadings" can occur in pursuit of a feminist ideal.

Creation of Eve

In Genesis 1:26, the deity says that he will make "Adam" (Humankind) in his image, and *they will rule* over the rest of the earth and its inhabitants. The narrator then reports, "God created Humankind in his image, in the image of God he created *him*; male and female he created *them*." The pronoun "them" is plural, as is the verb form (*they* will rule). Since "Adam" is a generic term for "Humankind" which has two sub-types, male and female, it can be read that Man and Woman were created as two separate beings, and that male and female, *together* and *equally*, are to rule over other creatures; there is no dominion of male over female.

In Genesis 2, the actual creation of Woman is elaborated upon. The text explains that the deity realizes Man needs a helper to match him. All of the animals parade past Man, but none qualifies. What is a "helper to match" Man?

Almost all occurrences of the word "helper" in the Hebrew Bible refer unmistakably to help from someone stronger, one who in no way needs assistance himself. It denotes a helper of the weak, or a helper in battle, and is used often as a proper name for a highly regarded priest or warrior (for example, in Hosea 13:4, God tells Israel, "You have never had a helper other than Me"). Of the twenty-one instances where the word is used as a noun, God is the "helper" seventeen times, and the remainder refer to military forces who come to Israel's aid. Only three occurrences could possibly be understood as help from equal or lesser forces, and even they need not be read that way, for the help referred to in all three instances is military strategy. Thus, this term, as used throughout the Hebrew Bible, designates a relationship which implies no inferiority on the part of the helper. In fact, the helper is necessary to continue the very existence or well-being of the person being assisted. To read Adam as a "perfect" being prior to the creation of Woman (his "helper") is to read Adam in opposition to the use of the word "helper" in the rest of the Hebrew Bible. More specifically, the *type* of helper Man needs is one who is a counterpart, an equal. Despite Man's relationship with the animals, their similarity does not imply the equality intended by the deity.

Traditional commentators have treated the original Hebrew word as implying a suitable, but *inferior* assistant, reinforcing the idea of female subordination by the familiar translation "helpe *meet*," a 16th-century expression used to describe a "small" or "subservient" assistant. Read this way, Woman's role *would* be to keep Man company, but *not* to rule co-equally.

The narrator then describes the actual creation of Woman:

> The Lord God cast a deep sleep upon Adam [humankind] and he [this earthling] slept; and he [God] took one of his [Humankind's] sides and closed up the flesh in its place. And the Lord God built the side which he took from the Man into a Woman and brought her to the Man. (Gen. 2:21–22)

Again, this raises issues. The first is the verb "build." Thus far in the narrative, the deity has "created" (the heaven and earth), "declared" that something should exist (for example, "there *will* be light"), "made" (the firmament), and "separated" (the waters above and the firmament below). However, it is necessary to "build" Woman, the first use of this verb in the text. Throughout the Hebrew Bible, "build" is used in contexts that suggest considerable labor, the "building" of towns, towers, altars, and fortifications. Apparently, the deity exerts little energy in providing for a heaven and an earth, light and darkness, stars and oceans, grass, seeds, trees, birds, sea monsters, beasts, or even Man: God merely *states* his intention and the narrator reports "and it was so." But the creation of Woman requires *considerable* effort.

And of what is Woman made? Unlike Adam, who was created out of the earth, the Hebrew text states that Woman was created from Adam's side. Like "build," this word is quite distinctive, used only in reference to the sides of the Tabernacle or the Temple and emphasizes the uniqueness of Woman. The narrator reports that the deity "builds" Woman, and then explains that it was out of Adam's "side," a word generally used in construction contexts. Significantly, this is the only biblical narrative where "side" refers to part of the human anatomy.

The popular translation, of course, is that Woman was created from Adam's "rib." ("Rib" does not appear to be a translation used anywhere else in the Hebrew Bible.) But perhaps "side" signifies too much importance for Woman, and not enough subordination: after all, there are only two "sides" to a person, but men have many "ribs." Certainly, one rib out of twelve can be spared to make a "helpe meet," but not one side out of only two for a "necessary helper."

Another argument used to support the inferior status of Woman is that she was the *second* human created, and thus secondary in rank. In fact, it *can* be argued that the text claims female *superiority* based on this same fact, if we note that animals are created in a Darwinian *ascending* series: creeping things; beasts; birds of wing; cattle and living things of the earth; fish of the sea; birds of the heavens; Man; and last, Woman. Thus, even if Eve *was* created after Adam, unless we accept Man as inferior to the creeping things because he was created *after* them, Woman cannot be viewed as inferior merely because of creation order.

Certainly, Man does not perceive Woman as having been created as an inferior. In fact, having recognized that Woman is indeed his equal, he exclaims: "This one, *this* time, is bone of my bones, and flesh of my flesh." That is, "at last a creature corresponding to *me*." Having rejected all that existed on the earth as his equal, Man is presented finally with someone with whom he can identify. And he identifies with her so closely that *he* uses a word which counterbalances his own identity. Until now only the generic term "Humankind" has been used. The deity refers to and calls "Adam." But once Woman has been created, the sociosexual terms of Man and Woman are used, and used first by Man. It is Man who recognizes that no word yet exists which fully denotes the equality implicit in their relationship, and he picks a twin-like name to express his affinity for and kinship with Woman. Significantly, he abandons the word which unites him more closely with the other animals who were inadequate to be his helper to match him.

Eating of the Fruit

The part of the Adam and Eve story that has received the most overlay of interpretation, however, is that of the eating of the fruit and perhaps the first (and most important) task is to distinguish between the narrative itself and the canonized overlay. A conversation takes place in Eden, one filled with textual ambiguity. Despite the fact that most interpreters view the serpent conversing only with Woman and not with Man also, the text does leave room for doubt.

First, from the moment the deity brings Woman to Man in Genesis 2, the narrator never mentions their being separated, never mentions Man doing one thing and Woman another. Second, in the dialogue of verse 16, the serpent speaks about "you" in the plural, and Woman answers in terms of "we," furthering the possibility that Man is standing there with her, also being addressed. Third, Genesis 3:7 says "and the eyes of *both of them* were opened." Since, strictly speaking, Woman's eyes should have been opened at the moment "she took of its fruit and she ate" (that is, *first*), this verse further substantiates the position that Man and Woman are tempted, take, and eat *together*.

However, the most serious argument for Man's presence is in the second half of Genesis 3:6. When Woman eats of the fruit of the forbidden tree, she gives some also to Man, and the text adds the phrase "to her husband *with her.*" Because of the grammatical construction, this part of the verse should properly be read as "to her husband (who *was*) with her."

If Man was present, and there seems to be no textual evidence to the contrary, then the narrator is portraying Man as silent and passive, a bland recipient. The narrator makes no attempt to depict Man as reluctant to eat of the fruit, or even hesitant. In fact, since it was only Man who heard the prohibition against eating of the tree of knowledge of good and evil directly from the deity (Woman having heard this prohibition second-hand, that is, filtered through Man), *he* is more guilty of having violated God's command than *she*.

Having eaten of the famous fruit, Man and Woman flee from the sound of the deity in the garden. God first questions Man regarding responsibility. Faced with his creator's anger over the transgression, Adam states: "The woman whom you gave [to be] with me, she gave to me from the tree and I ate." Adam does not claim that Woman seduced him; he does not call Woman wily as the narrator had previously described the serpent. If the text intended to make Woman the temptress, here was the opportune occasion. But the text is silent.

Yet, Woman *is* viewed as "temptress," and this portrayal of primeval Woman, stemming in particular out of the last half of Genesis 3:6, has continued. The Geneva Bible, for example, has in its marginalia "The woman seduced by the serpent, entiseth her husband to sin . . . [eating] of the fruit not so much to please his wife, as moved by her persuasion." The Rheims-Douay translators compare the serpent and the Woman in their marginalia: "She was beguiled by an inferior and subject; *as was Adam.*" The overwhelming consensus has been that Eve tempted, beguiled, lured, corrupted, persuaded, suggested, urged, used wicked persuasion, led into wrongdoing, proved herself an enemy, used guile and cozening, tears and lamentations, to prevail upon Adam; she had no rest until she got her husband banished, and thus she became "the first temptress." But substituting "tempts" and "temptress" for the literal "gave also to her husband who was with her" clearly strains the text. In a plain reading, it strains logic to read "she *gave* also some to her husband" as the equivalent of tempting and leading into sin. If they *are* synonymous, then it might be said that *God* is the cause of sin, for the deity "*gave*" Adam his wife, and "*gave*" Adam the garden to keep, with the forbidden tree in the middle of it.

The Punishment

One final point needs to be examined in re-reading this narrative: the "curse" on Woman in Genesis 3:16: "I will greatly multiply your pain in childbearing: in pain you will bring forth children; your desire shall be for your husband, and he shall rule over you." In the structure of Hebrew poetry, the second half of a line frequently is closely related in content to the first half: it carries the thought further, either repeating, clarifying, restating, or contrasting. "In pain you shall bring forth children" duplicates "your pain in childbearing." Therefore, "he shall rule over you" parallels "your desire shall be for your husband." The husband's "rule" lies either in the wife's need for her husband because of her desire to have children, or the strength of his sexual attraction for her. This is not an abstract statement of the subordination of Woman to Man in all relationships. Yet, that is how it has been interpreted, and that is how the narrative has been canonized. Traditional exegesis has characterized Adam as the quintessential "superior" male whose role in life is to dominate Eve. Eve is a deceptive temptress, morally inferior to Adam, stereotyped as "evil" and as a result, Woman is condemned eternally to be Man's "helpe meet."

CONCLUSION

In sum, looking at the Hebrew Bible through feminist lenses entails a shift in perspective with potentially profound implications. A feminist reading opens up the contents, revealing both its historical/cultural context *and* the religious possibilities its translating and editing conceals. A feminist approach can widen our historical and religious orientation by bringing to the fore material that previously may have gone unnoted (or intentionally overlooked). More importantly, it introduces another standard perspective—even, perhaps, another standard of *value*—by which we might judge and appreciate what we see. Feminist criticism forces us to look at who defines certain readings as normative, to what end, and with what implications. Insofar as feminism is characterized by concern and sympathy for women's experience, it demands we examine, reexamine, and take seriously the biblical texts that have spoken to and about women, and attempt to reevaluate our place in, and relation to, the wider tradition of biblical exegesis.

NOTE

It should be noted that feminist literary criticism, the precursor to contemporary feminist biblical criticism, became popular in the late 1970s. One of the major texts was Simone de Beauvoir's book, *Le Deuxième Sexe,* the main thesis of which is that woman is the "incidental," the "inessential," as opposed to the man who is the "essential." He is the Subject, he is the "Absolute"—she is the "Other." Thus, associating men with humanity more generally relegates women to an inferior position in society. Simultaneously, feminist literary critics focused on language as a tool of male domination, analyzing the ways in which language represents the world from the male point of view. Other feminist critics began examining how female characters are portrayed in the so-called literary "classics" emphasizing the implicit patriarchal ideology. Literary scholars also studied writings by women, examining female literary traditions.

REFERENCES

Alt, A. (1967). *The god of the fathers: Essays on Old Testament history and religion.* Trans. R. A. Wilson. Garden City: Doubleday.

Brenner, A. (1993). Women poets and authors. In Athalya Brenner (Ed.), *A feminist companion to the Song of Songs* (pp. 86–99). Sheffield: Sheffield Academic Press.

Cross, F. (1983). *Canaanite myth and Hebrew epic: Essays in the history of the religion of Israel*. Cambridge: Harvard University Press.

De Beauvoir, S. (1961). *The second sex*. Translated by H. M. Parshley. New York: Bantam Books.

Dobson, E. J., (Ed.). (1972). *The English text of the Ancrene Riwle*. London: Oxford UP.

Exum, J. C. (2010). Where have all the feminists gone? *lectio difficilior* 2/2010. http://www.lectio.unibe.ch.

Fewell, D. N. (1999). Reading the Bible ideologically: Feminist criticism. In S. L. McKenzie and S. R. Haynes (Eds.), *To each its own meaning: An introduction to Biblical criticisms and their application* (pp. 268–282). Westminster: John Knox Press.

Fiorenza, E. (Ed.). (2014). *Feminist biblical studies in the twentieth century: Scholarship and movement*. Atlanta, GA.: Society of Biblical Literature.

Haran, M. (1965). The religion of the patriarchs. *Annual of the Swedish Theological Institute 4*, 51–52.

Heine, S. (1989). *Matriarchs, goddesses, and images of God: A critique of feminist theology*. Translated by John Bowden. Minneapolis: Augsburg Press.

Hentsch, A. A. (1903). *De la litterature didactique du moyen age s'adressant specialement aux femmes*. Paris: Cahors.

Hyatt, J. P. (1955). Yahweh as the god of my father. *Vestus Testamentum 5*, 130–136.

Institoris, H. ([1486] 1970). *Malleus Maleficarum*. Translated by Montague Summers. New York: Bloom.

Kalmanofsky, A. (2015). Gender-bending in the Bible. Biblical interpretation. www.bibleinterp.com/opeds/2015/06/kal398016.shtml.

Macwilliam, S. (2011). *Queer theory and the prophetic marriage metaphor in the Hebrew Bible*. London: Equinox Pub.

Miscall, P. (1983). *The workings of Old Testament narrative*. Philadelphia: Fortress Press.

Myers, C. (2014). Foregrounding ordinary Israelite women. *AJS Perspectives*, Fall, 7–8.

Ozick, C. (1983). Notes toward finding the right question. In S. Heschel (Ed.), *On being a Jewish feminist: A reader* (pp. 120–151). New York: Schocken Books.

Plaskow, J. (1990). *Standing again at Sinai: Judaism from a feminist perspective*. San Francisco: Harper & Row.

Rashkow, I. (2000). *Taboo or not taboo: Sexuality and family in the Hebrew Bible*. Minneapolis: Fortress Press.

Sarna, N. (1989). The Jewish Publication Society Torah commentary: Genesis. Philadelphia: The Jewish Publication Society.

Stanton, E. C. (1895). *The woman's Bible*. New York: European Publishing Company.

Trible, P. (1978). *God and the rhetoric of sexuality*. Philadelphia: Fortress Press.

ADDITIONAL READINGS

Achtemeier, P. (Ed.). (1988). The Bible, theology and feminist approaches. *Int 42/1*, 3–72.

Bal, M. (1987). *Lethal love: Feminist literary readings of biblical love stories*. Bloomington, IN: Indiana University Press.

Brooten, B. (1982). *Women leaders in the ancient synagogue*. Chico, CA: Brown Judaic Studies.

Camp, C. V. (1987). Female voice, written word: Women and authority in Hebrew scripture. In Cooey, P. M., Farmer, S. A., and Ross, M. E. (Eds.), *Embodied Love* (pp. 97–113). San Francisco: Harper & Row.

Cannon, K. G., & Schüssler Fiorenza, E. (1989). *Interpretation for liberation*. Semeia 47. Atlanta, GA: Society of Biblical Literature.

Chopp, R. S. (1989). *The power to speak. Feminism, language, God*. New York: Crossroad Pub.

Fuchs, E. (1989). Marginalization, antiquity, silencing: The story of Jephthah's daughter. *JFSR 5/1*, 35–46.

Hackett, J. A. (1987). Women's studies and the Hebrew Bible. In R. E. Friedman and H. G. M. Williamson (Eds.), *The future of biblical studies: The Hebrew scriptures* (pp. 141–164). Atlanta, GA: Society of Biblical Literature.

King, K. L. (Ed.). (1987). *Images of the feminine in Gnosticism*. (Studies in Antiquity and Christianity series.) Philadelphia: Fortress Press.

Kraemer, R. (Ed.). (1988). *Maenads, martyrs, matrons, monastics: A sourcebook on women's religion in the Greco-Roman world*. Philadelphia: Fortress Press.

Kramer, R. (1983). Women in the religions of the Greco-Roman world. *RSR 9*, 127–139.

Milne, P. J. (1989). The patriarchal stamp of scripture. *JFSR 5/1*, 17–34.

Mollenkott, V. R. (1983). *The divine feminine: The biblical imagery of God as female*. New York: Crossroad Pub.

Moltmann-Wendel, E. (1983). *The women around Jesus*. New York: Crossroad Pub.

Myers, C. (1988). *Discovering Eve*. New York: Oxford University Press.

Pagels, E. (1988). *Adam, Eve and the serpent*. New York: Random House.

Procter-Smith, M. (1989). *In her own rites*. Nashville: Abingdon Press.

Russell, L. M. (Ed.). (1985). *Feminist interpretation of the Bible*. Philadelphia: Westminster.

Russell, L. M. (1976). *The liberating word: A guide to nonsexual interpretation of the Bible*. Philadelphia: Westminster Press.

Schaberg, J. (1989a). Biblical interpretation and critical commitment. *StTh 43*, 5–18.

Schaberg, J. (1989b). Text and reality, reality as text: The problem of a feminist historical and social reconstruction based on texts. *StTh 40*, 19–34.

Schaberg, J. (1987). Theological criteria and hermeneutical reconstruction: Martha and Mary (Lk 10:38–42). Protocol 53. Berkeley.

Schüssler Fiorenza, E. (1985). *Bread not stone: The challenge of feminist biblical interpretation*. Boston: Beacon Press.

Schüssler Fiorenza, E. (1983). *In Memory of her: A feminist theological reconstruction of Christian origins*. New York: SCM Press.

Tamez, E. (1988). Women's rereading of her Bible. In V. Fabella and M. Oduyoye (Eds.), *With passion and compassion: Third world women doing theology* (pp. 173–180). Maryknoll, NY: Orbis Books.

Tolbert, M. A. (Ed.) (1983). *The Bible and feminist hermeneutics*. Semeia 28. Atlanta: Society of Biblical Literature.

Trible, P. (1984). *Texts of terror. Literary-feminist readings of biblical narratives*. Philadelphia: Fortress Press.

Trible, P. (Ed.). (1984). *Black women in antiquity*. New Brunswick, NJ: Transaction Books.

Trible, P. (1982). The effects of women's studies on biblical studies. *JSOT 22*, 3–72.

Trible, P. (1978). *God and the rhetoric of sexuality*. Philadelphia: Fortress Press.

Weems, R. (1988). *Just a sister away*. San Diego: Lura Media.

Wegner, J. R. (1980). *Chattel or person: The status of women in the Mishnah*. New York: OUP.

Yarbro Collins, A. (Ed.). (1985). *Feminist perspectives on biblical scholarship*. Atlanta: Scholars Press.

Chapter 4

The Church, Woman, Leadership, and the Body

Silvia Geruza Fernandez Rodrigues

For centuries, the concept of man's superiority over woman has been built up through various means of communication. Through secular and religious literature, preaching, speeches, and teachings, women have been depicted as second-class citizens. According to "nature's laws" and in society as in church, women have been expected to accept submission unto man as an ordinance of God since creation. It has been taught that man was created to dominate both animals and women. Since he (Adam) was created first, by nature's law, woman must submit to his leadership and dominion and be able to distinguish the difference between their roles.

Many authors acknowledge the woman's anguish in her diminished role. They try to emphasize that even though the genders have different roles, they merely comply to hierarchic order, but woman's value remains intact. It has been emphasized that every society needs hierarchy to survive. However, others do not even try to cover up the fact that they believe women are indeed inferior to men. Therefore, their roles are different and women have more important tasks at home than in church or society. As a matter of fact, some even think—and state—that the only role the woman has in church is to be quiet, pray, and listen to the sermons delivered by the "legitimate and only" messenger of God—man.

Rita Lemaire (1997) finds it strange that in the literary construction of history, literature has consistently shown brilliant and heroic men, but has eliminated women, even though there are many women who have been brave soldiers and fighters. They have been listed as exceptional cases, pointing out that, in "men's affairs," there is no room for "normal" women. This only shows the masculine tendency to justify his power through origins in the past and his mapping of evolution, whether factual or hypothetical, up to the current day.

Through writing and literature men legitimate their present power status through the idea of ancestral inheritance:

> In this sense, in the human sciences discourses, the masculine representations over the woman, as the "natural essential and universally weak" can be considered one of the most radical ways of this kind of power legitimacy: it is not only about the ancestors' representation, once they were never different. (Lemaire, 1997, p. 180)

In literary history, women were systematically denied the propagation of their ideas and talents. The stories usually described some sort of insecurity about biological paternity, and the description of the lineage in paternal terms excessively emphasized cultural paternity as a mechanism of exclusion or denial of elements that would disturb the masculine monopoly.

Literary history has been, with very few exceptions, fundamentally ethnocentric and male centric. In European literary history, women were excluded or had their characteristics altered during the progressive process of oral transition into written forms. By choosing Latin as an elitist language, men were able to impose their worldviews. Until then, in European traditional communities, there were two differentiated cultures coexisting together, based on the economic work division between the sexes—men's culture and women's culture. Their universes developed in an atmosphere of equality, but each gender had its own kind of traditional knowledge and its own ways to deal with love, life, death, nature, and religion, as well as its own songs and literary identity.

Men basically used three methods of overpowering women: dominating the elite language, Latin, instead of using people's mother tongue; taking hold of symbols and rites from women's cultural world; and removing their discourse from context and inserting masculine speech.

In medieval literature, men and women were represented as active subjects, with their own desires, who took sexual initiative to satisfy their needs and desires. However, through literature, men identified themselves as active, as opposed to the passive identity attributed to women. They used several stylistic and rhetorical strategies, such as exaggeration, irony and ridicule, and the changing of concrete symbols into abstract metaphors to make women look passive, incompetent, or stupid. In Portuguese medieval songs, as well, there were several correlated transitions, where men were portrayed as active and as the only *Homo sapiens*.

The written literature despised oral tradition and culture and proclaimed itself as the only true civilized literature. The power of literature in forming social consciousness and concepts about women and men is undeniable, as, for example, the idea in Medieval and Renaissance Europe that women were lustier than men.

As every ideology comes with a promise, novels were written to encourage women to practice piety and be sexually pure. Samuel Richardson can be taken as example, in his book *Pamela*, written in 1740. Puritanical in his attitudes, he described well the sexual hierarchy wherein Pamela, the heroine, was an example of moral and sexual purity subject to the threats and tricks of lusty men. She would be rewarded if she resisted. The man who had threatened her fell in love with her, proposing marriage and becoming a changed man. Even when a woman is attributed "virtues" in men's written literature, the sexual hierarchy shown justifies and imposes a task division that at the same time gives man his power and his moral purity. Richardson portrays the woman as weak, without authority, and without autonomy.

WOMAN'S HISTORY IN RELIGIOUS LITERATURE

In religious literature, starting with the Bible, women's history has been treated as of little importance. For example, we might question why the women to whom Jesus appeared for the first time at Passover, and who were sent with news that would change history, are not mentioned either at the time or later in the New Testament narrative. Why, after such a great and extraordinary event, did those women have no say in the narrative, except for a brief report of Mary, Jesus's mother, who was present at the day of Pentecost?

It seems improbable that after years of intense ministry, these women went back to their homes to cook and to devote themselves to domestic tasks. But this is what we are expected to believe by the complete absence of reports about them.

If one reflects on what it meant for these women to follow Jesus at a time when their role was expected to be solely domestic, one can see that they were delivered from their traditional housewife role and now followed Jesus as his disciples. Probably, even Jesus's male disciples, whom they took care of, were not able to assimilate very well the different relationship they now experienced having women around them. By now they would have well understood the mission fellowship that Paul's letters show us and probably these women formed a group within their group.

For His women followers, Jesus was more than a promise of salvation. He became a real person to whom they had become close and that is why they were determined to follow Him in all His troubled moments. They would follow Him until His death, and after His burial, they had the courage to go to His tomb to anoint Him. This seems to have been possible for them to do because they were still considered unimportant by the authorities. Perhaps that scenario would change after Christ's resurrection, when everyone would be indiscriminately persecuted.

Their report of Christ's resurrection was rejected at first, probably because they were women, or because men felt humiliated for not being the first ones to witness such a relevant event.

Right after Pentecost, when the church started to find its role in the history of its time, male leadership was again established, setting women aside in their expected role of submission and insignificance. This was possible because Jesus was not there anymore to defy these tendencies, to call women to the center, and to affirm their roles as disciples and missionaries.

If we analyze Church history, we can also observe the considerable omission of feminine names, even though it is well established that women did participate in history making. Many historians cite women who left theological work, but very few of the women are quoted or included in the religious literature.

Mary Ward was arrested in Roma, Egeria, in 400 CE. Probably, this Galician monk wrote books about life and liturgy in Jerusalem; in her writing "Itinerarium" she recorded her peregrination to the Holy Land.

St. Gertrude the Great (1301), writer of five books entitled *The Messenger of Divine Love*, lived in a famous convent in Hefta that had an excellent school led by another woman, Matilde de Hackeborn, who wrote the *Book of Special Grace*.

Mechthild de Magdeburg (1282) was the author of seven books entitled *The Flowing Light of the Godhead*. In 1500, Teresa d'Ávila, from the order of Carmel, was declared a Doctor of the Church. In 1669, the young Juana Inês de La Cruz was recognized as the best poetess and the first great literarian of Spanish America. She defended women's right to culture in her "Letter to Sor Filotea de la Cruz," and in "Redondillas en defense de las mujeres," she satirized sexist prejudice. In a letter, "Carta Atenagórica," she raised a polemic argument against Pe. Vieira that showed understanding of patristic and scholastic theology.

In 1684, prejudice against women emerged when Elena Lucrezia Cornaro Piscopia went to the University of Padua, to take her doctorate in theology. They denied her the title of doctor in theology because she was a woman; instead they gave her a certificate of doctorate in philosophy.

It is necessary to mention male missionaries whose names became well known all over the world, but whose wives' names remain unknown, even when they played a large role in their husbands' ministry in the mission field. Usually, Christian literature attributes very little or no importance to those women.

We infer that the fears that motivate women's exclusion from the sacred have to do with relations of power. The masculinization of power was also inserted into the religious world, mirroring the patriarchic culture.

In the New Testament, Jesus related with women differently from Church institutions. His history with them did not include a power struggle. He empowered them to have a meaning that society had denied them. In this liberation, they were allowed to perceive Jesus's mission and to live it. Women's exclusion from the sacred comes from a fear of the feminine. According to Haughton:

> They are near home, in the house, however they are "the other, and they represent and feel the feminine in each one of them. They show their weakness in the dominant class. They are the enemy inside the house.(. . .) They represent that which the patriarchal culture fears: the uncontrollable, the unpredictable, life's own source, the vulnerability which is in the macho heart in the moment that domination fails and life begins. But life cannot be controlled, even though it can be destroyed. (1990, pp. 147–148)

Historically, the church lost contact with how Jesus acted in regard to women and consequently with the missionary liberation movement. It did not understand His main action toward women.

THE CHURCH RECORD WITH WOMEN

There are basically two main movements within the Christian church. According to the traditionalists, only men can have functions of leadership or hold positions involving education, authority, and ability. Women are the inferior part of a society while man is the main protagonist.

Robert Culver (1996) clearly states that man is the "head" of every Christian woman, not only his wife. "Head" means authority to him. According to him, a man must always have priority over a woman because she originated from him. I Corinthians 11:9 is used to establish man's authority in public liturgy, other social spheres, and obviously in the religious context. He believes that woman is made for man (Gen. 2:9); therefore, he must have authority over her in church, and woman must recognize this authority, supporting him in all matters. At home, as well, men are the main authority while women must conform and accept taking care of them.

As all ideology comes with a promise, Culver states that if women were to search for meaning by working with money or machines, they would go back home to their usual tasks to feel better. For him a woman's life is in its best aspect a "ceremony" (Weaver, in Culver, 1996, p. 57).

Anne Carr (1997) states that the dominant attitude up to today has been that the man is active, dominant, and more important in Christian history, and that the woman is naturally inferior and childish. Public ministries are reserved to men.

Many traditionalist theologians affirm the role of woman as procreator, and as man's helper. That task makes her inferior. She is merely a complement to the male.

In Christianity, woman's nature is always pictured as ruled by intuition and emotion and man's as active, reasonable, and self-controlled.

The concepts of marriage, children's education, teaching, business, law, and science form an ideological vocabulary that portrays the woman as "the other," the companion, the support; and the man as subject.

A great influence on that concept has come from the Fathers of the Church (100 to 800 CE), who lived right after the New Testament period. Their view of women was not very positive. Their attitude and ministries varied from place to place, but in the majority, they saw women as weak in body and intellect, tending to sin and heresy, sexually provocative, and a potential danger to Christian men.

The Church "Fathers," influenced by the Greco-Roman culture, declared that women were, *per definitionem*, the more fragile vase, slow in comprehension, mentally unstable, tending to deceit, and the source of rebellion, which ruined man—the image and glory of God—thus causing the death of God's son.

Women were not supposed to be in leadership in the church because, erroneously in the Church Fathers' exegesis, it was women who brought disaster to Paradise and because further disasters should be safeguarded against as well. Their responsibility for evil in the past was a sign that such trouble could repeat itself in the future unless care was taken.

Since the fourth century, through Augustine, one of the most influential Christian theologians, concepts of women have been pessimistic and sexist. The Church Fathers understood that a woman should be submissive to a man because of the natural and universal order. Ambrosio (fourth century) stated, for example, that women were not even made in the image of God, like men:

> How can you say that the woman is the image of God when she must submit to man as her master and she does not have any authority? She is not allowed to teach, nor to be witness in court, nor to make

> promises, nor to be a judge; even more is she incapable of leading! (Edwards, 1989, p. 91)

Augustine argued that even though Eve had in her body the same essence as Adam, her body was independent of his, implying that, by nature, men worry more about the spiritual, while women worry more about the physical and sexual.

Augustine taught that by "natural law" women should serve men, solving the tension between Genesis 1:26 and I Corinthians 11:7, arguing that the woman can only be in the image of God through her husband, even though there is the explicit declaration in Genesis that both male and female are made in the image of God.

The proposal that a woman will only be in the image of God through a man leaves unsolved the problem of those who do not get married. Is salvation only for married women? The race for husbands in the fourth century must have been fierce.

Ambrosio derived the name "woman" from the Latin word *mulher* (in Portuguese): *mulier*, woman, *molities mentis* (soft mind), contrasting with the derivation of *vir*, man, from the *animi virtus* meaning the *strength of the soul*. This was similar to the ideas of Aristotle, who believed that men were the norm and the ideal of perfection, and that women who had Faith could evolve and become like men.

The Church Fathers emphasized woman's submissiveness to man because of a negative attitude towards the human body and sexuality. They interpreted the natural female functions, such as menstruation and birth delivery, as part of the curse God placed on Eve because of her "sin." Many of the Fathers of the Church, contrary to the Old Testament blessing on procreation and considering children as blessings from God, preferred virginity to marriage. Influenced by religion, many women would walk around with torn clothes, fast excessively, and not take showers for long periods, denying sex and abstaining from sexual intercourse or any intimate relationship with the opposite sex.

> They encouraged young women to remain single and married women to leave their husbands, or to live with them in "continence" like brother and sister. Augustin and Jeronimo were extremely negative towards feminine sexuality. Saint Jeronimo stated that "the husband who embraced his wife with excessive passion was an adulterer because he loved her just to his own pleasure, like he would with a lover." (Duby & Perrot, 1990, p. 100)

When he was converted, Saint Augustine wrote: "There is nothing that I am more determined than . . . . to avoid intercourse with a woman. I feel that there is nothing more degrading to intelligence than for a man to hug a woman or to touch her body, without which it is impossible to have a wife" (Duby & Perrot, 1990). For Augustine, procreation should be done without passion or the loss of the woman's virginity, in a stage of "innocence" like she had before the fall.

Thomas Aquinas and other authors of the confession manuals in the 16th and 17th centuries reaffirmed Augustine's theory when they stated that passion in marriage condemned the passionate woman and made the husband libidinous. Even the positions in the sexual relationship were controlled in such a way that the woman could never be in an active position or above the man, which would be contrary to her social and subordinate role. The position *mulier super virum* was not considered "natural." Any position which brought pleasure and was not just for procreation was under suspicion.

Mary and her virginity were exalted to emphasize the supposed ordinary women's weakness and reinforce doubts about God's acceptance of sexual intercourse in marriage.

Reading the Fathers of the Church's papers help us to conclude that they viewed feminine sexuality as sinful and degrading.

The book *Malleus Maleficarum* (The hammer of the witches), published in 1487 by Kramer and Sprenger as a manual to identify and hunt witches (women), influenced the church for at least three centuries. During the period the book was in circulation, at least 500,000 witches were burned, 90 percent of whom were women. Some of the excerpts from the book show us the prejudice against women:

> Others again have propounded other reasons why there are more superstitious women found than men. And the first is that they are more credulous; and since the chief aim of the devil is to corrupt Faith, therefore he rather attacks them.
>
> The second reason is that women are naturally more impressionable and more ready to receive the influence of a disembodied spirit; and that when they use this quality well they are very good, but when they use it ill they are very evil.
>
> The third reason is that they have slippery tongues and they are unable to conceal from the fellow-women those things which by evil arts they know; and since they are weak, they find an easy and secret manner of vindicating themselves by witchcraft (. . .) All evil in the world is small in comparison to the woman's cruelty. (. . .) It is true that the Old Testament has a lot to say about women's evil because the one who was first tempted, Eve, and her imitators. (. . .) Since they are feebler both in mind and body, it is not surprising that they should come more under the spell of witchcraft. For as regards intellect, or the understanding of spiritual things, they seem to be of a different nature from men; a fact which is vouched for by the

authorities' logic, backed by various examples from the Scriptures. Terence says: Women are intellectually like children (. . .) But the natural reason is that she is more carnal than a man, as it is clear from her many carnal abominations. And it should be noticed that there was a defect in the formation of the first woman, since she was formed from a bent rib, that is, a rib of the breast, which is bent as it were in contrary direction to a man, and since through this defect, she is an imperfect animal, she always deceives. (. . .) For Cato says: "When a woman weeps, she weaves snares. And again, when a woman weeps, she labors to deceive a man" (. . .) The first woman showed that she had little Faith when she talked to the serpent, and all that is shown in the etymology of the word, because *Femina* comes from *Fe* and *Minus*, since she is ever weaker to keep and preserve the Faith.

Therefore, a wicked woman is by her nature quicker to waver in her Faith, and consequently quicker to abjure the Faith, which is the root of witchcraft. (. . .) And, as to her other mental quality, that is, her natural will; when she hates someone whom she formerly loved, then she seethes with anger and impatience in her whole soul, just as the tides of the sea are always heaving and boiling. We are not surprised, therefore, that there are so many women witches.

In the following texts, we can perceive their vision of women's sexuality:

And, now, let us examine the carnal desires of the body itself, whence has arisen unconscionable harm to human life. Justly we may say with Cato of Utica: "If the world could be rid of women, we should not be without God in our intercourse. For truly, without the wickedness of women, to say nothing of witchcraft, the world would still remain proof against innumerable dangers."

Valerius said to Rufinus: "You do not know that woman is the Chimaera, but it is good that you should know it; for that monster was of three forms: its face was that of a radiant and noble lion, it had the filthy belly of a goat, and it was armed with the virulent tail of a viper. And he learns that a woman is beautiful to look upon, contaminating to the touch, and deadly to keep. (. . .) Their voices kill the passengers emptying their purses consuming their strength, and causing them to forsake God." Again Valerius says to Rufinus: "When she speaks it is a delight which flavors the sin; the flower of love is a rose, because under its blossom there are hidden many thorns. (. . .) Her posture reveals vanity of vanities. They study as much on how to please men as men to please God."

(. . .) The woman is more bitter than death again, because that is natural and destroys only the body; but sin which arose from woman

> destroys the soul by depriving it of grace, and delivers the body up to the punishment of sin more bitter than death again, because bodily death is an open and terrible enemy, but woman is a wheedling and secret enemy.

We can picture many misconceptions about women, even in the exegesis of the Scriptures. It does not appall us that hatred toward women crossed the centuries; what really startles us is to see such prejudice and judgment of women nowadays, especially in Christianity, in general.

WOMEN AND THE FEMINIST MOVEMENT

The narrative of the original sin, wherein the woman was the one who listened to the serpent and ate the forbidden fruit, leads many theologians to believe and preach that the woman wanted to be like God, she was overtaken by pride, and she introduced sin into the world. As a result, women were given some tasks and men others, causing women to be diminished, submissive, and covered with shame.

Feminist theology calls women to get rid of the image of a woman who sacrifices, adapts, and is always amiable and altruistic, and to reject the masculine worldview of her in order to acquire self-love.

Through dualism, separation between man and woman, body and spirit, emerges an oppressive relationship, wherein the division between man and woman is also seen as a division between good and evil. Man is good and woman is evil. Therefore, there is an alienation where the characteristics of intellectuality, transcendence, and autonomy given to the woman left her without a body, labelled her as sensual and a subject, not the object of her own history.

To overcome sexism, we need to understand the exegesis of the Bible itself. It easily depicts three kinds of women: the sinner; the adulteress (evil possessed); and the pure, immaculate, which is an unreachable condition by most humans.

Eve; Mary of Magdalene; and Mary, mother of Jesus. Among them, Mary's purity is unreachable. For centuries, the body was punished, forgotten, poorly valued, officially despised, systematically hidden, and could only acquire any value when related to the higher "body of Christ," through communion and prayer, the community of the saints. In the 16th century the body was considered only a temporary habitat for the immortal soul, not without previously being punished to submit its evil to suffering to try to reach a higher, more holy condition.

The woman's body was mostly mortified and feared. The holy mystic women, such as Teresa d'Ávila, used to think that the dirtiest things were the holiest, considering lice "pearls of God."

Simone de Beauvoir, in her book *The Second Sex*, tries to deconstruct the concept of feminine nature, saying that the idea of woman's nature overrides the full humanity of women, as it causes conflict between being a woman and being a human being. The idea of woman's fragility by nature must be considered the result of social and cultural construction. For society in general to understand women's equality, it is necessary to demystify the "other" sex. According to Simone de Beauvoir:

> Nobody is born a woman: one becomes a woman. No biological, physical, economic destiny defines the form that the human female takes in society; it is the whole of civilization that elaborates this intermediary product between the male and the castrated that qualify the feminine. (1990, p. 9)

Children of both sexes are born the same; it is society's intermediation that makes them different, the way they are treated with the exaltation of the male organ and its virility, and boys being taught by their fathers from childhood that they are superior to the feminine sex. Girls, on the other hand, are raised to believe they do not need to go to school or to reason; it is enough to just play and learn how to be a mother, so they can get married to a man who will protect them with love and guidance. This behavior is a result of the fact that men condition women to think that way and to claim ignorance and incapability throughout the years.

A woman, therefore, is a product of the elaborations of civilization. She is not defined by her hormones any more than by her mysterious instincts, but by the way she sees herself through her strange consciousness, her body, and her relationship to the world.

Therefore, Simone de Beauvoir denounces the conditioning imposed by men on women. "Generally women accept what there is" (1990, p. 367).

Men mold women's world, rule it, and dominate it. Women accept their dependency and inferiority and they have not learned how to emerge as individual subjects. They feel like "eternal children," just as society has described laborers, Afro slaves, and the colonized Indians as "big children," accepting all the laws defined by men. So too are the women who owe obedience and respect to men, without questioning the reality that surrounds them, passively obeying the world cycle, ignorant that they can change the world's order through their actions.

A woman, by her blind faith, respects the rules for simply being a rule. For women, rights have to be conquered by force, while for men rights come by nature.

In the second volume of the book *The Second Sex*, Beauvoir makes a manifesto against the control and prison to which women are subjected by the masculine world, demanding action so that women acquire equality as human beings.

> Up to this date a woman's possibilities have been suffocated and lost for humankind and the time has come for everybody's interest to let her take all the risks and even try her luck. . . . How much time and strength are wasted away to finish, sublime, transfer complexes, speaking about women, seducing them and fearing them. Freeing them they would also be free. But it is precisely what they fear, therefore they stubbornly mystify woman to keep her imprisoned. (1949, pp. 483–489)

For Beauvoir, the promise that a woman's happiness is in taking care of her home comes from the masculine belief that she needs to be protected by her "legitimate tutors," and that women are able to perform these tasks under the false name of "femininity." Balzac described well this maneuver, advising men how to treat a woman by persuading her that she is a queen.

THE FEMINIST MOVEMENT AND WOMAN'S ORDINATION

The feminist movement wanted to reach all spheres of society and it also reached the church. In 1890, only 7 percent of the American evangelical denominations ordained women to the ministry. In 1900, 25 percent of them ordained women. Nine denominations authorized women to the ministry between the 19th and the 20th century. In 1970, there were more denominations ordaining women than in any other decade in the last 140 years. Seven of the largest American denominations started the process of women's ordination.

The process of women's struggle for equality in the church was parallel to their struggles in education and in the workforce. We cannot ignore the fact that the inclusion of women in the workforce has contributed to a major awareness of women's equality in the church, but we must also consider the fact that as the institutions became official, they excluded women from the pastoral ministry. The first major American and English denominations installed masculine power as they became official institutions, according to Chaves (1999).

In his studies he observed that the conflicts about women's ordination intensified around 1880, and that it was due to three different phenomena:

- When the churches had organizational political changes, women stopped being recognized officially.
- Evidence that in denominations that had restricted rules about women's ordination, they would still perform in the same roles as men did.
- Evidence that in denominations that officially believed in gender equality, women still faced many obstacles to their ministry in comparison to the male clergy.

Women's role in our society is still questioned in many different parts of the world. In most orthodox Islamic countries, men try to reinstate women in their traditional submissive and secluded role, removing them from their jobs, schools, or any other activity that is not at home. In some parts of Africa, men still argue about whether polygamy is right or wrong. In the Western world, following voting rights in the decade of the 1930s, professional opportunities for women and their role at home and with family continue to be discussed.

In the Christian church, the debate has become more intense in this century. In the last fifty years—and I refer to Western Christianity—and in the last ten years in Brazil, many Protestant denominations have opened their minds and doors to women in the ordained ministry and increased their opportunities for other forms of ministry, especially in the missionary field, where single women are the majority. However, not everyone in the Christian church accepts this quietly. Some still question whether this freedom for women is really compatible with the teaching of the Scriptures, and if the ecclesiastic leadership has not succumbed to secular values.

The Methodist church all over the world has largely ordained women pastors, as have the pentecostal churches in the United States of America and the neopentecostals in Brazil. However, the ordination of women to the pastoral ministry still finds much resistance among the orthodox pentecostals and in the historical churches in Brazil.

In 1999, the independent Presbyterian church council in Brazil approved the ordination of women to the position of pastorate and deaconess. There is a growing tendency in many denominations to extinguish the separation between laymen and the clergy. Many members of churches can preach, counsel, lead worship, and participate in the church council and in doctrine commissions, despite not being ordained. There are new ministries or new ways for old ministries: presbyters, counselors, chaplains, lay pastors and missionaries, deacons and deaconesses, and other ministries that enable a person to perform several different tasks in church and still have their secular jobs.

With all this opening up to lay involvement in the church, women continue to offer their potential and talents to Church service but are often met with rejection. At a time when women are competing in the workforce, in politics, and in the financial world, the church in Brazil has consistently closed itself to women's involvement in pastoral work. In the pentecostal world, women can be prayer leaders, Sunday school teachers for children, and missionaries, but they cannot be ordained ministers. In many of the historical churches, they are not even allowed to announce events from the pulpits. Women are needed as decorations, promoting tea events, visiting sick people in the hospitals and in their homes, helping with social work, but they are not allowed to make decisive contributions at meetings. While some churches accept and invest in women in the pastoral ministry, many others feel threatened by them and have looked for other ways to reaffirm traditional male domination.

Allied to this mentality, we have the theological revolution brought about by the modern critical approach to the study of the Scriptures and a new willingness to acknowledge that the Holy Spirit works in people's lives without the restriction of the official Church channels.

It is necessary to answer some questions brought about by the complexity of the relationship between the Old and New Testament, the society where the events developed, and the time it happened. Recently, contemporary theologians have scrutinized the Bible in a more elaborate, complex, and specialized way. To the textual and literary approach, they have added the form, the source, the narrative, the rhetoric used, criticism of the canon, and broader theological and historical criticism. They accept the principle of its inspiration and its mainstream application in the Christian doctrine, but they also recognize that the Bible must be studied in its context and that its teachings cannot be simply removed from their original setting and mechanically applied to the most diverse circumstances.

This attitude toward the Bible can lead us to deeper questions: Can we find in the Bible substantiation that men and women are equal? What is the relevance of the teaching about women's right to be ordained? How can we deal with ambiguous texts? Can we continue accepting the historical interpretation given by the first Fathers of the Church, which emerged in the second century, inspired by Platonic philosophy?

Several feminist scholars have proposed feminist theological anthropology in which women and men are equal, where no patriarchal views exist. These scholars note that by eliminating the inequality between women and men, violence against women would no longer exist.

Furthermore, if the church does not value gender equality, it will continue being imperfect, because it is led only by men, who are but part of God's creation. Fiorenza (1992) emphasizes that a church that is guilty of sexism, denying its equal ethos, also denies God's grace and kindness and it loses its Catholicism.

We cannot ignore the importance of secular feminism to bring to women in the Church an awareness of their value and place also before God.

The debate is still intense. Sexism resists despite all evidence. We do hope that in the very near future men and women will be equally able to serve their God and develop all the potential both have to build a strong church free from prejudice, futile rules, and the struggle for male domination.

REFERENCES

de Beauvoir, S. ([1949] 1990). *O segundo sexo. Vols. 1 and 2. A experiência vivida*. 7th ed. Rio de Janeiro: Nova Fronteira.

Carr, A. (1997). *A mulher na igreja*. Portugal: Tilgráfica.

Chaves, M. (1999). *Ordaining women: Culture and conflict in religious organizations.* Cambridge: Harvard University Press.

Culver, D., Foh, S., et al. (1996). *Mulheres no ministério.* São Paulo: Mundo Cristão.

Duby, G., & Perrot, M. (1990). *História das mulheres no ocidente.* Vol. 1.A Antiguidade. Porto: Afrontamento.

Duby, G., & Perrot, M. (1990). *História das mulheres. Do renascimento à idade moderna.* Vol. 3. Porto: Afrontamento.

Edwards, R. (1989). *The case for women's ministry.* Great Britain: University Press.

Fiorenza, E. (1992). *As origens cristãs a partir da mulher. Uma nova hermenêutica.* São Paulo: Paulinas.

Haughton, R. (1990). *A libertação da mulher. O anúncio de vida para o mundo que vem do feminino.* Petrópolis: Vozes.

Kramer, H., & Sprenger, J. (1487). *Malleus Maleficarum.* Speyer, Germany.

Lemaire, R. (1997). *O papel da mulher na passagem da tradição oral a escrita.* In Nádia Battela Gothb. (Ed.). A mulher na literatura. BH: ANPOLL.

Richardson, S. (1740). *Pamela.* London: Rivington & Osborn.

Chapter 5

Feminism Re-frames Who Wrote Hebrew Scriptures: 10th-Century Tamar, the "Master" Storyteller

Adrien J. Bledstein

This study proposes that Tamar, daughter of David, wrote great narratives preserved in the Bible. What she wrote is reconstructed from close reading of texts in Genesis, Exodus, Numbers, Judges, Ruth, Samuel, and Song of Songs. Reflection stories, repeated themes and phrases, and parallel episodes mirror Tamar's family experience. I suggest she first wrote the life of her father David in what is now called the Court History or Succession Narrative in 2 Samuel through 1 Kings 1. Her motivation begins in 2 Samuel 13. She is commissioned by King David to attend an ailing half-brother, Amnon, who brutally rapes her. For a literate woman, then as now, writing provides solace so one can move on (Desalvo, 2000). Until her father's death, she could compose his story from what she witnessed and heard while growing up listening to her father recount episodes in his life and hearing him sing his faith, anguish, hope, joy and grief to YHWH. After the rape, she would write from experience, observation, and questioning people in David's court. After completing her understanding of her father's fame and family turmoil, I suggest she could find happiness reflected in Song of Songs. Married with children, she would turn to recounting survival tales of the royal ancestors to Solomon's culturally mixed court of women, children, and servants. The texts we receive were edited primarily by men, but gems of Tamar's writings endure, attributed to so-called J, the "master" storyteller of the Bible, and the Court Narrator.

10TH-CENTURY TAMAR, THE "MASTER" STORYTELLER

Women as well as men channeled divine messages in Hebrew Scriptures—Deborah and Huldah are named prophetesses. Anonymous writings could be by either men or women. From archaeological evidence (Roberts, 2004) and biblical testimony we know elite women such as Jezebel (1 Kings 21:8) and Esther (Esther 9:29) were literate. What difference does it make to read with the preconception that texts were written by a woman?

Translations and interpretations, both misogynist and feminist, which assume only men wrote lead to disconnection with fundamental stories of faith. *The Book of J* proposes a woman wrote, but the translation is clearly by a man and the commentator is outspokenly non-religious (Bloom & Rosenberg, 1990; Bledstein, 1991a). In *Hidden Book in the Bible* (1998) and *The Bible with Sources Revealed* (2003), Richard E. Friedman identifies the "master" storyteller J with the Court Historian (also Bledstein, 1991a). Prior to this connection, in 1987 Friedman briefly entertained the idea that J could have been a woman. I will show how my assumption that J and the Court Historian are Tamar changes how we can appreciate views of women and their rights in Scripture. Translators who assume men wrote Scriptures tend to misconstrue a text to fit their preconceived opinion.

THE EARLY LIFE OF TAMAR

From biblical chronologies, David's reign of forty years and death at seventy, I construct the lifetime of Tamar and how she could know what occurred. In approximately 997 BCE, David is thirty-eight years old when Tamar is born to Maacah. David's eldest son by Ahinoam, Amnon, is five and Tamar's older brother Absalom three years old. By 994 BCE David is king of combined Israel and Judah and content in his palace in Jerusalem. He may well entertain his family with stories of his exploits interlaced with psalms. A year later four-year-old Tamar would witness the grand celebration of David's bringing the Ark to Jerusalem (2 Sam. 6). Another year and this favorite daughter (only she and Joseph wear the "coat of many colors," 2 Sam. 13:18–19; Gen. 37:3; Bledstein, 2000. Tamar is the one named sister of David's sons in 1 Chron 2:4; 3:9). Tamar could be present when the prophet Nathan tells the king he will have a dynasty, "house," but will not build a temple, "house," for YHWH (2 Sam. 7). Tamar would be puzzled by her father's disappointment and uncharacteristic prayer to YHWH, stressing ten times that he is YHWH's servant. Thereafter, her father is described as weary (2 Sam. 21:15). He stays at home while his armies go to war (11:1–2).

David appears rejuvenated when he marries Bathsheba, young widow of Uriah, one of the king's heroes (2 Sam. 23:39) who died in battle. A while later a baby is born to Bathsheba (2 Sam. 11:27). It is possible seven-year-old Tamar is sitting on her father's knee, tasting food he hands her from his own plate and drinking from his cup when astute prophet Nathan enters. David welcomes his friend and counselor, who presents a case to the king about a rich man who stole a poor man's "one little ewe lamb" that "was like a daughter to him" (2 Sam. 12:3) to feed to a stranger. Tamar would feel her father tremble with rage, jump off his lap, and hide behind his chair. David pronounces judgment on the rich man, whom he feels deserves to die, but will be punished fourfold for the wrong he did the poor man. Tamar would be startled to hear Nathan tell her father: "You are the man" (12:7). She would remember what each man says, but at seven not comprehend.

A few days later the infant born to Bathsheba is ill. David fasts and weeps (2 Sam. 12:15–23). The elders would not permit Tamar to comfort her father. When the infant dies, Tamar would see her father recover and partake of food. A year later, Bathsheba bears another son she calls Solomon. Tamar might love this little brother and be pleased to hear Nathan say that YHWH calls him Jedidiah, "Beloved of YaH" (12:25). Bathsheba bears three more sons, one named in honor of Nathan, who apparently favors this wife of David (1 Kings 1). Except for David's song of grief in Psalm 38, from my study of Psalms in narrative context (2015), I hear no psalms attributed to David from this time until nearly two decades later when he must leave Jerusalem because of Absalom's revolt.

THE COURT HISTORIAN

We meet Tamar in 2 Samuel 13. For me one clue to the identity of the "master" storyteller is the "coat of many colors," in Hebrew *ketonet passim,* in Scriptures associated only with Tamar and Joseph as mentioned above. The garment is a *me'il*, robe worn by priests, prophets, kings, and "daughters of the king." Sixteen women prior to Tamar were known as priestesses like Enheduanna, depicted wearing what is known as a "flounced garment" on a calcite disk displayed at the University of Pennsylvania.

Regarding 2 Samuel 13, Yale scholar Joel Baden (2013, pp. 191–193) recently noted remarkable similarities to the Joseph story and to the rape of Dinah. Amnon's rape of Tamar, according to Baden, could "only be told by one of the participants." From this he concludes the episode is a "literary creation" to account for Absalom's hatred of Amnon. I submit the reverse is more likely. A school of thought with which I agree suggests the rape of

Dinah and abuse of Joseph and the Court History were written in David's and Solomon's reigns (Friedman, 1987). I suggest the gifted storyteller, Tamar who indeed is a "participant" and survivor of rape, is deeply motivated to tell her story and record the *tsuris* in her royal family to uncover some meaning in her experience in relation to YHWH, the sole deity of her people. Until David takes Bathsheba and has Uriah killed, the portrait of David is remarkably positive as seen by this adoring daughter.

Tamar appears, and we hear her voice, only in 2 Samuel 13. Nowhere is she honored as "Tamar, daughter of David and Maacah, princess of Geshur." It is possible that male editors and chroniclers were embarrassed to favor this woman shamed by rape but acknowledge her as an ancestress they recall as "the female scribe," *HaSopheret* (Ezra 2:55, Neh. 7:57), matriarch of a family that survives exile and returns to Judah. We will honor her here. We will listen to her voice both as a character and as one of the greatest writers in the Western world. From careful reading of one chapter in the life of her father, I will show how we can appreciate an observant woman's experience of her family and history. Following is my translation in bold italics to distinguish from the JPS Tanakh (1985) translation followed by my commentary.

THE RAPE OF TAMAR

> **2 Samuel 13:1–2** This happened sometime afterward: Absalom son of David had a beautiful sister named Tamar, and Amnon son of David ***loved*** her. ***Amnon felt so frustrated he made himself ill on account of Tamar his sister,*** for she was a virgin, and ***it seemed too difficult in Amnon's eyes*** to do anything to her.

2 Sam. 13:1–2 "Sometime afterward" is after David's adultery with Bathsheba, the death of Uriah, the death of the first infant born to Bathsheba (2 Sam. 11–12), and eight years following the birth of Solomon. The phrase is heard in Tamar's stories of David (2 Sam. 2:1, 13:1, 15:1) and picked up by later writers. Absalom, the second-born son of David and firstborn of Princess Maacah from Geshur, has a beautiful sister named after David's ancestress Tamar, wife of Judah, matriarch of his tribe. The firstborn son of David with Ahinoam of Jezreel (not a wife of Saul as proposed by Halpern and Baden; Saul's wife Ahinoam was a daughter of Ahimaaz and at least 60 years old at the birth of Amnon), Amnon is "distracted," "cramped," "weakened" with passion for the beautiful virgin sister of a rival brother. A man taking any woman he chooses is a way of asserting power over her husband or protector such as a brother (like Gilgamesh taking a bride before the wedding, or a Pharaoh killing a husband to acquire the wife in the "Egyptian Tale of Two Brothers," or the mighty men in Genesis 6, or Shechem taking Dinah). Political power as well as sensual attraction is indicated by defining Tamar's relation with Absalom, protector of her honor which is bound to his.

> **2 Samuel 13:3–4** Amnon had a ***companion*** named Jonadab, the son of David's brother Shimah; Jonadab was a very clever man. He asked him, "Why are you so ***frail,*** O prince, morning after morning? Tell me!" Amnon replied, "Tamar, the sister of my brother Absalom, ***I love***!"

2 Sam. 13:3–4 Cousin Jonadab is a friend or adviser NIV, known to be a *hacham* meaning "wise person," in the immediate context of young men perhaps a "wise guy." Amnon mentions his reservation, Absalom is Tamar's protector. *Dal,* which I translate "frail" to remark on Amnon's diminishing masculinity, may mean: "lean" JPS, KJV, "haggard" NIV, "depressed" NAS, "mean," "scanty," "helpless," "wretched," "poor," "powerless," "insignificant," "dejected." Amnon's reply may be heard as whining.

> **2 Samuel 13:5** Jonadab said to him, "Lie down in your bed. ***You will be sick and your father will*** come to see you. Say to him, ***"Please let my sister Tamar come, and she will break my fast with bread; for she will perform before my eyes habbiryâ, and I will eat from her hand."***

2 Sam. 13:5 For Jonadab's advice, imagine fraternity brothers in their early twenties. Jonadab comes up with an obvious bright idea so Amnon can observe Tamar more closely. He describes a ceremony Tamar performs (Bledstein, 1992). His word choice of the food means to break a fast (*tivreyni*), a term used only here, regarding David's mourning the death of Abner (2 Sam. 3:35–36), with David's fast when praying for the life of his dying infant (2 Sam. 12:17), and in Lamentations (4:10). *Habbiryâ* is the name of the ritual Tamar is known to perform. The person who is ill will eat from her hand. These details in Jonadab's advice to Amnon, plus inside information that follows as we read on, point to Tamar's special status as a royal priestess who performs a healing ritual, emphasized three times.

> **2 Samuel 13:6** Amnon lay down, ***making himself sick***. The king came to see him, and Amnon said to the king, ***"Please let my sister Tamar come and make a couple of heart-loaves in my sight, so that I may break fast from her hand."***

2 Sam. 13:6 Amnon's request of his father is more casual and briefer than Jonadab's. Amnon lacks respect for Tamar's position and training as a priestess acknowledged in Jonadab's advice. Furthermore, he designates special food, *levivot* "heart-loaves" derived from *lev* "heart," perhaps Amnon's way of telling Dad his illness renders him impotent, adding an element of humor to an otherwise tragic episode, and he hopes will get a rise out of or motivate David to send Tamar. In Mesopotamia, therapeutic rituals conducted by a woman to restore vigor to an impotent man are called *SA.ZI.GA*, literally "rising of the 'heart'" (Biggs, 1967). Amnon does not employ the term *habbiryâ*.

2 Samuel 13:7 ***David sent a message to Tamar*** in the palace, ***"Please go to your brother Amnon's house and perform for him habbiryâ."***

2 Sam. 13:7 From Amnon's description, that she will make heart loaves and he will eat from her hand, David knows exactly what Tamar is to perform. The narrative captures the changing line of communication which affirms that what Tamar does is well known. David politely, with "please," commissions Tamar to perform *habbiryâ* in the house of Amnon. Women practitioners performed healing ceremonies in homes.

2 Samuel 13:8–9a Tamar went to the house of her brother Amnon, who was in bed. She took dough and ***shaped hearts before his eyes and cooked the heart-loaves. And she took the server and poured before him; but he refused to eat. And Amnon said: "Have out all men from me." And they went out every man from him.***

2 Sam. 13:8–9a David's brief message mentions only the name of the ceremony to be performed in the home. However, Tamar does what Jonadab envisions and Amnon implies with "heart loaves," making clear that this is a well-known ritual Tamar is designated to perform. Pouring a libation is part of the ceremony. The libation vessel may have a serpent depicted on it and "may have contained a decoction that was used medically and/or magically to cure the ills of the diseased" (Krumholz McDonald, 1994, p. 21). Tamar's preparation and goal have parallels to a Hittite ceremony by a woman practitioner who would interpret the ailing man's dreams. Dream interpretation is parallel to Joseph. Another parallel, before revealing his identity to his brothers Joseph commands, "Have out all men from me" (Gen. 45:1). Tamar remains, focused on the ritual she is commissioned by the king to perform.

2 Samuel 13:9b–11 After ***every man*** had withdrawn, Amnon said to Tamar, ***"Bring habbiryâ to the room so I may break fast from your hand."*** Tamar took the ***heart loaves*** she had made and brought them to her brother inside. But when she **brought** them **near** to him, he **took firm** hold of her and said to her, "Come lie with me, ***my*** sister."

2 Sam. 13:9b–11 Amnon firmly grasps her arm. His naming the ritual food accentuates his sacrilege as he urges her to commit incest with the same words Potiphar's wife speaks, "lie with me," when she urges Joseph to commit adultery (Gen. 39:7, 12).

> **2 Samuel 13:12–13** But she said to him, ***"No, my brother. Do not oppress*** me. Such things are not done in Israel! Don't do such a vile thing! Where will I carry my shame? And you, you will be like any of the scoundrels in Israel! Please, speak to the king; he will not refuse me to you."

2 Sam. 13:12–13 Now we hear Tamar's voice. She protests his grasp and clear intention to rape her. She urges him to think about the nature of such an act among their people, the consequences for him and for her. She is clearly knowledgeable about laws and history in Judah and Israel. "Vile," "senseless," and "outrage" are other translations of *naval,* linking her characterization of the violation he aims to commit to the sexual violence of the men of Sodom in Genesis 19 and to the rape of Dinah in Genesis 34. As Robert Alter points out, "The rape in both stories leads to murderous fraternal vengeance" (1999, p. 268). As both Polzin (1993) and Alter indicate, she uses the same words as the host of the Levite at Gibeah to dissuade a mob from gang rape of his guest (Judges 19:23). There too a woman is raped, which leads to civil war. Through allusion Tamar connects the terrible consequences of men acting like *elohim,* as if they are gods above any law, like raunchy deities in Sumerian and Egyptian myths. *Naval* is also the name of Abigail's "foolish" husband who belittles David whose men had protected the sheep being sheared (2 Sam. 25). As a last resort Tamar suggests the possibility that the king will bend the law against incest for Amnon so they can marry. This could be a lie to stall for time. The law regarding incest between siblings of one father but different wives is not yet codified. That is the excuse given by Abraham for marrying his father's daughter but not his mother's (Gen. 20:12). Not until the seventh century BCE did the priests and the Deuteronomist record with specificity family laws (Lev. 18:6, 9, 11; 20:17, Deut. 27:22). I suggest that the repetition and forcefulness of these laws were later included in the canon to condemn as well as deter someone like Amnon.

> **2 Samuel 13:14–15** ***But he was not willing to hear to her voice. Stronger than she, he oppressed her and lay her.*** Then Amnon felt a very great loathing for her; indeed, his loathing for her was greater than the love he had felt for her. And Amnon said to her, "Get out!"

2 Sam. 13:14–15 Amnon deliberately refuses to hear Tamar's "voice." The verb "oppress" means to "force," "humiliate," "subdue," and "violate." Like Shechem with Dinah, Amnon overpowers Tamar. His seduction rejected, Amnon is violent to get his way with her. In contrast to Shechem, whose lust turns to love of Dinah, Amnon's lust thwarted turns to hatred and disgust.

> **2 Samuel 13:16–17** ***She said to him, "No! Concerning this evil, to send me away, is greater than the other that you did to me."And he was not willing to hear her.*** He summoned his young attendant and said, ***"Please send this outside from me and bar the door behind her."***

2 Sam. 13:16–17 Tamar vehemently opposes his kicking her out. His current action is worse than the rape. The basis of her statement is reflected in the later law, Deuteronomy 22:28–29, where a man who takes a maiden must pay her father and marry her for life. Contrasting two actions, one surpassing the other, appears in the book of Ruth. Amnon's and Tamar's great-great-grandfather Boaz compares Ruth's second act, requesting he father an heir to take care of Naomi as even better than her first act, choosing him to be her husband over younger men (Ruth 3:10; Bledstein, 1993, "Female"). In deliberate contrast, a reversal of Boaz's appreciation of Ruth, Tamar compares Amnon's second vile act of sending her away as worse than the rape. Again he is not willing to hear her. Tamar's third-person narrator's view of the unfolding family disasters predicted by Nathan (2 Sam. 12) includes indications that each son of David, like father, deliberately chooses to despise YHWH's covenant. In contrast to his contemptuous command to Tamar, Amnon says "please" when he politely instructs his servant. "Woman" is not in Amnon's Hebrew, so the command is more dismissive of Tamar than translations which erroneously dignify his view of her by adding "woman."

> **2 Samuel 13:18** ***Though she had on a flounced garment, because virgin daughters of the king would wear such sacred-robes*** His attendant took her outside and barred the door after her.

2 Sam. 13:18 As Tamar is being cast out we learn she is wearing a sacred, ceremonial garment. In translations confusion reigns: *ketonet passim* most famously is the "coat of many colors," but also "ornamented tunic" TNK; "garment of divers colours" KJV; "long-sleeved garment" NAS or "long robe with sleeves" NRS, RSV; "ornate robe" NIV. Joseph in Genesis 37 is the only other person in the Bible who wears this distinguishing garment. Some translations of Genesis 37 differ from 2 Samuel 13. I translate "flounced garment" because a flounced multi-colored garment evidenced in Mesopotamia where Joseph and his brothers were born distinguishes high priests and priestesses who perform rituals, as talented managers and dream interpreters (Bledstein, 2000). The garment indicates Tamar is a favorite child of David as Joseph is favored by Jacob. A sacred garment is meant to protect the wearer but protects neither Tamar nor Joseph.

Other parallels between Joseph and Tamar are striking. Jacob and David send a favorite child wearing the distinguishing garment to see to the welfare of family members. Each is abused and cast out by brothers. There are at least half a dozen other parallels in the stories of Tamar and Joseph, strong indications that Tamar wrote the Joseph story as a reflection of her own experience.

> **2 Samuel 13:19** Tamar put dust on her head and rent the ***flounced garment*** she was wearing; she put her hands on her head, and walked away, screaming loudly as she went.

2 Sam. 13:19 Unlike abused women who feel somehow guilty, so suffer in silence, shame, and self-reproach, Tamar grieves publically, loudly, in the streets of Jerusalem. She tears the bloodied garment, parallel to the torn garment with goat's blood Joseph's brothers present to Jacob (Gen. 37:31). If justice reigns, the magistrate (King David) will require Amnon to take care of her as his wife all her life (Deut. 22:28–29). Tamar's public grief is to insure knowledge of the outrage.

> **2 Samuel 13:20–22** Her brother Absalom said to her, "Was it your brother **Aminon** who did this to you? For the present, sister, keep quiet about it; he is your brother. ***Do not take*** the matter ***to heart***." And Tamar remained in her brother Absalom's house, ***devastated***.

2 Sam. 13:20 Absalom's question indicates he is aware of "Aminon's" obsession with Tamar and animosity toward himself. Adding a syllable to his brother's name further indicates his contempt. In contrast to Tamar's public expression of grief which requires justice, Absalom shushes her to keep the outrage a family matter. Like Dinah's brothers Simeon and Levi, taking the rape of his sister as an attack on his honor, Absalom considers what he will do.

> **2 Samuel 13:21–22** When King David heard about all this, he was ***very angry.*** Absalom didn't utter a word to Amnon, good or bad; but Absalom hated Amnon because he had ***humbled*** his sister Tamar.

2 Sam. 13:21–22 Though angered, David as king, father, and magistrate does nothing to punish Amnon, does not even exile Amnon for his own safety nor does he require Amnon marry Tamar to restore her honor and provide for her. Contrast David's fury toward the fictional rich man who took the poor man's ewe lamb which "was like a daughter to him" in 2 Samuel 12:1–6 and his current wrath but inaction regarding the unconscionable behavior of his son toward his beautiful virgin daughter David sent to see to the welfare of his son. A decade following the death of

Bathsheba's infant, David's lack of action suggests he is morally paralyzed by his own wrongdoings, Nathan's prophecy, and his own part in commissioning Tamar to see to the welfare of Amnon. This violation by his eldest son is a second disaster predicted by Nathan. If David admits to himself that more catastrophes may come, his inaction as magistrate indicates his anger turned inward: he is depressed. From my reading of Psalms attributed to David interlaced with narrative, David prays Psalm 38 twice, first after the death of the infant and now after the crass abuse of his daughter by his oldest son. For another decade David is silent, cut off from YHWH until Absalom and his followers are moving toward Jerusalem to unseat his father.

> **2 Samuel 13:22** Responsible for protecting his sister's virginity and seeing no action from David to execute justice, Absalom conceals his hostility for two years. While Absalom channels his wrath to plot retaliation, I suggest that after Amnon's death, Tamar turns her humiliation and rage to trying to understand how the rape came about by writing her experience and inquiring from various parties to put together her construction of the life of her father and troubled family.

HASOPHERET WRITES HERSTORY

By my reckoning from approximate dates of David's reign and attention to details of the narratives regarding the passage of time, Tamar would be about seventeen years old (parallel to Joseph, her double) when raped by Amnon, who is about twenty-two years old. But how would Tamar know what happens before and after the rape? She hears or reads the message from David to her as well as experiences what occurs in Amnon's house. Legally it is likely that after Amnon is dead David would acknowledge Tamar as a widow of Amnon so she would be restored to a position in court where she would be privy to court gossip among women in David's harem, and have access to court counselors—such as Nathan and Jonadab—siblings, servants, and military personnel. Motivated to ferret out the truth, like any great writer doing meticulous research, she would question, question, question.

Regarding events before the rape, as a child she would have heard her father recount his exploits and chant his prayers. As mentioned above, she is about four years old when David joyously leads the procession with the Ark into Jerusalem. With her mother or a servant, she participates in the celebration, and may even witness the interchange between David and Michal (2 Sam. 6:20–23). Gifted like her father, she would recall such events, memories to draw on when she later needs to make sense of what happened to her.

Besides wearing the garment of a favorite, gifted child, another clue to Tamar's role in David's life is in Nathan's revelation in 2 Samuel 12, after David took Bathsheba. As suggested earlier, when Nathan tells the story of the rich man and poor man Tamar would not understand Nathan's "Thou art the man!" Contemplating later she could piece together a picture of her father's life prior to and following this searing event and David's fourfold punishments—the death of the infant, the rape of Tamar, the death of Amnon, and the death of Absalom.

Reflecting on her father before what she now understood as Nathan's disastrous prophecy (2 Sam. 12), Tamar would recall David's youthful, ecstatic prayers envisioning the grand temple he intends to build for his beloved YHWH (Psalms 26:8, 29:9, 18:7, 27:4, 5:7 [5–8], 138:1–2, 65:5, 68:28–29). As we saw, this adoring child could be present when Nathan informs David that YHWH provides a "house," dynasty, for David but is content with the portable Tabernacle. Not David but a son of his will build the "house" for YHWH (2 Sam. 7:1–16). She may well notice her father's disappointment—great kings in the ancient Near East build magnificent temples—but not understand at that early age the extent of her father's deflation at this news. Only later would she weave together her father's dashed plan to build the house for YHWH with David's weariness in battle, not going to war, then his being energized by the sight of Bathsheba. Details of the Bathsheba affair and Uriah's death she could glean from servants of David. Later editors interposed 2 Samuel 8–10 between 2 Samuel 7 and 11, interrupting the flow of Tamar's narrative connecting David's malaise with being denied the accolade due a king who builds an awe-inspiring temple.

Scholars view the turning point of David's career as his taking Bathsheba and miss his disaffection with YHWH, his need for rejuvenation due to his disappointment, and his deliberate decision to break the covenant by taking another man's wife. Like Abraham, David is tested. He must give up what he holds most dear, his vision of himself as temple builder. Unlike the man of faith Abraham, King David fails.

Joel Baden (2013) and Baruch Halpern (2001), accusing David of treacherous, multiple murders, read critically the positive spin of the narrative of David's life prior to his becoming king. These scholars do not consider what I believe is an important dimension of the David story—his prayers. Twice in fifteen years I read with inquisitive, literate adults in congregations my integration of psalms attributed to David with the narrative of his life (Bledstein, 2015). Hearing David's thinking at every stage of his difficult career reveals his dedication to YHWH and his effort to be a righteous good person who follows the covenant despite survival circumstances which force him to compromise his moral compass. With his prayers in mind it is no wonder that tradition suggests David is a man after YHWH's own heart (1 Sam. 13:14) so is anointed by Samuel

(1 Sam. 16). As noted above, David would regale his family with stories of his early years highlighted with prayers of anguish, hope, and gratitude to YHWH. An adoring daughter would present her father in the best light—until their lives change. The careful, fair-minded Succession Narrative is composed by a person who loves both David and Absalom. This is a family as well as a national story—thus Tamar becomes known as *HaSopheret*, the scribe. After Amnon's death and her return to court as a widow, she would be a quiet presence, witness to her father as he leaves Jerusalem, makes judgements along the way, and once again prays to YHWH. She would be present when David orders his commanders: "Deal gently with my boy Absalom, for my sake" (2 Sam. 18:5 TNK). She would witness and share David's grief at news of Absalom's death. She would return with her father to Jerusalem, hear his judgments along the way, then later have access to Hushai, who was in the court of Absalom during his attempted coup. She would hear of Absalom's taking his father's ten concubines, thus publically, ruthlessly, sealing his break with their father.

After suffering such pain and humiliation, this extraordinarily gifted, literate woman trained to be a priestess who heals—perhaps by invoking the dead ancestors or a goddess worshiped by her mother and indulged by her father—would feel compelled to make sense of what happened to her in relation to YHWH and achieve some peace with the past through writing. David dies when Tamar is thirty-two. She has many more years and her interests would change.

THE LATER LIFE OF TAMAR

I have long believed that Tamar also wrote from Eden through tales of the royal ancestors, portions of Exodus, Numbers, Judges, and Ruth. Recently I reviewed Phyllis Trible's groundbreaking and beautiful feminist treatment of Genesis 2–3 and Song of Songs (1973). For me she provides a key for unlocking a possible transition in Tamar's life. One may imagine that the woman who intoned Song of Songs is responsible for the Garden of Eden. For detailed treatment of parallel themes, literary style, and a non-patriarchal understanding, see Trible.

Here I focus on where I disagree with Trible regarding a word, *tesuqa,* translated "desire," which appears only in Song of Songs 7:10 (or 11), Genesis 3:16 and 4:7. "I am my beloved's, and his desire is for me" is a consistent translation parallel to "Your desire shall be for your husband, and he shall rule over you" (Gen. 3:16 NAS) and "sin (f.) is crouching at the door; and its (m.) desire is for you, but you must master it (m.)" (Gen. 4:7 NAS). Note how translators say the woman's man "shall" rule over her but Cain "must" or "can" master sin, which in Hebrew is feminine while references are masculine.

Alternatively, in 1993 I showed how the word translated "desire" may well mean "desirable" or "attractive." This does away with male domination and grammatically in Hebrew makes sense of Cain's relationship to sin. YHWH says to the woman in Eden: "You are desirable to your husband but he can rule over you" (3:16). God acknowledges the power of her attraction but warns her that her man can, is able to (not "shall" or "must"), rule over her. In my translation of Genesis 4:6, moving a *tov* from the end of "sin" to the beginning of the verb changes what YHWH says to Cain, who yearns to make a bad choice: "At an entry of sin (m.) you stretch out; it (m.) is desirable to you, yet you can rule over it (m.)" (Bledstein, 1993, "Eve"). Man, woman, and sin are "desirable."

Now let us turn to the lovers in Song of Songs. In 7:7–8 (8–9) he sings:

> Your stature is like a palm tree, and your breasts are *like its* clusters. "I said, 'I will climb the palm tree, I will take hold of its fruit stalks.' Oh, may your breasts be like clusters of the vine, And the fragrance of your breath like apples. (NAS)

With my translation the woman responds "I am my beloved's, he is desirable to me" (7:10 [11]), thus she joins him in love because she finds him attractive. Twice he likens her to a palm tree, in Hebrew *tamar,* which I suggest is a play on his beloved's name, Tamar.

Who is Tamar's lover? I propose Jonadab, the too "clever" youth who told Amnon how he could get closer to Tamar. Later he is a counselor to David (2 Sam. 13:32–36). He may well have been dismayed about his role in the devastation of Tamar, subsequent death of Amnon, and Absalom's revolt. He too may have adored Tamar and "wise" as he was may not have imagined that Amnon would callously abuse and dismiss her. Years later he would be more mature and approach her for forgiveness, revealing his role to her, thus filling in her rendition of 2 Samuel 13. Over a decade afterward, as Tamar completed writing her father's life, she and Jonadab might be drawn together by their shared understanding of mutual trauma and express their healing and new-found joy in songs of love.

THEMES OF THE "MASTER" STORYTELLER

From my study "What Is David Thinking?" (2015), it becomes clear that the tragedies in his family arise during a period when David's prayers are not recorded—he feels cut off from YHWH. When his eldest son claims he is ill, David does not pray to his healer, YHWH, as he did ten years earlier for the ailing infant of Bathsheba. Instead, as we have seen, he commissions Tamar as a priestess to perform a healing ritual. The rape of Tamar is a life-altering experience. The attack of her brother would prod her to reflect on the nature of YHWH, her family's relationship to their deity, and the history of her people. She might well interpret the disaster as a test of her, providing insight into themes reflected in narratives I attribute to this gifted writer.

For example, an episode which baffles interpreters of Hebrew Scriptures is an encounter of Moses and his wife Zipporah with YHWH in Exodus 4:24–26. The daughter of a Medianite priest, Zipporah saves the life of her husband by circumcising her son. Following is my translation with identification of each "him," "his," and "you":

> At a night encampment on the way, YHWH encountered him (Moses) and sought to kill him (Moses). So Zipporah took a flint and cut off her son's foreskin, and touched his (YHWH's) foot with it, saying, "You (YHWH) are truly a *father-in-law* of blood to me!" And when He (YHWH) let him (Moses) alone, she added, "A *father-in-law* of blood because of the circumcisions." (Exod. 4:24–26)

Zipporah knows exactly what to do and has the necessary equipment. Circumcision is not done to infants among her people so is a matter of contention between wife and husband. When YHWH, the god of her husband, appears to them threatening to kill Moses, Zipporah acts quickly. She speaks directly to YHWH addressing him (not Moses) as *hoten*, father-in-law, not *hatan*, bridegroom (the original Hebrew does not have vowels). Plural circumcisions, *mulot* (v. 26), include the circumcision of her heart which, under duress, is now open to worshiping YHWH, setting a precedent for "circumcise the foreskin of your heart" which, unlike male circumcision, applies to both men and women (Deut. 10:16).

This brief encounter is Zipporah's conversion experience, which I suggest reflects the effect on Tamar of being raped by a family member. Her healing ritual in the sacred garment may call upon ancestors or involve an idol representing the goddess Asherah. Tamar is just a child when she hears Nathan's oracle regarding David's not building the temple. On reflection she would realize how David and she had slipped away from calling upon YHWH as the sole God of the universe. Tamar's trauma frames how she understands and relates the survival stories of people who choose to trust YHWH that we read in the narratives. Belief in YHWH's ascendance over all deities is a primary theme in Tamar's stories of survivors.

Another confounding episode in the life of Moses becomes clear—and amusing. A notable difference between J narratives and the Court History is a sense of humor in tales of the ancestors not present in the Succession Narrative. That is why I hear Tamar telling the stories of the royal ancestors and Moses after she found peace from writing her experience in the life of her father.

Parenthetic additions indicate my interpretation of Exodus 3:12–15 where the divine name EHYeH, which unlike other names of God is neither male nor female, is proposed. Another limitation of Hebrew in presenting the single, asexual divine is that verbs, except I and we, are masculine or feminine. God tells Moses to go to Egypt and free the Israelites:

> "I will be with you." ***[and adds in case he needs proof]*** "When you have freed the people from Egypt, you shall worship God at this mountain." ***[Having witnessed the burning bush and hearing YHWH several time Moses anticipates the people might be dubious so says]*** "When I come to the Israelites and say to them, 'The God of your fathers has sent me to you,' and they ask me, 'What is His name?' what shall I say to them?" ***["Aha!" thinks God. "This is my opportunity to announce my preferred name that is neither male nor female and simply means 'I am' or 'I will be!' That is Eternal."]*** So God said to Moses, "*EHYeH-Asher-EHYeH.*" ***[Noting that Moses looks confused,]*** God repeated, "Thus shall you say to the Israelites, '*EHYeH* sent me to you.'" ***[Moses shakes his head. EHYeH is an unfamiliar name. Conceding to this overstressed man:]*** God said further to Moses, "Thus shall you speak to the Israelites: YHWH, the God of your fathers, the God of Abraham, the God of Isaac, and the God of Jacob, has sent me to you. ***[But EHYeH is thinking: Oy!]*** This shall be My name forever? This My appellation for all eternity?"

Gender free, the name *EHYeH* is an action verb. Judaism is about action (Joanne Greenberg conversation 9/2/2013). Thereafter the name EHYeH appears only in Exodus 4:12, 15; Hosea 1:9; Deuteronomy 31:23; and Jeremiah 11:4. Male designations for the deity of Israel predominate in texts edited by men.

YHWH TESTS FAVORITES

A theme in Tamar's writing is that EHYeH aka YHWH ("LORD"), Elohim ("God"), El-Shaddai ("mountain" or "breast"), tests favorites. The most well-known test is that Abraham is commanded to sacrifice Isaac, the child of YHWH's promise that Abraham's descendants will inherit the land and proliferate. Earlier this favorite is also tested by danger to his survival because of his beautiful wife. He feels vulnerable to a ruthless ruler who will kill him and take his wife evidenced in the Egyptian Tale of Two Brothers and David's taking Bathsheba and killing Uriah. Sarah is tested when she chooses to lie and to risk adultery in order to keep Abraham alive. She is childless, insulted by her handmaid, then blessed with an absurdly late birth (Bledstein, 1981). Rebekah is infertile for two decades, bears twins who wrestle in her womb, and she must act to assure the most competent son receives the blessing of YHWH. Parallel to Bathsheba (1 Kings 1), Rebekah orchestrates which son will carry on the blessing. Besides near death at the hand of his father, Isaac is prodded by his wife and Jacob's obvious deception to choose between his two sons regarding who shall receive his blessing. Esau fails Isaac's test. Jacob proves he wants the blessing and is a survivor by engaging in a ruse then is further tested by working for his unscrupulous uncle Laben for twenty years (Bledstein, 1993, "Binder"). Tricked into marrying Leah, Jacob also marries beloved Rachel. He is further tested by his loss of Rachel, then her son Joseph with whom he is reunited after decades of grieving. Joseph endures beating by his brothers, slavery in a foreign land, prison, the challenge of managing a seven-year famine, then reuniting with, testing, and forgiving his brothers.

Other favorites who are tested are Judah who loses two sons, and the first Tamar whose loss of two husbands leaves her a widow without children (similar to Ruth). Tamar takes command when Judah withholds his third son. She pretends to be a prostitute, seduces Judah, and is blessed as mother of royal descendants (Gen. 38). Miriam guards her baby brother, sees that he is protected by an Egyptian princess, and nursed by their own mother. Later she is punished for chastising Moses but her brothers come to her aid and her people wait for her before continuing their journey (Num. 12; Bledstein, 1991c, "Family"), reflection of support Tamar would have appreciated. Ruth and Naomi suffer loss of husbands with no descendants. They choose Boaz to marry Ruth and they have royal descendants as did the first Tamar (Bledstein, 1993, "Female"). A focus of 10th-century Tamar's narratives is on the challenges faced by each of her ancestors and how each survives. Experience in her father's house prepares her for entertaining Solomon's court by telling survival stories of her people.

Tamar's father David is given more press (seventy-three songs in the book of Psalms are ascribed to David) and he is tested more than anyone before prophets in the Bible. He conquers a giant; endures a crazed, dangerous boss; makes difficult choices to survive in exile; then he unites Judah and Israel to create a nation. He survives a three-year famine and chooses a location for the temple. David succeeds in all his tests until he is deflated when told he will not build the temple for YHWH. Weary, no longer leading the troops, he is energized by a forbidden woman. Nearly a decade later Absalom leads a rebellion and David is leaving Jerusalem when he prays after two decades of disaffection with YHWH. Under duress pressing him to act, he voices the source of his rupture with YHWH: "My zeal for Your house has been my undoing; the reproaches of those who revile You have fallen upon me" (Psalm 69:10 TNK). After venting his self-centered cause of estrangement from YHWH, David is energized and decisive so he survives a second exile and the death of his dear boy Absalom. He returns to Jerusalem and appoints Solomon heir to his throne. The rape of Tamar is a pivotal moment in her life, impetus to record her father's experience, then sing songs of love and tell tales of her royal ancestors.

READING THROUGH THE EYES OF TAMAR

How does the preconception that Tamar wrote change how we read? Consider the so-called "curse of Eve" that arises from faulty transmission and translation. The crafty serpent addresses the woman as "you" masculine plural because her man is present, a silent witness. "Did God say, 'You shall not eat from any tree in the garden?'" (Gen. 3:1 NRS). Repeating what she heard second hand from her man, she speaks up for both of them: "We may eat of the fruit of the trees in the garden; but God said, 'You shall not eat of the fruit of the tree that is in the middle of the garden, nor shall you touch it, or you shall die'" (Gen. 3:2–3 NRS). On the contrary, YHWH (note how the woman picked up the serpent's more general designation, *elohim*) specifically tells the man before the woman is formed from his rib: "You may freely eat of every tree of the garden; but of the tree of the knowledge of good and evil you shall not eat, for in the day that you eat of it you shall die" (Gen. 2:16–17 NRS). From her man the woman learns a vague, exaggerated command not to eat from nor "touch" the "tree in the middle of the garden" (Gen. 3:3). The serpent assures her that they will be like gods, knowers of everything from good to bad. Confusing knowledge with wisdom, she imagines they will gain sound judgment. After eating and sharing a taste with her man who is "with her," the woman is addressed directly by YHWH: contrary to her wish to be a goddess who gives birth in nine days without pain (Ninhursag), she will have increased pain in childbirth. YHWH warns her that even though she is "desirable" to her man, the woman *can* be ruled by him. Woman in the Garden of Eden is not cursed. The crafty serpent and the ground are "cursed." A clue to Tamar's storytelling is her sense of humor in spare presentation that captures different points of view revealing misperceptions so common among humans, and once upon a time a verbal serpent who takes advantage of human folly, perhaps commentary on the delusion Tamar entertained about administering a medicinal or magical healing potion made from something from a serpent.

Tamar has reason to draw parallels, such as brother kills brother: Cain murders Abel (Gen. 4); Absalom has Amnon assassinated (2 Sam. 13); the woman of Tekoa tells a similar story of her two sons (2 Sam. 14). Animosity of brothers results in maltreatment of a father's favorite who is cast out: Joseph and Tamar, wearing the *ketonet passim*, are abused by brothers. Both are known for dream interpretation. In youth Joseph foresees his future greatness but does not anticipate how his dreams will come about. Tamar expects to interpret Amnon's dream as part of the ritual she is performing (Bledstein, 1992). Later Joseph employs his gifts to save his family and all of Egypt from famine and Tamar applies her gifts to telling and writing stories that are read and interpreted to this day. Seductive "lie with me" is rejected by Joseph and Tamar with multiple reasons, and though innocent of wrongdoing, each suffers (Gen. 39:7–20; 2 Sam. 13:11–20). Before raping Tamar, haughty Amnon orders "all men out from me." In contrast, Joseph says the same in order privately to reconcile with his once scornful brothers who have proven they have changed (2 Sam. 13:9; Gen. 45:1). Judah becomes the leader of his brothers after being humiliated by his daughter-in-law Tamar. He is able to admit she is more in the right than he, as he did not provide her with a husband (Gen. 38). Together they become matriarch and patriarch of the Davidic dynasty.

When David takes Bathsheba he behaves like an *elohim*, a god who takes any woman he chooses (Gen. 6:2) and like a pharaoh, the fear of Abraham. The serpent tells the woman in Eden, they will become as *elohim*, knowers of good and evil (Gen. 3:5). "An angel of God, understanding good and evil" (2 Sam. 14:17) is how the woman of Tekoa addresses David. Other stories reflecting men who behave like *elohim* are the men of Sodom who demand "to know" ["The term 'to know' as a euphemism for sex (*yd'*) occurs five times in J but never in the other sources." (Friedman, 2003, p. 9)] the guests of Lot (Gen. 19), Shechem who takes Dinah (Gen. 34), and Benjaminites who rape the Levite's concubine (Judges 19). When "texts of terror" (Trible, 1984) are read as written by Tamar, atrocities by men are intended as criticisms: "every man did what is right in his own eyes" (Judges 21:25; Bledstein, 1993, "Judges").

In narratives only the serpent in Eden and David are described as crafty, *arum* (Gen. 3:1), a play on the word *aram*, naked in Genesis 2:25. Saul orders men: "Go now and prepare further. Look around and learn what places he (David) sets foot on *and* who has seen him there, for I have been told he is a very cunning *arum* fellow" (1 Sam. 23:22 TNK). *Hacham* is another term for "wise" and describes Jonadab who foolishly advises Amnon (2 Sam. 1–3:3–5) in contrast to the wisdom *hachmah* of the women of Tekoa (2 Sam. 14:1–21) and Abel (2 Sam. 20:16).

Absence of detailed war descriptions may be evidence of an ancient woman writer. Compared to Gilgamesh and Enkidu against Humbaba, tablet five alone is 269 lines. In the *Iliad*, book one is about 817 lines while the whole poem is 19,000 lines, with lengthy descriptions of battles. In contrast David versus Goliath is brief, a few verses, like a story told to children by David or a witness. Battles are mentioned, not described in detail.

CONCLUSION

Tamar meaning "date palm," the tree of life in the ancient Near East, channeled divinely inspired tales of matriarchs and patriarchs and the Exodus included in the Pentateuch or Torah, the scroll known as the Tree of Life in Judaism. Narratives and tales by Tamar and Psalms of her father inspire people of all faiths to this very day. Identifying with Tamar as the "master" storyteller in the Bible, we may claim our rights as women of faith.

REFERENCES

Alter, R. (1999). *The David story.* New York: W. W. Norton & Co.
Baden, J. (2013). *The historical David: The real life of an invented hero.* New York: HarperOne.
Biggs, R. (1967). *ŠÀ.ZI.GA: Ancient Mesopotamia potency incantations,* TCS 2. Locust Valley, New York: JJ Augustin.
Bledstein, A. (1981). The trials of Sarah. *Judaism, 30,* 411–417.
Bledstein, A. (1991a). Dear Harold Bloom. *Lilith, 16,* 28.
Bledstein, A. (1991b). So J was a woman? *Shi'a: A Journal of Jewish Responsibility, 21,* 49–51.
Bledstein, A. (1991c). Family matters: A multidimensional reading of Miriam's humiliation and healing. *Biblical Research,* XLVI, 1991 (sic) 2, 55–61.
Bledstein, A. (1992). Was habbiryâ a healing ritual performed by a woman in King David's house? *Biblical Research, 3,* 5–31.
Bledstein, A. (1993). Binder, trickster, heel, and hairy-man: Rereading Genesis 27 as a trickster tale told by a woman. In A. Brenner (Ed.), *Genesis: A feminist companion to the Bible.* Sheffield: Sheffield Academic Press.
Bledstein, A. (1993). Female companionships: If the book of Ruth were written by a woman . . . In A. Brenner (Ed.), *Ruth: A feminist companion to the Bible* (pp. 116–133). Sheffield: Sheffield Academic Press.
Bledstein, A. (1993). Was Eve cursed? (or did a woman write Genesis?) *Bible Review,* February 1993, *IX*:1, 42–45.
Bledstein, A. (1993). Is Judges a woman's satire of men who play God? In A. Brenner (Ed.), *Judges: A feminist companion to the Bible* (pp. 34–54). Sheffield: Sheffield Academic Press.
Bledstein, A. (1995, October). Dr. Tamar. *Bible Review,* 10–11.
Bledstein, A. (2000). Tamar and the 'coat of many colors'. In A. Brenner (Ed.), *Samuel and Kings: A feminist companion to the Bible* (pp. 65–83). Sheffield: Sheffield Academic Press.
Bledstein, A. (2002, November). *Zipporah at a crossroads.* Toronto: Society of Biblical Literature.
Bledstein, A. (2006, Spring). Woman's humor in the Bible? *Humanist Judaism, XXXIV.* No. II, 14–16 (Reprinted with slight changes from 1991 and 1998).
Bledstein, A. (in preparation, 2015). What Is David thinking? The dreams, values, and character of King David revealed through psalms in narrative context.
Bloom, H., & Rosenberg, D. (1990). *The book of J.* New York: Grove Weidenfeld.
Desalvo, L. (2000). *Writing as a way of healing: How telling our stories transforms our lives.* MA: Beacon Press.
Friedman, R. E. (1987). *Who wrote the Bible?* New York: Summit Books.
Friedman, R. E. (1998). *The hidden book in the Bible.* San Francisco: Harper San Francisco.
Friedman, R. E. (2003). *The Bible with sources revealed.* San Francisco: Harper San Francisco.

Gilgamesh: http://www.cidmod.org/sidurisadvice/Gilgamesh.pdf

Goitein, S. D., & Carasik, M. (1988). Women as creators of biblical genres. *Prooftexts*, 8.

Halpern, B. (2001). *David's secret demons: Messiah, murderer, traitor, king*. Grand Rapids, MI: Wm B. Eerdmans Publishing Co.

Homer, *Iliad*: http://www.gutenberg.org/files/6130/6130-pdf.pdf

Krumholz McDonald, D. (1994). The serpent as healer: Theriac and ancient Near Eastern pottery. *Source: Notes in the History of Art*, XIII, 4, 21–27.

Polzin, R. (1993). *David and the deuteronomist.* Bloomington: Indiana University Press.

Roberts, J. (2004). Enheduanna, daughter of King Sargon: princess, poet, priestess (2300 B.C.), Transoxiana 8, Junio 2004. http://www.transoxiana.org/0108/roberts-enheduanna.html

Trible, P. (1973). Depatriarchalizing in biblical interpretation. *Journal of the American Academy of Religion, 41*, 30–48.

Trible, P. (1984). *Texts of terror: Literary-feminist readings of biblical narratives,* (Overtures to Biblical Theology). Philadelphia, PA: Fortress Press.

Chapter 6

Women in the Holy Quran

Sayyed Mohsen Fatemi

The Holy Quran attributes the body to nature, whereas the soul is ascribed to God. The Lord said to the angels, "I am about to create a man from clay" (Chapter Sad, verse 71). "And so when I have fashioned him in perfection, and have breathed into him of My Spirit, fall ye down in submission to him" (Chapter Sad, verse 72). "And if they ask thee concerning the soul, say, 'the soul is by the command of my Lord; and of the knowledge thereof you have been given but little'" (Chapter Asra, verse 85).

In the meantime, the Holy Quran discusses the relationship between femininity and maleness in the context of nature and the material. "Was he not a drop of fluid emitted forth? Then he became a clot, then He shaped and perfected *him*. Then He made of him a pair, the male and the female" (Chapters Qiyamat, 36–39).

The Quranic view posits that the soul does not consider any gender for the soul. The human being's perfection, in the language of the Holy Quran, does not belong to his/her being a male or a female. The perfection and the sublimity of one's status is tied to the growth, development, enhancement, and transcendental process of the soul. From an Islamic point of view, the goal behind the divine revelation is to educate, to elucidate, to purify, to enlighten, and to awaken human beings. This, in the Islamic context, purports that the constitutional foundations of education is the soul of human beings and the soul has nothing to do with being a male or a female. Being a male or a female is related to the body and not the soul.

Purification, thus, goes back to the soul and the soul is essentially different from the body. The learner, in the Islamic school of thought, is the soul.

The soul, being immaterial, does not have any gender. "Thou, O man, art verily laboring towards thy Lord, a hard laboring; then thou art going to meet Him" (Chapter Al-Inshiqaq, verse 6). The message here indicates that human beings are travelers towards God. The body does not do the traveling, so the travelers are not divided into males and females. The soul does the traveling and in that the soul is not of any gender.

The etiological mission of the holy Prophets addresses the soul as the audience and the addressee. The Holy Quran argues that a human being's perfections and virtues get consummated in view of understanding the source, the holy revelation, and the day of judgment hereafter. In other words, human beings embrace their perfection through an ontological understanding of the source, namely, the creator of the world and His attributes, the hereafter, the life after death, and its implications as heaven and hell. The space between the commencement and the finale is embedded within a straight line where the divine revelation and prophethood are positioned.

The principles of the religion, according to the Islamic school of thought, underscore the relationship between the origin and the hereafter. Thus, understanding the origin, the hereafter, and the prophethood are the main features of a religious perspective. A saying is ascribed to the leader of the faithful Amir Almomenin (Salavatollah alayh): "May God's mercy be upon him/her who knows from where he/she has come, where he/she is, and to where he/she is going."

Understanding the abovementioned principles requires no gender. One needs to be neither male nor female to understand the aforementioned principles. No exclusive message has been sent to males or females in this regard.

Prophet Mohammad (Salallah alayhe va alehee va salaam) says, "Say, 'This is my way: I call onto Allah on sure knowledge, I and those who follow me'" (Chapter Yusuf, verse 108).

This is an invitation to all human beings. If a prophet writes an invitation to a male governor, another prophet sends another invitation letter to a female governor. The holy Prophet of Islam Hazrat Mohammad (Salallah alayhe va alehee va salaam) invited the male kings to Islam and Solomon the Prophet (Salamollah alayh) extended the invitation to a female king.

Therefore, all the invitations and the invitees are general and do not belong to any particular gender.

On the other hand, in examining the relationships between males and females in the Holy Quran, one needs to understand the underlying Qur'anic values, which make a distinction between what is considered the source of value or virtues.

The Holy Quran verses that focus on knowledge versus ignorance, faith versus paganism, sublimity versus meanness, virtues versus vice, right versus wrong, honesty versus dishonesty, obedience versus disobedience, trust versus treason, do not consider any of these features in the context of male or female. The subject of these attributes is neither the body of the male nor the female.

The reason and wisdom which are crystalized in the descriptive mode of human intellect, the heart which moves in line with the attempt to inquire into the nature of reality and intuition, as well as the soul that is described within the attributes of virtue or vice, are neither male nor female. Corruption or piety do not belong to any gender-oriented features; they are neither male nor female. Knowledge, either acquired knowledge or knowledge by presence, does not emanate from being a male or a female. In this regard, there is no superiority of male over female or vice versa.

In the domain of practical reason, there is no male or female categorization either. Issues such as will, faith, patience, and reliance on God are not specific to males nor females. The Holy Quran considers the soul as the owner of the values or what stands against values.

In some cases, the Holy Quran explicitly indicates the names of men and women to denounce pre-Islamic ignorant thoughts. The pre-Islamic ignorant thoughts discriminated men from women. They considered the virtues only in the realm of males. The Holy Quran condemns this viewpoint and declares that the soul does not belong to only a male or a female.

Prior to Islam, women were literally undermined and degraded. They were exposed to numerous forms of condescending behaviors. They were the subject of the wrath and anger of men. In the utilitarianism and consumerism of our world today, women are subjected to the denial of their identity and they are manipulated into objects of lust and exploitation.

None of the verses and chapters of the Holy Quran associate being a male as a prerequisite for any virtue, nor being a female as an impediment for obtaining a virtue.

In the Quranic viewpoint, being a male or a female does not, *ipso facto*, give rise to any source of pride or priority. In describing the original elucidation of the original human being, the Holy Quran sometimes describes clay, indicating that there is no pride in being a male or a female.

The only factor that can engender pride, in the Quranic viewpoint, is virtue and piety (Taqva) and that takes place away from any hubris, any arrogance, and any overbearing attitude of superiority. Taqva fights any form of egoism and egotism. It does not open up the path for any manifestation of solipsism and selfishness. Taqva liberates human beings from any form of pretentiousness shrouded in the ostentatious manifestations of materialism, utilitarianism, consumerism, racism, sexism, and self-centeredness. Taqva emancipates human beings from the manacles of supercilious selfishness.

The Holy Quran states, "O mankind, We have created you a male and a female; and We have made you into tribes and sub-tribes that you may recognize one another. Verily, the most honorable among you, in the sight of Allah, is he/she who is the most righteous among you" (Chapter Hujurat, verse 13). According to this verse of the Holy Quran and other verses, the creation of men is not superior to the creation of women. No racism or sexism is accepted.

Language and race merely act as features of identification. Facial complexion, language, race, dialect, and other superficial features belong to the realm of the body and not the soul. The soul is neither from the east nor from the west. It does not belong to any class or race. All are created as men and women. There is no cause of pride for being a male or a female. The transcendental leap for human beings goes beyond maleness or femininity.

The psychological problems and anti-ethical values that are discussed in the Holy Quran are ascribed to the heart and they are devoid of being male or female oriented.

Spiritual health and well-being are presented in the context of values and they are examined in the Holy Quran as attributes of the heart and the soul without any ascription to being a female or a male.

The Holy Quran says, "Whoso acts righteously, whether male or female, and is a believer, we will surely grant him a pure life; and We will surely bestow on such their reward according to the best of their work" (Chapter Nahl, verse 97).

This suggests that in order to embrace the pure life, two factors are of significance: the righteous act and the believing soul. There is no relationship to being a male or a female here as an indication of superiority. The language here applies to both men and women.

It is interesting to note that in the language of the Holy Quran, the only creature that can undertake changes in human beings are human beings. We are the only creatures that can serve as the agents of change and transformation. The changes transpire through the power of the will and the power of choice. In doing so, human beings can take it upon themselves to develop changes and transformations both in their inner and outside world. The changes, if they move in line with the ontological system within the monotheistic context, are considered righteous and if not they are taken as vice. In other words, human beings create different worlds through their options and choices. If their choices and options resonate with the etiological values of monotheism, they give rise to righteousness, and if they move against the monotheistic values, they give rise to vice.

Choices make human beings go above angels or below beasts. In doing so there is no superiority or inferiority for men or women. They both can make choices and they both can elevate their status or downgrade it. The criteria here are not gendered whatsoever. Both men and women can achieve the lofty status of becoming pure human beings through the choices they make. The elevation can apply to both men and women. Transcendental ascension and existential descent applies to both men and women.

Our choices can be revitalizing in that people can resuscitate their life and vivacity through moving in line with monotheistic values such as compassion, devotion, kindness, graciousness, benevolence, assistance, magnanimity, openness, forgiveness, and righteousness, or they can paralyze the transcendental leap through actions and choices such as brutality, violence, rancor, bitterness, animosity, corruption, oppression, racial discrimination, injustice, bellicosity, enmity, and backbiting. They all can take place in the realm of the soul and they are not exclusive to men or women.

The Holy Quran describes both men and women who are seemingly alive but are dead; people who seemingly possess hearts but their hearts are dead, they seemingly have eyes and ears but they are blind and deaf to the crucial issues. This may apply to both men and women who have departed from the transcendental values and have disconnected themselves from God.

The disconnection is not for only men or women. Both men and women can be disconnected or connected. Again, the subject here is the soul and not the body. One's authenticity belongs to his/her soul and his/her body merely serves as an instrument. The Holy Quran considers one's authenticity and truthfulness in his/her soul and considers the body neither the entire truth nor even part of the truth of one's being. The body is taken as the instrument or the means for the soul.

Prior to Islam, women were exposed to multifaceted forms of humiliation, so much so that the birth of a girl was considered as a sign of abjectness and misery. This was exemplified in the notorious acts of the men who buried their daughters alive upon the birth of their child. The Islamic school of thought denounces any violation of women's rights and condemns any form of injustice against the status of women. Men and women, according to the Holy Quran, do not possess any existential or ontological superiority over one another.

Imam Ali (Salavtollah alayh) cites the holy Prophet of Islam (Salallah alayhe va alehee va salaam), as saying:

> The Prophet came to our place. Fatima, the daughter of the Prophet and the wife of Imam Ali, was sitting in front of a cooking vase. I was cleaning the lentils. The Prophet stated that "Oh, Ali! Whoever helps his wife at home in doing the housework keeps away from hubris and arrogance in doing this. His name will be recorded among the martyrs by God. Oh, Ali, whoever does not feel arrogant in helping his wife in the household, his mortal sins will be expunged through his collaboration with his wife. God's anger will be removed through his assistance to his wife. The collaboration will increase his spiritual status. Oh, Ali, the men who help their wives will be among the righteous and the martyrs of the path of truthhood, or they will be among those who are exposed to God's special grace." (The book Alhayat by Hakimi, Hakimi, and Hakimi, Chapter 8, p. 495)

In another Haidth, Imam Javad, the ninth Imam of Shiites (Salavtollah alayh), citing Imam Ali (Salavtollah alayh) with a citation from the holy Prophet (Salallah alayhe va alehee va salaam), declares, "You cannot win all people's hearts through money and wealth, so win their hearts through good deeds and lofty human values" (The book Alhayat by Hakimi, Hakimi, and Hakimi, Chapter 9, pp. 613–648).

These examples would apply to both men and women, and both of them are encouraged to enhance the quality of their human life through abiding by the spiritual principles that bring elevation to life.

In another example, Imam Sadeq (Salvatollah alayh) states: "Do not assume that if you make a believer happy, you have only made him/her happy. I swear to God that You have made us happy and you have indeed made the Prophet (Salallah alayhe va alehee va salaam) happy too" (The book Usoole Kafi, Chapter 2, p. 189). The word "believer" in the abovementioned Hadith includes both men and women.

In discussing the characteristics of elevated men and women of awareness, Imam Sadeq, the sixth Imam of Shiites (Salavtallah alayh), mentions three characteristics that belong to the art of good thinking:

1. Good and decent public relations with people
2. Effective listening skills
3. Effective responses to people's questions

(The book Alhayat by Hakimi, Hakimi, and Hakimi, Chapter 9, p. 740)

The Islamic school of thought highlights the significance of brotherhood and justice in its multifaceted contexts and underscores the necessity of treating everyone, whether men or women, believer or non-believer, based on human principles and spiritual criteria. Imam Ali (Salavatolah alayh) explicates this by saying, "Treat every one based on respect and in accordance with the principle of human dignity and human elevation since everyone . . . either belongs to you as your religious companions or if not they are of your human companion!"

REFERENCES

Babeveyh, M. A. (1984). Oyoone Akhabar AReza (Alayhessalam). M. H. A'alami (Ed.). Beirut: Moassese Ala'lami Lelmatbooat.

Hakimi M. R., Hakimi, M, & Hakimi, A. (2010). *Alhayat*. Qom: Daleele Ma Publication.

The Holy Quran. Abdullah Yusuf Ali, trans. Mt. Holly, NJ: Islamic Educational Services.

Kulayni, M. Y. (1983). *Alkafee*. Tehran: Darol Ketabe Islamieh.

Nahjol balaghe of Imam Ali salavatolah alayh.

Usoole Kafi by Muhammad Ibn Ya'qub Al-Kulayni.

Chapter 7

Feminism in Hinduism: Female Deities and Their Influence on South Asian Culture

Divyaben Patel, Katherine Anne E. Scott, Paula K. Lundberg-Love, and Jeanine M. Galusha-Glasscock

Many Western cultures have a working concept of what Hinduism is, without having clarity as to how the religion influences Eastern culture. Hinduism itself can be very confusing to outsiders who are not familiar with the various manifestations of different divine entities and their complex relationships. However, what makes Hinduism all the more interesting is how it has profound effects on social mores in southern Asian countries, such as India and Pakistan. This chapter is intended to provide a historical context for Hinduism and discuss both the role of feminism within the religion and the impact on women's roles in society as a result.

THE ORIGINS OF HINDUISM

In contemporary times, the term "Hindu" is primarily thought of as solely describing an Eastern, polytheistic religion, i.e., Hinduism. However, originally the term described a population who lived beyond the Indus River in India. It is thought to have evolved from the Indo-Aryan word "Sindhu," which was the earliest known name of the Indus River (Flood, 1996; Narayanan, 1998).

Some scholars actually believe that the roots of Hinduism can be traced back to the Indus Valley civilization (ca. 2500 to 1500 BCE), as similarities between some aspects of this civilization and later Hinduism are quite striking (Doniger, 2015; Flood, 1996). However, it needs to be noted that there is no broad consensus regarding this issue (Flood, 1996). It has been suggested that a few of the images on seals that have been excavated in places like Harappa and Mohenjodaro may be precursors to the images of Hindu Gods and Goddesses that appear many centuries later in Hinduism (Doniger, 2015). The ancient religious texts may provide researchers with some clues as to how deep the connection is between the Indus Valley civilization and later Hinduism.

The Rig Veda, one of the four sacred religious texts associated with Hinduism, is chronologically the oldest, and may thus best elucidate Hinduism's roots (Doniger, 2015; Kinsley, 1988). The Rig Veda was most likely composed circa 1500 BCE by a nomadic people who lived in present day Punjab, in northwest India and Pakistan (Doniger, 2015). These nomadic peoples lived in the land of seven rivers, which included the Indus River, its five tributaries, and the river Sarasvati (Doniger, 2015). The Rig Veda is a collection of several hymns praising the Gods and consisting of ancient prayers (Kinsley, 1988). It also discusses the genesis of the world and contains many mythological and poetical accounts (Werner, 1994).

During the Rig Vedic period (ca. 1500 BCE to 500 BCE), male gods played a much more dominant role in religious life than their female counterparts, who were only mentioned in passing (Kinsley, 1988). One exception to this is the Goddess Usas, who is associated and identified with the dawn. Indeed, Usas has been placed within the hierarchy alongside the second-order male deities and will be discussed in detail later in the chapter. However, in general, women have been largely objectified in the Rig Veda because the Rig Vedic society was a patriarchal one. This is saliently illustrated by the fact that the most valued possessions of the Rig Vedic man were his cattle and his wife (Doniger, 2015).

GODDESSES IN THE RIG VEDA

Usas, the primordial goddess, is viewed as omniscient. Although she is described as a young and beautiful maiden, she also is seen as a motherly figure, a matron, and a protector (Kinsley, 1988). This is particularly noteworthy, because within such a patriarchal framework, Usas is an exception, as the role of the protector is typically ascribed to men.

Another goddess, Prithvi, is associated with the terrestrial sphere inhabited by human beings. She is closely associated with the male god of the sky, Dyaus. Together, they are said to kiss the center of the earth and are described as universal parents, who created the earth and the gods (Kinsley, 1988). The role of progenitor attributed to her clearly highlights her importance.

Some of the goddesses in the Rig Veda are not anthropomorphic, meaning that they are not as human-like as some of the other deities (Doniger, 2015). One such goddess is Aditi. Like Prithvi, motherhood is her most outstanding attribute. What makes Aditi unique is that she does not have a male consort, and is instead independent of that type of relationship. She maintains strict autonomy (Kinsley, 1988). She is conceptualized as a singular creator.

The Goddess Saraswati is associated with fecundity and fertility and is identified with a particular river, though there is controversy regarding with which river she is associated because the erstwhile river is very difficult to identify (Kalyanaraman, 2008). She is sometimes invoked for protection in areas that are not so fluvial, such as sheltering a tree or an iron fort (Kinsley, 1988). Other goddesses mentioned in the Rig Veda are Vac, goddess of speech; Nirrti, who is equated with ill-luck, death, and destruction in scattered references; and Ratri, the goddess of night, who is typically benign (Kinsley, 1988).

STATUS OF WOMEN IN THE VEDIC PERIOD AND LATER VEDIC PERIOD

Even though the Rig Vedic society was a patriarchal one, there is textual evidence to suggest that women enjoyed considerable social and political freedom and had access to education during the Vedic period (Wangu, 2003). They had access to the Vedas, the repository of sacred knowledge, and were able to pursue their respective educational interests. Hence, there are many examples of women teachers and theologians during this period (Altekar, 1959). Women also enjoyed considerable freedom in choosing their life partners and performing Vedic rituals jointly with men (Altekar, 1959; Wangu, 2003). Additionally, they took care of the household chores without the assistance of males and were considered as valuable members of the society (Wangu, 2003).

During the latter part of the Vedic period, a gradual decline in the status of women occurred (ca. 900 BCE to 500 BCE). Only the male members of the upper three *varnas*, or social castes (Brahmin priests, Kshatriya merchants, Vaisya merchants) could learn the Vedas (Wangu, 2003). Women who were interested in learning sacred knowledge were now only allowed to learn from secondary sources, such as their fathers, uncles, or brothers. In addition, there was also considerable curtailment of freedom of choice for women regarding political, social, and sexual matters (Wangu, 2003).

While this change in the societal atmosphere could be conceptualized as the rise of misogynism and the demise of existing feminism, it is important to contextualize these changes. The lens through which Westerners view Hinduism limits their understanding, simply due to extreme cultural differences. In fact, contemporary Indian activists, such as Madhu Kishwar, reject even the term "feminism" as they feel it is exclusively related to Western stereotypes (Narayanan, 1998).

MANUSMRITI

One of the most prominent dharma texts (*dharmashastras*) in ancient India was Manusmriti (the Laws of Manu). Dharma refers to the behaviors associated with Rta, the universal truth or cosmic order. Basically, dharma texts are religious codes of behavior, somewhat analogous to the Ten Commandments in Christianity and Judaism. Manu was most likely a mythological character said to be the first human, analogous to Adam in the traditions of the mainstream monotheistic religions of Christianity, Judaism, and Islam (Doniger, 2015). The Manusmriti consists of 2,685 verses on varied topics concerning the social obligations and duties of individuals and various castes. Unfortunately, Manu has earned considerable notoriety for his misogyny. He went to great lengths to justify wide-ranging repressive practices against women (Doniger, 2015). However, the concept of Manu is complex; he was not simply the first man created, as the tradition of Adam has been described. There have been multitudes of Manus and their lifespans can be hundreds of millions of years.

Unfortunately, even Indian activists such as Raja Ram Mohan Roy (1774 to 1883), who is sometimes considered the father of the Indian Renaissance, had to use Manusmriti in his fight against *sati* (widow burning), despite disagreeing with its principles, because of its prevalence (Narayanan, 1998). Other conservative texts were less well-known and thus had less of an impact on the development of social mores.

PORTRAYAL OF WOMEN IN THE GREAT HINDU EPICS

Overlapping with and following the Vedic period is what is now commonly referred to as the Epic period of India (ca. 1000 BCE to 300 CE). This aeon is when the great Hindu epics flourished and three stand out as defining the period: the Ramayana, the Upanishads, and the Mahabharata. The Bhagavad Gita, arguably the most well-known Hindu text, is a part of the Mahabharata and some consider it the foundation upon which contemporary Hinduism is built.

Draupadi, the wife of the five Pandavas, and Sita, the wife of Rama, are the two most notable women in the Hindu epics Mahabharata (300 BCE to 300 CE), and Ramayana (200 BCE to 200 CE), respectively (Doniger, 2015). One of the pivotal episodes in the Mahabharata is the stripping of Draupadi. One of the arguments to justify the treatment meted out to her is that she is promiscuous, due to her having multiple husbands and participating in polyandry (Doniger, 2015; Mukherjee, 1983). This is probably a pointed reminder to women that the ancient option of female promiscuity is no longer available to them and a warning that they too will be punished for participating in such acts (Doniger, 2015). She does not take down her hands and vows revenge, declaring that she will not tie her hair until she has drenched it in her enemies' blood (Diesel, 2002). The stand she takes against male violence has strong feminist undertones, in that she refuses to compromise her beliefs simply due to the fact that a male ordered her to do so and she defends her bodily autonomy.

Sita, on the other hand, is portrayed as a loyal, submissive, and uncomplaining woman. This is consistent with the patriarchal belief that women should endure suffering with a complacent attitude, regardless of the way they are actually treated (Mukherjee, 1983).

STATUS OF WOMEN IN THE EPIC PERIOD

In conjunction with the social norms being expressed in the major Hindu epics, there were two primary factors that contributed to the further decline in education of girls during the Epic period. First, the principle of endogamy was not strictly followed, meaning that marriage was not limited to specific ethnic groups within the greater population. Many tribal and folk peoples had intermarried within the various Brahmanic castes. The non-Brahmanic wives, who had become members of Vedic households, were unaware of the Vedic rituals and the liturgical language, Sanskrit (Altekar, 1959). With the passage of time, the religious rituals had become highly complicated. It was indeed a very long and arduous task to master the intricacies of the complex Vedic rituals, particularly for women who had to attend to other tasks as well (Altekar, 1959). Thus, the onus of maintaining order within the family fell on women and they moved away from pursuing religious and educational practices, prioritizing homemaking. Childbearing was a highly valued episode in women's lives, with the most auspicious occasion being the birth of a son (Wangu, 2003). It is important to note here that men similarly experienced a lack of options regarding everyday life. For example, men were simply not allowed to stay at home and nurture the children, and men of certain castes were severely limited in their choice of jobs.

In the later Epic period, there emerged a newfound focus on eroticism and the powers of water and vegetation. Sita, the heroine of the epic Ramayana, is the epitome of the emphasis on agricultural fertility. She was the daughter of the earth and the furrow, which symbolized female productivity (Wangu, 2003). Despite the fact that a goddess pantheon was gathering momentum during the Epic period, girls were being discouraged or even hindered from acquiring an education (Wangu, 2003).

LAKSHMI: THE ARCHETYPAL FEMALE DEITY

One of the important goddesses of the Hindu pantheon existing since the pre-Buddhist times is the goddess Lakshmi. Throughout her history, she has been associated with prosperity, well-being, royal power, and illustriousness (Kinsley, 1988). Though she began as a consort of a male deity, Vishnu, she has completely taken over the functions of the three major male gods, Brahma, Vishnu, and Shiva, by creating, sustaining, and periodically destroying the cosmos (Kinsley, 1988). In the Lakshmi-tantra, she is the supreme object of devotion. It is she who grants all desires, and her special incantations possess salvific qualities, meaning they have the power to provide redemption (Kinsley, 1988).

RADHA: THE UNLIKELY FEMINIST

Radha, the lover of Krishna, occupies a very interesting place in Hindu mythology. The Hindu texts and oral traditions that mention Radha make it amply clear that her dalliance with Krishna is clearly in defiance of social norms. The sexually explicit texts, such as Gita-Govinda, bring out in erotic detail the manifestations of Radha's manifold sexual desire in the arms of Krishna (Dhar, 2012). Though her devotion to her partner is completely consistent with patriarchal norms, her sexual desire makes her stand out as an improbable female icon within mainstream mythology (Dhar, 2012). She shakes the very foundation of patriarchy with her provocative agency.

GODDESSES IN THE PURANAS

The Puranas, which cover the aeon from ca. 400 CE to 1200 CE, provide a vibrant mythological narrative of a goddess who slays anti-gods and acts independently of males (Doniger, 2015). It is widely thought that Vyasa, the narrator of the Mahabharata, edited this collection.

The goddess who initially appears in the Puranas is known as Chandrika (the fierce). In later descriptions, she is often called Durga (hard to get to) or Kali (death or doomsday), a black goddess who wears a necklace of human skulls and a girdle made of the fingers of children (Doniger, 2015; Wangu, 2003). The complex mythological tales and religious sects surrounding these manifestations probably emanated from villages or tribal cultures, but began to spread under royal patronage, eventually assimilating into mainstream Hinduism (Doniger, 2015).

Durga is engendered from incredibly fierce energies of all the gods and she slays the buffalo demon (Menon, 2002). In her avatar as Durga, she initially finds it difficult to kill the buffalo demon. The gods then tell her that only a naked woman would be able to accomplish her task, so she takes off her clothes, unties her hair, and, lo and behold, the strength of the demon wanes and she is able to decapitate it (Menon, 2002). She then flies into a rage at the treachery of the gods, takes the form of Kali, and begins to devour the entire universe (Menon, 2002). The gods seek the help of Siva, her husband. Siva lies in her path and she unwittingly steps on him, after which she feels ashamed and begins to calm down (Menon, 2002; Hiltebeitel & Erndl, 2000).

In Hinduism, all goddesses can be considered manifestations of Devi, meaning female deities. It is thought that Devi's feminine power, Shakti, is inherent in all gods and mortals (Wangu, 2003). Yet it is interesting that, in general, Hindu women do not seem to be inspired by these goddesses. This may be because they see the qualities represented by female divinity as unachievable and cannot relate to them internally. It has been suggested that Hindu women focus solely on the physical appearance of the female deities, rather than the characteristics they represent (Wangu, 2003). For example, Durga, the slayer of the buffalo demon, bares her nakedness with no shame in order to complete her mission. She represents strength and determination, rather than the vulnerability and chagrin typically associated with female nudity during this time period.

THE BHAKTI MOVEMENT

The Bhakti movement was a religious reform movement that began in the twelfth century and gave rise to the bhakti cult (Sengupta, 2006). But to brand this movement as a mere reform movement would be an understatement. It was, in fact, an open revolt against the brahmanical and patriarchal construct of Hinduism (Fulkerson & Briggs, 2012; Sengupta, 2006). Serious attempts were made to incorporate elements of folk religiosity into the gamut of Hinduism (Fulkerson & Briggs, 2012).

People from all walks of life, irrespective of their gender, sect, caste, and class, joined this movement. The writings of women of the bhakti cult challenged the existing social mores. They depict an intimate and mystical relation with God that was often sexually charged. This was in open revolt against the system that did not permit women to offer their devotion through Vedic chanting of mantras to certain male deities (Sengupta, 2006).

As the liturgical language of the Vedas and the Upanishads was Sanskrit, it was beyond the reach of the lower caste and classes. In the brahmanical organization, women from lower castes faced double marginalization. So, it was only natural that the songs of the Bhakti movement were written in Prakrit, the spoken language of the masses (Sengupta, 2006).

The overwhelming desire to be freed from strictures of all kinds was so strong that we find women within the bhakti cult openly venting their displeasure at the patriarchy within the patriarchy, that is, at home and in the family (Sengupta, 2006). The recurrent theme of Lal Ded's songs is the mind-numbing triviality of domestic drudgery and the barbs aimed at her by her nemesis, her mother-in-law. Mirabai, too, renounces domestic life and rejects the conventions of her husband's home to be united with Krishna (Sengupta, 2006).

MIRABAI: THE QUINTESSENTIAL REBEL

Mirabai (ca. 1450 to 1498, or 1525 to 1597), the famous female bhakti saint, demonstrates autonomy and independence not generally present in the Epic period. Though she was forced to marry against her will, she shuns marriage and roams with mendicants and devotees of Krishna (Doniger, 2015). She was ahead of her time in that her poems mock both marriage and asceticism. Yet she continues to gain followers and devotees, even after her death (Doniger, 2015; Weber, 2009). She exemplifies free choice in choosing one's partner, which may be a source of inspiration for contemporary Hindu women who rebel against the idea of arranged marriage.

REINTERPRETATION OF ANCIENT SCRIPTURES

Indian women's first real encounter with modernity occurred during the colonial period (Bhatt, 2008). Raja Ram Mohan Roy (1774 to 1883), a religious and social radical, was thoroughly conversant with scriptures of many religions including his own, Hinduism. He reinterpreted ancient Hindu scriptures to fight against the custom of sati (Bhatt, 2008). *Sati* was the ancient Hindu custom of immolating a woman on her husband's funeral pyre (voluntarily or otherwise). Roy argued that sati was not a spiritual practice of great merit, specifically referring to the Upanishads. He said that it ensured only a temporary place in the heaven, not eternal liberation of the soul (Bhatt, 2008). This was a very clever ploy, in that Raja Ram Mohan Roy realized that the time was not yet right to argue strongly against sati from a secular point of view. In addition to sati, female infanticide, prostitution, child brides, and dowry deaths (newly married women who are burnt because they did not bring in enough money from their natal homes) were historically abundant (Narayanan, 1998).

A century later, at the height of the Indian independence conflict, Mahatma Gandhi advocated looking at the *smritis* and the *shastras* in light of his new doctrine of nonviolence, which according to him included gender parity (Bhatt, 2008; Ryland, 1977). Consistent with the Hindu belief that the ultimate responsibility of freedom rests with the individual, he said that women should not consider themselves weak and dependent (Ryland, 1977). Gandhi also suggested that the morally repugnant aspects of these texts should not be considered as divinely inspired (Bhatt, 2008). He argued that the heroines of the great epics, Sita and Draupadi, possessed the same moral authority as the scriptures by virtue of their pure moral character. He also cited the example of Mirabai to argue for women's participation in public life (Bhatt, 2008). Though it seems riddled with elitism and the male concept of idealized women, it is important to bear in mind that this was a part of an early reform movement.

From all this, it is clearly evident that the reinterpretive lens has been repeatedly used during various stages of Indian history to argue for equal rights for women. Hence, it can be said that one does not need always to look for inspiration outside religion to argue for gender equality. This is particularly relevant in the post-colonial period where the feminist initiatives have been largely secular. It is much easier to convince people about the merits of female empowerment from a religious perspective because religion is something which most people hold very dear to their hearts, as borne out by the examples of Raja Ram Mohan Roy and Mahatma Gandhi.

FEMALE ICONS IN FOLK AND REGIONAL HINDUISM

In Gujarat, a state located in the western part of India, the Mahi River has been portrayed as a bold, young, dark girl of the forest. She yearns to meet her true love, the ocean, and leaves her mountain home to marry him (Doniger, 2015). She undertakes a long and arduous journey to meet her lover, and the ocean initially rejects her marriage offer. She challenges him to a battle, and the ocean finally concedes (Doniger, 2015). This illustrates the ultimate triumph of the female will and power.

Kannaki, a Tamil goddess, avenges her husband's death. Her husband, Kovalan, is wrongly accused of stealing the queen's anklet and is put to death (Cush, Robinson, & York, 2008). She goes to the royal palace and exonerates her husband. Then she becomes apoplectic and rips off her left breast and throws it at the city of Madurai, burning the city to the ground (Cush et al., 2008). This symbolizes that a woman's strength lies in her bosom.

The Amman goddesses of South India are a far cry from most of the Brahmanical goddesses in the sense that they do not have any male consorts, rendering them independent of male control (Diesel, 2002). The virgin quality attributed to them does not represent sexual naiveté, but their indomitable and autonomous character. The appellation "Mother" is a metaphor for life-giving, creative powers (Diesel, 2002). Obviously, the Amman goddess religion of South India offers a potentially far more powerful set of role models for contemporary women than does the Brahmanical religion.

SHAKTI: THE IRRESISTIBLE FEMININE POWER

The concept of *Shakti* is so ubiquitous in the Hindu milieu that someone who is studying about Hindu gods simply cannot ignore it (Hiltebeitel & Erndl, 2000). Shakti stands for women's power. Surely, the oppression of women is a reality in Hindu society, but it varies in degree according to caste, gender, and other factors. There is clear evidence to suggest that the Shakta tradition is more inclusive of women than other Hindu traditions (Hiltebeitel & Erndl, 2000). This genre of Hinduism is more receptive of women as gurus and practitioners of the religion.

The concept of Shakti is connected to the life-giving female properties, as well as death. It is a complex amalgamation of female power in both positive and negative aspects (Hiltebeitel & Erndl, 2000). It is neither exclusively auspicious nor inauspicious. Holy women and female gurus are hailed as *mataji* (respected mother), which is eponymous with the name of the goddess (Hiltebeitel & Erndl, 2000). The holy woman identifies herself, and is identified by others, with divinity. There is a serious dearth of avenues of self-expression for women outside marriage, and divine possession by the goddess is one of the few culturally accepted ways of avoiding marriage (Hiltebeitel & Erndl, 2000).

The Tamil folk epic *Nallatankal (The Good Younger Sister)* clearly exemplifies the culturally acceptable notion of Shakti. A starving young woman returns to the house of her wealthy elder brother, only to have the door shut on her (Reynolds, 1980). But, the barred door cannot withstand the power that emanates from her. The potency of her power comes from the sexual fidelity of a married woman, the measure of her ability to control her sexuality, and the maintenance of her sexual purity (Reynolds, 1980).

Sharing the goddesses' ability to create, however, comes with a caveat. Reproductive ability necessitates participation in natural processes of menstruation and childbirth, as well as nursing and taking care of infants and children with all their accompanying pollutants (Menon, 2002). As a result, women keep alternating between conditions of relative purity and impurity. Consequently, there are certain do's and dont's that women have to follow during the so-called conditions of impurity, such as the kind of foods they eat and the places they visit.

FEMALE GURUS: A RELIGIOUS ODDITY

Despite being deeply involved in religious life, Hindu women seldom have held positions of institutional authority. One of the reasons why women have been barred from holding positions of religious authority is their supposed ritual impurity (Charpentier, 2010). However, despite restrictions being imposed on women's religiosity since Manusmriti, they still have found new avenues for religious expression. Women in Hinduism can be dubbed as invisible religious practitioners because their religious practices are largely restricted to the private domain and their religious legitimacy is not sanctioned by the shastras. However, women, along with men, can be seen as primary actors in folk religious narrative (Charpentier, 2010).

It is a welcome development that women have begun to wield greater religious authority and hold leadership positions in contemporary Hinduism. To achieve this, female gurus consciously discard scriptural restrictions and sometimes even oppose the scriptures that are regressive (Charpentier, 2010). The modus operandi of the female gurus is also somewhat different from their male counterparts. In Indian ethos, a stereotypical guru is pictured as a male renunciant who has given up the world in general and is living the life of an ascetic. On the other hand, we find that female gurus have not given up the world entirely. We see them striking a compromise between religious and social obligations (Charpentier, 2010).

MODERN TIMES AND FEMINIST ROLES IN INDIA

It wasn't until the late 1800s and early 1900s that Indian women began to openly strive for what can be loosely called feminism, but more realistically described as raising simple awareness of their presence and their needs. In 1904, hundreds of Indian women gathered for the Bharata Mahila Parishad (Ladies Social Conference) in Bombay and, for the first time, actively restricted men from attending. The speakers addressed topics on various social issues, including but not limited to education, lack of medical care for women, early marriage, child welfare, and working together to better their nation (Forbes, 1982).

While the original meeting was held as part of the National Social Conference, attendees quickly decided that they needed their own independent organizations. It was through these organizations—which were openly opposed by male reformers who preferred a joint organization—that the desire for women's rights were first verbalized and proposals were made to change the existing societal structure toward a more level playing field (Forbes, 1982). The National Council of Women in India (NCWI) was first founded in 1925 and became the first national organization to be associated with international women's rights. In fact, the NCWI was the first feminist organization to selectively attempt to become involved with politics, a previously unheard of possibility.

In 1927, what can arguably be called the most important Indian women's organization was founded, the All India Women's Conference. This group emphasized the disparity present among men and women in the educational sphere and was the first to simultaneously focus on social issues, such as child marriages. After all, what would be the point to plan for education for girls who were going to drop out of school once they were betrothed or married (Forbes, 1982)? This conference also led to rejection of the term "feminism" by the participants.

As mentioned previously, activists such as Madhu Kishwar wanted to gain individual rights without rejecting their patriotism, or their cultural beliefs, something that they felt the English ideal of "feminism" tried to do (Narayanan, 1998). They preferred the terminology "women's issues" and they struggled with the Western influence introduced by English imperialism. Sarojini Naidu (1879–1949) was one of the most prominent women who wrote on these themes, and she touched on both the secular (practical rights) and the spiritual (she believed that these "new women" were the spiritual descendants of the great female deities of the epics) (Forbes, 1982). While great political and religious changes have been effected during the last 100 years, including women gaining the right to vote and acquiring greater educational opportunities, there are still ongoing struggles for, and against, feminist themes.

CONCLUDING REMARKS

Even in the origins of Hinduism, we can identify some strains of feminism present within the patriarchal structure of the religion. We have seen that in the most ancient of the Hindu religious texts, Usas and other female deities have been given a prominent place. Similar undertones also can be seen in the great Indian epics. In the Mahabharata, Draupadi found avenues of self-expression despite being oppressed. In the Ramayana, although Sita embodied ideal female qualities (from a male perspective), going back to the furrow from whence she came was her final act of revolt. It can also be seen that in some traditions of Hinduism, the goddess Lakshmi has been given the position of an all-powerful deity.

We also have discussed the fact that some of the goddesses deviated from the prescribed social norms. The explicit nature of Radha's eroticism shows that she is completely aware of her sexuality, unlike other conventional goddesses. The goddess Durga has been portrayed as an epitome of female power, as she was born out of a synergy of the strengths of the various male gods.

Religious reform movements, such as the Bhakti movement, have popularized female icons such as Mirabai, who refused to conform to the existing social mores and chose the life of an itinerant. Importantly, facets of feminism within Hinduism have been used as compelling tools for logical argument by visionaries like Raja Ram Mohan Roy and Gandhiji to fight against the oppression of women. Therefore, the argument that some of the ancient scriptures can be used to fight for women's rights is not without merit.

Finally, it is noteworthy that in folk and regional Hinduism, women have been given their due importance. Though some of the goddesses are not so well known, such as Mahi or Kannaki, they are exceptional examples of female power, and in some traditions, Shakti (women power) has been given paramount importance by associating femininity with creation and also with death.

REFERENCES

Altekar, A. S. (1959). *The position of women in Hindu civilization, from prehistoric times to the present day* (2nd ed.). Delhi: Motilal Banarsidass.

Bhatt, N. S. (2008, October). A reflection on the challenges for Hindu women in the twenty-first century. Paper presented at the Religion, Women, and Society panel in the Conference on East/West in Dialogue: Religious Perspective on Global Issues in the 21st Century, Wellesley College, Wellesley. Retrieved from http://www.iop.or.jp/Documents/0919/shukla-bhatt.pdf

Charpentier, M. T. (2010). *Indian female gurus in contemporary Hinduism: A study of central aspects and expressions of their religious leadership.* Finland: Abo Academy University Press.

Cush, D., Robinson, C., & York, M. (2008). Encyclopedia of Hinduism. *Theological Librarianship: An Online Journal of the American Theological Library Association, 2*(1), 106–107.

Dhar, D. (2012). Radha's Revenge: Feminist agency, postcoloniality, and the politics of desire in Anita Nair's mistress. *Postcolonial Text, 7*(4). Retrieved on August 23, 2015, from http://postcolonial.org/index.php/pct/article/viewFile/1535/1424

Diesel, A. (2002). Tales of women's suffering: Darupadi and other Amman goddesses as role models for women. *Journal of Contemporary Religion, 17*(1), 5–20.

Doniger, W. (2015). Hinduism. In J. Miles (Eds.), *The Norton anthology of world religions.* New York: W. W. Norton Co.

Flood, G. D. (1996). *An Introduction to Hinduism.* Cambridge: Press Syndicate of the University of Cambridge.

Forbes, G. H. (1982). Caged tigers: 'First Wave' feminists in India. *Women's Studies International Forum, 5(6),* 525–536.

Fulkerson, M. M., & Briggs, S. (2012). *The Oxford handbook of feminist theology.* New York: Oxford University Press.

Hiltebeitel, A., & Erndl, K. M. (2000). *Is the goddess a feminist? The politics of south Asian goddesses.* Washington Square, New York: New York University Press.

Kalyanaraman, S. (2008). *Vedic river Saraswati and Hindu civilization.* New Delhi: Aryan Book International.

Kinsley, D. (1988). *Hindu goddesses: Visions of the divine feminine in the Hindu religious tradition with a new preface.* Los Angeles, California: University of California Press.

Menon, U. (2002). Making sakti: Controlling (natural) impurity for female (cultural) power. *Ethos, 30*(1/2), 140–157.

Mukherjee, P. (1983). The image of women in Hinduism. *Women's Study International Forum, 6*(4), 375–381.

Narayanan, V. (1998). Brimming with bhakti, embodiments of shakti: Devotees, deities, performers, reformers, and other women of power in the Hindu tradition. In Sharma, A., & Young, K. (Eds.), *Feminism and world religions* (pp. 25–36). New York: State University of New York Press.

Reynolds, H. (1980). The auspicious married woman. In S. S. Wadley (Ed.), *The powers of Tamil women* (pp. 35–60). Syracuse, NY: Maxwell School of Citizenship and Public Affairs.

Ryland, S. (1977). The theory and impact of Gandhi's feminism. *Journal of South Asian Literature, 12*(3/4), 131–143.

Sengupta, J. (2006). *Refractions of desire: Feminist perspectives in the novels of Toni Morrison.* Delhi: Nice Printing Press.

Wangu, M. B. (2003). *Images of Indian goddesses: Myths, meanings, and models.* New Delhi: Shakti Malik Abhinav Publications.

Weber, E. (2009). Hindu feminism, part I: The emancipation of Mirabai. *Journal of Religious Culture, 129*(1), 1–7.

Werner, K. (1994). *A popular dictionary of Hinduism.* Richmond: Curzon Press.

Chapter 8

Feminism in Buddhism

Linda Chiang

To the Western world, Buddhism is still a mysterious religion. Like many religions in the world, Buddhism is rich and deep. Its practices of meditation, mindfulness, and nonviolence have been translated into many languages and transported to numerous parts of the world. From the origins of Buddhism in India to its introduction into East and South Asia, people seem to have learned and heard about great masters and monks. However, unlike the Western world, the concept of feminism was not introduced to Asian—or specifically Buddhist-dominant countries in Asia, such as India, Korea, Burma, Thailand, Tibet, Japan, and pre-Communist China—until recent decades. Traditionally, Buddhist philosophy is considered to be gender-neutral and apolitical. So, how does feminism affect Buddhism, or does Buddhism have an impact on feminism? How did the concept of feminism in Buddhism begin? What are the implications? How does the concept of feminism in Buddhism affect the ordinary life of its believers? How is feminism demonstrated in Buddhism? These are questions with no simple answers. There are many facets of Buddhism. This chapter will focus on the nurturing and caring nature of mothering and its practice in Zen Buddhism, which reflects some of the characteristics of feminism.

A BRIEF HISTORY OF BUDDHISM

To discuss feminism in Buddhism, it is necessary to understand the development and establishment of Buddhism, especially during and around the time of Gautama Buddha, the master of Buddhism, and how his teaching led to the development of Buddhism.

As in human history, religion serves as a way of understanding and interpreting natural phenomena, life and death, and the structure of the cosmos. Among all religions, the oldest surviving religion is Hinduism, and this is where Buddhism has its roots and out of which it evolved and became popular around the 13th century (Coogan, 2005). The essence of Buddhism was carried from India to China around 520 CE by Bodhidharma, a monk known to be the first Zen patriarch. It was the Zen concept which was nurtured and spread throughout China and Japan (Reps & Senzski, 1985, p. 122).

According to the Buddhist tradition, a man named Siddhartha Gautama, who lived between 563 and 483 BCE, is considered to be the Buddha. He was a prince in the northern Indian kingdom of Shakyas, where his father was a ruler of the Shakya clan, which means he was rich and powerful.

There are many legends about the birth of Buddha. A more current one from around the seventh century CE claims that his mother was a virgin and his birth a virgin birth. This legend is similar to that of Jesus Christ in the Christian tradition. Many scholars believe it is part of a Buddhist apologetic developed in reaction to Christianity (Hexham, 2011).

Another popular story surrounding Buddha's birth is about a dream Buddha's mother experienced. It is said when she laid on her bed, a white elephant appeared, circled around her several times, and then entered her womb through her side. Startled by the dream, she called upon many wise men to interpret the dream. White elephants are very rare in India, and within the Hindu tradition white elephants are considered sacred; the wise men agreed the dream indicated some great news. This meant the child would become either a great warrior who would establish a greater kingdom, or a religious leader who had wisdom that would impact the whole world.

To prevent Buddha from wandering away from the kingdom and devoting his life to religion, his father was determined to keep him occupied with entertainment and showered him with lavish gifts. Legends indicate that he was entertained by over 40,000 beautiful dancing girls, had numerous palaces, and was constantly accompanied by friends (Haxham, 2011).

Unlike the mystery, controversy, and confusion surrounding his birth, Siddhartha's childhood is more easily examined and observed. By this time in his life, Siddhartha was surrounded with great wealth and security. He lost his mother seven days after his birth, and was raised by his aunt. At the age of sixteen Siddhartha was married to the beautiful Yasohara, his cousin and the daughter of a local ruler. He was shielded from the unpleasantness of everyday life and anything that might make him want to leave home or associate with religious people.

By about age 30, four experiences dramatically changed Siddhartha's way of life. While he was out riding, he encountered a young child full of energy and joy; an old man in great pain; a very sick man, near death; and a funeral procession carrying a decaying corpse. Witnessing such life changes caused Siddhartha to wonder about the meaning of life. As a result, he absorbed himself in meditation. One night, he left his palace quietly and found Alara Kalama, the teacher, to learn "the realm of nothingness" (Kerouac, 2008) and become "the awakened one." He continued to learn and preach until his passing.

FEMALE STATUS IN BUDDHIST SACRED BOOKS

Buddha means "enlightened one" or "awakened one." In Buddhist teachings, both genders have the capacity to become a Buddha. Buddhist sacred texts are thought of as guides on the path to truth, not truth itself. Therefore, there are many sacred books. These sacred books were translated and written in classical language, which prevented most ordinary people from comprehending them, thus leaving their interpretation to the monks or nuns and self-understanding.

The *Prajnaparamita Sutra* is considered the original text of Mahayana Buddhism. Scholars agree that it began to emerge into prominence in India around 100 BCE, which was about 400 years after the final nirvana of Shakyamuni Buddha. The original *Prajnaparamita*, the *Great Mother: The Prajnaparamita of 100,000 Lines*, purports to record the full audience given by Shakyamuni on Vulture Peak. This sacred book was called the *Heart Sutra* or *Prajnaparamita Heart Sutra* (Schireson, 2009). The Buddhist scholar Robert Thurman described the importance of this sutra as:

> The original *Prajnaparamita* is the text called the *Great Mother: The Prajnaparamita of 100,000 Lines*. It purports to record the full audience given by Shakyamuni Buddha on Vulture Peak with the greatest explicitness and completeness . . . over the centuries various abridged versions have emerged, including the very short *One Letter Sutra*, the short *Heart Sutra*, the concise *Diamond-cutting Sutra*, the *8,000 Line*, the *18,000* or *20,000 Line*, and the *25,000 Line Sutra*, for a total of eighteen Sutras. These are all considered the same Sutra, differing only in length and detail, never in basic import. (2005, p. 254)

These perfect wisdom texts served as the foundation for a systematic curriculum developed over many countries in the Mahayana Buddhist monastic universities, among the earliest universities on this planet. This ancient curriculum opened the minds of millions of practitioners for 1,000 years in India. In East Asia, it seems clear that *Prajnaparamita* served as the basis of the Ch'an and Zen traditions—the famous Sixth Patriarch of Ch'an in China, Hui Neng, recalled his own perfect wisdom upon a single hearing of the Diamond-cutting version of the Ch'an (Schireson, 2009, pp. 254–255).

This sutra is considered the essence of perfect wisdom; the goddess Prajnaparamita is the source of highest enlightenment for all Buddhas, and she is in the female form. Her teaching is the transformation and manifestation of the essence of life. Both the Zen and Tibetan traditions originated from the teachings of this sutra by both claiming Nagarjuna. The *Great Mother Prajnaparamita Sutra* directs followers of her teaching of the Mahayana bodhisattva practitioner and is decidedly female in nurturing terms.

> The bodhisattva will always maintain a motherly mind, consecrated to the constant protection, education, and maturation of sentient beings, inviting and guiding them along the path of all-embracing love. This Mahayana mind never succumbs to fear, anxiety, or depression, and is never overwhelmed by the strange adventures of awareness in the three realms of relativity—mundane form, sublime form, and formlessness. (Schireson, 2009, p. 255)

In order to help others to strive toward becoming the embodiment of the bodhisattva, practitioners need to practice nurturing to fulfill their mission.

GENDER EQUITY IN BUDDHISM

One might wonder if the great master of Buddhism, Gautama Buddha, discriminated against women. The best way to examine this question is from some of the Buddhist scriptures (Sutras). Nichiren (1222–1282 AD, a Japanese priest in the Kamakura Era) observed, "When I, Nichiren, read the sutras other than the Lotus Sutra (The Most Excellent Teaching Just Like the White Lotus, in Chinese Miao-fa-lien-hua-ching), I have not the slightest wish to become a woman" (in Ueki, 2001, p. 3). He further stated in his writing, "The Kegon-kyo says, 'One who looks at a woman even a moment will lose the virtuous functions of his eyes. Even though you may look at a large snake, you must not look at a woman.'"

Another important scripture, Hua-yen-ching, reads "A woman is a Great Devil King. She would often eat all people. She is the cause of evil passions in the present life, and in the future life will become a loathsome enemy" (Ueki, 2001, p. 4).

Among the Asian countries, many believe that Confucius's teachings limited the freedom of females. Females were under the care of their parents in their childhood, protected by their husbands throughout adulthood, and in their old age under the control of their sons. Women normally did not have the opportunity to be educated as they were considered to be without talents and were expected to be submissive and obedient. Such teaching diminished the status of women in Asian countries and influenced the practice of Buddhism, though it did not come from the original teachings of the Buddha.

Reading the statements above, one may wonder if Buddhism, which focused on the salvation of all people, really taught that women were inferior and would never obtain the status of Buddha. Traditionally, the practice of Buddhism is considered to be a patriarchal belief system. Female monastics were confined to inferior roles, and only permitted to serve food and clean for the men.

However, in Samyutta-nikaya, the Buddha used "chariot" to explicate the "wheels of righteous effort" (wheels of Dharma) and other teachings; "the learning board" and "drapery" correspond to "conscience" and "heedfulness." The norm (Dharma, universal law) is the "driver" and "right views" are the chariot (Ueki, 2001, p. 11). When teaching about the law of vehicle, Gautama Buddha used the following passage to describe the equality of men and women:

> And be it women, be it for whom
> Such chariot doth wait, by that same car
> Into Nibbana's presence shall they come.
> (Rhys Davids, trans., 1917, p. 45)

One can tell Gautama Buddha did not discriminate between male and female in the perfection of supreme Wisdom.

Gautama Buddha further taught the nobility of an individual is determined by one's behavior and deeds. He denied the authoritarian idea that simply because one was born into a family lineage, one is entitled as a person to respect. In his teaching, he answered the question of lineage and deeds:

> Ask not of birth, as the course of conduct.
> From any sticks verify fire doth take birth.
> The steadfast seer, though his descent be lowly,
> To intellect's aristocrats is lifted.
> By noble shame all that is evil curbing,
> Tamed by the truth, graduate in the taming,

> Of saving lore master, the good life living.
> (Rhys Davids, trans., 1917, p. 210)

It is evident that The Great One stressed the importance of conduct over one's birth. In his teaching of The Four Noble Truths, he made four points: All life is suffering, the cause of suffering is ignorant craving; the elimination of suffering can be achieved; and the way is the noble eightfold path (Kerouac, 2008). He further explained the Noble Eightfold Path as:

1. Right ideas, based on the Four Noble Truths;
2. Right Resolution to follow this way out of suffering;
3. Right Speech, tender sorrowful discourse with the brothers and sisters of the world;
4. Right Behavior, gentle, helpful, chaste conduct everywhere;
5. Right Means of Livelihood. Harmless food gathering is your living;
6. Right Effort, rousing oneself with energy and zeal to this Holy Way;
7. Right Mindfulness, keeping in mind the dangers of the other way (of the world);
8. Right Meditation, practicing solitary meditation and prayer to attain holy ecstasy and spiritual graces for the sake of the enlightenment of all sentient beings. (Kerouac, 2008, p. 31)

In his teaching, suffering knows no gender and everyone can reach the truth by walking on the right path.

According to Ueki (2001), Gautama Buddha preached for 45 years with a total of about 1,250 people who became his disciples—all men. When Buddhism was first founded, there was no Religious Order of Nuns. However, Buddha's stepmother, Mahaprajapati, asked the Buddha if she could become a Buddhist nun and renounce home, with another 20 women joining her. He was moved by her eagerness, and thus granted her permission on condition of the Eight Chief Rules. Buddha did not deny the possibility of women attaining enlightenment. The conversation between Buddha and Ananda, the Buddha's cousin and close disciple, who arranged for Buddha's stepmother to renounce the world, shows his attitude toward a female becoming Arhan.

> Ananda: Can't women attain the enlightenment of Arhan?
> Gautama Buddha: Yes, they can. Women can also attain Arhan. (Ueki, 2001, p. 9)

Arhan was translated into Chinese as *A-lo-han* and *Arkan* in Japanese, which means "one who is worthy of respect," or "one who is suitable for receiving obligation." Thus, Buddha instructed his disciples that women have the capacity to be respected and accept obligations.

Buddhism has gone through changes over the years since Buddha's passing. At around the third century BCE, Buddhist monks became more conservative. After the establishment of the schism of Hinayana Buddhists (lesser vehicle), discrimination against women began to appear (Ueki, 2001). They declared that only men could attain Buddhahood; women could never reach Buddhahood (p. 47).

Observing popular culture, the general public still sees Buddhism as a male-dominated religion. Arhat from Korea (1392–1910) and disciples from Japan (1881–1961) are all male figures. It is obvious that gender is still an issue in Buddhism in the 20th century.

THE COMMON PRACTICE OF BUDDHISM AND FEMINISM: THE LOVING CARE NATURE OF MOTHERHOOD

Females portray many characteristics that reflect the teachings of the great master of Buddhism, Gautama Buddha. Some scholars compare Buddhist and Feminist philosophies and conclude that these two philosophies share the same idea of perceiving all sentient beings as like one's own mother (Powers & Curtin, 1994). The Buddhism practiced in Tibet views mothering as the center of spiritual practice. Philosopher Sarah Ruddick (1989) claimed to be a mother and to take the responsibility of child care and "making its work a regular and substantial parts of one's working life" (p. 128). To take on such moral responsibility, therefore, is to take on other human beings' sufferings. It is the compassion and ethics of care which makes mothering the essence of the survival of human beings.

Ruddick (1989) further explained that mothering is a struggle to achieve nonviolence (p. 57) so that the world can be a place in which children will be nurtured and protected. In this sense, both Buddhism and feminism are inherently compatible (Powers & Curtin, 1994).

The mothering practice calls for transformation of experience from within. Female Buddhists are portrayed as protecting women and children and giving blessings in India. In Zen founder Suzuki Roshi's teachings, Zen meditation is described as a return to the mother so we can connect to the matrix of existence (Schireson, 2009, p. 236).

ZEN WOMEN AND BUDDHIST PRACTICE

In most Asian countries, Buddha followers as well as monks and nuns practice Zen. Zen practice helps humans to transform consciousness and lessen suffering (Schireson, 2009). Zen originated in China, where it was founded by Bodhidharma, who came from India in the sixth century (Reps & Senzaki, 1985, p. 19). The word *Zen* (*Ch'an* in Chinese, *Dhyana* in Sanskrit) means "meditation." Through meditation one realizes what

Buddha realized: the emancipation of one's mind. It implies that there is no barrier to the gate. For Zen masters, each worldly problem is a barrier; yet, those who have the spirit of Zen pass through it (Reps & Senzaki, 1985, p. 123).

A Zen spirit means not only peace and understanding, but also devotion to art and to work, the rich unfolding of contentment, opening the door to insight, the expression of innate beauty, and the intangible charm of incompleteness (Reps & Senzaki, 1985, p. 20).

The Zen Buddhists and Buddhist forebears declared that there are no fundamental differences when discussing spiritual capacity or experience to all human beings, regardless of class or gender. According to Schireson (2009), one of the four documented disciples of Bodhidharma (the founder of Zen in China) was a woman, Zongchi, who is described by Japan's founding Soto patriarch, Eihei Dogen. It is clear that women were practicing Zen from the very beginning. These Zen women have suffered and used their experience and transformation to model and to teach. Many stories and legends were told from Zen tradition and excerpts from these stories were organized into themes of love and sacrifice.

Love

Women practicing Zen philosophy are depicted in many stories in regards to love. Some of them fulfilled their duties as a wife and in motherhood, then pursued Zen. Some of them sacrificed their comfort to follow their sons' Zen practice. Some of them turned to Zen after their lives fell apart from various traumas.

In the book *Zen Flesh, Zen Bones* (1985), a famous female Zen philosopher, Shunkai (also known as Suzu), was compelled to marry against her will. Once the marriage was ended, she attended a university to study philosophy. In the university everyone who saw her fell in love with her, and wherever she went, she fell in love with others. Philosophy did not satisfy her and so she then visited the temple in Koyoto to learn about Zen. Because of her beauty and earnestness, she was mistreated by the head priest's wife who envied her beauty and accused her and another young Zen brother in the temple of impropriety. As a result, the young brother was expelled, and Shunkai was removed from the temple. She set a fire and burned down the 500-year-old temple and was consequently arrested and prisoned. Even then, both the young lawyer and the prison jailer were enamored of her. She met a Shinshu priest after she was released and learned the name of Buddha of Love. In that, she found solace and peace of mind. She wrote her story to support herself, which later reached the Japanese people after she passed away, and those who had hated her read her story with tears of remorse. Her whole life was saturated with love.

Sacrifice

One story described the sacrifice between a son and a mother. Shoun was a teacher of Soto Zen. When his father passed away, he had to take care of his mother. Whenever he went to mediate, he took his mother with him. In order to take care of his mother, he built a little house for her and copied sutras to earn money to support her. He bought fish for his mother for sustenance but was ridiculed by the public assuming the fish was for him, since Zen Buddhists are vegetarians. His mother therefore decided to become both a nun and a vegetarian. Shoun sacrificed his life in monasteries to instead make money to support his mother. His mother, on the other hand, gave up earthly enjoyment to save her son from being ridiculed. In their conduct, they cared for others more than themselves. This is the teaching of Buddhist selflessness or denying self to tend to others' needs.

Another story was from a mother's teaching. Jiun was a Shingon Master. He was a famous Sanskrit scholar of the Tokugawa era. His knowledge was in high demand and he frequently was invited to deliver lectures to his brother students. His mother did not consider him a follower of Buddha because he had a desire for glory and honor. She urged him to shut himself off and stay in a little temple in a remote area and devote his time to meditation to attain true realization (Reps & Senzaki, 1985, p. 55).

The stories above present examples of Buddhist compassion and caring for others at the cost of one's own enjoyment, and show how the people in the stories followed the Buddhist teaching to become "awakened ones." Buddha also teaches that when one develops the mind of loving-kindness one can achieve *nirvana*—ultimate truth, and peace (Villanueva, 2005).

CAN WOMEN ATTAIN ENLIGHTENMENT?

For Buddhism the highest status of mind is to obtain enlightenment. What is enlightenment? Attaining enlightenment (Bodhi) means taking vows to save suffering beings and carry out the practice of the "Six Paramitas" or "perfection of Buddhist practices." These are donation, keeping precepts, forbearance, assiduity, meditation, and wisdom.

According to Jack Kerouac (2008) there are various stages of enlightenment; therefore, it is possible to obtain enlightenment and still be prone to human failings. He concluded that one can become a bodhisattva simply by resolving and vowing to become perfectly enlightened in a future life either near or far, and by developing the knowledge and ability to free all sentient beings from suffering. In this sense, all bodhisattvas are human (p. ix). This may explain why Buddhist nuns and monks call their followers bodhisattvas. Karen Villanueva (2005) concluded that "within Buddhist philosophy, everyone is innately capable of transformation and awakening" (p. 69).

FEMINISM IN BUDDHISM

Is feminism in Buddhism increasing? Western feminist writers have extended a call for equality. The early female scholars of Buddhism are Caroline Rhys Davids, Mabel Bode, and Isaline Blew Honer (Collett, 2005). Their writings in the late 19th and early 20th centuries have paved the way for the study of women in early Indian Buddhism.

In Asia, nuns quietly follow the doctrines and perform deeds without thinking about self. This author's conversation with a few nuns in Taipei as well as in southern Los Angeles found that they did not see gender bias in Buddhism. When I asked whether they thought about the radical behavior of the Western feminist movement, their answer was no; they further claim Buddhism is gender neutral and that their teachers preach that whatever monks can do, nuns can as well. In fact, women in Asia were influenced and transformed by the Western women's movement. However, very few nuns were in the front line to fight for women's rights. They joined the effort to teach and preach and intended to create a clean world. The liberal individualists sought to humanize the capitalist market economy rather than the radical ones. This movement operated within the boundaries set by the state's legal and political system (Chang, 2009). Western feminism has been seen as aggressive. Therefore, most people in Asia who practice the Buddhist religion reject the concept of feminism.

CONCLUSION

The teaching of the *Lotus Sutra* is the principle that earthly desires are inseparable from enlightenment. Therefore, the sufferings of birth and death are in the realm of Nirvana. The truth of human suffering should be seen as the attainment of Buddhahood. It should be noted that the teaching of Buddhism did not exclude one gender or the other. Hughes (2012) stated that Buddhism is a way of living with compassion and insight. In his judgment, Buddhism is liberating for women. I do not think it is intentional or radical; on the other hand, it is the nature of its philosophy and the original teaching of the Master that one needs to be caring and compassionate toward human suffering. Therefore, it is important to recognize the female characteristics of nurturing and intimacy as described and practiced in Buddhism. What one might want to see is whether, after their enlightenment, practitioners take a proactive role to shape the society in which they reside and try to further change the world. Those who have attained enlightenment can do that by teaching or taking human suffering into the public arena, and help others to critically examine their lives and contribute to the peace of the world. It does not mean that they have to use any extreme means to awaken people. Tender and quiet love persistently flows to the community and eventually makes a difference. An old Chinese saying is that drops of water can penetrate huge stones. Women's soft power in Buddhism is waiting to show the world that moments of mindfulness and enlightenment are more influential than guns or weapons.

Buddhist practice has found its way into the Western world. Various organizations, such as Buddha Dharma Education Association and BuddhaNet have helped to educate society to Buddha's teaching. The world has embraced the practice of meditation and many people hope to attain enlightenment through awakening. Buddhism was recognized by the United Nation's International Women's Day in 2002, when they recognized and honored seven outstanding women in World Buddhism (Buddha Dharma Education Association, n.d.).

In summary, feminism's selfless caring and compassion to human beings can be found in Buddhism. However, it is not appropriate to conclude that Buddhism is feminism, because Buddhism does not take a militant approach as some modern feminists do; such behavior does not reconcile with Buddhism. Nevertheless, female Buddhists use their painful life experiences to break through gender stereotypes and encourage mutual acceptance to promote well-being for all humankind. There is no short cut or easy solution for them and they continue to endure long-term entrapments. They will continue to exercise feminist loving-kindness to reach both believers and non-believers of Buddhism. In essence, there is a need to continue the dialogue between feminism and Buddhism. This collaboration and joined effort just might shape the future of the world.

REFERENCES

Buddha Dharma Education Association. (n.d.). Buddhist studies: Outstanding women in world Buddhism. Retrieved from http://www.buddhanet.net/e-learning/history/women_world.htm

Chang, D. (2009). *Women's movements in twentieth-century Taiwan.* Urbana & Chicago, IL: University of Illinois Press.

Collett, A. (Fall 2006). Buddhism and gender: Reframing and refocusing the debate. *Journal of Feminist Studies in Religion 22*(2), 55–84.

Coogan, M. (2005). *Eastern Religions.* NY: Duncan Baird Publishers.

Davids, C. A. F. R. (1917) (Trans.). *The book of kindred sayings (Samyutta-nikaya).* Part I. Oxford: Pali Text Society.

Hexham, I. (2011). *Understanding world religions.* Grand Rapids, MI: Zondervan.

Hughes, J. (2012, March). The Moral Brain: Day One. Ethical Technology, Mar 30, 2012. Buddhist Feminism (Part 2), *Spring Wind: Buddhist Cultural Forum,* Mar 6, 2012.

Kerouac, J. (2008). *Wake up: A life of the Buddha.* London: Penguin.

Powers, J., & Curtin, D. (1994). Mothering: Moral cultivation in Buddhist and feminist ethics. *Philosophy East and West, 44*(1), 1–18.

Reps, P., & Senzaki, N. (1985). *Zen flesh zen bones.* N. Clarendon, VT: Tuttle Publishing.
Ruddick, S. (1989). *Maternal thinking: Toward a politics of peace.* NY: Ballantine Books.
Schireson, G. (2009). *Zen women: Beyond tea ladies, iron maidens, and macho masters.* Boston, MA: Wisdom Publications.
Thurman, R. (2005). *The infinite life.* New York: Penguin Group USA.
Ueki, M. (2001). *Gender equality in Buddhism.* NY: Peter Lang.
Villanueva, K. (2005). Mother love in Buddhism. *Journal of the Motherhood Initiative for Research and Community Involvement, 7*, 68–77.

Chapter 9

Femineity in the Gospel of John

Kamila Blessing

INTRODUCTION: WHAT DID WE MISS?

In her book *Written So That You May Believe,* Sandra Schneiders (2003) asks a stunning question: "Could it be that accepting the femininity of God will revolutionize our God-experience as radically as Jesus's divinity did in the First Century?" The question accompanies her observation that Christians have, for centuries, read John 3 "without realizing that the Fourth Evangelist here supplies us, through the voice of Jesus, with one of the clearest New Testament images of the femininity of God" by employing the metaphor of the new birth (p. 123). In fact, John's gospel is laced together—and can be summed up—with the metaphor of the new birth offered to those who believe in Jesus (John 1:12–13).

However, Schneiders's question is somewhat misdirected. As Ellens (2006) and others have observed, "God is not male or female, but God combines all that is characteristic of our two genders and more than that." In fact, made in God's image, we all have within us elements of male and female, and of homosexuality and heterosexuality, in varying degrees (p. 20). According to Ellens, that is what it means to be in God's image. So we are not looking to erase the masculine imagery of the God of the Bible, but to balance it with a nuanced understanding of God's entire nature. I propose to call what we are seeking "femineity": the womanliness in and of John's gospel. Let us define "womanliness" as having female-imaged capacities such as giving birth, but as part of a totality that is more than both female and male, and more than the intersection of them. The term "femineity" is here applied specifically to our understanding of the womanliness of the Deity.

This stance accords with John's overall approach to the gospel, beginning as he does with the eternal Logos, existing from before time and stretching to eternity.

GOD AS SYSTEMS THINKER

God is the original systems thinker. Anachronistic as the description may seem, it is in fact the backdrop of the gospel message. And nowhere is it more developed than in the gospel of John. It begins in John 1:1–4, where "through him [the Logos] all things came to be, and nothing that came to be began without him" (author's translation[i]). The Logos created the system. The "systems" description continues with images such as the vine of chapter 15, and it ends with the forever-open tomb, the proclamation of eternal life. In fact, what develops through John's account of Jesus's ministry, death, and resurrection is a radical redevelopment of the system—a reordering of the human system to realign it with the world as God created it. Human, earthly society is a puzzle that seems to make up an "obvious" picture but, being thrown up into the air, comes down again reordered to make an entirely new picture of a renewed humanity.

Many concepts that have been taken for granted in traditional interpretation look different when the puzzle comes down: God, Jesus, the family, women, Jews and pagans, and even salvation. The story itself, its literary characteristics and its elements, looks different. Just for one example, the theme of the new birth begins not with John 3 but with the cosmic Christ of 1:1–3, emphasizing (literally and figuratively) *genesis*. Genesis could not be more clearly cited. And, particularly in first-century culture, this primal birth also firmly invokes the femineity of the story to come.

This insight has particular significance when we look at the role of women—and the role of the womanly—in the story as a whole. Let us take a look at the traditional interpretations that are challenged by our point of view, at the specifics of femineity in John, and at the new insights that result.

OVERVIEW: INTERPRETATIONS OF WOMANLINESS IN JOHN

Among the assumptions that are common in traditional literature are these:

- Patriarchy/hierarchy dominates (and is therefore the intended order of things).
- A woman is routinely seen as inferior socially and legally, and conversations in the gospel are interpreted accordingly.
- Women in the story are sexualized, obscuring the woman as a type of the giver of new birth.

Brief as this discussion is, it is by no means exhaustive, but I will simply cite examples.

To address the patriarchal aspect of the gospel, Osiek and Balch (1997) acknowledge the issue and also propose a corrective to this stance:

> The overwhelmingly male images of paternal-filial relationship have been seminal for Trinitarian theology from Tertullian through Nicea and into the present era. This has been true to such an extent that some theologians argue, in the face of the obvious need for more balanced gender imagery in contemporary spirituality and worship, that the titles of Father and Son are definitively revealed, and thus normative and inflexible, language for the Trinity. There is a noticeable increase in father-son language as one moves through the canonical Gospels beginning with Mark and ending with John. (p. 143)

John, however, presents Jesus somewhat anomalously:

> The Johannine Jesus, however much he may seem to exemplify *andreia*, is also the incarnate feminine wisdom figure, agent of God's creation . . . and even feeds them [the disciples] with her own flesh like a nursing mother. (p. 144)

Thurston (1998) extends this observation: the Father God language in John is "essentially relational and not patriarchal . . . [Jesus uses] language that is intended to express the intimacy of family life . . . the intimate relationship with God which becomes possible through Jesus" (p. 92), re-forming the image of family.

Jesus is, in fact, the author of a new kind of family: a hierarchy of sorts, with Jesus as the head, but (theologically at least) equality among God's children. The totality of the gospel serves this singular purpose. Becoming God's child is, further, not like being given life through natural birth. It is a matter of birth from above, spiritual nurture, and an eternal heritage (3:3–7). The theme of birth is thus of central importance as a metaphor for the purpose of the book. What results from the new birth is not only a new family, but a new kind of family, based not biologically, and not along the lines of any religious institution, but based upon faith in, and relationship with, Jesus. Specifically, it is based upon eyewitness testimony to the resurrection of Christ and to his resurrecting miracles.

For an extended discussion of the way in which this new family comes about, see Blessing (2010, chapter 9). In that discussion, we have demonstrated that the very nature of creation is systemic, that is, based upon the interrelationships of all of the created. A "systems" approach also shows us how mistaken it is to assume that any one part of creation is more God's image than another.

If the disciples of Jesus are equals in this way, it follows that the women disciples cannot be of lower value or personal worth. Also, their meaning in the text, seen primarily as sexual, misses the point: they are ultimately there to develop the reader's concept of who Jesus is, and what a true disciple is. Yet, the traditional literature has devalued them and their meaning for centuries. For example, it is assumed that the woman at the well is unacceptable because she is a woman (just on the face of it), a Samaritan, and many times married. The "evidence" is that she is drawing water at noon and she is dismissed as lacking understanding. When the Samaritans say that they no longer believe because of her words, they are dismissing her witness.

On the contrary, in our systems view, her status is irrelevant. Her gender is not; she is in the image of the birth-giver. She draws water at noon to contrast with Nicodemus who comes at night, thus making her seeking after life visible to all. She delivers children for God (if not biologically) with the most effective witness in the gospel apart from Mary Magdalene. She is also a figure for adulterous Israel coming to entire faithfulness to the one God (as perhaps is the woman taken in adultery of John 8). Jesus clearly takes her seriously—Samaritan or not, woman or not—in revealing himself, only to her, as Messiah. Thus, we must take the women characters in the story very seriously to see the points that John is making apart from our Western and male-oriented "glasses."

FEMINEITY IN JOHN: WOMEN, JESUS, HAGGADAH

In what follows, we will look more closely at the roles of women in John, look at the femineity of Jesus himself, and then assess the effect of these deliberations upon the character of the story as John presents it.

Overview

It is generally acknowledged that each woman appears at a point where the author is bringing Jesus's ministry to a new level. Jesus's "I am" in the conversation with the Samaritan woman (John 4:26) is a prime example. Of course, Mary Magdalene is commissioned to proclaim the risen Christ. In Paul's letters (written several decades before John), the two criteria of apostleship are to have seen the risen Jesus and to have been sent to proclaim him. John 20:17–18 presents Mary Magdalene as the one person in John who most closely fits these criteria.

Apart from these special roles, however, it is probable that modern readers undervalue the traditional roles of women seen in John and in ancient Jewish society generally. Although women's sphere of action was usually the family, it must be remembered that their role as the bearers of children was regarded as the *means to immortality*. The woman in the home also had a spiritual significance that is foreign to moderns. For example, as recorded in the Mishnah (an early, authoritative form of Jewish law expanding upon the Pentateuch), Rabbi Phineas ben Hannah held that the woman in the home has an *atoning force not inferior to the altar of sacrifice*. Thus, what the Johannine community bestows upon women is not higher exchanged for lower, but one honor acknowledged along with another.

More than that, however, atonement and immortality are the two gifts promised *in nuce* in John 1:12–13, and the specific attributes of the risen Christ. While he atones for humanity beyond the limited (in time and space) effect of altar sacrifice, it is never stated that he supersedes the role of women. Put another way, the women in John represent the ideal of humanity reflecting the person of Jesus himself. These ideal disciples (of either gender) exercise atoning force by bringing believers to the Atoner himself. It is imperative that we pay close attention this theme throughout the gospel.

This development is most easily seen in the apparently matched conversations between Jesus with men and Jesus with women.

The Samaritan Woman Contrasted with Nicodemus

The first two conversations occur in John 3:1–21 (Nicodemus) and John 4:1–42 (the Samaritan woman). Nicodemus is a man, a Jew, and a leader of the Jews, a highly acceptable person who must bear a great deal of theological knowledge. Yet among the conversants, Nicodemus is the only one who never expresses belief in Jesus *as a result* of the conversation. The scene begins with Nicodemus coming to see Jesus "at night." Nicodemus announces the seeker's faith: Jesus's miraculous signs must mean that he is "from God." Jesus's reply introduces the major theme of the conversation, that of being "born from above," or "born again." Jesus states further that to see the kingdom of God, a person must be born "by water and the Spirit." Nicodemus misunderstands each of these statements, seeing only the material, reductionistic sense of Jesus's words.

Jesus goes on to explain that only with the spiritual view of himself will the world understand and follow him. Nicodemus never responds. He appears only twice more in John, in John 7:45–52 and in John 20:39–40, never proclaiming his faith openly. In the latter passage, Nicodemus and Joseph of Arimathea (who also has hidden his faith "because he feared the

Jews," John 19:38) claim and bury Jesus's body. This is an act of personal devotion and sacrifice, and yet not one of proclamation. Thus Nicodemus's faith in Jesus does not bring others to Jesus physically or religiously.

The Samaritan woman (John 4:1–30 along with John 4:39–42), unlike Nicodemus, is unnamed, female, and an unacceptable Samaritan. Her conversation also revolves around a misunderstanding about water and the spirit. Like Nicodemus, she hears and responds to Jesus on the most material level ("You have nothing to draw with," John 4:11). However, she comes at noon rather than at night, signaling that what she does in relation to Jesus is open to the world. Upon hearing that Jesus is offering eternal life (John 4:14), she responds by asking for some of it. Far from asking merely to avoid the work of drawing and carrying, evidently she is thirsty for the spiritual life. One indication is that she does not hesitate to say, "I can see that you are a prophet."

The subject then changes to a central point of contention between Jews and Samaritans, the place of true worship. Jesus tells her that God will be worshiped neither in Jerusalem nor at the Samaritans' mountain, Gerizim. Rather, "A time is coming and now is when true worshipers will worship the Father in spirit and truth" (John 4:23). Jesus is declaring that, from the time of Jesus on, no physical temple will be able to hold the Spirit. The body of Jesus is the true locus of the Spirit of God and the appropriate object of worship.

The Samaritan woman responds with heartfelt longing: "When [Messiah] comes, he will explain everything" (John 4:25). Jesus then declares (John 4:26): "I who am speaking to you am he." Literally, in Greek, this is . . . "I am; [that is,] the one speaking to you," or more to the point: "I am; the one speaking to you [is the 'I am']," using the name of God given to Moses in Exodus 3:14. Thus the first and only pronouncement of Jesus's messiahship is made to a woman, simply because she is "thirsty" for that knowledge—open to it, and eager to drink it in.

In contrast with Nicodemus, the Samaritan woman goes into the city and brings her fellow Samaritans to faith in Jesus. Thus, according to Gench (2004), the Samaritan woman "proleptically fulfills Jesus's final prayer for his disciples and those who 'will believe in me through their word' (John 17:20), for the story concludes by noting that 'Many Samaritans from that city believed in him' (translating literally) 'because of the word of the woman bearing witness' (John 4:39)" (p. 128).

The story closes with the Samaritans' declaration that they now believe because of Jesus himself, rather than the woman's testimony alone. It is they (alone in this gospel) who call him "the Savior of the world." The expanding awareness of Jesus's true identity—within one person, then within the community—is replicated for and in the reader by means of a literary device. This "device," however, is also the author's witness to the reader; it is the escalation of Christological titles, throughout John 4:1–42.

Jesus is first a Jew (John 4:9), then Lord (John 4:11), greater than our father Jacob (John 4:12), prophet (John 4:19), Messiah (John 4:25), Christ (John 4:25, 29), the "I am" (John 4:26), and finally, Savior of the world (John 4:42). So, in the very structure of the narrative, the Samaritan woman has been used by the Lord also to bring the reader along in faith.

Thus, this woman is fruitful for Christ, whereas Nicodemus is not. She contrasts with other disciples also because she enters into a theological discussion with Jesus. Characteristically in John, the male disciples are passively present, for example, in John 2:1–12; they fail in persistence—for example, in John 20:10, they leave the tomb upon finding it empty; and they fail to speak their mind to Jesus, John 4:27, 33; John 6:60–61; John 16:12–20. This woman is the sower whose planting the other disciples are to reap (John 4:35–38)! In a powerful way, she carries out the functions of a true disciple.

One other dimension of this story must be addressed: it incorporates Jewish imagery of sexuality and marriage. Each of the conversations with women contains such imagery. For example, though the author calls Mary "mother of Jesus," implicitly she is also the bride of God; she bore his son. In the Old Testament, well imagery often refers to God's relationship with Israel (e.g., Proverbs 5:15–18; Song 4:12; Jeremiah 2:1–15). Jesus's "spring of living water" recalls, e.g., Jeremiah 2:13, wherein God is "the spring of living water." In these terms, the Samaritan woman is a symbolic wife to Jesus who brings him many offspring. Her disciple-love for him is the love of the bride of Christ. She is an active part of the rebirth by faith of God's new people and a paradigm for the true disciple (man or woman).

In view of the spiritual nature and high calling implied by the purpose—bearing children to God—it is the more inappropriate to assume a merely sexual role or any negative attributes for the Samaritan woman. If, as some have suggested, she represents the ancient Israel who had many *ba'alim* (husbands, but more to the point, lords, or *gods*), she has come at last to the one God at the one "temple"—the person of Jesus—that is eternally efficacious. In her response to Jesus, the woman also effectively answers Nicodemus's question: can a man enter again into his mother's womb (John 3:4)? The answer is Yes, because the mother is God, the rebirth is offered to all who believe in the name of Jesus, and the true disciple is the one who models (her)self on that God by bearing Jesus out to others and thus bearing them over again to God.

Thus the Samaritan woman is foremost a type of the *womb-for-God*. She also reflects Jesus's own role, as we will see in a later section.

Martha and Mary Magdalene; Thomas and Peter

Jesus's conversations with Martha (John 11:21–27; 11:38–40), Mary Magdalene (20:10–18), Thomas (20:24–29), and Peter (21:15–19) bear a complex relationship with one another. We begin with Martha. After her long wait for Jesus, Martha accuses him: (11:21), "Lord . . . if you had been here, my brother would not have died." However, immediately upon being told by Jesus that her brother will rise again, she acknowledges the resurrection on the last day. Jesus replies (11:25–26): "I am the resurrection and the life . . . Do you believe this?" Without hesitation, and without requesting a miracle, Martha confesses (11:27): "I believe that you are the Christ, the Son of God, who was to come into the world." Thus, she expresses faith in the person of Jesus, apart from any promise or miracle. At the conclusion of the story, Jesus calls Lazarus to life using the classic birthing formula of the ancient midwife: "Lazarus, come forth!" (vs. 43). For more on this topic, see Blessing (2002).

Mary Magdalene also is centered wholeheartedly upon the person of Jesus, seeking his body. She will not desist, despite the other disciples having left in confusion after seeing the empty tomb (20:10). Her tearful persistence is a lovely embodiment of Jeremiah's prophecy (Jeremiah 29:13–14, RSV), "When you seek me with all your heart," says the Lord, "I will be found by you." Having been called by name by the man she thought was the gardener, she recognizes him as the risen Jesus. When he commands her (20:17), she obeys immediately, going to tell all of the disciples: "I have seen the Lord!" (vs. 18). She thus becomes the first to be sent by Jesus to witness to the resurrection and the first actually to witness to the other disciples. For this reason, she is often called "the apostle of the apostles." Mary Magdalene thus "rebirths" Jesus's own disciples by bringing them into their first knowledge of the risen Christ, soon to be reiterated by the Lord himself.

John intentionally contrasts Thomas with the two women. Having missed the appearance of the risen Christ to the other disciples, Thomas declares: "Unless I see the nail marks in his hands and put my finger where the nails were, and put my hand into his side, I will not believe it." *Unless I see, I will not believe.* Perhaps he is afraid to believe that he will see Jesus again. Perhaps he thinks he has been "fooled" once before, into believing in Jesus's miraculous power. For whatever reason, he rejects the disciples' word of testimony and puts a condition on his faith, unlike Martha.

Nevertheless, Jesus accommodates Thomas, even using Thomas's own words in granting his desire (20:27). Thus, Jesus actually *heals* Thomas's petulantly expressed fear of disappointment and *confirms* his demand for a personal visitation. This is paradoxical, but with it, John predisposes the reader to take John's word for it. It is in this way that the reader's faith is to be based upon the signs—the ones that (20:31) "are written that you may believe that Jesus is the Christ, and . . . that by believing you may have life in his name."

John hopes that, on the basis of this text, the reader will rise and say along with Thomas the forever resounding words, "My Lord and my

God!" (20:28). However, like Martha and Mary Magdalene, the reader is to take the *Word* as the needful sign—at least for the time being, until she sees for herself. This is, perhaps, a sign of the times of John's community of faith, but not by any means a denial of the gift of signs directly observed.

If we add the conversation with Peter, additional dimensions of the message emerge. As Thomas is confronted against his unbelief, Peter is confronted (21:15–19) with having denied Jesus three times. He must be commanded to feed God's sheep—three times—whereas the women have simply fed the "sheep" through their proclamation. Thus, Thomas and Peter contrast with the simple, acted-out devotion of Martha and Mary Magdalene, offered and carried out unconditionally.

Thus, the women represent the bride of Christ, "the new Jerusalem . . . prepared as a bride beautifully dressed for her husband" (Rev. 21:2). *The women represent all true discipleship—that of men and of women—in the metaphor of the ancient prophets: God's people as God's true love.* Hence the carefully placed references to certain disciples solely as "woman" (4:1–42; 2:4; 19:26) evokes the image of *all* who are devoted to Christ. Nevertheless, a great honor has been bestowed upon actual women in John's use of the woman-as-disciple.

It may be objected that this symbolic schema still leaves God in the image of the male. One of the most powerful messages in John derives directly from this fact, however. For John to use feminine imagery to define any of the functions of Jesus (who is one with the Father) is extraordinary. He does so in few but crucially placed instances. Besides the one mentioned earlier, where he is midwife to Lazarus, the most powerful of these are the birth and death imagery relating to Jesus himself. We now turn to this imagery and to the meaningful presence therein of Jesus's mother.

Jesus's Mother and Jesus *as* Mother

Jesus's two encounters with his mother (who is never named in John) contain John's most striking uses of the term "woman." Unique in ancient Greek-language literature, Jesus's addressing his mother as "Woman" can be understood only against the backdrop of the overall meaning of the woman cited above—as a metaphor for true discipleship. However, these encounters exactly bracket Jesus's public ministry before his death on the cross. They thus tell us something about the nature of Jesus himself and the shape of his ministry.

The first encounter, in 2:3–4, is part of the first sign, the provision of wine at the wedding in Cana. The passage says that when the wine provided by the host was gone, "Jesus's mother said to him, 'They have no more wine.'" This statement of need without a direct request is a typical courteous form in which a Jewish woman of the time might ask a man for something. (Compare John 11:3, where Martha and Mary of Bethany "sent word to Jesus, 'Lord, the one you love is sick.'" Obviously, they wanted Jesus to come and heal Lazarus, but this is the only way in which it is expressed.) From this point in the Cana story, however, almost all translations confuse Jesus's answer in one way or another, attempting a nearly impossible idiomatic translation. Literally, in Greek, what Jesus says is: "What [is that] to me and to you, Woman? My hour has not come."

This question, along with the key terms "woman" and "hour," provide a clue to the entire meaning of the passage. Each term has at least two meanings, and here, John uses them with literary precision. Let us take the direct address "Woman" first. John is marked by direct address to the reader, and such direct address might occur anywhere in a narrative. Given that "woman" is a term which, by the end of the gospel, means the true believer (of either gender), it is fully possible that the author here both records Jesus speaking to his mother, and, as the author, addresses all believers. If so, John is literally asking the believer a pointed and highly charged question: "What *is* this to you and to me?" Thereby he says: Notice this! "This" is both the lack of wine, and the miracle that is about to happen. The real question is, "What is the significance of these things in Jesus's life and in your own?" If you cannot answer, you have not understood; you are not an insider. The correct answer is: "In this sign, I, Jesus, show you my identity." (Hence, John 2:11: through this miracle, Jesus "revealed his glory, and his disciples put their faith in him.")

The phrase "my hour" is used in only two ways in John. It refers to Jesus's ultimate purpose, his death and new birth for the sake of the world. It also refers to the woman's "hour," the hour of giving birth. The latter, however, is a metaphor for Jesus's leaving (his death) and its effect on the disciples (16:21). Thus, the seemingly incongruous mention of his hour during the wedding at Cana is an example of familiar "in group" language among the Johannine community. It tells us that Jesus's death and resurrection are the real subject of the Cana story.

As the story goes on, Jesus's mother says, "Do whatever he tells you"—another word to characters in the story (the servants), but also to the reader. Upon Jesus's command, the servants fill stone jars with water and present some of it to the master of the banquet. The master calls the bridegroom and says (2:10): unlike everyone else, "you have saved the best [wine] till now," that is, till the end. This is both the end of the banquet in John 2, and the end of the gospel story, the crucifixion and resurrection. The water and wine (usually assumed to be red wine) here are seen to serve a double purpose. The water and wine of John 2 are symbols of the genuine, earthly water and blood that are shed during earthly birth. They also foreshadow the blood and water that will flow from Jesus's earthly body on the cross. The presence of Jesus's mother, addressed as "Woman," reinforces the reader's association of the wedding at Cana with Jesus's natural birth—even while he is performing the first sign of his death. This complex of symbols thus affirms the incarnation—the Son of God taking on a mortal body. Also, in Jesus's first miracle at Cana, the entire story of God's purpose, worked out through Jesus's birth, death, and resurrection, is presented *in nuce*.

In the sole other appearance of Jesus's mother, John 19:25–27, we read that only she, three other women including Mary Magdalene, and the Beloved Disciple stayed with Jesus at the cross. In the last act of his earthly ministry, Jesus presents his mother and the Beloved Disciple with each other *as a new family*. It is significant that literally in Greek, Jesus "says to *the* [not his] mother, 'Woman, behold your son'. . . [and] to the disciple, 'Behold your mother.'" "Behold" (*i'de*) is a revelatory formula, not simply "here is" as in many translations. These commands to Mary and the Beloved Disciple double as prophetic pronouncements for the reader. To Jesus's mother and to the believer, Jesus is *also* saying, "Behold your God's-Son—behold me on the cross." He reinforces this by a command to the disciple (including the reader) to behold his new mother—*also* Jesus on the cross, about to shed his blood for the new birth of the world. So the inclusio, bracketing Jesus's entire earthly ministry, highlights his mission as the new birth-giver, and giver of the new birth.

Jesus, Mother of Believers

Now, finally, Jesus gives up his spirit (20:30). Then (vs. 34) a soldier pierces his side with a spear, "bringing a sudden flow of blood and water"—unmistakable birth imagery. Jesus himself understood his death, its manner, and its effect on the believer in this way (recall 16:21–22). Like a woman in labor, he literally pours out his blood for the life of the world. This is why, just after the water and blood, the author stops the story to reinforce its importance (vs. 35): "The man who saw it has given testimony, and his testimony is true. He knows that he tells the truth, and he testifies so that you also may believe." The theological point of Jesus as birth-giver could not be made more strongly than in the repetition of wine/blood-water imagery here and at Cana, each time with his mother as witness.

There is one more element in the death of Jesus. This is, symbolically, the last birth in which the "mother" will experience anguish and pain. John may be alluding in this imagery to Isaiah 66:7–11, one of the most graphic prophecies of the new creation in the Old Testament. Isaiah 66 is one of two passages (along with Psalm 22) in which God is described as midwife. It is also a promise that when the new creation is complete—in the resurrection—it will be as it was before the fall of humankind. Isaiah 66:7 says: "Before she goes into labor, she gives birth." The curse of painful birth will be reversed; God's people are freed from the effects of the fall. Thus in the manner of Jesus's death, he takes on and incipiently takes away the pain, the curse of disobedience to God, and not only for women, but for the whole world.

Here we have Jesus as the author of atonement, the healer of the pain and suffering of the world. And here it is most evident that Jesus echoes the role attributed to women—or more to the point, authors that role—being a force for atonement. With Jesus, however, it is once for all effective as *the* sacrifice in and of the temple, Jesus himself.

Since God is the author and presider over this death-and-birth (e.g., 19:11), further Old Testament allusion may be present here. Psalm 22:9 says, "You [God] brought me out of the womb; you made me trust in you even at my mother's breast." It is notable in this context that in both Matthew 27:46 and Mark 15:41, Jesus on the cross quotes another part of Psalm 22 (vs. 1), "My God, my God, why have you forsaken me?" Matthew and Mark thus make Jesus the speaker of this psalm—the one who is brought forth from the womb by God. There are further and complex quotes and allusions to this psalm in these three gospels' account of the Passion. For example, in John, Jesus's flow of blood and water alludes to vs. 14, "I am poured out like water . . ." Thus John—perhaps having read these other gospels—is naming God as the midwife both of the new creation birthed by Jesus on the cross, and of Jesus himself, reborn from the tomb.

The image of God as midwife to the one who is simultaneously dying, giving birth, and about to be reborn is striking, particularly to the reader who knows the Old Testament. God as midwife and birth-giver is far from incidental. Thus John punctuates the male images of both Jesus and the Father with profound images of the feminine—the more powerful because of their placement at the beginning and end of Jesus's earthly ministry. *And Jesus himself is no less than Mother—Mother as the author of immortality and as the bringer of atonement for any who wish to be reborn with him. That is the power of John's message of the disciple as woman and the power of the disciple as the perpetuator of the blood line of the descendants of the cross.*

Thus the femineity of the Gospel of John is thoroughgoing and crucial to our understanding of its message.

The Haggadah

One further observation may be made: the story, the telling of it, also embodies a distinct femineity. The *inclusio* of the blood-and-water stories is itself an aspect of femineity. These pericopae are the (literary) womb of the story, the womb of the development of the ministry of Jesus, and the womb of the new believer who, witnessing these signs through John, is formed along the way.

CONCLUSION

No greater affirmation of femineity can be given than for Jesus to take on a role that, in the first century, is strictly the province of women—and to do so as a part of his essential nature, being one with the Creator. This image of God would have been clear to the first-century reader. Thus, John is not exclusively male-dominated as it may seem on first glance. Women's roles in the Fourth Gospel as well as the feminine imagery used to describe Jesus show that the feminine response to God—and women's contributions to the community of the faithful—are to be greatly honored. The believer is to be born of God; next to that, human birth (and human gender as well) are secondary as a source of worth. Thus, the spiritual potential of *all* humankind is affirmed, and this is the greatest reason to affirm the spiritual callings of all believers.

However, God created the whole system, defined by its interrelationships, and specifically as each person's relationship directly to God. That God cannot have created a fractured image of himself in his word. We would do well to look for his femineity all along the way, through history, and throughout the Word-Jesus—especially in the Gospel of John.

REFERENCES

Blessing, K. (2002). Midwifery and birthing practices. In C. C. Kroeger & M. J. Evans (Eds.), *The IVP women's Bible commentary* (pp. 286–287). Downer's Grove, IL: InterVarsity Press.

Blessing, K. (2010). *Families of the Bible.* Santa Barbara, CA: Praeger.

Ellens, J. H. (2006). *Sex in the Bible: A new consideration.* Westport, CT: Praeger.

Gench, F. T. (2004). *Back to the well: Women's encounters with Jesus in the Gospels.* Louisville, KY: John Knox Press.

Osiek, C., & Balch, D. L. (1997). *Families in the New Testament world: Households and house churches.* Louisville, KY: Westminster John Knox Press.

Schneiders, S. M. (2003). *Written that you may believe: Encountering Jesus in the fourth Gospel.* NY: Crossroad Pub. Co.

Thurston, B. (1998). *Women in the New Testament: Questions and commentary.* Eugene, OR: Wipf & Stock Publishers.

Chapter 10

Feminism in the Eastern Orthodox Church

Maria Stoyadinova

In the winter of 2010, my now husband and I had a church wedding in Bulgaria. The location we picked was the Bachkovsky Monastery—one of the most famous and picturesque monasteries in Bulgaria located right outside of my husband's hometown. As we pulled up gleefully to the location with our wedding party, everyone was commenting on the awe-inspiring architecture and location, while we reveled in our decision to hold our church wedding at such a historic and respected Bulgarian institution. Our confidence in this decision would be quickly eroded upon meeting the pastor officiating at the ceremony.

Instead of the dignified and spiritual figure that I had been envisioning, said pastor arrived from his chambers after a non-trivial delay and looked visibly tipsy and even more visibly irritated to see us. I started worrying that we had interrupted something important, but since nothing of the sort was mentioned, I brushed the abrupt welcome off so as not to ruin an otherwise wonderful day. Soon the pastor, while still preparing for the ceremony, started actively engaging with some of our female guests. "How are you doing, sweetheart?" he asked one of my close friends in a tone that was flirtatious and patronizing all at once. This naturally struck me as both inappropriate and oddly misplaced coming from a respected church representative. My friend luckily did not speak Bulgarian, although she was still fittingly thrown off by both the creepy tone of the question and, even more so, by the unsolicited touch on the cheek that she received from our officiator which did not require a translation. The pastor soon moved on to another one of my female guests and proceeded with a very similar and equally ill-suited interaction. She also thankfully did not speak Bulgarian and my husband-to-be and I tried to relay what was happening to both guests who looked rightfully perplexed, though neither one of us managed to come up with any meaningful explanation. What were we supposed to say? Don't worry, our pastor just seems to be hitting on you? This is pretty standard pre-wedding procedure in Bulgarian churches? We were (and still are) at a loss of words.

Despite all of that, I still held hope that we would be able to avoid additional incidents and get through the upcoming ceremony. I had been looking forward to this ceremony for months but was now starting to contemplate running away from it even before it had started, not in the least because of my wonderful man I was about to marry. I did not run, mostly for fear of getting lost in the surrounding woods in late December and possibly having my body discovered by a search party around New Year's Eve, mauled by wolves, with a face still wearing a wedding veil and look of bewildered desperation (which would only marginally have been affected by the wild animals attacking me).

Things did not get better when the actual ceremony started. Some parts of it I was mentally prepared for—the segments of the sermon instructing me to serve and obey my husband were expected and sadly quite a standard part of any religious wedding, by no means limited to Orthodox Christianity. The part where the priest stopped the ceremony to loudly admonish me for inaccurately holding the prop wine glass and to cheerfully comment that I obviously did not know what I was doing, as I needed to rush things like a "typical woman"—knowingly winking at the male guests and visibly proud of his witty remark—I was certainly not anticipating. Seeing my friends harassed and being myself subjected to boorish and sexist comments at my own wedding was surely not how I had imagined my special day. Several similar remarks later I was seriously regretting our entire decision for an Orthodox Church wedding. I had planned on immersing myself in the rich cultural and religious heritage of our country that day. What I got was indeed a throwback to a different era—though in a very different and unpleasant sense.

I wish I could say that what happened that day was an isolated incident driven by one particularly inappropriate Church figure, even if a revered and popular one, but that would be naive. Blatantly reductive attitudes toward women remain quite standard in Bulgaria to this day and, perhaps, I should not have been that surprised that a Church existing in the midst of such attitudes and additionally encumbered by the traditional conservatism of Orthodox thought would provide for an unpleasant atmosphere for women. And yet, I was. I knew better than to expect progressive attitudes toward gender equality from our pastor. And, as amazing as it would have been to have a stimulating exchange of ideas on gender politics, that was in any case not the goal of our trip to the monastery that day. However, I did not expect the level of dismissiveness and disrespect I and the other women at the ceremony encountered, from a revered Church representative nonetheless—and one who seemingly was utterly unaware of his offensive behavior.

This experience made me wonder about the broader position and role of the Eastern Orthodox Church in gender politics and the Church's attitudes toward gender equality nowadays. I do not pose this as a theological question and do not intend to analyze scripture or the evolution of Orthodox Christian theology over the centuries. My main goal in this chapter is to look at the position of modern-day members and supporters of the Orthodox Church toward the roles and rights of women in society. I additionally explore how these attitudes translate into the actual participation of the Church in the lives of women in the largest Orthodox Christian country in the world—Russia.

A trend emerging across several of the Orthodox works on the topic of women's rights seems to be a fundamental misunderstanding of the actual concept of feminism and its core components. Of course feminism as a social movement and philosophy is continuously evolving and feminists are a widely diverse group of people who have different opinions on numerous topics and diverging views on how to perceive, analyze, and solve a variety of social issues. That diversity within the movement is what makes it a vibrant and powerful social force and what allows feminist concepts to keep pace with the wider context of social and political developments across the world. The Orthodox views of feminism that I came across, however, seem to ignore every aspect of this feminist diversity by portraying feminism in highly simplistic and inaccurate terms and attempting to reduce it to a single concept. Moreover, these interpretations of feminist ideas illustrate a complete lack of desire or effort to understand even the very basic building blocks of feminist philosophy and the core principles guiding the movement. Instead, the Orthodox opinions I came across present several widely inaccurate ideas of what their authors believe and, more importantly, fear feminism represents, portray these as descriptive of everyone who defines themselves as a feminist, and then make the leap to conclude how dangerous and irrational the entire movement is based on that myopic and erroneous depiction of it.

Delving into each intricacy of the feminist movement is too monumental a task to be addressed in this chapter or, in fact, any single literary work. However, it is fair to say that one of the core building blocks of feminism is the basic belief that women and men deserve equal rights and treatment in society, politics, the workplace, and every other sphere of life. A number of Eastern Orthodox writings addressing women's rights seem to have a different view. One curious overarching theme that emerges from several of these pieces is the belief that feminism attempts to negate the existence of any biological differences between the two sexes. None of the authors explain the source for that belief, which is both inaccurate and painfully simplistic. Feminism does resist and deconstruct the ingrained pillar of patriarchal ideology which dictates that many of the widely nuanced physical differences both between and within sexes should predetermine the "appropriate" social role and general conduct a person needs to adopt. Additionally, feminism points to the countless ways in which many of these differences that have been described as "ingrained," "biological," and "pre-destined" are in fact cultural constructs and have been used for centuries as means of classifying women (or men exhibiting what were labeled as "feminine characteristics") as the inferior, more inadequate, and irrational sex. Simply postulating that feminism negates physical differences between the sexes and that this proves the entire feminist philosophy is irrational and not worthy of attention is highly skewed and reductive and an ironic illustration of the same cultural constructs that feminists have been pointing to for decades.

Yet, this is the precise route that Archimandrite Chrysostomos takes in his essay "Women in the Orthodox Church"—a work from 1981 that is yet, to this day, a main publication about women in the Church on the Orthodox Christian Information Center website. The author makes promising strides in his critique of the feminist arguments by placing the word feminist in quotation marks and equating it with being irrational in the same sentence: "as regards the so-called 'feminist' position (of which we hear so much today), there are certain issues on which the Orthodox Christian (if not, perhaps, the rational individual) cannot yield" (Chrysostomos, 1981). The quotation marks would have actually been appropriate as a means to fittingly distance the author's definition of feminism from any slightly more involved and accurate description. Of course, the context of the piece makes it clear that the quotation marks in this leading sentence were not designed to prepare readers for the distorted portrayal of feminism that follows, as the author seems oblivious to his own bias and confusion. Rather, they are being used as vehicles to express the author's condescending derision of the whole concept of feminism, or at least what he believes feminism to mean, which he sees as deserving so little attention that it cannot even be mentioned without being delegated to the inferior status of fake concepts cited in quotation marks.

Chrysostomos paints a picture, according to which a large goal of feminism is to refute women's physiological ability to bear children: "We border on the insane (not an unusual thing in these bizarre times) if we deny the biological roles of men and women in procreation" (Chrysostomos, 1981). The author further expresses concern that an increasing number of women are trying to negate their femininity and "unique identity" in their quest for equality (Chrysostomos, 1981). Chrysostomos's conclusion is that women and men are naturally and obviously different physically *and* psychologically and that God has different visions and roles for them, but insisting that none of this means that women have a "lowly" status in society or the Church (Chrysostomos, 1981). Thus, the article reinforces some of the very basic concepts that have been utilized for centuries to maintain the status quo and keep women at an appropriate distance from power, authority, and decision-making about both their own lives and social developments in general, while at the same time purporting to have an utmost respect toward them—or at least toward those women who conform to a set of prescribed social roles. All other women are classified as irrational, extremist, and not worthy of attention.

Additional support for the skewed depiction of the women's rights movement comes from a recent discussion called "The Church and Feminism" that took place in Bulgaria's capital and was organized by the Orthodox site Pravoslavie.bg. The panelists included Sister Serafima—a Bulgarian Orthodox nun—and Dr. Toneva and Dr. Stoyadinov—religious studies professors at Bulgarian universities. The three of them shared somewhat different, though largely converging, views and apprehensions about what they perceived as the essence of feminism and its critique of the Orthodox Church.

Dr. Stoyadinov offered his view of the origins of feminism by comparing the women's movement to racism, sexism, nationalism, and nazism and explaining that all of these phenomena emerged as extreme reactions to various social events in Western societies, none of which have any relevance to Bulgarian culture (Sister Serafima, Toneva, & Stoyadinov, 2015). Casually placing feminism in the same bucket as the toxic and hateful philosophies that made up the rest of Dr. Stoyadinov's list demonstrates a deeply ingrained fear that feminism is hugely harmful and dangerous while at the same time illustrating a profound resistance to understanding any part of its history or core components.

Dr. Stoyadinov's co-panelist, Sister Serafima, focused on responding to one of the main feminist critiques of the Orthodox Church, namely, the opposition to the exclusion of women from the priesthood. She viewed those critiques as arrogant and illustrative of the fact that some women have no appreciation for what they already have within the institution, which is their roles as mothers and assistants to male authority figures. In Sister Serafima's view, there is no room for discontent within the Church; one needs to either accept the institution with all of its current rules or remove oneself from the Church entirely by rejecting it (Sister Serafima,

Toneva, & Stoyadinov, 2015). Participating in the Church while attempting to reform it is not left as an option. Perhaps the most confusing part of Sister Serafima's presentation, however, is the oxymoronic statement that women can be anything they want to be within the Orthodox Church, so it makes no sense for them to be coveting additional roles that are not accessible to them (Sister Serafima, Toneva, & Stoyadinov, 2015). How women are given access to every role within the Church and simultaneously banned from participating in some of the key roles within the institution is not addressed.

Lastly, Dr. Toneva went outside of the issue of priesthood to discuss the problems with modern-day society more broadly. She asserted that today's societal issues are at least partially due to the fact that men have lost their authority within the family unit, for which she predominantly blames women (Sister Serafima, Toneva, & Stoyadinov, 2015). Overall, the forum seemed less focused on addressing the interaction between feminism and the Church, as its title indicated that it would, and more preoccupied with directly rejecting feminism as an ideology by painting a curiously imprecise picture of it and pinning that against the positive social forces in society—such as the Church and the family unit—both of which, based on the general sentiment expressed during the panel, are entirely dependent on male authority to function properly.

In addition to creating that odd and vastly distorted depiction of what feminism stands for, several publications by Orthodox Church representatives paint a traditional and regressive picture of women's roles in society and the Church. The website Pravoslavieto.com, which offers a number of opinion pieces from Church members on the intersection of Orthodox Christianity and feminism, is infused with descriptions of what the "natural" and "predestined" traits of femininity are and how any deviation from these accepted roles is detrimental to women themselves and to society as a whole. Moreover, in most instances these pre-determined guidelines for appropriate female behavior are sneakily presented as compliments and testaments of women's power.

In one such piece, Archbishop Konstantin—a member of the Russian Orthodox Church—starts off with the illusory attempt to describe the significance of women in religion and spirituality. His approach to that is to define the sources of female power in the context of religion which, according to him, stem from the strong inherent intuition that makes women naturally more connected to the Holy Spirit (Archbishop Konstantin, 2003). He further explains that when women "take men's place" in life, they are essentially "not contributing anything special" to society (Archbishop Konstantin, 2003). In a few broad strokes this viewpoint aims to provide a strict outline for female behavior as passive and nurturing while at the same time condemning women who do not adhere to it as unwomanly and useless, trying to unproductively tag onto roles already being fulfilled by the men around them instead of dutifully resigning to being the bearers of spirituality and feminine energy.

The author additionally decries the emergence of a godless modern culture full of "man-like" women, which, according to him, is also correlated with higher degrees of desperation in society (Archbishop Konstantin, 2003)—though the latter concept is not defined or clarified. The implication here is that women are implicitly responsible for the overall well-being of all of society and if they make the choice to step away from traditional roles and be, in the author's own words "man-like," they somehow impede everyone's development and comfort. Women who lose touch with their "femininity" and Church-prescribed life roles are thus blamed for contributing to the communal spiritual downfall and unhappiness. By implying that, the piece does indeed end up ascribing a huge amount of power to women's choices and behaviors, although a type of mythical, magical power, where ordinary life choices made by women lead to dramatic and detrimental social changes. At the same time, this model effectively strips women of any actual power to exert agency over their own lives by attempting to shame them back to their "predestined" roles.

A related stream of thought flowing through that and a number of other Orthodox Christian opinion pieces on feminism (and generally in many conservative viewpoints about women's roles in the U.S. and Eastern Europe alike) is the idea that the woman is also primarily responsible for the spiritual development of her family, especially her husband. Taking Archbishop Konstantin's argument to its logical conclusion, if women are so uniquely connected to the Holy Spirit, they are obligated to be the transmitters of spirituality to those less intuitively attuned to it, i.e., the men around them. The Metropolitan Seraphim of Johannesburg and Pretoria makes this point explicitly when he says that the woman is the one who "brings to God all those within her **own** family" and who "puts on her love for Christ through her fellow man" (Metropolitan Seraphim of Johannesburg and Pretoria, n.d.). The author calls these functions a woman's "first priority" (Metropolitan Seraphim of Johannesburg and Pretoria, n.d.). In summary, not only do women have a very specific set of character traits that are acceptable for them to exhibit—their intuition, motherliness, and spirituality—and social roles they are expected to take on—protectors of the family, dutiful and stabilizing wives and mothers, but they also bear responsibility for the spiritual development of the men in their lives. In other words, a woman's failure to connect to God or to evolve spiritually is her own fault, but a similar failure on the part of her husband is not his responsibility but rather hers as well.

So, how do these ideals of feminine conformity transpose themselves into the everyday lives of women in Eastern Orthodox countries? Perhaps there is no better or more fascinating case study for that than the intersection of the Church and women's rights in the largest Orthodox Christian country in the world—Russia. The conflation of politics and religion there, especially under the long-lasting rule of Vladimir Putin (as both President and Prime Minister), have led to a widely regressive set of laws and social developments, all of them extensively detrimental to the lives of women and the cause for gender equality.

In 2013, the Russian Orthodox Patriarch Kiril made headlines worldwide with a proclamation of his views on feminism. In a single statement, Kiril gave voice to a backwards, myopic, and destructive view of women's role in society, while at the same time clearly demonstrating how these perceptions are essential to the ideology holding together the Russian post-Soviet dictatorship. The punchline of Patriarch Kiril's quote was that feminism is "very dangerous"; the underlying reasons for it were that women seeking what he called "pseudo-freedom" outside of the home would result in the virtual demise of society and of Russia as a whole. In Kiril's own words: "(i)t's not for nothing that we call Russia the motherland" (Elder, 2013).

The ignorance and absurdity underlining Patriarch Kiril's statement and the implication that women cannot be "free" and are in fact a menace to society unless they assume the roles of wives and mothers are apparent if not surprising. At the same time, there is one part of that opinion that is quite true—the current form of Russia's society and the fragility of the Putin regime would not be able to survive a culture where the indestructible, horse/racecar/snowmobile-riding (Taylor, 2011), impossibly good at sports (Feeney, 2014) macho character is no longer elevated to the heroic stature that Putin has built for himself. As with every cult-driven regime in history, Putin's power is dependent on a carefully manufactured public image of the leader as an invincible and impossibly strong figure. That image, in turn, aims to symbolize Russia's dominant position on the domestic and international arena (Sperling, 2015, locations 1837–1849).

This image-crafting has two main components—the stifling of any voices revealing the dysfunctional and abusive nature of this governance model, enforced by numerous human rights abuses on the one hand; and the shared social reverence toward the exaggerated macho leadership figure on the other. This model is thus internally consistent and easily reinforces itself—the more dissidents get publicly penalized or sent to jail, the fewer cracks in the system get exposed while at the same time the strong leader image is upheld and further celebrated.

The first part of this formula—the suppression of any opposing voices and opinions—is no secret to anyone who has followed political events in Russia in recent years. Human Rights Watch documents numerous instances of political power abuses, many of them directed at punishing critics of the administration or social groups threatening the masculinity paradigm of the country. Moscow made headlines in 2013 with its "gay propaganda" law, effectively making even public discussions of same-sex relationships open to prosecution. Other human rights abuses include the widespread tolerance of hate crimes toward gay people, legislation penalizing critics of the administration, as well as outlawing any public expressions that could be construed as "insult[ing] the feelings of religious believers" ("World Report 2014: Russia," 2014). Feminism comes into play in this context by being one of the movements seeking to express discontent with the various harmful and discriminatory social policies in the country, such as Russia's laws (or lack thereof) on domestic violence, contraception and reproductive rights, and the position of the Orthodox Church on these issues.

One example of the backlash against feminist expression in Russia that turned into a high-profile case across the world several years ago was the Pussy Riot trial. In early 2012, members of the punk-rock feminist group Pussy Riot performed what they labeled a Punk Prayer at an Orthodox Church (Brooke, 2012) in protest of the Church's symbiotic relationship with Putin's regime (Stanglin, 2013). The protestors were arrested and two of the group members received two-year prison sentences, but were released in late 2013—toward the end of their prison terms and shortly before the Winter Olympic Games that Russia hosted in early 2014—in what was ostensibly a staged act of international goodwill by the president, which the group members themselves called a "PR move" (Stanglin, 2013). The Pussy Riot trial revealed deeply entrenched attitudes about appropriate female behavior in Russian society, a misogynistic judicial system, and, not least of all, a reactionary and fearsome approach to feminist expression within the Orthodox Church. Not only was the performance deemed "heretical" during trial, feminism as a whole was equated with heresy "when proclaimed inside a church" (Elder, 2013). Patriarch Kiril went as far as calling the Pussy Riot protest "the work of the devil" (Amos, 2012).

After their release, the band members continued their activism. In response, they have been physically attacked on several different occasions by law enforcement members, some of whom even assaulted them with whips during the Sochi Olympic Games (Gentleman, 2014). Activists expressing allegiance with Pussy Riot have been subjected to similarly vicious assaults and backlash from politicians and self-appointed defendants of the Church as well. Several years ago, during a demonstration of Pussy Riot supporters, a Russian politician punched one of the protesters and used a combination of religious (Pomerantsev, 2012) and mysoginist rhetoric (Sperling, 2015, location 7484–7488) to address his actions. On the religious front, he said that Jesus's words urging us to "turn the other cheek" only apply to "people you know" (Pomerantsev, 2012), implying that physically assaulting strangers would be well within the range of activities that Jesus would condone. On the misogyny front, he commented that the protestor he had assaulted was a "feminist lesbian" (Sperling, 2015, location 7488), which seems to have been intended both as an insult and as an excuse for his act of violence.

The second part of the personality and masculinity cult-building that underpins modern Russian rule is well-described by Valerie Sperling in her book *Sex, Politics, and Putin: Political Legitimacy in Russia.* That component is the establishment of male gender as the stronger one responsible for protection and leadership, leading to a zero-sum view of gender relations where femininity must necessarily be meeker, softer, nurturing, and, of course, obedient (Sperling, 2015, location 7531–7541). Feminism jeopardizes that necessary superiority of the male leader and thus puts into question the dictatorial and abusive decisions put forward by him, making the whole ideology threatening to the current social state of the Russian regime (Sperling, 2015, location 7531–7541).

So, while it is clear why gender equality would be seen as threatening to the Putin governance model, why is the Orthodox Church part of this discourse that appears to have mainly political ramifications? To answer that, one needs to understand the close ties between church and state in the country. In Russia, the incorporation of the Orthodox Church into political affairs has been scrutinized by many in the international community in recent years. This symbiotic relationship serves a few goals at once. On the one hand, it is utilized as a way to consolidate the power of the regime by garnering additional social support for the administration's political decisions (Malashenko, 2012). At the same time, the Church has long been used as a foreign policy tool to exert Moscow's influence on the international arena (Curanovic, 2013). Two decades ago, a number of Church officials were exposed as having past careers within the KGB (Pomerantsev, 2012).

Nowadays, in Russia, the Church is a complement to the Putin administration, perpetuating the forced and cartoonish portrait of masculinity that underpins the dictatorial power typical of his regime (Tzanev, 2011). In return, Church leadership members are getting significant political support for their backing of the government (Tzanev, 2011). In addition, over the past few decades, the Russian Orthodox Church enjoyed numerous state-sanctioned financial benefits as well, from tobacco trade profits to energy industry donations (Pomerantsev, 2012). A 2011 corruption probe into an Orthodox archpriest revealed the accumulation of large amounts of wealth, including multiple luxury vehicles and real estate properties (Osborn, 2011a). Patriarch Kiril himself was at the center of a corruption scandal involving his possession of a $30,000 Swiss watch and the Church's unsuccessful attempt to hide the watch by modifying a photograph of Kiril wearing it (Schwirtz, 2012).

The Church's role in undermining the rights and freedoms of women in Russia is quite extensive. On the social front, the Russian Orthodox Church has been very actively involved in efforts to pass legislation that severely restricts women's access to reproductive healthcare. Earlier this year, Patriarch Kiril lobbied Russian lawmakers to move toward a "total nationwide ban" on abortion. The Church has long tried to intervene in policymaking related to women's health and has spoken out strongly not only against abortions, but also surrogacy ("Patriarch Seeks Abortion Ban," 2015). Last year, Christian lobbyists in Russia even went as far as proposing a ban of certain types of "contraceptives with an abortive function" ("Christian Lobby Seeks," 2014). Members of the Church have also taken a highly retrograde position on sexual violence, shaming women and placing blame on victims for sexual attacks perpetrated against them. In early 2011, a Russian Orthodox Church archpriest was quoted as saying that women wearing "provocative" clothing and drinking should practically expect to be raped as a result (Osborn, 2011b). Archpriest Vsevolod Chaplin also compared women whose attire he disapproved of to prostitutes, strippers, and clowns in the same statement (Osborn, 2011b).

The situation is equally bleak on the subject of domestic violence. Russia to this day has no official law criminalizing domestic violence, despite the fact that, according to some sources, as many as 33 percent of Russian women are domestic abuse victims and between 10 and 14 thousand women are killed by a domestic partner annually (Monaghan, 2015). On the grassroots level, some Orthodox Church representatives are participating in efforts to address domestic violence, such as supporting shelters for abuse victims (Monaghan, 2015). At a political and legislative level, however, the Church has contributed to the glacial pace of legislative reform (Bitten & Kerim, 2013). The Church has opposed the work of activists seeking the establishment of a law against domestic assault in the country (Meyer & Galouchko, 2013) and have themselves worked against that legislative measure (Folbre, 2013). According to the Russian journalist Elena Kostyuchenko, as cited by Tzanev in a *Deutsche Welle* article, sexual and physical assault of women is considered standard in many parts of Russia and is accepted by the state (Tzanev, 2011). Unless a domestic violence incident ends in death, the authorities are rarely able to get involved (Tzanev, 2011).

Having a religious institution that exhibits so little respect or concern for the health, safety, or human rights of women is in itself deeply troublesome. Women who seek support from Church members for spiritual growth and comfort should not have to face regressive and dangerous attitudes by the very people tasked with providing them religious guidance. When the Church additionally crosses over into the political realm to actively build and support a political and judicial system aimed at suppressing and abusing women, as is the case in modern Russia, then that religious misogyny becomes a menacing political force that needs to be actively exposed and resisted.

NOTE

The views and opinions expressed in this chapter are solely those of the author and do not necessarily reflect the views and opinions of any company or organization with which the author is or has previously been associated.

REFERENCES

Amos, H. (2012). Russian punk band were doing devil's work, says leader of Orthodox Church. *The Guardian.* Retrieved on August 20, 2015, from http://www.theguardian.com/world/2012/mar/25/pussy-riot-devils-work-kirill

Archbishop Konstantin. (2003). Служението на жените в Църквата [The service of women in the Church]. *Pravoslavie.com.* Retrieved on August 20, 2015, from http://www.pravoslavieto.com/feminism.htm (Reprinted from Църковен вестник [Church Newspaper], Vol. 15, 2003).

Bitten, N., & Kerim, T. (2013). The Duma and Russian Orthodox Church vs feminism. *Open Democracy.* Retrieved on August 28, 2015, from https://www.opendemocracy.net/5050/natasha-bitten-tatiana-kerim-zade/duma-and-russian-orthodox-church-vs-feminism

Brooke, J. (2012). Moscow's 'Punk Prayer' protesters get 2-year sentences. *Voice of America News.* Retrieved on August 1, 2015, from http://www.voanews.com/content/pussy-riot-found-guily-of-hooliganism/1490081.html

Christian lobby seeks constitutional ban on abortions in Russia. (2014). *RT.* Retrieved on August 26, 2015, from http://rt.com/politics/206479-russia-abortions-ban-christian/

Chrysostomos, Archimandrite. (1981). Women in the Orthodox Church: Brief comments from a spiritual perspective. *Orthodox Christian Information Center.* Retrieved on August 19, 2015, from http://orthodoxinfo.com/general/women.aspx (Reprinted from *Orthodox Life,* Vol. 31, No. 1, Jan–Feb, 1981, pp. 34–41).

Curanovic, A. (2013). Religion in Russia's foreign policy. *New Eastern Europe.* Retrieved on August 22, 2015, from http://neweasterneurope.eu/interviews/812-religion-in-russia-s-foreign-policy

Elder, M. (2013). Feminism could destroy Russia, Russian Orthodox patriarch claims. *The Guardian.* Retrieved on August 23, 2015, from http://www.theguardian.com/world/2013/apr/09/feminism-destroy-russia-patriarch-kirill

Feeney, N. (2014). Watch Putin play hockey and score suspicious number of goals. *Time Magazine.* Retrieved from http://time.com/95533/vladimir-putin-hockey/

Folbre, N. (2013). President Putin's patriarchal games. *The New York Times.* Retrieved on August 23, 2015, from http://economix.blogs.nytimes.com/2013/12/23/president-putins-patriarchal-games/?_r=0

Gentleman, A. (2014). Nadya Tolokonnikova: "I suppose we have nothing more to lose." *The Guardian.* Retrieved on August 27, 2015, from http://www.theguardian.com/theguardian/2014/sep/19/nadya-tolokonnikova-pussy-riot-interview-nothing-to-lose

Malashenko, A. (2012). Religion in Russia: Politicization and disengagement. *Carnegie Moscow Center.* Retrieved on August 23, 2015, from http://carnegie.ru/publications/?fa=49273

Metropolitan Seraphim of Johannesburg and Pretoria. The role of women in the Church. *Orthodox Research Institute.* Retrieved on August 12, 2015, from http://www.orthodoxresearchinstitute.org/articles/misc/seraphim_role_of_women.htm

Meyer, H., & Galouchko, K. (2013). Putin allies let abuse law linger despite killings. *Bloomberg Business.* Retrieved on August 23, 2015, from http://www.bloomberg.com/news/articles/2013-10-27/putin-allies-let-abuse-law-linger-as-a-woman-is-killed-each-hour

Monaghan, J. (2015). Domestic violence in Russia: Optimism as country faces up to the 'silent crisis.' *The Independent.* Retrieved on August 28, 2015, from http://www.independent.co.uk/news/world/europe/domestic-violence-in-russia-optimism-as-country-faces-up-to-the-silent-crisis-10239053.html

Osborn, A. (2011a). Russian Orthodox Church embroiled in corruption scandal. *The Telegraph.* Retrieved on August 18, 2015, from http://www.telegraph.co.uk/news/worldnews/europe/russia/8790457/Russian-Orthodox-Church-embroiled-in-corruption-scandal.html

Osborn, A. (2011b). Russian woman who wear miniskirts 'should not be surprised if they get raped.' (2011). *The Telegraph.* Retrieved on August 23, 2015, from http://www.telegraph.co.uk/news/worldnews/europe/russia/8266752/Russian-woman-who-wear-miniskirts-should-not-be-surprised-if-they-get-raped.html

Patriarch seeks abortion ban in Russia in parliament speech. (2015). *RT.* Retrieved on August 11, 2015, from http://rt.com/politics/225087-russia-church-abortions-ban/

Pomerantsev, P. (2012). Putin's God squad: The Orthodox Church and Russian politics. *Newsweek.* Retrieved on August 14, 2015, from http://www.newsweek.com/putins-god-squad-orthodox-church-and-russian-politics-64649

Schwirtz, M. (2012). $30,000 Watch vanishes up Church leader's sleeve. *The New York Times.* Retrieved on August 7, 2015, from http://www.nytimes.com/2012/04/06/world/europe/in-russia-a-watch-vanishes-up-orthodox-leaders-sleeve.html?_r=0

Sister Serafima, Toneva, K., & Stoyadinov, M. (2015). Църквата и феминизмът [The Church and feminism]. [Webinar]. In Православие и съвремие *[Orthodoxy and Modernity].* Retrieved on August 23, 2015, from http://www.pravoslavie.bg/пол/църквата-и-феминизмът

Sperling, V. (2015). *Sex, politics, and Putin: Political legitimacy in Russia* [Kindle Fire HD]. Retrieved on August 4, 2015, from Amazon.com

Stanglin, D. (2013). Freed Pussy Riot members call Russia amnesty a PR stunt. *USA Today.* Retrieved on August 15, 2015, from http://www.usatoday.com/story/news/world/2013/12/23/pussy-riot-member-released/4173379/

Taylor, A. (2011). Vladimir Putin: Action man. *The Atlantic.* Retrieved on August 23, 2015, from http://www.theatlantic.com/photo/2011/09/vladimir-putin-action-man/100147/

Tzanev, K. (2011). Послушание вместо сексуална просвета [Obedience instead of sex education]. *Deutsche Welle,* Retrieved on August 9, 2015, from http://www.dw.de/послушание-вместо-сексуална-просвета/a-15544746

World Report 2014: Russia. (2014). *Human Rights Watch.* Retrieved on August 23, 2015, from http://www.hrw.org/world-report/2014/country-chapters/russia

Chapter 11

The Mystical Feminine in Baha'i Scriptures

Paula A. Drewek

The year was 1986—my feminist awakening. The source was the recitation of "The Maid of Heaven" passage at a Baha'i women's conference at Louhelen Baha'i School in Davison, Michigan. The opening of this passage I have added to the close of this chapter. At this point I was unaware of female images of the divine in Baha'i scriptures—at least they caused me little notice. But this image was beautiful and compelling and powerful. It planted a seed. I had originally made plans to return to graduate school at the University of Ottawa to obtain a Ph.D. in religious studies. I was set to leave in a couple of months and I planned to research something along the lines of the Baha'i teaching of the equality of the sexes. It is a key social principle of the Baha'i faith and I was interested in how it was understood and being implemented.

As fate would have it, I entered U. of O. at a time of feminist revival. Many of the grad students and some teachers were interested in women's issues in academe. We planned a women's conference at University of Ottawa in 1991 with prominent Canadian and American presenters on diverse aspects of women's issues. Many were trying to bring their patriarchal faiths out of "the dark ages" into a world where women had a valued place as more than just supporters of men—in the congregation, the community, the scriptures, etc. They did so in multiple ways, but often by highlighting personal experience. I became even more interested in the representation of women in the Baha'i faith and published an article on it in 1991 in the *Journal of Baha'i Studies*. The way I saw it, Baha'i teachings already gave women a prominent place, scripturally and socially, but the realization of equality ideals had a long way to go to catch up with the images and injunctions in the Baha'i Writings. I propose to examine with you three major images of the mystical feminine in the Baha'i Writings, but first, some groundwork.

CHARACTERISTICS OF BAHA'I THEOLOGY

The Baha'i Writings are not the first to utilize feminine imagery of the divine in its scriptures. We have, for example, Shekina and Lilith in Hebrew tradition, Sophia in the Greek, Isis in ancient Egypt, Shakti and the many goddess figures in Hinduism, and Kuan Yin in the Buddhist context. It is not my purpose to make comparisons between them. I leave that to you. But, having female images of divinity is important to women. If the divine is the locus of power, authority, and value, women need to find those attributes accessible to them as well. Female images of divinity are empowering and inspiring. Women need feminine images of divinity if we are to argue for an equal place in the social order. But to locate feminine images of divinity in material forms such as ancient goddesses, Earth Mother, Gaia, Isis, and the like seems to me not very liberating. Women have been associated with physical fecundity for thousands of years. Spiritual fecundity is more necessary to the current need for wholeness and balance. And that wholeness requires feminine forms of divinity in interaction with masculine forms.

There are two features of Baha'i theology which illumine the context within which such a discussion of the interaction of feminine and masculine forms can occur. Those are:

1) The impossibility of knowing God, and
2) The Manifestations[1] as avenues toward what we *can* know of God.

> The door to the knowledge of the Ancient Being hath ever been, and will continue forever to be, closed in the face of men. No man's understanding shall ever gain access until His holy court. (Baha'u'llah, *Gleanings*, p. 49)

So the *forms* through which we can know of God are not adequate to apprehend the Reality of divinity. That is why we have God's Messengers

(Manifestations) as intermediaries to give us physical beings we can know, observe, come to love, and Who reflect divine attributes.

> As a token of His mercy, however, and as a proof of His loving-kindness, He hath manifested unto men the Day Stars of His divine guidance, the Symbols of His divine unity, and hath ordained the knowledge of these sanctified Beings to be identical with the knowledge of His own Self. (Baha'u'llah, *Gleanings*, pp. 49–50)

These holy beings are the signs of God on earth through whom we can come to know, appreciate, be attracted to, and love God, the Divine Essence.

> These sanctified Mirrors, these Day Springs of ancient glory, are, one and all, the Exponents on earth of Him Who is the central Orb of the universe, its Essence and ultimate Purpose. From Him proceed their knowledge and power; from Him is derived their sovereignty. The beauty of their countenance is but a reflection of His image. . . . These Tabernacles of Holiness . . . are but expressions of Him Who is the Invisible of the Invisibles. By the revelation of these Gems of Divine virtue all the names and attributes of God . . . are made manifest. (Baha'u'llah, *Gleanings*, pp. 47–48)

Baha'i Writings make no distinction between the Manifestations of God in terms of prominence or authority, greater or lesser. All are validated and equal. While these are Signs of God on earth, we need to beware of God-ideas that come from our own imaginations which would constitute idolatry; the world of names and forms (i.e., characteristics of physical reality) is multiple, not unitary.

The images through which we glimpse divinity in Western culture have become fixed in masculine forms. No wonder feminists have felt left out of ultimate religious values. But let's not confuse the *forms* through which divinity is expressed with the God essence they are intended to convey. Our helplessness to comprehend the mystery of divinity is the acme of human understanding—to know that you cannot know.

MYSTICISM AND THE USE OF METAPHORS

Hence we arrive at the evocative, but perhaps misty, territory of the mystical as a way to convey or approach the ineffable, that which has no physical presence or form. Mysticism usually refers to the human desire for transcendence and identification with the Godhead. I use the term "mystical" in its general sense as ineffable, beyond mundane, practical experience, suggesting a spiritual reality beyond this physical one. While calling upon sensible particulars, mystical imagery points beyond them. In his book *The Purpose of Physical Reality*, John Hatcher deconstructs some of the elements in a variety of symbolic devices used to convey the abstract by physical means: allegory, symbolism, metaphor, parables, analogies. Such devices include "the tenor," that which is described (in this example, the Maid of Heaven); "the vehicle," or what is compared ("inmate of the Exalted Paradise"); and "the meaning," the connection or similarity between the two. The meaning relates the Maid as the vehicle of Baha'u'llah's revelation. Thus, she is a mystical image pointing beyond herself to the divine presence as she addresses us "in a most melodious voice, the anthem of praise, for a remembrance of Him Who is the King of the names and attributes of God (Baha'u'llah)."

Hatcher speaks of the metaphorical *process* which forces us, the reader in this case, to make a connection or find the meaning of the comparison. What qualities of the known "Maid" are applicable or help disclose "the Exalted Paradise"? Hatcher proposes that the most important feature of the metaphorical process is education—not simply of the mind, but of the soul also. "The improvement of the soul through the metaphorical dramatization of spiritual attributes is hardly a new idea" (Hatcher, 1987, p. 83). Recall morality plays and the classical Greek dramas. What *is* the *process* at work here? We recognize the abstract quality in the physical dramatization (hubris, for the ancient Greeks). Such recognition may lead to attraction, to a desire to develop such a quality in our own lives, or warn us away from negative characteristics as in the fables of Aesop. Such attraction or repulsion has the potential to develop habits as we internalize the attractiveness of certain spiritual qualities ("broidered Robe of Light" or "wondrous accent of the Voice") as connoting light, love, wisdom, beauty, and such. Metaphors thus become a tool for the development of spiritual attributes (through their attraction or repulsion). For Baha'is this is one of life's essential purposes.

The *language* of the metaphorical process is but another tool in the functioning of metaphors for our education. Metaphorical language, while relying on characteristics of the physical world, evokes ideas, feelings, and attraction to the spiritual worlds.

> Think not that we have revealed unto you a mere code of laws. Nay, rather, We have unsealed the choice wine with the fingers of Might and Power. (*Kitab-i-Aqdas*, pp. 11–12)

The language is also a sifter, an assayer of the intent or frame of mind of the listener/reader. Because metaphors have both outward and inward meanings, we are challenged mentally and spiritually to discover the inner within the outer meaning. Baha'u'llah speaks of the twofold language in this excerpt from the *Kitab-i-Iqan* (pp. 254–255):

> It is evident unto thee that the Birds of Heaven and Doves of Eternity speak a twofold language. One language, the outward language, is devoid of allusions, is unconcealed and unveiled; that it may be a guiding lamp and a beaconing light whereby wayfarers may attain the heights of holiness, and seekers may advance into the realm of eternal reunion. Such are the unveiled traditions and the evident verses already mentioned. The other language is veiled and concealed, so that whatever lieth hidden in the heart of the malevolent may be made manifest and their innermost being be disclosed . . . In such utterances, the literal meaning, as generally understood by the people, is not what hath been intended.

I'm reminded of a verse with a similar intent from Matthew in the Gospels when the disciples came to ask Jesus why he spoke in parables:

> To you it has been given to know the secrets of the kingdom of heaven, but to them it has not been given. For to him who has will more be given, and he will have abundance; but from him who has not, even what he has will be taken away. This is why I speak to them in parables, because seeing they do not see, and hearing they do not hear, nor do they understand. (Matt. 13:10–13)

"The secrets of the kingdom of heaven," and the "Throne of Thy Lord, the Inaccessible, the Most high" are like references to those spiritual worlds beyond the minds of men which, nevertheless, attract the heart of the mystic and the believer alike. Succinctly, metaphors and their cousins are capable of "separating the sheep from the goats" by developing spiritual acumen.

This chapter responds to feminists who use gender as a cultural construct. Like a prism, the cultural lens breaks down the divine reflection into its component features and into multiple names and forms. So today we have multiple goddess figures and heroines from all possible cultural and religious legacies who are empowering women to recapture spiritual qualities such as knowledge and power, wisdom and courage. I am interested in finding in the Baha'i scriptures examples of the mystical or divine feminine that enrich our understanding of the multiple names and forms of the divinity without tying it to political or cultural contexts. That would be another chapter in and of itself.

THE MYSTICAL FEMININE IN BAHA'I WRITINGS

The feminine divine is prominent in Baha'i scripture in several forms; I will focus on three of these forms: the creative or Mother Word, the Queen of Carmel, and the Maid of Heaven. The last two are both divine dramatizations of the interaction of masculine and feminine principles of divinity in the Baha'i revelation, but in each case, their interaction with masculine principles is evident. The complementary nature of masculine and feminine interaction is more akin to yin and yang than to Western dualism. It shifts the perspective from either/or, competing opposites, to a balanced and whole framework wherein each component completes the other and needs the other.

As Mother Word

The Mother Word is the revelation of God from its multiple sources in the scriptures of the world's religions. In Baha'i scriptures it functions as the creative force of the universe. Mother Word describes an active "principle," not a being. This force or *word* recalls for some of you the opening of the Gospel of John, "In the beginning was the Word . . ."

It is the power of creation, that which rears and nourishes human growth on this planet (not a projection of feminist desires for a larger role on the world's stage). Power and procreation become identified in the following from Baha'u'llah:

> The moment the word expressing My attribute "The Omniscient" issueth forth from My mouth, every created thing will, according to its capacity and limitations, be invested with the power to unfold the knowledge of the most marvelous sciences, and will be empowered to manifest them in the course of time at the bidding of Him Who is the Almighty, the All-Knowing. Know thou of a certainty that the Revelation of every other Name is accompanied by a similar manifestation of divine Power. Every single letter proceeding out of the mouth of God is indeed a mother letter, and every word uttered by Him Who is the Wellspring of Divine Revelation is a mother word and His Tablet a Mother Tablet. (*Gleanings*, p. 142)

The mothering images are used to suggest the divine *creative principle* of the Word of God. Baha'u'llah identifies the birthing powers of God with the word "Fashioner":

> No sooner is this resplendent word uttered, than its animating energies, stirring within all created things, give birth to the means and instruments whereby such arts can be produced and perfected. All the wondrous achievements ye now witness are the direct consequences of the Revelation of this Name. (*Gleanings*, p. 142)

Here the divine feminine is identified with the *power* of creation, not with a fixed condition of sexuality applied to objects or persons in the created world. In yet another passage, Baha'u'llah refers to the animating properties of the Word, when uttered by humans.

> Whoso reciteth . . . the verses revealed by God, the scattering angels of the Almighty shall scatter abroad the fragrance of the words uttered by his mouth, and shall cause the heart of every righteous man to throb. (*Gleanings*, p. 295)

The Mother Word is the channel of divine power, of transformation, of the change of heart leading to the inclination toward God, as well as of the wonderful arts and sciences on which civilization prides itself. The Mother Word is the power of life in the world of creation and gives an interactive and dynamic dimension to the mystical feminine. Receiving the Word then opens the recipient to the creative energies latent within it. "Should the Word be allowed to release suddenly all the energies latent within it, no man could sustain the weight of so mighty a Revelation" (*Gleanings*, pp. 76–77). Hence the Word is released in relation to the capacity of its hearers. The gradual release of God's creative power through the world sets the stage for Progressive Revelation, a key Baha'i principle underpinning the unity of all religions as timely expressions of God's Will for successive generations of human development. It embraces all the holy books as successive chapters in the unfoldment of this Divine Will, a never-ending process.

Another reference to the preeminence of the Word of God is found in the *Tablets of Baha'u'llah*:

> O friend of mine! The Word of God is the king of words and its pervasive influence is incalculable. It hath ever dominated and will continue to dominate the realm of being. The Great Being saith: The Word is the master key for the whole world, inasmuch as through its potency the doors of the hearts of men, which in reality are the doors of heaven, are unlocked. No sooner had but a glimmer of its effulgent splendor shone forth upon the mirror of love than the blessed word 'I am the Best-Beloved' was reflected therein. It is an ocean inexhaustible in riches, comprehending all things. Everything which can be perceived is but an emanation therefrom. High, immeasurably high is this sublime station, in whose shadow moveth the essence of loftiness and splendor, wrapt in praise and adoration. (*Lawh-i-Maqasud*, p. 173, *Tablets of Baha'u'llah*)

So this Mother of all life is the unlocker of love and of the connection between the visible world and that invisible world of Divine Essence. The references above to "the Great Being" refer to the God Essence, while "the Best-Beloved" is a reference to the Manifestation, or, in this instance, Baha'u'llah.

The Tablet of Carmel and the Queen of Carmel

In the Tablet of Carmel (Baha'u'llah, *Tablets of Baha'u'llah*, pp. 3–5), we have a divine dramatization of two forces coming together: the ancient of Days as the Manifestation of God, and a feminine personification of the Mountain of God, the Queen of Carmel, the site of the Manifestation's holy seat or throne. One might recall the relationship of Isis and Osiris from ancient Egypt in the ruler and throne duo. Isis was identified as the seat of power or the Throne and Osiris as Ruler of the Underworld.

The tablet resembles a courtship dance with feelings of separation and longing for reunion followed by movements ever closer culminating in a consummation recalling the divine marriage of heaven and earth, a theme to be found throughout the Western religions. The wedding dance closes with a circling around the sacred spot and tidings of rejoicing moving out to the entire earth as "both land and sea rejoice at this announcement" (Baha'u'llah, *Tablets*, p. 5). I have described the pattern of development in this tablet as a dance-drama because it alternates successively between a divine call and an earthly response. The holy mountain responds to the summons:

> Haste thee, O Carmel, for lo, the light of the countenance of God, the Ruler of the Kingdom of Names and Fashioner of the heavens, hath been lifted upon thee. (p. 3)

Note how God is personalized in this drama by reference to his countenance. Next, the terms "Ruler" and "Fashioner" suggest masculine divinity. Ruler is often identified with the Lord of Heaven and Fashioner with the hand of God creating humankind in Genesis. The hand was the physical form evoking God in Early Christian art such as in the church in Ravenna, Italy. These are familiar, cultural associations to be sure, as any references to masculine and feminine must take some cues from our cultural contexts.

The mountain of God now bursts forth: *Seized with transports of joy, and raising high her voice, she thus exclaimed: "May my life be a sacrifice to Thee, inasmuch, as Thou hast fixed Thy gaze upon me, hast bestowed upon me Thy bounty, and has directed towards me Thy steps"* (p. 3). This is literally true as Baha'u'llah did visit Mt. Carmel during his exile in Acca, Palestine. The personal quality of association and movement is touched by "raising . . . her voice" and receiving his "gaze" and "steps." Then she laments her separation from him and is quickened to life by "the vitalizing fragrance of Thy Day" and "the shrilling voice of Thy Pen" (p. 3). The entire creation "shakes" in response to this Pen. Here, the Word of God, symbolized by the Pen, is a masculine force identified with the potent forces that quicken all earth to life. Note how the imagery touches upon several of the physical senses such as sight, hearing, and touch:

> When the ocean of My presence surged before thy face, cheering thine eyes and those of all creation, and filling with delight all things visible and invisible. (p. 4)

The earth receives her Lord as Lover. Her body is identified with the revelation of His Glory: *Well is it with him that circleth around thee, that proclaimeth the revelation of thy glory, and recounteth that which the bounty of the Lord thy God hath showered upon thee* (p. 4). This same meeting has "turned thy sorrow into gladness, and transmuted thy grief into blissful joy" (p. 4). In response, the holy mountain is to give thanks and to:

> Call out to Zion . . . . and announce the joyful tidings: He that was hidden from mortal eyes is come! His all-conquering sovereignty is manifest; His all-encompassing splendor is revealed. Beware lest thou hesitate or halt. Hasten forth and circumambulate the City of God that hath descended from heaven, the celestial Kaaba round which have circled in adoration the favored of God . . . And the company of the most exalted angels. (p. 4)

This rousing image of actively meeting the Glory of God (the English translation of Baha'u'llah) also recalls the previous revelation of Islam by its reference to the celestial Kaaba. The Jewish covenant is referenced in the Call to Zion. "The City of God" is the time of unity between heaven and earth of any of the revelations of God through these Chosen Beings or Holy Manifestations. Rather than a place, it is a time referent to the coming of the Manifestation, humanity's expectation of His coming, and of the eagerness of accepting Him when He reveals Himself (the consummation). Then we also have the response as a circumambulation recalling the Muslim pilgrims' movement around the earthly Kaaba.

The majesty of the masculine images of sovereignty and splendor meets with the actively receptive images of listening, quickening, delight, and thanksgiving: *all the atoms of the earth have been made to vibrate* in response to this reunion and *the Tongue of Grandeur hath been moved to disclose that which had been wrapt in His knowledge and lay concealed within the treasury of His might* (p. 5). The forces now disclosed from hiding resemble the children issuing forth from the divine meeting. At length *will God sail His Ark upon thee, and will manifest the people of Baha* (p. 5).

The divine feminine in this tablet is the holy mountain of God destined to reveal God's splendors. Today, Mount Carmel is indeed a witness to the presence and power of Baha'u'llah's revelation as its shrines and gardens rise high above the city of Haifa, Israel. The progression of nine terraces below and nine above the Shrine of the Bab invite the visitor to ascend unto God's Holy Mountain. The union of Heaven and Earth that this tablet proclaims will "manifest the people of Baha," the children of this divine marriage. Interaction of masculine and feminine images is once again central to the fertility characterized by consummation. The dance-like call and response weaves these elements together until they are nearly indistinguishable, illustrating our theme of masculine-feminine complementarity and interaction. Scholars may also recall similar divine marriages within Judaism and Christianity. In the Torah, God is the bridegroom and Israel is His Bride; in Christianity, Christ is the husband and his bride, the Church. Perhaps these allegorical unions supplied the prototype for the Queen of Carmel as a symbol of mystical union.

This tablet is doubly significant since the Baha'i Holy Places are located on Mount Carmel. Here stands the Shrine of the Bab who began the dual revelation and announced the coming of Baha'u'llah. Also situated is the administrative center of the Baha'i world housed in the building of the Universal House of Justice and its attendant Archives, Center for the Study of the Holy Texts, and International Teaching Center, as well as shrines to Baha'u'llah's wife, son, and daughter. Seldom in religious history have both the sacred and administrative arms of a faith been joined in one location.

The Maid of Heaven

The most pervasive feminine images of divinity (and the one that first excited my interest) are those portraying the Maid of Heaven as the personification of the Holy Spirit or the Revelation. The attractive or charismatic features of both male and female find their source in the Creator of all life. Male and female imagery are wedded in partnering of the Manifestation, Baha'u'llah as King of Glory, with his mystical partner as the Maid of Heaven. Beginning with her appearance to Baha'u'llah in the Siyah-Chal prison, she embodies connection to God in a form of luminous beauty whose central characteristics are joy, brightness, purity, and glory. She calls to Baha'u'llah in "a most sweet voice":

> Turning My face, I beheld a Maiden . . . suspended in the air before Me. So rejoiced was she in her very soul that her countenance shone with the ornament of the good-pleasure of God. (Baha'u'llah, as quoted in *Shoghi Effendi, God Passes By,* pp. 101–102)

Her appearance personified two themes in the relationship of Creator and creatures: the splendor of the hidden is made manifest, and the Manifestation discloses or unveils the beauty and attractiveness of the revelation of God. Both themes require interaction of male and female principles. Note the conjoining of opposites as she continues:

> Betwixt earth and heaven she was raising a call which captivated the hearts and minds of men. She was imparting to both My inward and

> outer being tidings which rejoiced My soul, and the souls of God's honored servants. (p. 102)

The beauty and attractiveness of the Manifestation is emphasized as she proclaims:

> By God! This is the Best-Beloved of the worlds . . . This is the Beauty of God amongst you, and the power of His sovereignty within you, could ye but understand. (p. 102)

The creative connotations of the female principle commingling with the male in a kind of mystical coitus, complete with heavenly womb, is found in another appearance of the Maid of Heaven from the writings of the Bab (Baha'u'llah's forerunner):

> By the righteousness of the One true God, I am the Maid of Heaven begotten by the Spirit of Baha, abiding within the Mansion hewn out of a mass of ruby, tender and vibrant. (*Selected Writings of the Bab*, p. 54)

The most extended imagery of the Maid of Heaven is found in *Gleanings from the Writings of Baha'u'llah*. We are prepared for the grand entry of this Maid by references to previous revelations, recalling the radiance of Sinaic splendor in its lightening glimpse of crimson light. Then she enters by the command of God. Light and immortality become the enduring features of her apparel: "Drape thyself in whatever manner pleaseth Thee in the silken Vesture of Immortality, and put on, in the name of the All-Glorious, the broidered Robe of Light" (pp. 282–283). The silken vesture recalls Tahirih's nuptial garments.[2] Our vision having been awakened, the next command is directed toward our ears: "Hear, then, the sweet, the wondrous accent of the Voice that cometh from the Throne of Thy Lord, the Inaccessible, the Most High" (p. 283). Next, her countenance is to be unveiled to reveal the beauty associated with a black-eyed damsel, an image that will be familiar to students of the Quran as a description associated with the heavenly houris. The veil is a symbol of modesty and chastity and is a characteristic especially associated with the feminine in Baha'i scriptures. Likewise, the veil of God's Revelation is always the mysterious and unexpected circumstances of its appearance. It appears counter to the hopes, desires, and preconceptions of the majority of people.

The Maid of Heaven uses the beauty of physical and sensual attributes as a gateway, a door to the Revelation. The sensual nature is to awaken our consciousness of the beauty and attractiveness of the attributes of God. The Maid image addresses all the dwellers of heaven and earth in a stunning image compressing sound, sight, light, and longing into a majestic presence that leaves paradise quivering in expectation. This is no ethereal or sterile feminine. She commands our senses and joins them to spiritual purpose—that heart's attraction to the beauty of God.

The attractiveness of the Maid of Heaven refocuses creative power in a dimension of spiritual fecundity, rather than physical fecundity. As such it serves as a vehicle that enables us to transcend our present limitations and tap into the root of transformation—the feminine power of Revelation to give birth, to create anew. The Maid of Heaven continues the personification of the feminine as the New Eve. More than creature, she is the power of Creation—the power without which seeds do not grow, attraction is not generated, human culture does not develop. She is to awaken in us a sense of our beginnings and directions as we endeavor to formulate and express them in the world of creation.

In several tablets revealed in Baghdad, Baha'u'llah describes his relationship with the Maid of Heaven as part of the process of the intermingling, complementarity, of male and female principles. In the Tablet of the Maiden *(Lawh-i-Huriyyih)* and the Wondrous Maiden *(Hur-i-Ujab),* both not translated into English from Arabic, "He portrays in dramatic terms the appearance before Him of the Maid of Heaven, personifying the 'Most Great Spirit' . . . " (Taherzadeh, *Revelation of Baha'ullah* vol. 1, p. 213). Taherzadeh says, "The dialogue between the two is fascinating. It reveals, on the one hand, the unique station of Baha'u'llah and, on the other, the afflictions which had befallen Him through the misdeeds of a perverse generation" (p. 125). The divine attributes are depicted "as if in a sublime drama" (p. 125). It is interesting that Taherzadeh describes Baha'u'llah's relation with the Maid as a dialogue, since this form is also the dramatic device in the Queen of Carmel image and emphasizes complementarity of the masculine and feminine principles. Elsewhere, Baha'u'llah speaks of the Maids of Heaven as celestial inhabitants ("Tablet of the Holy Mariner," *Gleanings,* pp. 32, 136, 327; *Tablets of Baha'ullah,* p. 189).

CONCLUSION

Consonant with Western religious traditions, the Baha'i scriptures associate the mystical feminine with heavenly sources and spiritually potent forms; thus, I have used the term "mystical feminine." This reference is in stark contrast to some modern feminists who wish to embody the feminine divine in tangible or earthly beings. The major earth-references are the power identified with the creative Word as the Mother of Life and the Queen of Carmel, which is a mountain. We are all children nurtured to our individual expressions of spirituality through partaking "every morn and eve" of the Mother Word. It gives life to us and continues to nourish our spiritual growth through all stages of life. Our maleness or femaleness is not important to this relationship. We are all as children at the breast, taking our fill. In this form, the divine may be taken within humanity—may be eaten, absorbed, ingested, and digested—to be expressed outwardly in deeds of service, detachment, compassion, humility, and other virtues.

How do I as a feminist regard the divine feminine images in Baha'i scripture? They preserve and nurture what I have come to regard as feminine qualities such as beauty, purity, fecundity, and luminosity without trivializing them in forms that are too defined and limiting. One may argue that even the above qualities are defined and limiting. Yet, they are among the multiple divine attributes (recall the multiple names and forms from the introduction) which Baha'is are to cultivate in this earthly life. Any concrete forms bear the danger of reifying images of divinity by catering to fashions of the period or tempting us to conceive of the divine in solely human terms. By providing us with multiple images of a single divine spirit, the Baha'i writings point away from gender as a primary point of identity and toward multiple spiritual attributes and qualities. The multiplicity of these qualities gives us a more comprehensive understanding of God, and of our own growth potential than single-sex images could provide, such as Father and Son, Mother and Daughter, or Husband and Wife. They invite continuing dialogue with the text. Such a dialogue depends on what we bring to it as we grow in faith and understanding.

The dialogue of male and female imagery that we identified in both the Tablet of Carmel and the Maid of Heaven protects us from the tyranny of either sex by giving us the framework of complementarity within which to process and understand the social changes we will confront. Such a dialogue emphasizes the foremost importance of unity in the consultative process,[3] and preserves the balance of male and female attributes and characteristics.

Instead of being divided and polarized, masculine and feminine attributes are united in the social body we all share. The process of change in concert leaves little room for entrenched positions of the sexes behind an imaginary firing line. The worlds of divinity revealed by Baha'u'llah have reinvested our understanding of God with mythic and symbolic catalysts to empower our spiritual *and* social growth.

Portions of this chapter have been adapted with permission from Paula A. Drewek, "Feminine Forms of the Divine in Bahá'í Scriptures," *The Journal of Baha'i Studies*, Volume 5, n. 1 (March 1992).

Quotes are from the RSV unless otherwise noted.

NOTES

1. Manifestations are the Baha'i reference for Messengers of God, Chosen Beings as intermediaries between the human and the divine.

2. Tahirih was a Babi heroine who dressed as for a wedding before being ushered from the Governor's house to be tossed into a well and buried by the religious authorities.

3. The process of consultation is used in all Baha'i collaborative efforts. It involves prayerful meditation, absolute truthfulness, participation by all and acquiescence to the group's decision.

REFERENCES

Baha'u'llah. (1962). *Epistle to the son of the wolf.* Wilmette, IL: Baha'i Publishing Committee.

Baha'u'llah. (1963). *Gleanings from the writings of Baha'u'llah.* Wilmette, IL: Baha'i Publishing Trust.

Baha'u'llah. (1978). *Tablets of Baha'u'llah.* Great Britain: W. & J. Mackay Ltd.

Baha'u'llah. (1989). Kitab-i-Aqdas. (Trans. 1992). U.S.: Baha'i Publishing Trust. (Original work published c. 1873.)

Baha'u'llah. (1989). Kitab-i-Iqan (The Book of Certitude). (Shoghi Effendi, trans., 1930). U.S.: Baha'i Publishing Trust.

Effendi, S. (1979). *God Passes By*. Baha'i World Centre.

Hatcher, J. (1987). *The purpose of physical reality: The kingdom of names.* Wilmette, IL: Baha'i Publishing Trust.

Selected Writings of the Bab. (1982). Baha'i World Centre.

Taherzadeh, A. (1974). *The Revelation of Baha'u'llah, Baghdad 1853–63.* Vol. 1. Oxford: George Ronald.

Part II

Religious Philosophy in Feminism and Feminist Action

Chapter 12

Martial Religion, Ravaging Warfare, and Rape: Polytheistic Greek and Monotheistic Israelite Views

Kathy L. Gaca

INTRODUCTION

In my research on martial rape against girls and women, I aim to raise our level of historical and moral knowledge about martial rape, female war-captive enslavement, and compulsory procreation in populace-ravaging warfare from antiquity to modernity.[1] I define and provide a historically grounded explanation of ravaging, martial rape, and the rest of this organized violence in the first section below. My main interest in this research is to explain this aggressive treatment of women and girls and its principles in order to disclose its harmful effects across generations on civil society, freedom, and the life worth living. In this essay, my focus is on the religious dimension of this violence and its core principle, which I identify and explain as the martial power over life and death (in brief, martial power).

Martial rape in war ravaging, I argue, is organized religious aggression going back to the ancient Near East and Mediterranean, and it exerts this martial power either as live enslavement or as lethal force over the girls and women of ravaged peoples. Ravaging, martial rape, and enslavement are justified on martial religious grounds and administered under religious powers, rites, and personnel, such as prophets. The knowledge gained from investigating martial power demystifies the idea that such a power emanates from a divine realm beyond civil right and wrong and impervious to moral reasoning and challenge, an idea key to making martial power religious. This knowledge enlightens also because it brings into focus the ethno-religious hostilities and steep inequities based on sex, age, and social status that have been perpetuated by martial ravaging and its coercive customs of procreation and child-rearing. Overall, this research topic deals with aspects of human cruelty, guile, and exploitation at its worst, but my aim is constructive. The greater clarity we gain about ravaging, rape, and the hatred and injustices brought in their train should help facilitate global efforts to reduce martial aggression and to free girls, boys, women, and men from its adverse effects.

In this chapter, I argue that religions going back to the ancient Mediterranean and Near East have historically functioned in important ways to implement, run, and justify ravaging warfare and martial rape for the enrichment of some men and dependents in martial ethno-religious groups at the destructive expense of outside peoples and of one another, especially in the lower echelons. Martial aggression has been rooted since antiquity in the organized bureaucracy of martial power, a bureaucracy that was more multi-faceted in antiquity, when polytheistic religions and their war gods in this region were still active as vehicles of popular devotion and morality. In the first section of this essay, I explain my published findings about martial ravaging over its history and its agenda to rape, enslave, and exploit the girls and young women of ravaged peoples. In the second, I explain the religious framework of this organized aggression from antiquity to modernity. For antiquity, I draw on Greek polytheistic and Israelite monotheistic accounts about ravaging and martial rape as presented in the *Iliad*, the Hebrew Bible, and in ancient Greek history. For modernity, I sketch the persistence of the religious ethos of martial power from humanitarian testimonials about forced conversion in the martial Serbian ravaging of Bosnian Muslims in 1992 and from investigative reporting about the current martial aggression of ISIS in Iraq and Syria. In light of this religious framework, the social and moral history of ravaging and martial rape proves of major import for the theme of this essay collection, religion, feminism, and women's rights.

To be clear at the outset, my argument in this essay is not that religions in general are the cause and perpetuating mechanism of martial ravaging and rape. My position is that religions in and developing from the ancient Mediterranean and Near East are problematic to the extent that they support this aggression and the fear-inducing inequities of martial power by which this violence is conducted and perpetuated. The Abrahamic religions, Judaism, Christianity, and Islam, have historically been used to extend and buttress martial power, Judaism developing in part from the martial religious legacy in ancient Israel, Christianity from Hellenistic Judaism, and Islam since the early medieval period building from Judaism and Christianity. These religions are not alone in carrying the burden of martial power going back to antiquity, for the same is true of a number of polytheistic religions in this region that persisted through late antiquity. One Hellenized late antique martial ruler, for instance, used to boast that he was a son of Ares. On this basis, he commandeered and dominated girls, young women, and boys of ravaged peoples in Arabia and Ethiopia, a number of them to serve him, and the rest for his beneficiary supporters (Gaca, 2014, pp. 332–337). Yet, because the worship of Ares and other defunct gods and goddesses of war are no longer active in religious devotion and morality, they no longer motivate or serve as justification for martial outbreaks of ravaging aggression. The Abrahamic religions, however, are still very active worldwide in shaping popular devotion and morality. While this can be positive in many ways, it is seriously problematic when their embedded constructs of martial life-and-death power gain normative hold, for then it is not long before war ravaging or other martial aggression begins with a sense of divinely authorized entitlement against peoples considered ethno-religious enemies.

The close historical overlay of martial power on religion is such that at times the two can seem different names for the same ruthless social control, such as during the martial spread of Islam and of the Christian Crusades. Yet to identify religion as martial power would be too narrow and reductive, for religions in this region have also been a basis for trying to keep the exercise of this power at bay,[2] such as male Druids being exempt from war campaigns, and even to dismantle this power. An example of the latter effort includes the view in Judaism, Christianity, and Islam that the Lord God or Allah is a divine power of mercy and love, an idea worth keeping in mind as we turn to war ravaging and martial rape, where cruelty and anguished hatred claim divine authority and have the upper hand.

WAR RAVAGING, MARTIAL RAPE, AND ENSLAVEMENT: A RESEARCH SUMMARY

Populace-ravaging or ravaging warfare (*diarpazein, diripere, bazaz* [בָּזַז]) is a strikingly sex- and age-based practice that begins with the effort to massacre either all the fighting-age males or all the males, little boys and infants too, among targeted peoples, and that culminates in the rape and enslavement of girls and women, mainly young women. Martial rape is of two kinds. The first kind is lethal and exemplifies the martial power to kill. It is exercised as unrestricted gang rape directed mainly at the grown and mature women of a ravaged people. The second kind is a life-threatening and enslaving intimidation scheme directed mainly at girls and young women. This is the sex and age group sought out and wanted alive from the ravaged people to enrich the rewarded men and their dependents among their forces and beneficiary peoples (Gaca, 2014, pp. 306–307; 2015, pp. 281–291). This kind of martial rape exemplifies the enslaving martial power over human life, for here the power to kill is used as a suspended death threat hanging over ravaged and bereaved young female war-captives in order to exert an exploitative control over them and their sexuality, reproductive capacity, and other labor skills and talents (Gaca, 2016a; 2016b). The threat to kill can be activated if the girls and young women put up a fight.[3] Killing resistant war-captive girls and young women is meant to induce an unquestioning compliance from the rest of them and to underscore the false impression that they too are worthless and expendable, even though forcibly utilizing procreativity and other skills are pivotal to the building and maintenance of the martial lower echelons. Hence, the girls and young women are generally wanted alive. They are sought out to be slavish reproductive vessels, and to perform other labors considered women's work in martial societies, including forced prostitution.[4]

Historically, the men who have gained war-captive girls and young women by ravaging wars and the number they each gain has depended on whether their martial societies are monarchies, aristocracies, or brotherhoods. In monarchies, young female captives are the crown property of the king. In addition to keeping his lion's share, he distributes this largesse in war-captive females as he sees fit among his male elite and family members, including his own main wife or wives and daughters, in effect as open-ended loans to ensure their loyalty and obedience to him. This female crown property is revocable in case the recipients turn out insubordinate and disloyal. The king lets them know who is boss when he carries out a repossession. This monarchic ability to repossess and reallocate the women is well expressed in the martial theology of Israel. Because the men of Israel have become wayward, the Lord God declares, "I will give their women to others and their fields to conquerors" (Jer 8:10, cf. 6:14).

In aristocracies, oligarchic men, hostile to the custom of the kingly lion's share, attempt through agreements among themselves as a kind of class of princely officers to hoard the female war-captives in groups among themselves, as exemplified in Homeric epics (*Il.* 2.224-42). In the *Iliad,* for example, the insubordinate Achilles is furious over the reclaiming of his war-captive Briseis by Agamemnon to punish him for his insubordination. To Achilles, the Greeks are a martial aristocracy. Briseis belongs to him and in his crew of female captives, yet Agamemnon is acting like a big king by repossessing her.

Brotherhoods, by contrast, are hostile both to the monarchic lion's share and to aristocratic hoarding. Each man in the forces should get his own female war-captive as a spear-conquered wife or domestic inmate, rather as though war-captive girls and young women should be like army-issue gear doled out to each man in the brotherhood as recipients. Just as every man a satchel, so too a coerced female war-captive to call his own wife and to treat as his servile attendant.

Hence, in ancient monarchies, the kings remained the ultimate owners of female captives and could repossess and reallocate them, but in aristocratic hoarding this was not so. The oligarchic male elite themselves sought to be the owners without monarchic oversight and strings attached. In ancient brotherhoods, such as among the pre-monarchic Israelites, every man should get his own spear-conquered girl or woman before any man gets two or more.[5] The martial culture of raping and enslaving ravaged young female war-captives thus was historically embedded in and mediated through the divergent types of martial governance in antiquity and female war-captive distribution patterns. These girls and young women were enslaved crown-property labor pools owned and managed by kings, concubines of aristocratic men or crews of enslaved laborers attendant on aristocratic men and their families, and individual spear-conquered wives or domestic inmates in brotherhoods.[6] In aristocracies and brotherhoods, they could also be forced slave prostitutes for lower echelon men.[7]

As seen in the following historical sketch from ancient and modern examples, there are two basic components of populace-ravaging warfare. On the one hand, there is a systematic effort to kill the males of targeted people, either the fighting-age males en masse or all the males, boys and infants too. On the other hand, there is a systematic effort of martial rape, the lethal or enslaving penetrative sexual aggression against captured females.[8] Modern testimonials about ravaging techniques bring the ancient evidence into clearer focus, such as the *Iliad* and Xenophon's *Anabasis*. Conversely, the ancient accounts disclose the historical roots of this organized violence and cross-generational imposition of martial customs on human society through armed takeover, occupation, and colonization, girl after girl and woman after woman among the ravaged and enslaved female war-captives who stayed alive. The sex- and age-based aggression of ravaging is organized and consistent from antiquity to modernity, and it indicates that the enslavement of war-captive girls and women is a fundamental purpose of ravaging warfare over this extensive time. In this sketch, I concentrate mainly on ravaging incidents that feature the killing of fighting-age males, but I do touch upon and point out several incidents that feature the killing of the entire male lineage, boys and infants too.

In the breakdown of the former Yugoslavia in 1992, as the young Bosnian Muslim woman Emina states, "The [Serbian] Chetniks entered our village with their tanks and armored cars. . . . They killed men between the ages of fourteen and sixty right off."[9] Emina's account describes one fundamental practice of ravaging warfare, the systematic killing of fighting-age males. The Greek historians Herodotus, Thucydides, Polybius, and Diodorus further show that the killing of fighting-age males, including their capture and slaughter in cold blood, is one recurrent method of ravaging warfare from the Persian and Peloponnesian Wars onward to the early Roman empire. Roman and later Greek historians confirm that this is one standard practice of ravaging warfare through to the end of the Byzantine era in 1453 CE (Gaca, 2010, pp. 128–156; Gaca, 2014, p. 306).

Like Emina, the Roman historian Livy states that males in the Balkans who were fourteen or fifteen to sixty years old considered themselves fighting-age (26.25.11). Justin's epitome of the Hellenistic history by the Roman historian Pompeius Trogus similarly states that sixty years of age was the conventional upper limit of fighting-age men in Macedonia under Philip II (*Epitome* 11.6.6). Sixteen is further attested as the lower age limit of males sought out for massacre among enemy ethno-religious groups in the heavily ravaging 1912–1913 Balkan Wars (Carnegie, 1993/1913, p. 180). The youthful age is not fixed because the determinant of being fighting age is the onset of pubescence. When ravaging martial aggressors seek to kill the targeted group of fighting-age males, they do not ask the younger-looking captured males how old they are or consult birthdate records to decide which of them to slaughter. They check whether the male captives have developed armpit hair. Even if their faces are still without any shadow of a beard, those with hair under their arms are fighting age and are to be slaughtered.

The social customs of identifying this wide age range of males as fighting age, between fourteen and sixteen to sixty years old, and the martial ravaging project to slaughter them among targeted peoples are an indication that ravaging martial massacre in recent and modern times has a historical continuity with antiquity. The systematic killing of this age range of males as fighting age was not separately invented in the Persian and Peloponnesian Wars during the fifth century BCE, the twentieth-century Balkan Wars of 1912–1913, and Bosnia in the early 1990s. Rather, this is one consistent pattern of ravaging martial aggression, and it indicates that there is an ingrained culture of extreme organized violence from antiquity to modernity in which the martial power over life and death is exercised in structured and recurrent ways.

Unrestricted lethal gang rape or other sadistic and injurious rape is the historical norm against women of the targeted people not wanted alive, mainly the grown and mature ones.[10] Intimidating death threats but generally survivable practices of single-assailant or limited serial rape are the historical norm against girls and young women wanted alive, many to be treated as coerced reproductive vessels. After the massacre of the fighting-age men in Emina's village, the "Chetnik" or Serbian martial forces rounded up Emina and other Bosnian Muslim girls and women and started stripping, beating, and subjecting them to martial rape in public and in detention camps, killing a number of them. They kept others alive to forcibly impregnate them with offspring raised to identify with being Serbian (Gaca, 2016a; Stiglmayer, 1994, p. 97; UN Document S/1994/674/230i). These forms of extreme sexual violence against girls and women constitute martial rape and are the second fundamental component of ravaging warfare.

War ravaging is described in the Homeric *Iliad*, an epic that is an oral composition in origin, is rooted mainly in early Iron Age Greek cultural memory, and precedes the advent of ancient Greek historiography, that is, the Greek invention of writing historical narratives.[11] As stated in the *Iliad*, by one kind of ravaging, the aggressor forces "kill the men (*andres*)," the fighting-age males, and "lead away the children and women" (*Il.* 9.593–594). This early portrayal of the two-stage ravaging procedure highlights only one aspect of the second stage, the leading away or commandeering abduction of women and children seized alive. In the *Iliad*, however, martial rape is acknowledged as part of the second stage in a provocative euphemism as part of Nestor's order to the Greek forces: "Let no man go home until each one has slept with a Trojan wife" to avenge Paris's taking of Helen.[12]

The orders to carry out martial rape are further reflected in a soldiers' oath in the *Iliad* to uphold a ceasefire. The Greek and Trojan forces have sworn this oath, and its organized violence applies to the Trojans once the ceasefire is broken by a transgressor on their side. "Let the women" of the Trojan enemy "be sexually penetrated (*migeien*)" by the Greek forces upon carrying out the male massacre of Trojans (3.301–302), here a massacre of the entire male lineage, as further discussed below. Hector and Priam likewise are blunt, not euphemistic, in foreshadowing the extreme violence of the aggravated sexual assault in store for girls and women of ravaged Troy (Gaca, 2015, pp. 286–288). While enslaving martial rape against girls and women wanted alive is emphasized in the *Iliad*, lethal martial rape is tersely acknowledged in this epic too.[13] Starting with Herodotus, Greek and Roman historians confirm that women not wanted alive were tormented and killed, often through lethal gang rape, such as mature adult and elderly women (Hdt. 8.33, Tac. *Hist.* 3.33, Paus. 10.22.4).

Nestor reinforces his martial rape order by threatening to kill any Greek forces who would try to take to their ships and go home instead (2.354–359). This threat offers a concise insight into the martial power of superiors to have disobedient inferiors summarily killed. Here the threat is directed not at female war-captives through death-threat rape and domination by ravaging forces, but at the forces by one of their own superiors to stop them from acting on their own non-compliant volition. The Greek forces have just rushed to their ships because they want to go home and forget about ravaging Troy, but Nestor stops them cold. He will have them killed if they try.

Ravaging is also represented in the *Anabasis,* the late classical-period memoir by Xenophon (ca. 428–354 BCE) about his experience as a Greek mercenary soldier for the Persian Cyrus the Younger. Xenophon reaffirms that still in his day each member of his Greek mercenary forces insisted on keeping at least one personal war-captive woman or child as his coerced bedmate from the war-captives they ravaged recently (*neôsti*), the prettier the more likely to be chosen for this purpose (4.1.8, 4.1.14).[14] The ravaging that Xenophon and his men carried out is one basic reason why Carduchian men, an ethnic branch of the Armenians, took their women and children with them in their flight up the mountains to escape from Xenophon and his ravaging mercenaries. The Greek forces wanted the children and women of the Carduchians, and mainly young women and girls, both as personal slaves to keep and as coerced objects of their sexual desire, and others as slaves to sell (6.6.38). To gain them required killing Carduchian men, and to try to stop this commandeering required killing Greek mercenaries (4.1.10, 4.1.22). The killing of Carduchian men and enslavement of their women and children was not systematic because these mountain men, women, and children were nimble and effective in their defense strategies, such as rolling boulders down in an effort to crush and block the mercenaries' way.

As borne out by these historical examples, the two foundational practices of populace-ravaging warfare are shown to be male massacre of the targeted people, fighting age or all ages, and martial rape against the girls and women, thereby killing them or keeping them as live slaves to exploit.[15] Martial rape is consequently not random, anarchic, or the result of seizing moments of opportunity. It is included as part of the ravaging orders and pacts in the *Iliad* (2.354–359, 3.297–301), and it is understood as a standard procedure of ravaging in Deuteronomy (21:14, 28:30).

This commandeering of girls and women through death-threat martial rape is recognized in the *Iliad* as female enslavement, "taking the day of freedom away" from the girls and women of a ravaged people. What is more, ravaging female enslavement is a stated purpose of war ravaging in this epic.[16] From antiquity to modernity, to ravage their people and abduct the young women and girls under the threat of killing them for resisting has marked the beginning of their being treated as slaves. A number of them are actually called slaves, but they need not be called slaves to be martially enslaved. The danger, pain, and humiliation of being held captive, subjected to aggravated sexual assault, and forced to perform unwanted labors under the threat of death for resisting is paradigmatic enslaving treatment, as Weil and Patterson have persuasively argued.[17] By my argument, further, the death-threat workings of enslavement were well understood in antiquity as historically fundamental to how martial societies were hierarchized and run. As with Nestor, superiors wielded the martial power of life and death with impunity over inferiors and could have them tormented and killed for failing to do as they were told with the required submissiveness and loyalty. For example, when the headmen and elders in a city surrendered to the Assyrian king Ashurnasirpal II (reigned 883–859 BCE), they acknowledged that he held this power by embracing his feet and beseeching him, "If it is your pleasure, slay! If it is your pleasure, let live! That which your heart desires, do!"[18]

The martial power to kill slavish inferiors if they fail to remain subordinate and pleasing to their superiors was known to the Romans as "the power of life and painful death" (*vitae necisque potestas*), and it has been a pervasive and defining feature of martial power since antiquity. Though presently understood mainly as belonging to sovereign monarchs in Western history and to fathers in early Roman law and legend (Nyquist, 2013, pp. 193–226), this power has not been left solely in their hands. By the Iron Age, men in martial aristocracies and brotherhoods have wielded this power over the war-captive women and children in their possession, including children fathered by them through martial rape. This made men autocratic, personal tyrants over the war-captive women and children in their possession (Gaca, 2016b). This power is best known on the historical record from Roman *patria potestas*, where the man in principle can have his wife and children killed with impunity for being insubordinate, but it is not limited to Roman society and not restricted to antiquity.[19]

The power over life and death in manifold guises is basic to how martial society has been run since the emergent Iron Age, and it has given societies so run their fearsome and oppressive tenor. For example, in Roman armies, a general could kill every tenth man among his contingents judged insubordinate or ineffective so that the ninety percent left alive learned to mind their place and follow orders without question (Frontinus, *Strat.* 4.1.37). Another clear example from the late Roman republic is the Celtic martial custom of torturing and killing the man who showed up last when a mustering of forces was called. This was done in full view of the main troops (Caesar, *BG* 5.56.2). What still needs recognition is that this martial power since antiquity has been wielded over war-captive girls and women by the men to whom they are distributed. Here the martial power over life has largely taken the form of raping to forcibly impregnate female war-captives in order to populate the lower and relatively poor echelons of martial society with male and female offspring conditioned from birth to be treated as slaves and to show unconditional loyalty and obedience to those with martial power over them.[20] Even if those held under this power have not all been called slaves, they have been enslaved as lower echelon forces or as spear-conquered wives, concubines, and prostitutes, for they were pressed into doing things they would choose not to do if they were free from the threat of being tormented or killed with impunity by their martial masters for being insubordinate, not following their dictates. This threat and the behaviors it extorts from those under this domination are basic to enslaving martial power, be it raped and terrorized girls or grown Greek forces being impelled to stay and ravage Troy because otherwise their superiors will see to it that they are killed.

At this point I have explained the organized violence of war ravaging, its techniques and aims of mass killing and martial rape, and the enslaving terror of the power by which it runs. Now let me sketch the place of ravaging and the mindset of martial power in the broader history of armed conflict. Ravaging is historically one form of warfare and expression of martial power, albeit a prevalent one in and since antiquity. Not all armies and not all soldiers practiced this kind of warfare or committed martial rape when they took up arms, just as today not all soldiers and armies practice warfare in this manner. In antiquity, for instance, many fought to defend their own peoples and neighboring allies from being ravaged, so long as the allied coalitions of regional defense were still intact and neither bribed into being complicit with the ravagers nor intimidated by their wielding of martial power. As ancient military defense policy, children and mothers were the ones "for whom wars are customarily taken up" to protect them from ravaging martial aggressors (Justin, 26.2.3; Synes., *Calv. enc.* 21.9–11). Soldiers on the defense prided themselves on being modest but effective and smart (Aesch., *Sept.* 447–452, 473–480). They defended their own and allied peoples, female relations especially, from ravaging predations and from surrendering and undergoing forced labor under martial power. By contrast, martial aggressors were braggart soldiers crowing about their rich plunder in female war captives and the other ways they were made to feel like status warriors in martial society ("Hybrias," *PMG* 26, Alciphron *Epist.* 2.34.1–3).

Further, ravaging does not exhaust the forms of populace-targeting aggression run by martial power. Another form should be distinguished from ravaging and likewise has roots in the ancient Near East and Mediterranean. It is a campaign to slaughter a people in their entirety regardless of sex or age, best known from the book of Joshua as martial *herem* (e.g., Josh. 10:40, 11:11), and thus it removes the young female-plundering stops on killing that are in place in ravaging. This policy, memorably summed up in Deuteronomy 20:16 as leaving no creature that breathes alive among the people under attack, humans and domesticated animals alike, is not only a Semitic martial practice in antiquity, despite the common view that it has this circumscribed range (Zorn in Nadali and Vidal, 2014, p. 88). Total slaughter is also known in the Indo-European martial sphere, as is clear from the Athenian-led Thracian aggression against Mycalessos.[21] This form of martial aggression against targeted peoples is historically rarer in antiquity than the recurrent practice of ravaging (e.g., Polyb., 5.111.1–7; Caes., *BG* 7.28.4), notwithstanding its twentieth-century prominence as a practice by the Nazis in the Holocaust and by the Hutu in the latter weeks of their genocide of Tutsis in Rwanda (Human Rights Watch/Africa, 1996, p. 41). Total slaughter is not ravaging, for the commandeering and traumatic isolating of live young female captives for exploitative sexual and other purposes is integral and fundamental to the mass killings that inform the ravaging war norm.

War ravaging in antiquity was not understood as tantamount to massacre. This is a valuable corrective to present tendencies to merge ravaging and total slaughter together, portray incidents of war ravaging as reducible to massacre (e.g., Carlton, 1994; Katz, 1994), and treat the war-captive girls and women kept alive as though they never existed. In antiquity, ravaging was known as slaughter and captivity, and "a big slaughter" (e.g., Hdt., 7.170.3) and "plentiful captivity" (e.g., Theoph., *Chron.* 257) when the ravaged people had numerous women and children (Gaca, 2014, p. 327; Procop., *Goth.* 6.21.38).[22] The captivity involved a doing of "incurable" harms so painful to the women and girls kept alive that a number of them pleaded to be killed, but they were denied this release (Procop., *Goth.* 5.9.24). Those in charge wanted them alive and subservient.[23] A number of mature adult and elderly women, however, were tormented and killed, often through lethal gang rape (Hdt., 8.33; Tac., *Hist.* 3.33; Paus., 10.22.4). The women and girls seized as captives had their clothing torn off as a lead-in to the rapes, such that even the stripping could cause injuries.[24] They were then allocated by contingent or tent among the martial forces (Eur., *Tr. Wom.* 28–31; Din., *Demosth.* 24). Martial rape and ravaged female captivity are thus unambiguously acts of war as well as fundamental aspects of martial power historically and socially.

The compulsory procreative workings of death-threat martial rape are key to what has made war ravaging seem productive since antiquity to the many ethno-religious groups who have run and gained from ravaging operations. From an upper-echelon martial perspective in antiquity, this practice helped create and populate the lower echelons with slavish and exploitable human resources, female and male alike. This seemed desirable to those in charge or on the ascendant in the martial running of society, but only so long as the underlings remained loyal and obedient to their superiors.[25] From a lower-echelon perspective, to gain young female war-captives and sexually use them in this way provided fresh infusions to enrich the men and their dependents who gained them, and to augment their groups and ethno-religious identities with offspring born and raised to identify with their conquerors (e.g., App., *Hann.* 244–246).

Since antiquity, martial forces have also been utilized to threaten to ravage peoples unless they surrender and become forced laborers for their conquerors (Deut. 20:10–14; cf. Hdt. 2.102.1–106.5), and to further threaten them with ravaging upon their surrender unless they remained subordinate. When a people surrendered to the coercive terms of martial power, they did so in order to forestall being liquidated through the mass killing, rape, and abduction characteristic of being ravaged, and thus to retain what they still could of their former kin groups and culture. Nonetheless, they were still drawn into being martially run and held under the ravaging threat. For example, their fighting-age males could bring ravaging punishment down on their people for the insubordination of ignoring a summons to participate in a martial campaign. This is exemplified in the punitive ravaging by Israelite forces against the town of Jabesh-gilead, a town in league with the Israelite brotherhood. According to Judges, the men of Jabesh-gilead failed to show up for the Israelite martial call-out to take exact vengeance on the Benjamites of Israel for the lethal gang rape of the Levite's concubine.[26] In response, the Israelite forces killed the men, grown women, and boys of all ages in the Jabesh-gilead. The Israelite forces also seized and handed over the war-captive virgin girls of Jabesh-gilead as spear-conquered wives to the remnant Benjamite forces who still survived, now widowed and on the verge of extinction, but reconciled to the Israelites (Judg. 21:1–15).

Similarly, punitive ravaging is in store when a surrendered people rebel against being treated as slavish forced laborers, whether as lower-echelon martial forces or in other sorts of toil. For instance, the forces of the Persian king Darius ravaged his subject Greek city of Miletus in 494 BCE. Darius in his own eyes was entitled to do this, for he was quelling a large-scale slave revolt. Men of Miletus led by their puppet tyrant Aristagoras helped instigate the rebellion of Ionian Greek cities against him. The Persian kings regarded the Ionian and Aeolic Greeks as slaves they inherited in their paternal lineage (*patrôioi douloi*, Hdt. 2.1.2), passed down to them since their conquest by Cyrus. Darius punished the defiant Ionians accordingly by making a punitive ravaging example of Miletus. He had his forces ravage Miletus, kill all the captured fighting-age males, commandeer the girls and boys, and castrate the boys.[27] Ravaging thus functions as a stunning punitive instrument to intimidate subjects into believing that there is no way to get out from under martial power. To try is to go the way of Jabesh-gilead and Miletus.

In the martial running of societies since antiquity, the forces trained in ravaging aggression acquired formidable techniques of organized violence. In addition to arson methods, the men learned, as a version of martial arts, how to kill, rape, and plunder a targeted people. For a few specifics, this includes how to slash the carotid arteries of men and how to grab women's breasts with clenching force so as to overwhelm them with pain and make raping them a cinch (Stiglmayer, 1994, p. 157; Vranic, 1996, pp. 93, 113). Hence ravaging was the product of group male training. Their superiors worked to instill this behavior and to keep it under their control. They sought to discipline these men to ravage targeted peoples strictly on authorized orders, and to punish them and their women and children to the extreme of ravaging them if they proved insubordinate in the face of such orders. This punitive treatment discloses that these forces and their dependents were violable to the point of being killed and raped en masse for disobedience. This means that they and their children and women were treated as slaves under martial power. The men were not bold warriors acting on their own volition. In theory, then, ravaging forces were supposed to be unconditionally obedient to their superiors, rather like kill dogs, letting loose their ravaging aggression only when given their go-ahead, and required to do so without hesitation when given this nod.[28] Martial religious rites and beliefs have historically played a critical part in this control project to mandate, justify, and regulate martial ravaging, rape, and enslavement, as I now argue.

THE RELIGIOUS FRAMEWORK OF RAVAGING AND MARTIAL RAPE

Ravaging forces in and since antiquity have been taught to believe that their leading gods witness, endorse, and even issue their ravaging orders. The chain of command goes beyond the men's mortal superiors in the martial hierarchy. The superiors are the ones with access to this divine mandate, which the god or gods either witness or issue as an order. As a result, war ravaging has long been imbued with religious and theological beliefs and rites, as is already recognized for biblical *herem* or total slaughter (Stern, 1991). In this martial religious belief system, the ultimate authority, approval, and efficacy of ravaging belong on the divine level, and its power is believed to derive from the gods.

For example, in Deuteronomy 20:10–18 the Lord God transmits through his prophet Moses the commands and conditions under which Israelite martial forces are to carry out ravaging and total slaughter—Deuteronomy 20:10–15 for the Israelite martial ravaging policy and 20:16–18 for the *herem* policy. Further, in Numbers 31, Moses again mediates the Lord God's orders when he summons Israelite martial fighters to a ravaging war against the Midianites. To explore Deuteronomy 20:10–15 more closely, in ancient Israelite martial society, the coercion and enticement to ravage targeted peoples are treated as the authentic word of the Lord God. Unlike *herem,* which applies to the lands claimed as Israelite patrimony, ravaging applies to resistant cities at a distance: "When you draw near to a city to fight against it, offer terms of peace to it. And if its answer to you is peace and it opens to you, then all the people who are found in it shall do forced labor for you and shall serve you. But if it makes no peace with you, but makes war against you, then you shall besiege it; and when the Lord your God gives it into your hand you shall put all its males to the sword. But the women and the little ones, the cattle, and everything else in the city, all its spoil, you shall take as booty for yourselves; and you shall enjoy the spoil of your enemies, which the Lord your God has given you."[29] The Lord God not only orders and spells out the procedure of ravaging for distant cities that resist surrendering to martial power. He is also the one who "gives" the besieged city "into the hand" of the attacking Israelite forces.

To turn to some of earliest known ancient religious roots of ravaging and martial rape, the *Iliad* offers a polytheistic Greek understanding of martial power and the coercive rituals that surround its practice from the top down in the martial hierarchy. In this epic, "the best (*aristoi*) of the Trojans and Achaean Greeks" as princes (*basileis*) are the ones empowered to establish a ceasefire for a winner-take-all duel between Paris and Menelaus. At the top, the Greek and Trojan elite agree among themselves to a retaliatory ravaging of their forces and their forces' dependent women and children in the event of ceasefire treachery from the Greek or Trojan side. The overlords and princes, all the honchos, make and formalize this agreement, Agamemnon and Odysseus by name on the Greek side (3.270, 274). Agamemnon as Greek overlord is the one who calls upon Zeus, Helios, and chthonic gods to be its guard-keeping witnesses (3.280). The elder Trojan king Priam is not present with the Trojan martial elite at this decision-making, but he is summoned from the city and he participates in rites formalizing the agreement (3.259–262). Thus, the pact is made, struck among the overlords and their martial elite and the gods as guarding witnesses.[30]

The Greek and Trojan forces are not consulted or allowed to offer any deliberative input into the terms of the pact, even though its terms put everyone they hold dear at risk, including their own persons. The retaliation for breaking the ceasefire is imposed as binding on both forces and their dependent women and children—the latter an otherwise little noticed auxiliary group on site in the Greek camp. The forces are pressed into rituals to show their compliance. Through martial communion and oath-taking, they uphold that they and their dependent women and children must be punished by ravaging if anyone on their side transgresses the ceasefire. Ladling wine into their cups, each member of the forces, Greek and Trojan alike, pours a wine libation on the ground, and they each keep saying an oath (*eipesken*), perhaps a group chant or a turn-taking solo declaration. They swear that the men and boys on the side with any treacherous agents in their midst must be killed and that the men's female bedmates or wives (*alochoi*) must be raped by the forces who uphold the ceasefire. As they put it, the warriors on the double-crossing side and their children (*tekea*) must have their brains spilled out just like the wine they are pouring in libation (3.297–301). These brain-bashed children are strictly boys, as Agamemnon later makes clear (*Il.* 6.55–60). But the punitive aggression does not stop there. As the main body of men further swear, the wives of the fighters with transgressors in their midst must be "copulated with (*migeien*)" or "dominated and tamed (*dameien*)" by the forces on the righteous side that upholds the oath. Thus, the vowed retaliation includes killing the boys and raping the wives among the men's female dependents.

This soldiers' oath is not a pact among free men given a genuine choice, but among forces treated slavishly under martial power to ensure their unconditional obedience. The men on the Greek and Trojan sides and their dependents are assumed violable to the point of having their male lineage killed in its entirety and their female affiliates subjected to martial rape. These are the religiously authorized terms of Camp Martial in and since antiquity, as first attested in the *Iliad*. You and your people are pressed to enter, and you are not allowed to leave unscathed. For those held under the martial power of life and death, men have to accept that they, their sons, and mature female affiliates can be exterminated for insubordination in their midst, the women by lethal gang rape. Further, their young female dependents, including their sisters and daughters, can be seized and possessed by angry kings, aristocrats, and brotherhoods' fellow elite when the men have not followed orders. Thus, while the incidents of Jabesh-gilead and Greek Miletus show the martial forces of ravaging wrath unleashed, the soldiers' oath provides the added insight that lower-echelon men could be put through rites to solemnly swear that they accept and uphold this dire treatment for being insubordinate.

As a result of the soldiers' oath, ravaging with an aim to kill the males of all ages becomes the divinely mandated outcome for Troy once Pandarus, a Lycian archer and Trojan ally, breaks the ceasefire and inflicts a non-fatal thigh wound on Menelaus from afar (*Il.* 4.85–147). From a martial religious perspective, this makes the mass killing and martial rape envisioned against Troy seem righteous and inexorable, and it is supposed to look that way even to the Trojan forces (Gaca, 2015, pp. 286–288).

The soldiers' oath in the *Iliad* thus highlights that the threat of ravaging is historically pivotal to making people slavish under martial power, that is, violable through the sex-and-age patterns of being killed and raped en masse for acting against authorized orders. While the men and their auxiliary women and children are wanted alive from an upper echelon perspective, so long as they remain obedient, disobedient men are to be eliminated like mad dogs, and their women and children have no standing as innocent bystanders or civilians with immunity. The men's attachés of children and women are collateral to ensure the men's compliance with orders authorized by their superiors and gods.[31] When that insurance does not work, the women and children are there to be violated and killed or enslaved again once their targeted males are massacred, just as in Miletus and Jabesh-gilead.[32] Hence ravaging is a linchpin in the martial power over life and death. It functions as a predatory way to acquire and terrorize girls and women from external peoples into being reproductive and submissive slaves in martial society. It also serves as a threat of imminent punishment held over men and their dependents unless the men follow their orders, a punishment the men can be pressed through rituals to swear they deserve, as seen in the soldiers' oath.

Perhaps the most insidious aspect of religious martial power is the cunning twist it gives to love and bonding, core traits of human decency, by turning them into an incentive to rape and kill. If you love anyone else enough to risk your life for them, then under martial power you can be manipulated to kill and rape—rape if you are male. Men and boys have mainly been the ones worked over by this religious martial power in the martial running of society, perhaps because martial rape is a pivotal function of ravaging.[33]

Even today, the threat to men who resist and their loved ones is no hoax. The retaliation can take the form of killing resistant men or raping their sisters for refusing to join the martial call-out to ravage the people targeted as ethno-religious hostiles. As also noted by the Bosnian Muslim woman Kadira, "There were three [local Serbian] men I knew, they're dead now, they refused; they didn't want to go along with it," the assigned massacre and rapes of neighboring Bosnian Muslims, "and so they [Serbian paramilitaries] killed them" (Stiglmayer, 1994, p. 120). So too in the 1912 and 1913 Balkan Wars: "An Arab Christian soldier of the Gallipoli army, . . . when asked why he had taken part in these atrocities, forbidden by his religion, replied confidentially in Adrianople, 'I did as the others did. It was dangerous to do otherwise. We had the order first to pillage and burn, then kill all the men'" (Carnegie, 1993/1913, pp. 133–134).

Similarly, when the young Serbian man Rade refused to take part in ravaging his Bosnian Muslim neighbors, Serbian paramilitaries seized his twelve-year-old sister Zeljka and sent her to the rape camp populated primarily by Bosnian Muslim girls and young women, including the seventeen-year-old Mirsada, a friend of Rade and Zeljka from the same village. As stated by Mirsada, "The [Serbian fighters] arrived in our village, Kalosevic. They wore masks, and White Eagle insignia on their uniforms . . . I could see from my window how they rounded up people. They dragged my neighbor [Rade], a Serb, and his entire family out of the house. As he was not a member of the Serbian militia and had refused to kill Muslims and Croats, they took his 12-year-old sister Zeljka to the camp."[34] This cautions against seeing martial rape as a manifest sign that male sexuality has naturally been rape-oriented since prehistory. If men rushed to rape women and girls en masse, there would be no need to coerce and manipulate them in this way, using their own female dependents as sexually violable collateral to impel them to ravage and rape other men's women and girls on command.

The intensity of religious martial coercion also suggests that the men generally found martial aggression a "no exit" job imposed on them through martial power, not a meaningful enterprise worth the risks. If the men were satisfied with their work as ravaging martial assailants, their overlords would not have needed to work in league with priests, prophets, and gods to develop strategies of counter-ravaging threats to stop them from rebelling or defecting.[35] A number of Israelite men, for example, if given a choice, would have preferred a safe and secure family, house, and vineyard (e.g., Deut. 20:5–7), just as Greek forces would have rather gone home. This simple and peaceable way of life is hard to attain when your own and neighboring societies are martially held and run, everyone in the lower echelons violable by their own wrathful leaders and gods and those of rivals if they try to say no to martial power.

As another revealing part of the martial religious outlook, Deuteronomy 21:14 recognizes that sexual copulation was rape in ravaging spear-conquest marriage, and yet condones the practice. Deuteronomy 21:10–14 prescribes the rites that ravaged young female war-captives must go through to become forced wives, spear-conquered inmates of ravaging Israelite forces. For example, the young woman must have her head shaved, her nails clipped, and be given a month to mourn the deaths of her father and mother, and then the man can sexually copulate with her. Even though Deuteronomy allows this sexual activity, it makes no pretense that this was legitimate husband-wife sex of the conventionally recognized civil religious sort. In and since antiquity, legitimate marriage and its inauguration by wedding rites presume the approval of the parents and kin of the betrothed, not, as in the Israelite war ravaging of the Midianites and Jabesh-gilead, the massacre of the girls' parents and many of their relatives, and the forcible commandeering of their unmarried daughters by ravaging soldiers. Deuteronomy 21:14 does not try to conceal or make light of this fact. Instead it openly refers to the permitted copulation as the Israelite man debasing his slavishly treated wife by raping her. Similarly, the root signifies Shechem debasing Dinah by raping her (Gen. 34:2); the Benjamite thugs debasing the Levite's concubine by raping her (Judg. 19:25, 20:5), leaving her to die; Ammon debasing Tamar by raping her (1 Sam. 13:14); and martial forces of Assyrians and other martial groups debasing the women in Zion and the virgins in Judah by raping them (Lam. 5:11).

Spear-conquest marriage was wrong from the civil religious perspective in antiquity. It was pseudo-marriage, contrary to religion and custom, nothing that should ever be confused with joyful kin-approved weddings like that celebrated in the city at peace in *Iliad* 18.490–496. In these traditional marriages of the civil religious sort, genuine love-making and partnership remained both a viable option and the preferred kind of interaction between wives and husbands.[36] By contrast, martial rape that posed as marriage was from a Greek religious perspective tantamount to a ravaging assault on Aphrodite herself. It was the behavior of a "soldier religiously wronging the marriage bed (or spouse), a ravager of the goddess Aphrodite," as the Hellenistic Greek poet Lycophron puts it. This phrase aptly conveys the outrage in and since antiquity about seizing daughters as war-captives, revoking their religiously ordained marital birthright, and laying waste their procreative and regenerative community obligations in order to make them reproduce ethno-religious martial enemies through spear-conquest rape and enslavement.[37] Deuteronomy 21:14 recognizes this sexual wrong by referring to it as debasing rape, yet at the same time it glosses over the wrong by condoning it. It would only prohibit Israelite men from selling their spear-conquered wives as coin-transacted slaves to other buyers—the ravaged girls and women the Israelites rape they have to keep. By maintaining this position, Deuteronomy shows its martial religious hand by accepting that the sexual copulation between Israelite forces and their ravaged young spear-conquered inmates constituted a normative rape culture in which the girls had to acquiesce to survive.[38]

To appreciate this moral compromise in Deuteronomy, consider a modern example of ravaging spear-conquered marriage as experienced by the Tutsi Ancille of Rwanda. Ancille was twenty-three years old when about forty Hutu militia broke into her family home and killed her four brothers and her mother in front of her. This is the same technique of ravaging as that used against the Midianites and Jabesh-gilead—killing of grown, sexually active women like Ancille's mother in addition to killing all the males. At the time, Ancille was engaged to be married, but that was not allowed to matter anymore. One of the Hutu assailants claimed her as his own. Marking Ancille as his own, he "started hitting me," she states. "He cut me on the leg and told me that I was going to be his wife." Along with the hitting, the cutting in particular meant Ancille belonged to him. In civil society from antiquity to today, there is an extensive and gracious protocol of courtship for strangers to get to know one another and to pick spouses or have their parents pick them. None of that is at work in spear-conquest marriage. The Hutu man took Ancille to his house, locked her in during the day while he was gone, and forced her to be his so-called wife in the evening. That meant she had to cook for him and submit to him raping her upon his return, and there she remained until she was rescued by Tutsi resistance forces (Human Rights Watch/Africa, 1996, pp. 56–57). Deuteronomy acknowledges that the Israelite counterpart to this Hutu martial practice is rape, but nonetheless goes along with the practice.

The Peripatetic Greek philosopher and historian Clearchus (ca. 340–ca. 250 BCE) imparts added complexity to the ancient religious dimension of ravaging and martial rape in his account of Tarentine Greek martial aggression against the ethnically mixed Apulian-Messapian city of Carbina in southern Italy. This incident took place before, and likely soon before, a counter-ravaging incident inflicted on the Tarentine Greeks and their Rhegian allies in 473 BCE. Clearchus discloses a Hellenized religious disapproval of this incident, which contrasts with the Greek Tarentine religious viewpoint that their aggression was divinely mandated and justified.

Clearchus states that after the Tarentine Greek forces overthrew Carbina, they collected together girls, virgins, and young women of the Apulian-Messapian city, stripped them naked, and subjected them to martial rape in the most outrageous public setting imaginable—the very temple precincts of the gods in the city. They desecrated the city's sacred ground by turning it into a rape camp. The fighters, "after rounding up girls, virgins, and the women at their sexual peak into the sacred precincts of the inhabitants of Carbina, staged the bodies of these female captives naked for everyone to view during the daytime." Then, in a manner strongly suggestive of predatory wolf-men, each of the Tarentine soldiers "jumped as he wished" on this "luckless herd and sexually devoured the youthful beauty of their bodies that were rounded up," stimulated as the forces were by their "sexual desires."[39]

In Clearchus's ensuing narrative, the god Zeus retaliates against the Tarentine forces by striking them with his lightning bolt (Athen. 12.522e). This pious legend is Hellenized lore, and it discloses a strongly negative religious reaction to having your own own or allied people subjected to ravaging warfare. In the biggest martial slaughter of Hellenes known to Herodotus, Apulian-Messapian forces in 473 BCE retaliated in kind against the Tarentine forces and their Rhegian Greek allies for trying to forcibly uproot them from their cities in southern Italy (Hdt. 7.170.2–4), of which Carbina is known in some detail, thanks to this account by Clearchus.[40]

It is of great interest that this counterattack against Tarentine Greek forces by Apulian-Messapian forces was seen as a divine punishment from Zeus, father of the Olympians and dispenser of divine justice. This indicates that the southern Italian avengers of Carbina were Hellenized in their religious practices and beliefs to a degree, for southern Italy had numerous Greek colonies in addition to Tarentum, and the legend puts Zeus on the side of the Apulian-Messapians.[41] So furious were these forces as a Zeus-ordained lightning squad that they killed an untold number of Tarentines and three thousand of their allied Rhegian forces, according to Herodotus. This counterattack was likely in part a rescue mission to the extent that girls and women of Carbina may have been found and restored to any of their remnant families and people.[42]

Why was Zeus so angry? From the perspective of the Apulian-Messapian forces and of any survivors and allies of Carbina, Zeus punished the Tarentines for perpetrating the lawless "incurable" in Carbina. What the Tarentine forces did to these inhabitants, and especially to the girls, virgins, and women, was an atrocity that called for the perpetrators to be killed off before they could continue their effort to uproot other Apulian-Messapian communities, in which killings en masse and the martial rape and commandeering of young female inhabitants loomed large. This was why the flashing blue anger of Zeus was on their side.

However, from the perspective of the Tarentine Greek forces and their allies, and more broadly in terms of martial religious beliefs, ravaging was a basic, though ruthless, tool of warfare. Forces trained to ravage and commanded to carry it out exercised this aggression in response to their gods and in league with them. Seen from this perspective, Zeus punished the Tarentine depravity in using Carbina's sacred precincts for the mass rape of the rounded-up girls, virgins, and women in the city,[43] not for the sexual mauling itself—where they did it, not what they did.

What is more, from the aggressors' viewpoint, a divine impetus or nod of approval in advance was believed critical to attain in order to ravage a targeted people.[44] The deity or deities believed to authorize this aggression were then made beneficiary recipients of the plunder gained through ravaging. The designated beneficiary gods were given their share of the plunder, or of its monetary proceeds, as thank offerings by armies flush with young persons ravaged alive, female exclusively or in the majority, depending on whether boys among the ravaged peoples were kept as live captives or killed. Historically, youthful human captives were the most valuable plunder regularly seized, with oxen a distant second in value.[45] An offering that included captive human plunder, as opposed to monetary proceeds, thus would include young female (or mainly young female and some young male) war-captives handed over as temple personnel.[46] So standard was this protocol of thanking the gods that a conventional percentage of the plunder or its proceeds was regularly brought to the gods' sacred precincts, in Greek martial society the *dekatê* or ten percent, in pre-monarchic Israelite martial society a more humble two percent or less for the Lord God's share.[47] Thus, sacred temples were given their conventional cut of the ravaging windfall in the form of young captive personnel and/or monetary proceeds.

The Tarentine forces followed the religious protocol of thanking their gods for the ravaging aggression that they carried out. They dedicated a bronze representation of their ravaging conquest over Iapygian-Messapian inhabitants to Apollo at Delphi, and possibly even of the conquest of Carbina itself: an offering "from Tarentines, horses in bronze and women taken captive from Messapian people." As Pausanias adds, this sculpture dedicated to Apollo was the work of no low-profile figure in the making of religious art world of classical Greece, for the Argive Ageladas (ca. 520–450 BCE) was the sculptor. Ageladas was reputed to have taught Polyclitus, Myron, and Phidias, and he was repeatedly commissioned by Tarentines and others for dedicatory works, albeit mainly to commemorate athletic victories.[48]

Thus, in terms of the assumed arrangements between ravaging forces, superiors, and their deities, the Tarentine forces could not have gotten their hands on the girls, virgins, and women of Carbina without the backing of Apollo and Zeus. Yet the Hellenized Apulian-Messapian survivors and allies of Carbina could not have disagreed more, and as ostensible proof they could point to their bloody weapons slick from the big slaughter. The anger of Zeus was all theirs because of what the Tarentine forces did to the girls, virgins, women, and other devastated inhabitants of Carbina. Thus, there was no universal ancient consensus approving, or even accepting, the so-called law of the ravaging conqueror: "It is the perpetual law among all peoples that when a city is captured among those waging war, the bodies and goods of those in the city are the captors' own" (Xen. *Cyr.* 7.5.73).[49] Sharply divided views were the norm. Every triumph of the ravagers and their allies was a rage-inducing atrocity, an incurable injustice, to ravaged survivors and their allies.

That temples and their gods were beneficiaries from populace-ravaging makes it all the more striking that temples as sacred places became refuges where suppliants of the gods were in principle not to be ravaged (Sinn, 1993, pp. 88–109). For temples to be refuges to protect against ravaging appears to be a temple-based movement of dissent and resistance to ravaging and martial power. Temple personnel who were ravaged and enslaved themselves or descended from ravaged and enslaved ancestors made an effort to resist martial religious norms and to change society for the better from their limited corner of workable power. They turned sacred precincts into safe havens, or at least tried to do so. This is another reason why it is important not to regard martial religious power as the only voice of religion in the ancient Near East and Mediterranean.

In Hellenistic Judaism, the book of Judith makes the gravity of ravaging clear. It portrays this martial aggression as something that should never be done to your people, but only to those who have provoked your enmity because of their egregious wrongdoing to your people. In this tale, the Hivite enemies of Israel receive their due comeuppance from the Lord God when, as narrated in Genesis 34:25–29, Simeon and his brothers ravaged the Hivites in retaliation for the Hivite Shechem raping their sister Dinah. As stated with approval in Judith, to punish the Hivites for this wrongdoing, the Lord God surrendered the Hivite men to be massacred, princes and slaves alike, and "he gave their women as plunder and their daughters as captives," using Simeon and the other sons of Jacob as his instruments for this punitive purpose of ravaging male massacre and enslaving female acquisition (Jud. 9:3–4). But in Judith, nothing could be worse than to have your own peoples ravaged. The Lord as the omnipotent dispenser of martial power is beseeched by the people of Israel not to allow any more martial aggression to be done to them. They have suffered enough. Though the Israelites in Judith do not mention these incidents in their pleas, the suffering would include the destruction of Samaria and mass deportation of many in its populace by Assyrian forces in 722 BCE, and the Babylonian ravaging and ensuing martial occupation of Jerusalem in 597 BCE (e.g., Jer. 9:22, 12:3, 14:18), which led to the mass deportation of many of its inhabitants, some to Babylon (cf. Jer. 40:7), a deportation that took place in stages over the next decade, through 586 BCE. As stated in Judith, may the Lord not hand over the people of Israel to be ravaged, such that their women and children are turned into plunder and their ravaging enemies subject the people to the stinging "censure exultation" (*oneidismon epicharma*) that goes along with ravaging them (Jud. 4:8–12). Judith makes the gravity of ravaging clear by wishing this divine retribution only on enemies who have carried out such aggression against your own. The Babylonians are public enemy number one in this respect in Jeremiah 25:12: "Then after seventy years are completed, I will punish the king of Babylon and that nation, the land of the Chaldeans, for their iniquity, says the Lord God, making the land an everlasting waste."[50] Consequently, martial aggression against your own or allied peoples in and since antiquity has historically been an atrocity that could impel enmity to the degree of wanting enemy men, women, and children massacred, raped, and enslaved, and seeing this atrocity as divine justice. In response to Carbina, the Apulian-Messapian forces abhorred the Tarentines and their Rhegian allies for similar reasons, and they took it upon themselves to be Zeus's agents of avenging martial power.

CONCLUSION

Martial ravaging and rape can at first seem inexplicably pointless in its cruelty, too old to trace, and impervious to change. There it goes again. Coercive martial call-outs transform what was a civil society into a ravaging war zone, with the men driven by their summons to carry out the assigned killing, raping, and abducting of targeted ethno-religious peoples based on their age and sex, be it in the Troad, Jabesh-gilead, Miletus, Jerusalem, Bosnia, Darfur, and presently in Iraq and Syria. These outbreaks drive many into displaced refugee camps, another human encampment showing the effects of martial power where life is on edge and nothing is secure, not even subsistence needs and basic hygiene. Yet the close interconnections between martial ravaging, rape, and religion can and should be made intelligible and more open to effective challenge. This essay is a contribution toward this end.

Ravaging is the religious martial power over life and death conducting its cunning routine of mass murder, rape, and predominantly young female enslavement in a manner that has persisted from antiquity to modernity. Over this extensive time, there have been differences in religious rites to authorize this aggression, in the ethno-religious identities of the ravagers and ravaged, and in ideas about whether the gods witness or give the orders for ravaging assaults. The number of gods believed to approve ravaging has also gone down from many to the still competing monotheistic few, the Lord God tolerating no other gods before him and there is no god but Allah. Yet the human bodily aggression of ravaging remains consistent in its sex-and-age protocol: Kill the males, fighting-age or all the males down to the littlest baby boy, and kill a number of the grown females among targeted peoples, partly through lethal gang rape. Seize the girls and young women, and rape, enslave, and exploit them along with their ensuing slavish male and female progeny, as though the gods authorized this windfall in abject human resources and are pleased to receive their share. Ravaged young female war-captives are subjected to death-threat rape as the entry point of compulsory procreation in this making of "the poor you will always have with you" as instrumental and expendable lower echelons. But this seemingly inevitable inequity holds only so long as societies remain martially run or under the lingering inequitable influence of having been so run, for these societies need the *vulgus* for their martially run projects in life. As explained above, this martial religious idea informs the *Iliad,* the Hebrew Bible, and Greek historical sources. Its outlook persists in the modern martial practices of Christian Serbian Chetniks, Muslim Arab *janjaweed* in Darfur, and ISIS. Yet every ravaging strike has stimulated a response of outrage, hatred, and enmity from the remnant survivors, from the ones who knew and loved the abducted and the so-called expendables.

Martial rape, long a forbidden subject for open public discourse, has persisted from antiquity into recent and modern times while remaining covered in fear, shame, denial, and oblivion.[51] This concealment has helped allow ravaging and martial rape to persist, for martial rape has until now been the missing film reel showing the other half of ravaging warfare. Only by watching it do we clearly see the striking coercion of martial power. Martial rape does not show men of valor acting on their own volition to massacre and rape. It shows men held as slaves under martial power, coerced and enticed into being cruel and believing that their gods mandate that they have to behave this way to prevent killing and rape from befalling them and their dependents. This belief is not without due cause. As seen in the twentieth-century Balkan wars, men who refuse to take part in a ravaging martial call-out can be killed and the women and girls in their families can be raped and enslaved.

To comprehend and counter the martial religious practice and justification of mass killing and rape that have persisted from the ancient Mediterranean and Near East is a key step in the educative project to free society from martial power. A basic part of this project would be for contemporary religions with roots in this ancient legacy no longer to claim that martial ravaging has no religious overlay in the cultural and moral history of this region (e.g., Armstrong, 2014). Deuteronomy, for instance, is a repository of ancient martial religious norms of Israel, and this is no fringe writing in Judaism and Christianity. It condones spear-conquest martial rape as well as ravaging and total slaughter (*herem*).[52] To work toward becoming universally human-affirmative, Judaism, Christianity, and Islam should acknowledge their historical share in making massacre, martial rape, and slavish compulsory procreation seem not merely acceptable but divinely ordained. If we comprehend and hold ourselves accountable for the martial religious traditions of massacre and enslavement in our history, modern public policy and religions still active as vehicles of devotion and morality would become more effective at challenging martial religious aggression. We would also be better equipped to trace and resolve the ethno-religious hostilities that historically derive from and perpetuate mass murder, rape, and enslavement, and to dismantle the coercive martial power and insistence on religious conversion that sustain it. To reach this point would be a significant step toward attaining human dignity and freedom worldwide, starting with girls and women from the sexual and procreative ground up.

My study of martial rape, ravaging, and their religious framework accordingly seeks to encourage a heightened standard of respect for mutually consensual sexual relations and for the worth of human life by moving beyond the denials about martial rape to explain this lurid sexual aggression and its key functions in the religious lineaments of the martial power. In a just society, an informed female sexual volition would be a basic human right or similar cardinal principle of human decency. It would be interwoven into everyday life that raping any girl or woman is a sexual transgression against her will and status as an inviolable person, an act of *biazein,* that is, a bodily breaking and entering that is inherently wrong regardless of her creed or ethnicity. No religious teachings would prevail over this principle. It would be common knowledge learned from early childhood that for civil society to exercise any of its already articulated rights, such as the right to life, liberty, and happiness, requires in a fundamental way that all women and girls are free from rape and from any kind of sexual and reproductive coercion.

Similarly, to come to terms with war ravaging challenges the desensitized habit of thinking that men exist to kill or be killed in wars. This conditioning too is shaped by martial power, which has long marked fighting-age men as disposable. Lower-echelon men, many of them descended from ravaged women in their near or distant maternal lineage, are "persons of no importance" from an upper-echelon martial perspective when they are targeted and massacred as hostiles in an outbreak of martial ravaging (Carnegie, 1993/1913, p. 297). Their expendability is made unforgettable in the testimonials of men who survived being targeted with systematic massacre, for it is no cliché that they are slaughtered like sheep. Christo Dimitrov, a Bulgarian miller from Serres, was sixth in line to be massacred by Greek forces in the second Balkan War of 1913. Pretending to be dead after being struck with a blade four times, he could still tell by listening that more Bulgarian male compatriots were massacred that day: "I heard a sort of gurgling, like the sound which sheep make when they are being slaughtered, in the room next door" (Carnegie, 1993/1913, p. 293). Dimitrov's testimony is a reminder that societies run by martial power are inherently inequitable and produce ravaging wars. This is basic to what they do for their killing and their living. They are slavishly run and enslaving cultures of lower-echelon men put to killing men in quasi-herds, just as they are a culture of lethal and death-threat rape and exploitation imposed on war-captive girls and women.

Seen rightly, humble men like Dimitrov are irreplaceable persons, just like the women and girls, both in their families and villages and in human heritage as a whole. If given the choice, these people would rather have gone home and lived modest lives secure and respected in their family and community ties. The men did not want to be goaded into braggart soldier supremacy and pitted against one another like fighting cocks en masse in the use of acquisitive and retaliatory ravaging among martial monarchies, aristocracies, and brotherhoods. They were impelled into this role largely out of a religiously induced fear of divine and human retaliation against them and their dependents, as though ravaging on authorized orders were the only way to protect them.

Going back to antiquity, religious martial power has instated the template that human prosperity is inequitable, wasteful, and prone to violence, benefitting the rich at the expense of the frugal. People are still rewarded for using coercion and cunning to exploit lower-echelon persons of supposedly no importance, female and male alike. To respect every girl, woman, boy, and man as inviolable persons who matter would help make martial power and its lingering adverse effects passé and encourage the development of an inclusive prosperity.

NOTES

1. Gaca, 2008, 2010, 2011a, 2011b, 2012, 2014, 2015, 2016a, 2016b. Translations from Greek and Latin are my own unless otherwise indicated. Translations from the Hebrew Bible are generally my adaptations from RSV in light of the Hebrew. I generally cite Greek and Roman works by the abbreviation list in the *Oxford Classical Dictionary*, 4th edition 2012, but my abbreviations can be longer in the interest of clarity. Biblical references generally follow the *Chicago Manual of Style* online/16th edition.

2. This was one of the strong attractions to join the Druids in ancient Gaul, Caesar *BG* 14.1.

3. "Further, officers and soldiers violated several girls; they even killed one, named Agatha Thomas, the daughter of a gardener, because she resisted them." "One [Bulgarian] girl of eighteen named Matsa Anton Mancheva resisted stoutly and offered money. . . . The Greeks [i.e., ravaging Greek soldiers] took her money and still attempted to violate her. She resisted and was killed," Carnegie, 1993/1913, pp. 297, 307.

4. Slavish reproductive vessels, Gaca, 2016a, and see too Eur. *Troj. Wom.* 562–567, Nic. Damasc. fr. 53, and cf. Hdt. 6.138.1–4, Anna Comnena 15.7.1–2, Leo Chalcocondyles 64D (Migne).

5. Judg. 21:1–15, cf. 1 Sam. 30:24, and so too Cretan ravaging bands; Pritchett, 1991:366–368.

6. Monarchic crown-property, Batto 1974:26–28, Xen. *Cyr.* 5.1.1; aristocratic-owned crews of war-captive female laborers, Hom. *Od.* 9.39–42, 22.433–473 (here Odysseus's, the *dmôiai* put to death for being insubordinate and insolent to his family), and Gaca, 2015: 284–286 for the *Iliad* on the aristocrat-owned and managed female war-captive laborers seized from ravaging Troad communities and interned in the martial Achaean Greek camp. For slave (*andrapoda*) concubines of aristocratic men, see Chalcocondyles (*pallakidas apo andrapodôn*, 64D). On forced wives in brotherhoods, see Deut. 21:10–14, 23.18.9–16.

7. The use of female war-captives as forced slave prostitutes is historically important but not my focus in this essay, e.g., Gaca, 2015: 290–291; 2014: 339–349.

8. Gaca, 2010: 127–156; 2012: 85–89; 2014: 305–306; 2015: 281–284.

9. Stiglmayer, 1994, p. 97, and so too UN Document S/1994/674/230i. On Stiglmayer, 1994 as reliable source for Bosnian Muslim testimonials, see Wing, 1994 and Kent, 1997, pp. 1107-–1108.

10. Hdt. 8.33, Tac. *Hist.* 3.33, Paus. 10.22.4. Lethal gang rape, however, is not necessarily the only way to kill grown and mature women. They can be run through with a sword, as attested in antiquity, Ervin, 1963: pls. 21b, 27. They can also be burned alive, the latter first attested (to my knowledge) in the 1912–1913 Balkan Wars, Carnegie, 1993/1913, p. 279.

11. Gaca, 2011b, p. 114 n. 10.

12. Totten and Bartrop, 2009, pp. 219–221.

13. *Il.* 22, pp. 124–125, discussed in Gaca, 2016b.

14. In Xenophon's martial culture, the war-captive children kept as their personal sexual inmates could be girls or boys, *Anab.* 4.6.1–5, 7.4.7–11.

15. Gaca, 2010: 127–156, 2012: 85–89, 2014: 305–306, 2015: 281–284.

16. "Women" in the sense of "womenfolk" (*genos gunaikôn*) includes girls and women: Gaca, 2014, n. 1. Homeric evidence for targeting womenfolk to "take away their freedom": *Il.* 6.450–461, 8.164–6, 9.325–329, 9.590–594, 10.421–422, 15.496–499, 19.291–294, 20.193–194, *Od.* 9.39–42, cf. Gaca, 2008, p. 159 and Finley, 1998, p. 54. The revocation of freedom applied to little girls too, *Il.* 16.7–11 cf. Eur. *Tr. Wom.* 1089–1095; Gaca, 2008, pp. 145–171 and n. 57. The deliberate commandeering and subjugating of young female captives of ravaged peoples are also at work in post-exodus Israelite ravaging policy and practice: Deut. 20:10–15, Num. 31:1–54, Judg. 21:6–12. The repeatedly stated Greek martial aim in the *Iliad* to seize and enslave female captives is confirmed by the fact that all the specific references to war-captives in the Greek camp are to early adolescent girls (*kourai*) and women (*gunaikes*). Chryseis as *kourê*: *Il.* 1.98, 1.111; Briseis as *kourê*: *Il.* 1.275, 1.298, 1.336–337, 1.392, 2.377, 689, 9.106, 9.637–638, 18.444–445, 19.55–58, 19.261, yet a young bride at the time of her conquest, *Il.* 19.290–299. Other named young female captives: *Il.* 9.664–668, 11.624–627, 14.6–7. The unnamed *gunaikes* set forth as contest prizes to victors in Patroclus's funeral games, *Il.* 23.263, 512–513, 704–705.

17. Weil, 2003: sections 7, 21, 14; Patterson, 1982, pp. 26, 44–45, 337.

18. Luckenbill, 1926: 144, lightly updated, using "your" in place of "thy." Lineaments of this monarchic sovereign power can even be traced somewhat speculatively to the second-millennium Bronze Age Hittites (e.g., Beal, 1992, p. 79).

19. Westbrook, 1999, Yaron, 1962. On the applicability of *vitae necisque potestas* as the principle of martial power wielded over ravaged young female war-captives, see further Gaca, 2016b, where I draw partly on von Byern, 1833, pp. 65–67, and Human Rights Watch/Africa, 1996, pp. 53–54, to show the martial aggressor's latitude to kill a ravaged female war-captive held in martial servitude to him.

20. To appreciate how this power works, imagine how you would behave if you were locked in a room with a person who could kill you with impunity if he or she judged you to be insubordinate. For starters, it is not likely that you would give backtalk. If you were told to grovel, you likely would. If sexual activity were imposed on you, it is unlikely you would openly resist.

21. Thuc. 7.29.1–30.3; Kern, 1999, p. 1, is the first to notice this important point.

22. Aspects of this important point are appreciated in several pioneering studies on ancient war ravaging that have helpfully gone beyond identifying ravaging with massacre to explore the sexual aggression against the war-captive women and children, Pritchett, 1991; Finley, 1998; Kern, 1999; Ducrey, 1999; Goldstein, 2001; De Sensi Sestito, 1999; Eckstein, 2007; Scheidel, 2009; Nadali and Vidal, eds. 2014. Important modern accounts of martial ravaging and rape include Askin, 1997 and de Brouwer, 2005.

23. See too Human Rights Watch/Africa, 1996, p. 39. To be killed, they would have had to fight back, not beg to be killed. Begging and pleading show submissive conduct, a desired behavior trait.

24. Gaca, 2012, pp. 99–101.

25. For example, the Persian queen Atossa wanted ravaged Greek girls and young women as maids, and this was one factor in the Persian king Darius's decision to ravage the Greeks before the Scythians, Hdt. 3.134.5.

26. Whether this vengeance against the Benjamites is ravaging or total slaughter is not expressly stated in Judges.

27. Greek ideas of freedom (e.g., Raaflaub, 2004) are a deep-seated resistance to martial power because of incidents like these. The Athenians, for instance, were outraged and grief-stricken by this incident, Hdt. 6.21.2. This reaction shows more than a touch of selective ethno-religious memory at work. The Athenians counted the men of Miletus as their own people, because Athenian men in the late Dark Age played a major role in ravaging and colonizing Carian Miletus, killing the Carian men and boys alike and turning the Carian women and girls of Miletus into their ravaged war-captives and coerced sexual inmates, Hdt. 6.21.2, 1.146.2.

28. For instance, Camin. *Expug. Thess.* 52.4. This is true even of ravaging mutinies and rebellions—the defiant forces followed the dictates of their ringleaders, such as the Roman mutineer Fimbria leading his troops to ravage Ilium (Troy) and its vicinity in 85 BCE.

29. Deut. 20:101–104; Thistlethwaite, 1993, pp. 59–75.

30. Vranic, 1996, p. 141; Anonymous/Hiller, 2005, p. 63. See also Eustathius, *Capt. Thess.* 467B (ed. Melville Jones), on ravaging forces conspicuously trying to humiliate and disgust by bending over and aiming their runny feces at war-captive men in custody, including Eustathius. See Dio 9.39.5–9 for a Roman legend about projectile defecating by a drunken Tarentine Greek on the garment of Postumius

Megellus, a Roman legate sent in 282 BCE to demand restitution from Tarentum. This insult is said to have led Postumius to declare that the Tarentine Greeks would wash his cloak with their blood. Tarentum was ravaged by Roman forces in 209 BCE.

31. "Attachés" refers to *aposkeuê*, for which see Lee, 1972, pp. 430–437; Holleaux, 1926, pp. 355–366; Burstein, 2012; and Pritchett, 1991, pp. 173–174.

32. In the book of Jeremiah, this use of the ravaging threat again shows its martial religious hand as a form of social control, here over men in agricultural occupations, not only in martial forces. Because the men of Israel have become wayward, the Lord God declares, "I will give their women to others and their fields to conquerors" (Jer. 8:10, cf. Jer. 6:14).

33. This practice could drive a wedge of detachment of adult males from the women and children in their midst as a counter-strategy to martial overlords trying to keep men obedient by playing off their fears about the well-being of their women and children. A striking example of this detachment is the stance of Egyptian mercenaries who defected from a pharaoh to become martial forces for a Libyan overlord. When the pharaoh tried to bring them back, they responded that their women and children were wherever their penises were, Hdt. 2.30.4.

34. There are heroic figures in societies torn apart by ravaging, and Rade is one of them. As Mirsada further states, "Finally, we reached the camp. It was very crowded—all women, children, and old men. It looked like some kind of forest motel. . .They separated me from my mother and sister. They told us we would later be together, but I never saw them again. I stayed with the girls and the younger women. They raped us every night . . . One night, Zeljka's brother Rade helped twelve of us escape. They caught two of us. We spent days hiding in the forest, in improvised underground shelters, and we managed to get away. If it hadn't been for Zeljka's brother, I would not have survived," Searles and Berger, 1995, pp. 174–175. Likewise, if the Trojan War ended with victory for the Trojans, their takeover of the Greek army camp would have been a similar rescue venture, for many of the women and girls detained there belonged to satellite villages of Troy (cf. *Il.* 9.325–333). Retaliatory rape would be reserved for any women and girls who belonged to the Greeks.

35. This further supports 1968, p. 187: "If human beings were endowed with an innate proclivity for war, it would not be necessary to indoctrinate them with warlike virtues; and the mere fact that in so many societies past and present so much time has been devoted to such an indoctrination proves" or at least suggests, "that there is no instinct for war," Andreski, 1968, p. 187.

36. This is clear from Mesopotamian models of beds with heterosexual couples making love on them, including the woman mounting the man, e.g., Postgate, 1992, p. 104, fig. 5.7. This marriage ideal, in which husbands and wives are of like mind in their interactions, is beautifully expressed in Ovid's portrayal of the humble Baucis and Philemon (*Met.* 8.636, 705–706), and it also appears in Odysseus's well-wishing for a fine marriage to the adolescent Phaeacian princess Nausicaa, *Od.* 6.180–185.

37. *stratêlatên / athesmolektron, Kupridos lêistên theas, Alex.* 1142–1143, and see too *Encomium ducis Romani*, Anon. 497.9–17, p. 1941 (= p. Flor. 2.114).

38. In the modern day, variants on this practice are now aptly known as "survival rape" (Penn and Nardos, 2003, pp. 41–56), the shaping of coercive social conditions

such that the girls and young women subjected to them are compelled to submit to being raped to avoid being treated even more harshly and possibly killed.

39. Clearchus fr. 48 in Athen. 12.522e. For why *paides* refers strictly to girls, see Gaca, 2014, pp. 303–326. This section on Carbina is adapted with permission from Gaca, 2014, pp. 324–331.

40. On the ravaging nature of this counter-attack, see Gaca, 2014, p. 327.

41. Herodotus attributes Cretan ethnic ties to the Iapygian-Messapians, 7.170.2.

42. Whether any such rescues took place is not known for the girls, virgins, and women of Carbina. However, rescues were one aim of counterattacks. For instance, Pompey's overthrow of Mithridates and his forces in the late 60s BCE led to rescuing some of Mithridates's forced concubines and restoring the young women to their parents, Plut. *Pomp.* 36.2.

43. A warning against such desecration is voiced from a martial perspective by Heracles in Soph. *Philoct.* 1440–1443: "Keep this in mind. Whenever you ravage a land, be reverent to matters pertaining to the gods, for Zeus thinks that everything else is second to that."

44. See further Pritchett, 1991, pp. 365, 368.

45. Gaca, 2014, p. 329, n. 6.

46. See Pritchett, 1971, p. 96. In addition to the primary evidence Pritchett cites, note the scholia on Eur. *Phoen.* 202 (ed. Schwartz), for which see Gaca, 2014, p. 329, n. 65.

47. For instance, Hdt. 9.81.1–2. See further Pritchett, 1971, pp. 93–100 on the *dekatê*. In Numbers 31, the Israelites are more sparing in the share distributed to the Lord God. All the plunder from the Midianites, the virginal girls first on the list, is distributed, half to the Israelite forces who carried out this campaign and half to the rest of the Israelites, with a tribute in girl and animal bodies from each group to be set aside for the Lord and to be managed by the Levites and the priest Eleazar, 1 of every 500 or 0.2% from the 12,000 Israelite forces; and 1 of every 50 or 2% from the rest of the Israelites, Num. 31:32–47.

48. Pausan. 10.10.6, cf. 4.33.2, 6.8.5-6, 6.10.6, 6.14.11, 7.24.4, 10.13.10, *Grove Class. Art. Arch.*, s.v. Ageladas.

49. The ideology of the law of the conqueror retains its currency in the 16th century CE, but is attested by this point with a Christian protest against granting the practice any divine endorsement: "And if someone takes female war captives in war, it is allowed for him to do whatever he wants to them without hindrance. So then, how can it be from God that one legislates for whoredom and the corruption of virgins?" in the extended chronicle of Macarius Melissenus, as built from Sphrantzes and a pastiche of other sources (*Chronicon maius,* p. 490 in Grecu, 1966). While the substance of this protest is valuable to the extent quoted here, it is biased in positioning Mohammed as though he were an Islamic lawgiver resolutely in favor of populace ravaging and other lawless practices. For Melissenus, see Setton, 1976, p. 316, n. 206.

50. Similarly, in Psalm 137, the Jews in exile are presented not only weeping by the rivers of Babylon to remember, but yearning for the destruction of the city and saying, "Happy will be the one who takes your little children and dashes them against the rock" (Ps 137:9).

51. "The problem is that women and girls don't say what happened to them," as noted by Jeanne, a young Tutsi woman who provided testimony about being

martially raped by Hutu forces in Rwanda, Human Rights Watch/Africa, 1996, p. 59. Yet there are reasons for not speaking. Martially raped girls and women risk retaliation for speaking up, and they have reason to think that there is no point to taking the risk, that to say something will change nothing, Human Rights Watch, 2002, p. 80.

52. Deut. 30:15–20 also represents the Lord God as the ultimate martial master of life and death over the Israelites—choose life through religious obedience, or else face death.

REFERENCES

Andreski, S. (1968). *Military organization and society.* Berkeley: University of California Press.

Anonymous/Hiller, M. (2005). *A woman in Berlin: Eight weeks in the conquered city.* Translated by Philip Boehm. New York: Henry Holt.

Armstrong, K. (2014). *Fields of blood: Religion and the history of violence.* New York: Knopf.

Askin, K. (1997). *War crimes against women.* The Hague: Nijhoff.

Batto, B. (1974). *Studies on women at Mari.* Baltimore: Johns Hopkins University Press.

Beal, R. (1992). *The organization of the Hittite military.* Heidelberg: Carl Winter Universitätsverlag.

Burstein, S. (2012). Whence the women? The origin of the Bactrian Greeks. *Ancient West and East, 11,* 97–104.

Carlton, E. (1994). *Massacres: An historical perspective.* Brookfield, VT: Ashgate.

Carnegie Commission for International Peace. (1993/1913). *The other Balkan wars: A 1913 Carnegie Endowment Inquiry in Retrospect.* Washington, D.C.: Carnegie Endowment.

de Brouwer, A. (2005). *Supranational prosecution of sexual violence: ICC, ICTY, and ICTR.* Antwerp: Oxford.

De Sensi Sestito, G. (1999). Schiave di guerra tra *dikaion* ed *ômotês.* In F. Merola & A. Storchi Merino (Eds.), *Femmes-esclaves,* 111–128. Naples: Jovene.

Ducrey, P. (1999). Le *Traitement des prisonniers de guerre dans la Grèce antique.* Paris: de Boccard.

Eckstein, A. M. (2007). *Mediterranean anarchy, interstate war, and the rise of Rome.* Berkeley: University of California Press.

Ervin, M. (1963). A relief pithos from Mykonos. *Archaiologikon Deltion, 18,* 37–75.

Finley, M. I. (1998). *Ancient slavery and modern ideology.* Princeton: Markus Wiener.

Gaca, K. (2008). Reinterpreting the Homeric simile of *Iliad* 16.7–11: The girl and her mother in Ancient Greek warfare. *American Journal of Philology, 129,* 145–171.

Gaca, K. (2010). The andrapodizing of war captives in Greek historical memory. *Transactions of the American Philological Association, 140,* 116–171.

Gaca, K. (2011a). Manhandled and 'kicked around': Reinterpreting the etymology and symbolism of *andrapoda* (*Indogermanische Forschungen*). NY: Palgrave.

Gaca, K. (2011b). Girls, women, and the significance of sexual violence in ancient warfare. In E. Heineman (Ed.), *Sexual violence in conflict zones from the ancient world to the era of human rights.* Philadelphia: University of Pennsylvania Press.

Gaca, K. (2012). Telling the girls from the boys and children: Interpreting *paides* in the sexual violence of populace-ravaging ancient warfare. *Illinois Classical Studies, 35–36,* 85–109.

Gaca, K. (2014). Martial rape, pulsating fear, and the sexual maltreatment of girls (*paides*), virgins (*parthenoi*), and women (*gunaikes*) in antiquity. *American Journal of Philology, 135,* 303–357.

Gaca, K. (2015). Ancient warfare and the ravaging martial rape of girls and women: Evidence from Homeric Epic and Greek Drama. In M. Masterson et al. (Eds.), *Sex in antiquity (278–297).* New York: Routledge.

Gaca, K. (2016a). The martial rape of girls and women in ancient and modern warfare. In F. Aolain, N. Cahn, D. Haynes, & N. Valji (Eds.), *The Oxford handbook of gender and conflict.* New York: Oxford University Press.

Gaca, K. (2016b). Getting rich at her expense: Continuities in rape and tyranny in martially run society from antiquity onward. In S. Budin (Ed.), *Women in antiquity: Real women across the ancient world.* New York: Routledge.

Goldstein, J. (2001). *War and gender.* New York: Cambridge University Press.

Grecu, V. (1966). *Memorii: 1407–1477,* with Pseudo-Phrantzes, Makarios Mellisenos, *Cronica: 1258–1481.* Bucharest: Editura Academiei Republicii Socialiste România.

Holleaux, M. (1926). Ceux qui sont dans le baggage. *Revue des études grecs, 39,* 355–366.

Human Rights Watch. (2002). *The war within the war: Sexual violence against women and girls in Eastern Congo.* New York: Human Rights Watch.

Human Rights Watch/Africa. (1996). *Shattered lives: Sexual violence during the Rwandan genocide and its aftermath.* New York: Human Rights Watch.

Katz, S. (1994). *Holocaust and mass death before the modern age.* New York: Oxford University Press.

Kent, S. (1997). Writing the Yugoslav wars (1992–1996). *The American Historical Review, 102,* 1085–1114.

Kern, P. (1999). *Ancient siege warfare.* Bloomington, IN: Indiana University Press.

Lee, J. A. L. (1972). *Aposkeuê* in the Septuagint. *Journal of Theological Studies, 23,* 430–437.

Luckenbill, D. (1926). *Ancient records of Assyria and Babylonia,* volume 1. Chicago: University of Chicago Press.

Nadali, D., & Vidal, J. (Eds). (2014). *The other face of battle: War on civilians in the ancient Near East.* Münster: Ugarit Verlag.

Nyquist, M. (2013). *Arbitrary rule: Slavery, tyranny, and the power of life and death.* Chicago: University of Chicago Press.

Patterson, O. (1982). *Slavery and social death: A comparative study.* Cambridge, MA: Harvard University Press.

Penn, M., & Nardos, R. (2003). *Overcoming violence against women and girls: The international campaign to eradicate a worldwide problem.* New York: Rowman & Littlefield.

Postgate, J. N. (1992). *Early mesopotamia: Society and economy at the dawn of history.* New York: Routledge.

Pritchett, W. K. (1971). *The Greek state at war,* Vol. 1. Berkeley: University of California Press.

Pritchett, W. K. (1991). *The Greek state at war.* Vol. 5. Berkeley: University of California Press.

Raaflaub, K. (2004). *The discovery of freedom in Ancient Greece.* Translated by R. Franciscono. Chicago: University of Chicago Press.

Scheidel, W. (2009). Sex and empire. In W. Morris & W. Scheidel (Eds.), *Dynamics of ancient empires.* New York: Oxford University Press.

Searles, P., and Berger, R. (eds.). (1995). *Rape and society: Readings on the problem of sexual assault.* Boulder, CO: Westview Press.

Setton, K. (1976). *The papacy and the levant, 1204–1571,* Vol. 1. Philadelphia: American Philosophical Society.

Sinn, U. (1993). Greek sanctuaries as places of refuge. In N. Marinatos & R. Hagg (Eds.), *Greek sanctuaries: New approaches* (pp. 88–109). New York: Routledge.

Stern, P. (1991). *The Biblical herem. A window on the religious experience of Biblical Israel.* Atlanta: Scholars Press.

Stiglmayer, A. (1994). *Mass rape: The war against women in Bosnia-Herzegovina.* Lincoln, NE: University of Nebraska Press.

Thistlethwaite, S. (1993). You may enjoy the spoils of your enemies: Rape as a biblical metaphor for war. *Semeia,* 59–75.

Totten, S., & Bartrop, P. (2009). *The genocide studies reader.* New York: Routledge.

UN Document S/1994/674/230i/Annex IX. (1994). The Final Report of the United Nations Commission of Experts Established Pursuant to Security Council Resolution 780 (1992), Annex IX "Rape and Sexual Assault."

von Byern, E. (1833). *Bilder aus Griechenland und der Levante.* Berlin: Hande & Spener.

Vranic, S. (1996). *Breaking the wall of silence: The voices of raped Bosnia.* Zagreb: Biblioteka Antibarbarus.

Weil, S. (2003). *The* Iliad *or the Poem of Force.* Edited and translated by James P. Holoka. New York: Peter Lang.

Westbrook, R. (1999). Vitae Necisque Potestas. *Historia, 48,* 203–223.

Wing, A. (1994). Review: "Mass rape. The war against women in Bosnia-Herzegovina by Alexandra Stiglmayer. *The American Journal of International Law, 88,* 849–851.

Yaron, R. (1962). Vitae Necisque Potestas. *Tijdschrift voor Rechtsgeschidenis, 30,* 243–251.

Chapter 13

Judaism and Feminism

Ilona Rashkow

BASIC BACKGROUND INFORMATION ON JUDAISM

The question of how many Jewish Americans there are does not have a simple answer because the number of Jews in the U.S. depends on how one defines a Jew, as explained in the Pew Research Center's major new survey of Jewish Americans (Pew, 2013). There are roughly 5.3 million adult American Jews (2.2% of the adult U.S. population) as defined by the Pew Report. This number includes about 4.2 million American adults who say they are Jewish by religion (1.8% of the U.S. adult population) and 1.2 million Jews who consider themselves "Jews of no religion," a group of people who say they are atheist, agnostic, or "nothing in particular" when asked about their religion but who were reared Jewish or have a Jewish parent and who still consider themselves Jewish aside from religious beliefs and/or practice. Two other groups were not counted as Jews in the report. There are an additional 2.4 million adults in the "Jewish background" category—that is, people who were reared Jewish or had at least one Jewish parent, but who now either identify with a religion other than Judaism (most are Christian) or say they do not think of themselves as Jewish or partially Jewish, by religion or otherwise. Also, there are 1.2 million adults in the "Jewish affinity" category—people who were not raised Jewish, do not have a Jewish parent, and are not Jewish by religion but who nevertheless consider themselves Jewish in some sense.

"Judaism" does not lend itself to a facile definition, although it is described often as "the religion, philosophy, and way of life of Jews" (*Encyclopedia Judaica*, 2007, p. 511). The Talmud (Shab. 31a) tells the well-known story of a gentile who wanted to convert to Judaism but only on the understanding that he would be taught the whole of the Torah while standing on one foot. Hillel accepted him and, in response to his request, replied: "That which is hateful to you do not do to your neighbor. This is the whole of the Torah. The rest is commentary. Go and study." Hillel's definition was only one of the many attempts to discover and define Judaism—its main ideas and particular viewpoint—in order to differentiate it from other religions and philosophies. Developed and adapted to diverse circumstances throughout its long history, it contains varying emphases as well as outright contradictions. Extending over thirty-five centuries of history and a significant portion of the world, Judaism has not retained the same form and character. Biblical period Judaism differs from exilic and post-exilic Judaism; rabbinic Judaism is quite different from Mosaic Judaism; and post-19th-century Judaism differs yet again. That said, there appear to be some tenuous threads which make various aspects of contemporary Judaism a unified whole.

Contemporary Judaism includes the intricate religious and cultural development of the Jewish people incorporating the social, cultural, and religious history of a widespread and diverse community, both people who do and do not think of themselves as "religious." From the perspective of "peoplehood," Judaism is the group memory of the communities and cultures formed by Jews through the ages. It consists of the religious texts and commandments; the diverse Hebrew, Yiddish, and Ladino languages; the visible markers of religious observance, such as the *kippah* or the *payot* or the *tzitzit*; the communal structures; and the whole range of Jewish education, family life, food, festivals, music, dance, customs, and humor. "Each part of the Jewish tradition is integrally related to the whole. Jewish religion and Jewish culture are more than complementary, they are symbiotic; one is inconceivable without the other" (Harvard University Pluralism Project).

BASIC BACKGROUND INFORMATION ON FEMINISM

In its essence, "feminism" seeks social equity for women and analyzes a wide range of issues in terms of gender politics. But that definition is too simplistic, as any perusal of feminist theory bibliographies shows.

It is common to speak of three phases of modern feminism, the first of which began at the Seneca Falls Convention in 1848 when 300 men and women rallied to the cause of equality for women. Elizabeth Cady Stanton (died 1902) drafted the Seneca Falls Declaration outlining the new movement's ideology and political strategies, including feminist biblical hermeneutics.

The second wave of feminism began in the 1960s and continued into the 1990s. This wave unfolded in the context of the anti-Vietnam War and the civil rights movement as well as the growing self-consciousness of a variety of minority groups around the world. American Jewish women, including Betty Friedan, Gloria Steinem, and Letty Cottin Pogrebin, were in the forefront of the second wave of American feminism. While these Jewish feminists became well-known activists within wider American society, an equally significant Jewish brand of feminism developed as well with far-reaching implications for American Judaism.

The third phase of feminism began in the mid-1990s and due to the influence of post-modern scholarship destabilized many constructs including the notions of "universal womanhood," body, gender, sexuality, and heteronormativity (Rutenberg, 2003).

THE IMPACT OF AMERICAN JUDAISM ON AMERICAN FEMINISM

All Jewish feminists have at least three things in common: they are women, they are Jews, and they are feminists. These separate facets of their identity may conflict with other members within each subcategory, as when Jewish women face anti-Semitism from other feminists, or experience sexism within the Jewish community. However, efforts to integrate these three aspects have brought feminist insights to the Jewish community and Jewish insights to the feminist movement.

Many Jewish women who became feminist leaders generally attribute their activities to two contrasting experiences of Judaism. Some speak of a *positive* influence: the Jewish tradition of social justice. They identify Judaism, and their experiences as a minority group, as the source of their commitment to social justice. For these women, Judaism and feminism are complementary partners in the work of *Tikkun Olam* ("repairing the world"). As Letty Pogrebin has described her own roots:

> I grew up in a home where advancing social justice was as integral to Judaism as lighting Shabbat candles . . . Having learned from [my parents] to stand up for my dignity as a Jew, I suppose it was natural for me to stand up for my dignity as a woman, which, after all, is what feminism is all about. (Jewish Women's Archive, "Letty Cottin Pogrebin")

On the other hand, some Jewish feminists say that *negative* Jewish experiences contributed to their involvement in feminist movements, such as being excluded from the *minyan* (prayer quorum, traditionally composed of ten men), not being allowed to say *kaddish* (mourner's prayer) for a parent, or the opportunity for as good a Jewish education as males. As a result, many women embraced feminism as a reaction against patriarchal Jewish values and as an alternative to a model of community based on traditional gender roles. As a consequence, some feminists have worked to "change the system" as discussed below ("The Impact of Feminism on American Judaism").

The status of American Jewish assimilation in the postwar period was a major factor in the role of Jewish women in the American feminist movement. Although assimilation was sufficiently underway that Jewish women were able to go beyond the boundaries of their community and mingle with non-Jewish women, Jews were still new enough to America that they were identified by others, and identified themselves, as "outsiders." Generally upwardly mobile, Jewish women in this period tended to be well educated and sensitive to injustice, which fostered their feminist activism. Individual Jewish feminists have made a major impact in American judicial and political life. (Among the many are United States Senators Barbara Boxer and Dianne Feinstein; Congresswoman Bella Abzug; Congresswoman Elizabeth Holtzman; N.Y. Supreme Court Judges Birdie Amsterdam and Judith Kaye; and Supreme Court Justice Ruth Bader Ginsberg.)

While Jewish female activists such as Friedan, Steinem, and Abzug became well known in American society as a whole, another aspect of Jewish feminism developed: some of the American Jewish publications published in the 1970s began to change the perceptions of women in modern Jewish life generally and in rather disparate fields. For example, *The Jewish Catalog* (1973) contains a chapter on Jewish women emphasizing "consciousness-raising" and suggesting new "areas of priorities for interested Jewish women"; *Lilith* magazine was established in 1976 by Susan Weidman Schneider and Aviva Cantor; and Blu Greenberg's *On Women and Judaism* was published in 1979. As Anne Lapidus Lerner wrote in 1973, "Queen Esther no longer reigns supreme in the hearts of young Jewish women. More and more of them are admiring Vashti's spunk instead" (Lerner, 1973, p. 3).

THE IMPACT OF FEMINISM ON AMERICAN JUDAISM

American Jewish life has been transformed radically by American feminism. While many feminist celebrities are Jews, the focus of their feminism has not been specifically Jewish in nature. On the other hand, the Jewish feminist movement (women such as Rachel Adler, Paula Hyman, and

Aviva Cantor) have centered their activities on changes within contemporary American Judaism. As a result, they are recognized primarily within the Jewish community as having changed many aspects of Jewish religious, intellectual, cultural, and communal life in the United States.

Non-Orthodox American Judaism

That said, one of the greatest challenges to Judaism in America has been the women's movement. For most of its history, Judaism was patriarchal; women's role was to maintain a kosher home while activities that took place in the public sphere (such as study and prayer) were considered mandatory for men only. While the Reform movement of the 19th century adopted some measures intended to equalize the role of women in the synagogue, such as mixed seating, it was not until the 1970s that the structure of Judaism began to change in response to feminist activities. To the secular feminist and the conventional Jew alike, American feminism and American Judaism may seem to present contrasting belief systems. Yet since 1971, a number of significant changes in American Jewish life have been made and they have effected a partial reconciliation between contemporary feminism and American Judaism.

Conversely, modernity saw also a few non-synagogue female-only spheres of women's traditional expressions of Judaism minimized or eliminated by non-Orthodox Jews, such as *mikveh* observance (immersion in the ritual bath following menstruation and childbirth) which declined radically in the modern era (although it has been revived in the late 20th century by the Conservative movement). Since the *mikveh* served as a gathering place for women only to socialize and exert authority in the absence of men, its decline diminished women's opportunities to assemble away from male presence. Further, the liberal branches' decline in adherence to Rabbinic law (important to Orthodox Judaism) weakened women's status as sources of domestic and gendered experience-based experts, particularly concerning laws of *kashrut*. Traditionally entrusted with responsibility for the laws of *niddah* and *kashrut*, women had been viewed with the moral trust, intellectual ability, and religious commitment necessary for their strict adherence to those often complex laws.

The most dramatic change in Judaism for many centuries came with the equality of women in Reform, Conservative, and Reconstructionist synagogue worship. The public honoring of young women in non-Orthodox congregations, the *bat mitzvah* ("daughter of the commandment," discussed below), became widespread by the late 1960s, followed by decisions by these branches to include women in the *minyan*, call women to the Torah, and allow women to lead synagogue worship services. Perhaps the most striking transformation from previous Jewish practice has been the ordination of women as rabbis.

In 1972 the Reform seminary (Hebrew Union College–Jewish Institute of Religion) ordained Sally Priesand (the first woman rabbi in America), and in 1973 the Reconstructionist Rabbinical College ordained Sandy Eisenberg Sasso. The Conservative movement did not ordain women until 1985 when Amy Eilberg was ordained. But the issue deepened the divide between Orthodoxy, which does not allow women to lead services, and the other Jewish branches (see below, however, for a discussion of the first American Orthodox seminary for women). It should be noted, however, that in 1990 Nishmat, an Orthodox institution, was founded in Israel by Rabbanit (wife of a Rabbi) Chana Henkin to bring higher Torah learning to women. Nishmat has become a world center for women's scholarship, leadership, and social responsibility, and a world leader in paving a new path for women in Orthodox Jewish life. Ten years after its founding, Nishmat created the new religious role of *Yoatzot Halacha* (women *halakhic* advisors), opening the way for women in Orthodox religious leadership.

Orthodox Judaism

Orthodox Judaism constitutes the smallest major Jewish branch in America (about 10% of the Jewish population) and it is by no means monolithic: there is a diversity in practice, there is no ultimate authority or hierarchy of authorities, and it has never been able to mobilize even one national or international organization in which all of its groups would speak as one.

Ḥaredim

The Haredi proportion of the overall Jewish population is higher in the United States and the United Kingdom than in Israel.

According to the 2013 Pew Survey, about a quarter of American Orthodox Jews are *haredim* (referred to often as "ultra-Orthodox"). America is home to the second largest Haredi population, which, according to predictions based on its current growth rate, will double approximately every 20 years. In 2000, there were 360,000 Haredi Jews in the United States (7.2 percent of the approximately 5 million Jews in the United States); by 2006, the number had grown to 468,000 or 9.4 percent (Wise, 2007). Although they have changed over time, haredim have made far fewer compromises with contemporary secular culture or essential changes in the way they practice their Judaism from what the tradition and *halakhah* (Jewish law) have followed throughout history. Haredim establish and maintain their traditional identity and separation by dressing (and grooming themselves) in ways that make them distinct. For men this means having a beard and long earlocks as well as black caftans and black hats (fur hats or *shtreimels* on the Sabbath and holidays for married or adult men), and often some form of knee pants and black shoes. For women it means dressing in modest clothing that covers most of the body, and for married women, a head covering (such as a kerchief covering their hair, a wig, or even a wig covered by a hat or kerchief). Variations in attire are determined by sectarian affiliation within the haredi world.

Haredim struggle actively against the influences of secular culture. Although there are many elements that distinguish haredim from other American Jews, perhaps the most outstanding is their attitude toward sexuality. Unlike Modern Orthodox and non-Orthodox Jews who allow the free mixing of males and females in social and educational settings, haredim separate the sexes from the earliest years of life. Not only do they offer separate education of males and females, they also discourage dating and the free selection of marital partners but rely instead on arranged marriages (usually by the very early twenties or late teens) to other haredim. Studying Torah for as long as possible is the ideal for men, while women are expected to give birth and rear children who will be Torah scholars or the wives and mothers of Torah scholars. As a result, American feminism has made virtually no impact on ultra-Orthodox American Judaism.

Modern Orthodox

Approximately 168,000 American Orthodox Jews (about three-quarters of American Orthodox Jews) are "Modern Orthodox" Jews who choose a middle way between whole-hearted acculturation to America and strict insulation from it (Wise, 2007). These are Jews who, although following *halakhah*, value and receive a secular education in addition to their intensive Jewish one, attend university, and are found in most professional careers.

The mantra of Modern Orthodoxy is expressed in the motto of Yeshiva University—*Torah u'Madda* ("Torah and science"), the parallel values of Jewish observance and involvement in the secular world.

One of the greatest controversies in Modern Orthodoxy is women's roles in religious life. During worship services, men and women are separated by a curtain or low wall, and only men are allowed to lead services, read, and bless the Torah. Women are exempt from time-mandated *mitzvot* and, for the most part, cannot become rabbis (however, see below for a recent innovation).

It was in the context of the second-wave feminist movement of the 1960s and 1970s that Orthodox women began to question their roles in the family, the workplace, society at large, and religion. As a result, institutions emerged in Israel and the United States that offered advanced text-based Jewish learning (including the study of Talmud) for Orthodox women. These institutions, like Matan in Jerusalem and Drisha in New York City, created a cadre of learned Orthodox women who wanted to take on public roles in religious life. American feminism, combined with stronger Jewish education for Orthodox girls, has caused some dissatisfaction with traditional gender roles and restrictions among many Orthodox women (and men). Being Orthodox, they retain their adherence to *halakhah* but have sought changes within the limits of Jewish law through creative re-interpretations as well as by attempting to shift some aspects of Jewish culture or by creating new opportunities for female religious participation.

Perhaps as a by-product of second-wave feminism, in 1977 the first International Conference on Feminism and Orthodoxy was held in New York City which led to the creation of the Jewish Orthodox Feminist Alliance (JOFA). The JOFA's position is that traditional Jewish legal processes should be pressed to deal with questions of Jewish women's leadership and participation. Orthodox women now have opportunities for studying rabbinic texts (limited previously to men) and with training in particular areas of Jewish law, women serve as legal advisors to Orthodox women regarding issues connected with divorce and *niddah* observance. Orthodox women have established women-only prayer groups and institutions for studying rabbinic texts, and a few Orthodox synagogues have started to permit women to deliver a sermon (usually after the service). Several clauses have been proposed for inclusion in the *ketubbah* (religious marriage contract) that would provide recourse for a woman whose husband refuses to grant her a Jewish divorce. The problem of the *agunah* (a woman whose husband refuses, or is unable, to grant her an official bill of divorce, known as a *get*) remains a central issue for Orthodox feminists and organizations of Orthodox women are attempting to address the problem of the *agunah*.

Some Orthodox women have assumed para-rabbinic roles in their communities, although these women have not been given the title "rabbi." Working as rabbinical advocates, family purity experts, and synagogue leaders, these women perform tasks that were once the domain of male Orthodox rabbis exclusively. Although the women who hold these positions might look like rabbis and sound like rabbis, they are careful not to call themselves rabbis. Although Jewish law prevents women from being witnesses or counting as part of a *minyan*, women *can* do most of the jobs that male rabbis do.

Since the late 1990s, a handful of Modern Orthodox synagogues in the United States have created congregational leadership positions for women. While each synagogue has chosen a different title (community scholar, assistant congregational leader, education fellow, spiritual mentor), all of these positions carry a job description that resembles much of what pulpit rabbis do, incorporating teaching and pastoral care.

While a few women have received private ordination from Orthodox rabbis, they have not been recognized as rabbis in mainstream Orthodoxy.

In March 2009, after a course of advanced study equivalent to that of male rabbis, Sara Hurwitz received ordination from Rabbi Avi Weiss of the Hebrew Institute of Riverdale as a *Maharat*, an acronym Weiss devised, which stands for "*halakhic*, spiritual, and Torah leader. Committed to training more women to serve as religious leaders of synagogues, schools, and college campuses, Weiss opened Yeshivat Maharat in New York in fall 2009. As of August 2015, twenty women have enrolled in Yeshivat Maharat's programs and five have been ordained. Of the five women who have been ordained by the yeshiva (three in 2013 and two last year), four are working in synagogues, serving essentially as assistant rabbis. (The fifth is a Jewish educator in Montreal.) Yet even as they have found jobs, the Maharats and the institutions they serve are grappling with how to define their roles as clergy in a movement that still does not accept women as rabbis. "We recognize that the path toward female leadership is slow and is an evolution, and part of the mission of *Yeshivat Maharat* is to open communities up to the possibilities of women serving in leadership positions," said Sara Hurwitz, the dean of Yeshivat Maharat (whom Weiss ordained in 2009 as a "rabba"). "We know that there are parts of the Orthodox community that are not open and not ready for Orthodox female leadership, but many are" (Hellman, 2015).

Only time will tell if there will be additional jobs and positions for the graduates of Yeshivat Maharat, or if the Orthodox sensitivities to a woman being called "rabbi" will change as more qualified and learned women are seen in religious leadership roles. In the modern world, where women hold public positions in so many areas, it is certainly likely that an increase in the numbers of women with advanced religious education and leadership experience will continue to make a serious difference to and in the Orthodox community.

AMERICAN FEMINISM'S INFLUENCE ON JEWISH RITUALS

American feminism's influence on Jewish rituals has been seen in two ways: adapting existing rituals and creating new ones. Anthropologists label many activities as "rituals," ranging from private ceremonies (including those with just one person or only a few participants) to large gatherings, and from single acts to long sequences spread over months or years. The occasions for ritualized behaviors vary also, either contingencies such as illness or misfortune, life events (such as birth, "coming-of-age," and death), or recurrent religious holidays with their attendant rituals.

Feminists critical of adaptive rituals (sometimes referred to as "add women and stir") have questioned the value of putting their energies into making women's versions of the rituals that Jewish men are performing, or fighting for the right to perform those rituals in communities that forbid them to do so. Instead, they have proposed creating distinctively female alternatives, derived from insights and practices that are unique to lives of Jewish women, which will transform Judaism into what Judith Plaskow described as "a religion that women as well as men have a role in shaping" (Plaskow, 2014, p. 134).

Both adapting existing rituals and creating new ones exist in both the recurrent daily and seasonal/holiday patterns of Judaism as well as the nonrecurring moments of personal life which celebrate or mark times of new beginning and transition from one life stage to another. Moments of passage with their attendant rituals provide the means of transition from one life stage and one sphere of responsibility to another. As such, they confirm the hierarchies of value of the community and they project an ideal sequence of personal development which women can anticipate.

Birth is naturally the first major moment in a person's individual and communal life. When a boy is born, a circumcision rite called a *brit* ("covenant," short for "covenant of circumcision") takes place eight days later. This ceremony, of great antiquity, confirms the transition of the male infant from being a child of Adam, as it were, to a member of the Jewish people. Thus, the boy enters the "covenant of Abraham." The *brit milah* ritual has been regarded historically as a vital Jewish tradition, and the *mitzvah* to honor the rite with a festive meal became an opportunity to celebrate the birth of a son and welcome him into the Jewish community.

Originally, Judaism had no special celebration to welcome female infants into the covenant. Traditionally, fathers were given an *aliyah* (the honor of reciting the blessing before and after a section of the weekly Torah portion is read) at the synagogue on the first Shabbat after a girl was born. The child received her Hebrew name at the same time. After services, both mother and father were honored at a congregational *Kiddush* (refreshments served after prayer services).

As Jews became more sensitive to the importance of including females in Judaism's most important rituals, the need to welcome daughters became apparent. Because welcoming rituals for Jewish baby girls are a recently developed phenomenon, there is no single *Simchat Bat* ("joy of a daughter") ritual. Welcoming daughters with contemporary Jewish rituals has exploded in popularity in the last decade. Though it is not yet universally practiced, daughters' welcoming ceremonies are held by families across the spectrum of Jewish identity—from those who tend toward the secular to those that are modern Orthodox. Whichever form of celebration is followed, Jewish families are increasingly finding formal ways of expressing joy on the birth of a girl as well as the birth of a boy.

The study of Torah begins quite early and, according to custom, this event is inaugurated by having the child find and trace the letters of his or her name, which are covered with honey. This act symbolizes the hopes for the sweetness of life devoted to Judaism. However, a boy is not a "formal" member of the community until he is thirteen years old. At that time he will become a *bar mitzvah*, literally a "son of the commandment(s)." He can then perform all the commandments and is required to do so with full responsibility for his religious behavior. When the boy is first "called up" to the Torah, symbolic of his attainment of majority, the father says a blessing commemorating this transition to adulthood.

Traditionally, a girl achieves majority at twelve years and a day, a time symbolic of the onset of menstruation. Since the impact of American feminism, girls are given fuller instruction in the traditional literature (though this varies by group) and in liberal contexts a *bat mitzvah* ceremony ("daughter of the commandment") has been developed to mark a girl's rite of passage. The degree to which this ceremony is part of the traditional service depends upon the strictness of the community. Some congregations give a girl the same Torah ceremony as a boy, others only give her some ritual part in the Friday evening service, and still others limit this involvement to some celebratory action outside the framework of a religious service. There is a high correlation between how a girl celebrates her majority status and the role of women in a given ritual community. Strict traditionalists, concerned with the separation of these and other ritualistic roles of the female, tend to regard the moment as a "female" affair. Those groups that variously reject traditional rules about women (particularly matters of segregation in prayer, formal exclusion from the prayer quorum, and fewer required positive commandments) will correspondingly consider the girl's majority as a more ritual event along the lines enjoyed by boys. These issues are subject to local rabbinic-communal regulation, although the communities are subject to the authority of different rabbinical institutions and their rulings on these matters.

For traditionalists and nontraditionalists alike, the wedding canopy is a major moment of personal and social transition. The male and female take their place as equal, productive communal citizens with the obligation to fulfill the first *mitzvah* of the Torah: "be fruitful and multiply." The wedding is thus the transition to the basic Jewish institution of the home and to the responsibility for the continuance of Judaism.

In addition to appropriating traditionally male rituals, new women's rituals have been evolving since the 1970s and share certain common characteristics.

First, they mark the unmarked events linked to women's experiences that previously have not evoked formal Jewish responses. These include the onset of menstruation, pregnancy, giving birth, and menopause.

Second, they foster a sense of "female community." Many of them are held in all-women groups, and encourage supportive sharing. This aspect reflects the influence of the consciousness-raising sessions of early secular feminism and has been preserved primarily in *Rosh Chodesh* groups. (*Rosh Chodesh*, literally, "head of the month," is a significant festival day. It remains a custom in some communities for women to refrain from work on

Rosh Chodesh, as a reward for their refusal to participate in the incident of the Golden Calf.) Evoking the mood of a support group, the rituals emphasize the participation of a community of equals and create opportunities for women's bonding across lines that might otherwise be divisive, such as age, economic class, marital status, and ideology.

Third, unlike traditional rituals, these women-only rituals allow for improvisation and personalization. Most new women's rituals are not meant to change or challenge laws or be legally binding, Thus, they do not have fixed liturgies, specific words that must be said, or a series of actions that must be performed to make the ritual valid. The preference for improvisation, personalization, and choice that the rituals reflect leaves a wide opening for creativity. For example, suggestions for *Rosh Chodesh* meetings that one might receive from the Hadassah organization or a newer group, "Moving Tradition: It's a Girl Thing" (Ochs, 2007) which promotes *Rosh Chodesh* observance among young girls, are presented as inspirational templates from which one can pick and choose. Likewise, in Debra Nussbaum Cohen's book of rituals for baby daughters, the reader is given a template for most ceremonies, as well as hundreds of elements to consider incorporating, in an easy-to-follow menu of options (Cohen, 2001).

Fourth, women's-only rituals provide ideas for additional ceremonies that foster the spirituality of the individual in addition to that of the entire Jewish people. While the new women's rituals foster the growth and cohesive feelings of communities, they tend to emphasize the psychological and spiritual well-being of individuals within the group. Because of the emphasis on the individual over the group, it is worth noting that American Jewish feminists have not attempted to create brand-new holidays to be celebrated by all Jews or even by all Jewish women. Many Jewish feminists as well as Jewish organizations have published guidelines to help women establish new rituals within their communities. For example, the Jewish Women's Center of Pittsburgh is a community of women of all Jewish backgrounds that provides educational opportunities and spiritual experiences rooted in Jewish values and feminist ideals. In addition, P. Adelman wrote a ground-breaking book (*Miriam's Well: Rituals for Jewish Women Around the Year*) that has been used by many congregations as well as smaller groups of Jewish women (1973). JOFA has a pamphlet ("Orthodox Jewish Women and Ritual: Life Cycle Guides") that has personal stories and suggestions from women who have felt excluded from traditional life cycle events. The guides illustrate how women can expand their roles in the Orthodox Shabbat rituals, celebrating their daughters' births and *bat mitzvahs*, and in mourning loved ones.

Fifth, these innovative rituals take place in a less regulated space. As Paula Hyman discusses (2009), the earliest new women's rituals typically took place in homes or in nature. They were enacted away from institutionalized settings, both physically and metaphysically, so as to avoid being subject to rabbinic, communal, or male jurisdiction. There were feminist *seders* that moved from one woman's apartment to another each year and then expanded so that they now take place in community centers and catering halls. There are pre-wedding *mikveh* parties that take place, among women friends, in the ocean, under the moonlight. There are gatherings of Lubavitch Hasidic women in basement recreation rooms for designing and decorating Miriam's tambourines. Only later, as the new rituals became more familiar, have they been held in synagogues and Jewish community centers.

Sixth, the new women's rituals are timed more flexibly. They are created when a situation calls for ritual marking and intensification and are set to fit the emotional needs and schedules of the celebrants. A baby girl's naming ceremony, for instance, rarely takes place on the eighth day of the infant's life or during the first time Torah is read after birth. Instead, it is usually held when the mother has regained her strength after childbirth and when relatives can arrive more conveniently. The feminist *seder* is also flexible: it can take place before Passover or during one of the intermediate days, any time that does not place it in direct competition with family observance.

Seventh, these new rituals promote a feminist agenda within the context of Judaism. This is accomplished through fresh readings of traditional sources which can be a formidable project for women who identify as "*halakhic* Jews" and are reluctant to be viewed as radical or disloyal.

Thus, one of the most significant expressions of the creation of feminist Judaism and its influence on the Jewish people is women's involvement in the full range of rituals and ceremonies that exist both within and beyond *halakhah*. The most prominent is egalitarian ceremonies, which create and express the desire for equality between women and men in religious ritual, from which women were either actively excluded or in which they were in the past permitted only minimal participation.

The *bat mitzvah* ceremony, which began to develop in the early twentieth century, blazed the trail to equality. This egalitarian consciousness paved the way for the creation of new ceremonies that express the feminist desire for cultural equality, reflect the female life cycle, and have no precedent in normative *halakhah*. Most of the new ceremonies are based in one way or another upon older female traditions, such as preparation ceremonies for a wedding, fertility rituals, or ceremonies that marked old age, which existed on the fringes of masculine culture. The renewal of these feminine folk traditions led finally to feminist interpretations of those ceremonies in *halakhah* which are intended for women, particularly the monthly immersion in the *mikveh*. Finally, other ceremonies reflect the empowerment of women via creative-feminist development of the *halakhic* and folk traditions connected with the Jewish calendar. (The best-known examples of this are women's *seders* and *Rosh Chodesh* ceremonies.)

CONCLUSION

Historical studies of American Judaism seem to have downplayed women's lives. The growth of academic Women's Studies Programs helped establish a counterpart within Judaic Studies Programs.

Feminist analyses have criticized masculinist biases in describing the Jewish past, and have used historicism to justify feminist innovations. For example, feminist analyses of rabbinic literature have uncovered legal precedents for changing *halakhic* prescriptions regarding women (Hauptman, 1998) and interpretive patterns of leniency in establishing Jewish law (Biale, 1995). The impact of feminism on Judaism has highlighted patterns of gendered rhetoric in rabbinic literature that create the masculinity of God (Boyarin, 1993; Baskin, 2002; Eilberg-Schwartz, 1994).

In the early years of women's studies, the task seemed to be fairly straightforward. Textual expressions of misogyny and male-centeredness were demonstrated, and even if the thinker had been dead for centuries, his influence continued as part of a long chain of patriarchal tradition. More recently, however, feminist scholars of Judaism have developed more complex analyses, demonstrating ambivalences toward women within the same thinker and text, and also turning to metaphorical uses of masculine and feminine imagery in matters not explicitly related to men and women.

Judaism *has* made an enormous impact on the feminist movement. Likewise, the feminist movement has influenced contemporary American Judaism more than many scholars had foreseen. Both Judaism and feminism continue to evolve; hopefully they will continue to do so in tandem.

REFERENCES

Adelman, P. (1973). *Miriam's Well: Rituals for Jewish women around the year.* New York: Biblio Press.

American Jewish Yearbook. (1977). G. Himmelfarb (Ed.). Philadelphia: Jewish Publication Society.

Baskin, J. (2002). *Midrashic women: Formations of the feminine in rabbinic literature.* Waltham, MA: Brandeis Press.

Biale, R. (1995). *Women and Jewish law.* New York: Schocken.

Boyarin, D. (1993). *Carnal Israel: Reading sex in Talmudic culture.* Santa Barbara: University of California Press.

Cohen, D. (2001). *Celebrating your new Jewish daughter: Creating Jewish ways to welcome baby girls into the covenant.* Jewish Lights Pub.

Eilberg-Schwartz, H. (1994). *God's phallus and other problems for men and monotheism.* Boston, MA: Beacon Press.

Encyclopedia Judaica. (2007). M. Berenbaum and F. Skolnik (Eds.). Vol. 11, 2nd ed. Detroit: Macmillan Reference USA.

Greenberg, B. (1979). *On women and Judaism: A view from tradition.* Philadelphia: The Jewish Publication Society.

Harvard University pluralism project. Retrieved on August 1, 2015, from http://www.pluralism.org/religion/judaism.

Hauptman, J. (1998). *Rereading the rabbis.* New York: Westview Press.

Hellman, U. (2015). Jewish Telegraphic Agency. Retrieved on August 3, 2015, from http://www.jta.org/about-us.

Hyman, P. (2009). Jewish feminism in the United States. *Jewish Women: A comprehensive historical encyclopedia.* Jewish Women's Archive.

Jewish Women's Archive. "Letty Cottin Pogrebin." Retrieved on August 1, 2015, from http://jwa.org/feminism/pogrebin-letty-cottin-1.

Lerner, A. (1973). Who hast not made me a man: The movement for equal rights for women in American Jewry. *American Jewish yearbook.* Philadelphia: Jewish Publication Society.

Ochs, V. (2007). *Inventing Jewish ritual.* Philadelphia: Jewish Publication Society.

Pew Research Center. (2013). A portrait of Jewish Americans.

Plaskow, J. (2014). *Feminism, theology, and justice.* Boston, MA: Brill.

Rutenberg, D. (Ed.). (2003). *Yentl's revenge: The next generation of Jewish feminism.* New York: Seal Press.

Wise, Y. (2007, July 23). Majority of Jews will be ultra-orthodox by 2050. *University of Manchester News.*

Chapter 14

A Room Prepared: Women and the Mystic Experience

Anna Byrne

"There is no time. I can't find a priest I like. I don't know the scriptures, the sacraments, the rituals. I don't know where to start. I'm not spiritual . . ."

For many women, spirituality is another thing *to do*. Something to do well; another chance for failure. Alternatively, spiritual longing is seen as a luxury, a thing for which there is little time or space. God seems aloof, away, or out of touch. There is the belief that you either "have God" or you do not; you are either "spiritual" or you are not.

The demands of everyday life, culture, and often organized religion cloak a woman's true identity as both connected to the divine and infinitely loved. The right to an inner way of knowing, the right to be cherished, to be replenished, and to find the holy in the ordinary is essential for life. Severed from these, a woman feels dry, devoid of meaning, inadequate, and alone.

This disconnect from the sacred is an illusion. Spirituality is not limited to a small sect of human beings, but is the universal search for meaning, depth, belonging, and growth (Teasdale, 1999). Women may begin the spiritual search by returning to their most precious resource—the self. It is the body, the heart-space, the daily workings of the hands that bring the divine to life, even in the midst of chaos, boredom, or loneliness. It is the returning to consciousness in this very moment, here and now, present in your kitchen, your loved one's tears, your creative work—present within you.

MYSTICISM

This is mysticism, the face-to-face encounter between the human heart and the Other, whether named as Great Spirit, Brahman, Goddess, Tao, Allah, God, or Enlightenment (Lanzetta, 2005). Mysticism reveals that the obstacle in the human–divine relationship is not separation, but the *perception* of separation. Mysticism requires no clergy, no place of worship, no single practice. Enfolded within its meaning are the pathways women choose toward unity, the ways greater consciousness is revealed to women, and the transformative effects of this experience (McGinn, 2006).

The mystical way is the tradition of Islamic Sufis, Jewish Kabbalists, Christian contemplatives, and Buddhist and Hindu gurus and sages. It is often termed "'hidden' or 'secret' because the divine is not known by mental effort but is taught through love" (Lanzetta, 2005, p. 30). Mysticism "rearranges energy" from the inside (Teasdale, 1999, p. xvi), stripping illusion, untruth, and ego to return woman to herself. It moves the paradigm from finite to infinite and knowing to unknowing, binding the bodily to the transcendent. Mysticism is a radical affirmation of the material world and of the human form, having chosen both for its expression. It results in an enlightened awareness that finds its end in human and ecological justice.

The lineage of female mysticism is a unique encountering. Femininity both impacts, and is impacted by, mystical consciousness (Lanzetta, 2005). For women who are often excluded from formal education and ecclesiastic roles, mysticism offers a room prepared, a door unlocked. Here, women may find full spiritual identity and expression. In turn, the matrix of feminine heart, mind, and body distinctly shape how Ultimate Reality is embodied and expressed in the world.

ANCESTRAL GROUNDS

> The beginning of the universe
> Is the mother of all things.
> Knowing the mother, one also knows the sons.
> Knowing the sons, yet remaining in touch with the mother,
> Brings freedom from the fear of death.
> (Lao Tsu, 1997/6th c. BCE, ch. 52)

Before the dawning of the world religions was the mystical. "Silence precedes being; *ein sof* [the Infinite] . . . flows into *ayin;* the womb of the mother is the source of the ten thousand things" (Lanzetta, 2005, pp. 33–34). Mysticism is the universal fore-text that predates, births, and informs religion (Lanzetta, 2005) and to which religion returns at its highest level.

Each of the major faiths began with an illuminating encounter between a human being and a Greater Consciousness, Other, or Divinity. It was the awakening under the bodhi tree of Siddhartha Gautama, Jesus's transfiguration on the mount, the cave encounter between Muhammad and the angel Gabriel (Teasdale, 1999). These spiritual awakenings led each to radically progressive views of society.

Buddha changed the context for women in sixth- and fifth-century BCE India, granting them entrance to the Sangha as *bhikkhunis* (nuns). In so doing, he offered a viable alternative to domestic duties and declared Nirvana accessible to all who followed the Four Noble Truths (Bancroft, 1987). Women were Jesus's intimate friends and followers, an egalitarian stance for first-century Judaism (Jantzen, 1995). Mary Magdalene is recorded as the sole person to have both witnessed Jesus's death and proclaim his resurrection. After Muhammad's revelation, his wife Khadija validated and encouraged his experience. Their daughter, Fatima, is often cited as Islam's first mystic (Adams Helminski, 2015).

Despite the early inclusion of women, the formalization of religion replaced personal experience with dogma, select inerrant texts, and fixed hierarchies. These became yoked with patriarchy and the self-interest of men, the wealthy, and the educated. Accompanied by an emphasis on male-dominated imagery, creedal language, and rituals, men became and remain gatekeepers of spiritual experience (Jantzen, 1995).

Ancient associations with the earthly, the emotional, and the sensual have equated women with temptation, sin, and an inability to self-actualize (Jantzen, 1995). In most traditions, women have been considered inferior and "actual obstacles to men's spiritual progress" (Bancroft, 1987, p. x). Women's spiritual rejection has coexisted with her socio-economic, cultural, and sexual oppression. This breach from the intuitive, the intimate, the inclusive, leaves no one truly liberated.

Rather, theologian Lanzetta (2005) describes women's relationship with mystical spirituality in this way:

> Women live with an intuitive, if unrealized, sense of the mystical. They consistently display qualities of consciousness depicted as divine or holy; interdependence, mutuality, intimacy, pathos, moral outrage, passionate pain, righteous anger, caring, courage, compassion, and unself-interested love . . . They also participate in life processes and roles associated with awe, mystery, magic, and transcendence: biologically through menses, pregnancy, birth and lactation; as midwives, mothers, clergy, and caregivers; and as visionaries, shamans, mystics, prophets, and saints. (p. 157)

As the "living source" of faith, mysticism moves within but is not bound by structural, corporate, or devotional ideas (Teasdale, 1999, p. 11). Mysticism also has an inverse relationship to power. It favors the ego's annihilation over its accumulations. It positions itself in the desert more often than in cathedrals. It works toward simplicity, sacrifice, and powerlessness rather than authority, wealth, and status. It sheds the cloth of certainty in order to present the self in naked unknowing. In this way, it not only remains open to the unlearned, the novice, the poor, but finds within the open and ordinary heart rich conditions for consciousness to emerge.

DAKHINI

"A spark seems to have fallen suddenly upon it that has set it all on fire" (Teresa of Avila, 1991/16th c., p. 119).

The female mystic finds dynamic and resourceful ways of living between the clergy and the cosmos. In every century and religion, she has been found as rich, as poor, as wife, as witch, as nun. She has been desert *amma*, *sanyasini* (renunciate), mother to many, traveller, and reformer, often bridging religious traditions and working for social change (Teasdale, 1999). Female contemplatives wrote mystical itineraries, letters, and autobiographies, many of which were condemned, destroyed, or concealed by anonymity (Hollywood, 2002). Sufis, in particular, used poems and songs to convey their experiences (Adams Helminski, 2015). Their writings are raw, revisionist, and at times, erotic. Most worked against the norms of their time and many suffered greatly, enduring illness and persecution (McGinn, 2006).

Some of the best known include fourteenth-century anchoress Julian of Norwich; Mirabai, the sixteenth-century Hindu mystic; and Rabia of Basra (717–801), the first Sufi to articulate the relationship with the divine in the poetry of Lover and Beloved (Adams Helminsky, 2015). Many exist as unknown holy women who found the divine in the daily workings of their lives.

In eleventh-century India, Sukhasiddhi, mother of six, was cast from her home by her husband after she gave the last of the family's rice to a beggar. She began brewing her own rice wine and opened a restaurant. When she heard that Virupa, a famous yogi, lived nearby on a mountain, she began to send him free beer. In turn, he became Sukhasiddhi's teacher. She manifested *dakhini*, the female embodiment of enlightenment (Simmer-Brown, 2001).

Left ill following the difficult birth of her first child, Margery Kempe recovered after experiencing a vision of Christ. A housewife and home brewer, the fifteenth-century Englishwoman was known to have a proud and difficult nature. After bearing fourteen children, she convinced her husband to live a chaste life, finally leaving the family to travel on pilgrimages through Switzerland, Venice, Jerusalem, Prussia, Spain, and England. Kempe was labelled a heretic and insane. She was also the first woman to record her autobiography in English (Atkinson, 1985).

Spanish mystic Teresa of Avila (1515–1582), who entered the convent at nineteen, founded the Order of Discalced (Barefoot) Nuns as a sign of renunciation and poverty. She believed the Catholic Church needed reforming from within. By the time of her death, she had succeeded in establishing seventeen monasteries for nuns and fifteen for friars (Harkness, 1973). She remains the only woman to have founded religious orders for both men and women.

Born in Ukraine in the nineteenth century, Hannah Rachel Verbermacher studied Jewish texts from a young age. She spent much time in seclusion, experiencing visions and voices. She also opened her home in order to teach, give blessings, and to heal. She is recognized as one of the only female Hasidic leaders (Maroney, 2013).

Simone Weil (1909–1943) was a French Jewish woman who studied Catholicism and experienced repeated visions. She wrote about the relationship between religion, secular society, and technology. She is regarded as one of the century's most influential philosophers, social critics, and spiritual writers (McGinn, 2006).

THE GUHA

In the hidden *guha,* the cave of the heart, we meet the divine in honesty and freedom. The guha is the still point of true self where the deepest center (*atman*) is at one with the center of the universe, the Brahman. This is the dwelling place of eternal essence (Teasdale, 1999) and the place of return to deepest identity.

In Africa, the concept *ubuntu* "asserts that each person is endowed with inner energy" (Lanzetta, 2005, p. 183). Judaism, Christianity, and Islam use "soul" to describe this holy spark. God recognizes and yearns for God's self in the soul, drawing it upwards with great love (McGinn, 2006). When awakened, the soul responds in happy willingness to return to its primordial singlehood in God (Hollywood, 2002). For Buddhists, consciousness is the nature that is cultivated. The Buddhist concept of no-self (*anatman)* is not an individualistic state, but part of an eternal and universal whole that "unites love and knowledge" (Teasdale, 1999, p. 63).

THE LIVING BOOK

All lineages use practices to prepare for, and support, spiritual experience. Disciplines themselves are not the aim, but are used to clear any obstacle that maintains a sense of separation. Unhelpful daily habits, emotional responses, and mental patterns need clarity and rebalancing. It is the Sufi's *fana* or "passing away" of the lower self that requires constant sensory input and pursues its own security, comfort, and image (Lanzetta, 2005). In Hinduism, the world is *maya*, an illusion created by temptation that must be overcome (Teasdale, 1999). The space that remains within is one of surrender, mystery, and receptivity for consciousness to enter (Lanzetta, 2005).

Spiritual practices find expression in a cultural kaleidoscope. Study of holy scripture, as well as ritual, liturgy, and prayer, have been common in Christianity (Lanzetta, 2005), while Eastern traditions have drawn from meditation and simplicity. Both include silence, solitude, and a renunciation of personal will and material comfort (Teasdale, 1999).

In the sixth century, an anonymous Christian writer, known simply as Pseudo-Dionysius, distinguished between two ways of "contemplative consciousness": the *via positiva*, or way of affirmation, and the *via negativa*, or negative way (Lanzetta, 2005, p. 14). Both are necessary as the mystical path flows between the active and passive, named and unnamed, intellectual and bodily, in an interconnected dichotomy of contemplation and action. The paths of affirmation and negation are assumed and personified by women in ways that differ from men.

Via positiva uses names, physical, and emotional traits to describe and relate to divinity. It relies on established, passed-down traditions of ritual, good works, and virtue (McGinn, 2006). Practices include *lectio divina* of Christianity, the mantra-chanting and yoga of Hinduism (Teasdale, 1999), and the ecstatic dances of the Sufi dervishes.

Supported by ecclesiastic and political authority, male spirituality has largely been ritualistic, sacramental, and scholarly (Lanzetta, 2005). Historically, women had little access to academic and theological training except through monastic orders. When the Grand Inquisitor of Spain forbade the reading of mystical and devotional texts, some of the only written material Teresa of Avila and her nuns had access to, God appeared to Teresa in a vision saying, "Do not be distressed, for I will give you a living book" (McGinn, 2006, p. 110). It is from this "living book" of experience that feminine spirituality has drawn.

For the female devotee, the body becomes tool and text for mystical union (Lanzetta, 2005). Having some control over their bodies, female mystics often chose somatic disciplines, and the body became the site for the unitive experience. In thirteenth-century Christianity, women fasted, held night vigils, and confessed regularly. In some cases, they used extreme forms of asceticism that centered on holy inedia (refusing all food but the Eucharist), difficult physical work, and the imitation of the Passion of Christ (McGinn, 2006).

The body was also the site of revelation. Powerful visions, voices, and ecstasy were more frequently experienced by female mystics than by male ones (Jantzen, 1995). Although some of the more austere practices brought women close to starvation, illness, and death, many also recovered from serious illness due to encounters with the divine (McGinn, 2006).

For many, these powerful but temporary experiences were "only preparatory and peripheral," a stage to a higher level of consciousness (McGinn, 2006, p. xiii). Beliefs in the Middle Ages viewed woman as more "porous and imaginative than men and, therefore, open to possession (whether divine or demonic)" (Hollywood, 2002, p. 9). Though extreme cases exist, for many women, somatization was an empowering and transcendent act that used the most intimate means available to them—their own bodies—as "a profound expression of Incarnation" (Bruneau, 1998, p. 9). "Women mystics do not just know about or unite with divinity; they incarnate and embody Her, bearing in their bodies the marks of a realized intimacy" (Lanzetta, 2005, p. 98).

Here, the female mystic reclaims its ancient association with the bodily, the sensual, the emotive. The body becomes the bodhi tree, the mountain of transfiguration, the cave of encounter. It is the apostolic robe, the priestly medium of sacraments, and the intermediary between God and the world (Bruneau, 1998, p. 8). An embodiment of higher consciousness, the body is no longer reviled but becomes a vessel for truth, compassion, and awareness.

There is a well-known story of Rabia of Basra. One day, she was seen running with both a torch of fire and a pot of water. When asked the meaning of her actions, she replied, "I am going to quench the fires of Hell and burn Heaven, so that both these barriers to understanding shall vanish from the eyes of pilgrims, so that they may seek Truth without hope or fear" (Sakkakini, 1982, p. 3).

This is the *via negativa,* the "pathless path," in which nothing is desired but God (Lanzetta, 2005, p. 14). Negation recognizes that human principles, concrete language, and rational thought are not only limited or unhelpful, but dangerous when applied to an Ultimate Reality that is formless and inexpressible (Lanzetta, 2005, p. 15). Instead, will, desire, and activity are detached from and surrendered. It is a place of vulnerability where doubt, emptiness, and mystery are readily found (McGinn, 2006).

In Buddhism, meditation brings awareness that the true nature of reality is impermanence and emptiness. The "no-self" will pass away; only the eternal Buddha-nature survives. This reveals the futility of striving, of attachment, of individual identification. Contemplation and meditation practice letting go into a state of nothingness (Teasdale, 1999).

For women, this nothingness is not the nothingness experienced when viewed as property, sexual instruments, or domestic help. Instead, it differs from male mystical experiences in that, "It is not primarily about letting go of power, ego, and will, as it is passing through women's gendered 'nothingness' to finally gain perspective and wisdom over their own lives"

(Lanzetta, 2005, p. 96). Expectations and labels that are both false and harmful fall away and return women to true identity that is free, beyond worldly authority, and ultimately honored and secure (Lanzetta, 2005). A position of repose, negation rests in pure presence.

Affirmation and negation are also found in spiritual symbolism. Divinity has largely been imaged in male form, representations which limit and exclude vital characteristics of Ultimate Truth. Though mystics report difficulty describing their experiences, written attempts often use feminine metaphors for describing the soul's receptivity to the Divine, as well as the relational dimensions of mystic experience. This is true for both male and female mystics (Lanzetta, 2005; McGinn, 2006).

In mystical texts, the Divine finds expression as *Theotokos,* the Mother of God in Eastern Orthodox tradition. In Judaism, she is *Sophia Wisdom* and *Shekhinah,* the feminine indwelling. She is Buddhism's and Hinduism's *bodhisattva* of compassion, and Islam's *rahim* or womb of the All-Merciful. Taoists hold her as the source of all, the Ten Thousand Things (Lanzetta, 2005, p. 45).

Christian mystics such as Julian of Norwich, Gertrude of Helfta, Hildegaard of Birgen, and Mechthild of Magdeberg wrote extensively of Jesus and God as Mother. To Origen in the third century, "every devout soul was both bride and mother" (McGinn, 2006, p. 402). In the Qur'an, each *surah* or chapter opens with "In the Name of God, the Beneficent, the Merciful." Both "beneficent" and "merciful" derive from the root of the word "womb," and underscore Allah's nurturance and generosity (Adams Helminsky, 2015, p. 5).

In Christianity and Sufism, language is intensely personal, describing the divine and soul in relational terms. It is the mutual gaze and passionate embrace between Lover and Beloved. In its ultimate form, it is expressed as the long-awaited marriage union of Bride and Bridegroom (Adams Helminsky, 2015; McGinn, 2006).

As well as affirming the feminine, mystic writing also expresses the linguistic *apophatic* or "un-saying" tradition that is an undoing of religious icons and pronouns that eliminate the feminine (Lanzetta, 2005). Negation is the basis of Judaism's unutterable name of God, *YHWH,* and Hinduism's "*neti,neti:* God is not this (neti), and not that (neti)" (Teasdale, 1999, p. 59). "For the higher we soar," wrote Pseudo-Dionysius, "the more limited become our expressions . . . we pass not merely into brevity of speech, but even into absolute silence, of thoughts as well as of words" (McGinn, 2006, p. 287). Silence holds the "'immense remnant' of everything in human experience that has not been tamed and symbolized by language" (Bruneau, 1998, p. 6).

It is in this "immense remnant" that experience moves from affirmation to negation, identity to intimacy, and finally beyond these dualities. When the draw of paradise and the threat of hell are no longer motivators, Love alone becomes the intention. Emptiness is an enigma; it is a void, and yet, it is also the state where absolute interconnectedness, peace, joy, and compassion are found (Teasdale, 1999). It creates a spaciousness within to be used by inspired forces.

THE FINAL INTEGRATION

> "What, do you wish to know your Lord's meaning in this thing? Know it well, love was [the] meaning. Who reveals it to you? Love. What did [the Lord] reveal to you? Love. Why does [the Lord] reveal it to you? For love." (Julian of Norwich, 1978/14th c., p. 342)

What is the nature of this final stage? At the apex of experience, the kaleidoscope of lineages integrate into a final understanding of the inherent unity between creature, creation, and Creator (Smith, 1976, p. 3). The soul reaches divinization and consummation; the atman returns to Brahman; freedom from attachment results in Enlightenment (Teasdale, 1999).

There is often a connection between suffering and transformation of consciousness as a devotee experiences alternating states of painful self-realizations and blissful revelations of the divine. The mystic experiences the angst of their own failings, limitations, and habitual patterns of suffering that have kept them separate from the love of God (Lanzetta, 2005). They desire to overcome these at any cost, showing even a "willingness to be consigned to hell, if that be God's will" (McGinn, 2006, p. 366). Fear, trembling, great distress, loss of faith, and feelings of abandonment are reported. Christian mystics also write of intimately sharing the agony of Christ's Passion (McGinn, 2006). Just as powerful are feelings of overwhelming love, ecstasy, awe, rapture, and joy. Buddhists describe deep peace, compassion, and loving-kindness (Teasdale, 1999).

Though sensory experiences vary, mystics report that divisions between time and eternity, separation and space, and the material and spiritual, are overcome. The mystic experiences great internal freedom and becomes, if not for a moment, ageless and deathless (Teasdale, 1999). For women, encounters with a radically loving presence are "more than a one-time *experience* of divine presence, or even a sustained and infused *feeling* of divinity," but are instead a condition that removes "everything and anything that stands in the way of the original freedom between God and the person" (Lanzetta, 2005, p. 82).

It is noteworthy that science is beginning to affirm this experience of Oneness. Quantum physics finds, at both micro and macro levels of the universe, interrelated energy fields that profoundly influence each other and connect individuals and environments across time and space (Wheatley, 2006).

One vital difference between mystical experience and other euphoric states is its transformative result. When a person becomes self-actualized, takes on the Christ Consciousness, or embodies the love of the Creator, this state finds fulfillment in a lifestyle of humility and simplicity, steadfastness and joy in the face of suffering, a deep commitment to *ahimsa* or nonviolence, and selfless, compassionate service to others (Harkness, 1973; Teasdale, 1999).

THE BODHISATTVA

> Ultimately, we have just one moral duty: to reclaim large areas of peace in ourselves, more and more peace, and to reflect it towards others. And the more peace there is in us, the more peace there will be in our troubled world. (Hillesum, 1996/1981, p. 226)

Transformation of consciousness does not occur in isolation. Deep solidarity with the universe moves healing from an individual to a social salvation embodied in ecological responsibility and human rights (Lanzetta, 2005, p. 182). Christian mystics speak not only of being reborn by divinity, but of bearing and birthing divinity to the world (McGinn, 2006). This is also the way of the bodhisattva, the one who delays personal enlightenment to labor instead for the liberation of all beings (Harkness, 1973, p. 170).

Contemplation is a way of re-visioning the world. It is "always revolutionary, for it takes apart what is comfortable and convenient, asking us to see the world from God's perspective" (Lanzetta, 2005, p. 66). The ousting of the individual ego allows us to more clearly see the collective one of structural poverty, war, genocide, capitalism, and consumerism.

Female mysticism has often found its end in social justice. The Beguines were an order of lay women in thirteenth-century Europe who struggled particularly with the integration of poverty, preaching, and social action. Taking no formal vows, they supported themselves by manual labor and devoted their lives to serving the poor and sick (Petroff, 1991). Teresa of Avila's encounter with God's goodness stood in sharp contrast with the mistreatment she suffered because of her womanhood. Rather than deny her suffering, she joined it to the suffering of the world, using both to reform Catholicism (Lanzetta, 2005). A contemporary example of spiritual social justice is found in Sister Helen Prejean, an American nun and advocate for the abolition of the death penalty (Flinders, 2006).

A pressing global issue today is the status of the Earth as a living entity. Drawing inward to silence, solitude, and simplicity offers insight and an alternative to a culture of continuous stimulation, consumption, and acquisition. Simplicity, as a mystical practice and outcome, lessens our dependence on other species, restores life balance, and frees energy for other uses (Teasdale, 1999). The mystic's ability to hold paradox and mystery fosters patience to steadily work toward change.

Women, who hold life in their flesh and give life to new flesh, are inextricably "wed to creation" (Lanzetta, 2005, p. 166). Theirs is a physical, connected spirituality that is expressed as a *way of being*. Relationally, women go beyond the moral code to hold within their bodies tolerance, justice, and mercy. Buddhist teacher Pema Chödrön, Christian contemplative Cynthia Bourgeault, spiritual leader Ammachi, and Sufi Camille Adams Helminski are women working toward social justice, interreligious dialogue, and the alleviation of suffering. It is women's ability to "integrate the highest states of mystic contemplation with the pastoral needs of their sisters, neighbours, and friends that sets apart women's mystical legacy" (Lanzetta, 2005, p. 81).

CONTEMPORARY MYSTICISM

Of what relevance is mysticism today? What does enlightenment, salvation, and liberation mean in the twenty-first century?

In wealthy countries, life is marked by a new set of dichotomies: an increase in the quantity of personal connection without a corresponding increase in quality; education in isolation from wisdom; an abundance of luxuries and a growing dissatisfaction with possessions; leisure time without creativity (Harkness, 1973, p. 17). Women confront a collective voice urging them to *do, be, and have* more, both inside and outside the home, an accomplishment that demands greater fracturing of self (Lanzetta, 2005). We are desensitized to our own life force, numbed by an "intoxicating culture that dispenses the narcotics of dissipation and superficiality" (Teasdale, 1999, p. 106). Women have become disconnected from the "Mother-Line" of spiritual women to which they belong (Flinders, 2006, p. 3).

Women have sought spiritual refuge in the forest, the desert, the cave, as well as in convents and the sangha (Teasdale, 1999). But to where does a woman return today for contemplation, for rest, for sanctuary?

Within each woman is "an inner monastery where she and her beloved divinity are alone" (Lanzetta, 2005, p. 168). This monastery requires no conditions. It is not one of selfish retreat; the woman who is depleted and splintered cannot be truly effective, loving, or life-giving. It is within this monastery, this guha, that a woman regains her grounding, finds resiliency, and is reestablished in the world with clarity, strength, and new levels of intimacy. Family and other close relationships increase the capacity for connection with the divine (Adams Helminsky, 2015). The ordinary, the daily, the mundane, become doorways to awaken moment by moment (Lanzetta, 2005).

In addition to affirmation and negation, Lanzetta (2005) offers the *via feminina*, or "feminine way," which recognizes and encourages alternative practices, metaphors, and pathways to God, meaningful for both women and men who seek a new approach to spirituality (p. 13). The *via feminina* esteems spiritual leadership and action based on inclusivity, compromise, and nonviolence.

CONCLUSION

Though finding expression through specific faith traditions, time periods, and personalities, mystical encounters are remarkably alike: "a reality in the depths of the self that is, paradoxically, Other and irrevocably separate from us" (Armstrong, 1994, p. xii). Mysticism brings ever-fresh revelation to ancient beliefs while offering participation in the "community of consciousness," a way of seeing that reveals unity within spectacular diversity and works toward interspirituality, ecological interdependence, and human liberation (Teasdale, 1999, p. 241).

For women who walk the threshold of spiritual experience, the Room Prepared offers an intimate way of being known that is always affirming, restorative, and energetic. It rebuilds authority on authenticity, where revelation, vision, truth, and love continuously unfold at a personal level. In this room "every woman is a conduit, translator, prophet, redeemer, and mother of the sacred world—she who is female power to create and generate change" (Lanzetta, 2005, p. 167). A woman enters the room because refreshment of soul and of self is necessary, because there is no chance at failure, because it is her birthright. She enters it "for Love." The Room is Prepared; one needs only to enter.

REFERENCES

Adams Helminsky, C. (2015). Women and Sufism. Retrieved on August 4, 2015, from http://sufism.org/articles/women-and-sufism-by-camille-adams-helminski-2

Armstrong, K. (1994). *Visions of God: Four medieval mystics and their writing*. New York, NY: Bantam Books.

Atkinson, C. W. (1985). *Mystic and pilgrim: The book and the world of Margery Kempe*. Ithaca, NY: Cornell University Press.

Bancroft, A. (1987). Women in Buddhism. In U. King (Ed.), *Women in the world's religions: Past and present* (pp. 81–103). New York, NY: Paragon House Publishers.

Bruneau, M. (1998). *Women mystics confront the modern world*. Albany, NY: State University of New York Press.

Flinders, C. L. (2006). *Enduring lives: Living portraits of women and faith in action*. Maryknoll, NY: Orbis Books.

Harkness, G. (1973). *Mysticism: Its meaning and message*. Nashville, TN: Abingdon Press.

Hillesum, E. (1996). *An interrupted life and letters from Westerbork*. New York, NY: Henry Holt and Company Inc. (Original work published 1981).

Hollywood, A. (2002). *Sensible ecstasy: Mysticism, sexual difference, and the demands of history*. Chicago, IL: University of Chicago Press.

Jantzen, G. M. (1995). *Power, gender and Christian mysticism*. Cambridge, England: Cambridge University Press.

Julian of Norwich, Saint. (1978). *Showings*. Mahway, NJ: Paulist Press. (Original work published ca. 14th c.)

Lanzetta, B. J. (2005). *Radical wisdom: A feminist mystical theology*. Minneapolis, MN: Fortress Press.

Lao Tsu. (1997). *Tao Te Ching*. G.F. Feng and J. English (Trans.). New York, NY: Vintage Books. (Original work published 6th c. BCE.)

Maroney, E. (2013, March). Erased from tradition: The maiden of Ludmir. *The Montreal Review*. Retrieved on August 8, 2015, from http://www.themontrealreview.com/2009/Maiden-of-Ludmir.php.

McGinn, B. (Ed.). (2006). *The essential writings of Christian mystics*. New York, NY: Modern Library.

Petroff, E. A. (1991). The mystics. *Christian History, 30*. Retrieved on August 8, 2015, from http://www.christianhistoryinstitute.org/magazine/article/women-in-medieval-church-mystics/.

Sakkakini, W. E. (1982). *First among Sufis: The life and thought of Rabia al-Adawiyya*. London, England: Octagon Press Limited.

Simmer-Brown, J. (2001). *Dakini's warm breath: The feminine principle in Tibetan Buddhism*. Boston, MA: Shambhala Publications.

Smith, M. (1976). *The way of the mystics: The early Christian mystics and the rise of the Sufis*. London, England: Sheldon Press.

Teasdale, W. (1999). *The mystic heart*. Novato, CA: New World Library.

Teresa of Avila, Saint. (1991). *The Life of Teresa of Jesus*. (Translated by E. Allison Peers). United States: Image Books. (Original work published ca. 16th c.)

Wheatley, M. J. (2006). *Leadership and the new science: Discovering order in a chaotic world*. San Francisco, CA: Berrett-Koehler Publishers, Inc.

Chapter 15

The Feminine Spiritual

Deborah Brock

INTRODUCTION: THE MISNOMER

One quest threads through all of humanity: a spiritual source of identification. The religions that have formed and maintained them seem to provide spooling for various threads of spirituality, but it is spirituality itself that is the life blood. There is a delicious wealth of feminist literature and culture focusing on feminine spirituality. The feminine and the spiritual are seemingly synonymous in much of human history, and especially when perceived through Goddess history, which as a major cultural phenomena, stands on its own historical merit.

The Mother Goddess of ancient civilizations provides what seems like a primal understanding of this entwinement of spirituality and the feminine. Because the female body was perceived to be the magical portal through which life recycled, it became an object of reverence and worship. Only through the physical cave of the female could life resurge, and consequently the feminine body became godlike and hence the Goddess. Because it was from the moist vaginal earth that life was created and substance was found, creation and life came to be represented in the Goddess. There was no separation between the life-giving body of the Goddess and the life-sustaining gifts from the earth. The Mother Goddess was, in and of herself, the essence of spirituality as it was then understood: woman as divine and earth as medium through which one met the divine. The worship of Mother Goddess was intrinsic to life itself. However, the Mother Goddess got lost over time and space in the long generations of human shifting.

In the throes of the great Liberation Movement of the 1960s, however, the Mother Goddess returned in full force. As Carr (1986) wisely suggests, spirituality is "individually patterned but culturally shaped" (p. 50). The feminine was assigned to spirituality as an exclusive equation through the resurgence of the Goddess culture. This equation was a feminist effort to exorcize the spiritual out of an oppressive patriarchal religious context. The efforts of the Goddess reframe as a feminist adjunct was essential to bring into the feminine equation a non-religious but sacred affiliation. Today, countless women across the world actively engage in ritual Goddess ceremonies, in worship of the Goddess, in participation as Goddesses, and in a social network of feminine fun. This lovely and lively display of personification serves its own purposes for the ever-present need for ritualistic and symbolic connections to the divine as well as connections to a like-minded community—both essential pieces of a matured spirituality. This return to the Mother Goddess as a banner cry for feminine freedom, specifically in a spiritual sense, restored what had been seemingly lost in the memory of history. This restored feminine highlighted the ever present flow of a strong feminine nature in everyday spirituality; passion itself. For many, this Goddess rediscovery was a first gasp of fresh air following a long stale history of personal, social, and gender suppression. Not only did the Goddess movement demonstrate that women possessed a strong spiritual nature, it reiterated some of the most important components or traits of spirituality: independent strength, purpose, and personal identification.

While spirituality in a feminine context has its roots in the Goddess tradition, a full feminine spirituality cannot be limited to an exacting transfer of Goddess worship, even though there are powerful components that we dare not lose again, such as our connection and responsibility to the web of the earth. Spirituality is more than Goddess worship, which alone could become yet another religion. Goddess religion alone would stifle the flow of a genuine spirituality, potentially slipping into absolute templates of demand and oppression. Spirituality cannot be staid; it must be given its own right to flow through time and space so that the cultural context itself is the impetus for its direction. In other words, it has to be discovered through individual life force to move cultures forward in a tangible way.

Perhaps the single best word for the essence of spirituality as demonstrated in the feminine is *passion*. In Walsch's (1995) classic attempt to humanize spirituality through blatant conversation with the divine, he suggests that passion is simply "God wanting to say Hi" (p. 102). I admire both the simplicity and profundity of Walsch's suggestion that true human passion is the divine seeking connection. Depending on our perception, passion can be simple or infinitely complex. Passion is an unintended surge of direction or a calling. People do not assign passions to themselves; passions are assigned to them, and often, seemingly rise up from unknown places. Hillman (1996) says that each of us is in possession of our own unique daimon, a "soul-companion," responsible for nudging us into our passion. Hillman dares to say that our daimon is the carrier of our destiny. These are strong words with a serious intention, but I believe that he is correct. If deterred or ignored, passion culminates in a life of great disappointment. If passion is ignored or unfulfilled, the basic purpose of life is unfulfilled, undirected, and "un-spirited." As Walsch suggests, when passion is destroyed or dismissed, the divine is lost. We cannot live without it and without it the divine is lost in us.

Passion as a primary definition of spirituality is important for the feminine. In examining women's spiritual search through rhythm, Redmond (1997) says, "behind this surging feminine energy is a yearning to understand who they are and what their purpose in life is. They long to live meaningful lives in harmonious rhythm with the sacred energies of the earth and heavens" (p. 7). Whether we retrace our origins to the ancient Goddess or the God of the Old Testament, we find the most primal and basic rhythm of all: breath, the only constant of life and death. Breath, the life force that either extends or terminates our physical condition, is equally a spiritual metaphor for passion. As we breathe and inhale the very substance of life, air, we can also inhale divine spirituality, through which we discover our direction and fulfill our purpose. Without breath there is no life, no personal awareness, no artistic inspiration, no drive toward action. Divine breath initially filled our outer clay molds with mobility and function while filling our inner sense with purpose and hope. Without such breath we are inanimate, insignificant, and lifeless. With divine breath instilled, we experience an inner insistence to reproduce that with which we have been instilled. When we are filled with spiritual breath and consequent passion, we must both sense and act. Passion can often lie dormant for years in an individual and for generations in a culture. Passion must simmer and brew, and then come to a full boil in its rightful time. Passion must come to activity to be truly spiritual. Breath must circulate.

One of my greatest Gestalt therapist mentors, Richard Olney, taught me a mantra as both a self-regulation and an ignition for passion: "I give thanks for life. I honor life." The giving thanks is inhaled: humbly accepting the goodness of life. The honoring of life is the exhale: appreciating and returning life's goodness. I still use this mantra for myself and I teach it to my clients with the intention of helping them circulate the goodness of their feminine passion. In circulating passion, we each identify our best qualities and then discover how to access those qualities so that we can present our contributions to life at large. We activate our spirituality in the physical and relational world.

In this present discussion I attempt to examine the passion of breath as it is exemplified by the aesthetic mothers, both those of the desert and of the early and middle century monasteries. These great spiritual women are some of our earliest examples of feminine spiritual breath. They exhibit the essential qualities of a flowing spirituality: independent strength and impassioned purpose and drive demonstrated in concrete and practical ways that nurtured themselves and served others.

THE ASCETIC MOTHERS

We find in the early Desert and Monastic Mothers a common passion that drove them out of the world and into themselves, nurturing privacy for the purpose of introspection and as a means of rediscovering a personal spiritual nurturing. Like the great Persian queen Esther, who was consigned to the closed doors of the palace, we might sense that providence, across time and space, planned for the early mothers to close the doors upon themselves so contemporary mothers could open them back up. The early Desert and Monastic Mothers, with their internalizing breath, incubated a passion so essential that it would ride through generations and rattle all the way to present history in a movement toward social justice. In other words, as we explore these female lives individually or collectively, we find the great Feminine Spiritual, rhythmically breathing in and out, preserving life, enhancing life, and restoring life as necessary.

Identifiable Traits of the Ascetic Mothers

The most clarified traits personified in the lives of the Desert and Monastic Mothers are two significant components, seemingly paradoxical: 1) a *call to be apart* that required a sense of bold independence and a qualitative level of self-acceptance, and 2) a *draw to community* that ultimately served as a source of sustenance as well as companionship. Both separateness and community relied on a concrete reality and on connection.

The Call Apart

Ryan (1998) boldly states "most of us, myself included, would rather defend ourselves *against* our own potential greatness, because we know the sacrifices that living such greatness would require" (p. 19). The aesthetics of the early to middle centuries apparently knew that activation of their greatness was an absolute requirement for the sustaining of a feminine spirituality. Knowing this, they dared to retreat from the social-political crises of the times as a means of self-preservation. This retreat was no easy task given that the environments to which they retreated were potentially hostile in and of themselves. Ryan also suggests that there is urgency innate to any call, an urgency not to be confused with a frantic self-condemnation but rather a clarification and intent toward its end. The Desert Mothers, in particular, recognized this urgency and took a tremendous risk. The church they knew, through which they had discovered and impassioned their spirituality, was experiencing a dangerous whiplash. To stay in the emerging social, i.e., public, environment as it was headed was an obvious dissolution of its personal content as well as an increasing forfeiture of their female status within that context.

The Desert Mothers knew they needed to draw apart from society to preserve the personal quality of their spiritual strength. Their call was to separate. They had already acquired a self-acceptance through their spiritual experience. That was the initial or authentic gospel message: personal freedom through realized truth. This spiritual confidence was lodged deep within these early women and served them well not only in their trek to the desert, as it were, but in their self-maintenance as well. Their spirituality was manifested through passion, as intensely joyful as it was arduous in service. Bolen (1984) might attribute the archetype Hestia, a goddess of wisdom, to these early Desert Mothers in that they possessed an inner groundedness, an internal sense of connectedness despite the chaos around them. Bolen reminds us that "The Self is what we experience inwardly when we feel a relationship to oneness that connects us to the essence of everything outside of us" (p. 114). Bolen's noted paradox of "connecting and detachment" is similar to the lives of the Desert Mothers as well as the Monastic Mothers. These ascetics heeded a call to private and individualized service to maintain the quality of a personal spirituality. Their detachment was in the form of the desert or the monastery. Their connection was in their community of one another in service and with the earth.

TO WHERE DID THIS CALLING TAKE THEM?

While the Desert Mothers wandered into the isolation of the wilderness, the Monastic Mothers sought sanctuary in mortared communities. The centrality of simplicity and earth's sustenance within both of these environments was predominate and served as a spiritual tether. These drawings, similar but different, were sources of sustenance as well as companionship. The Sustenance component is evident: to survive in an isolated or cloistered environment required determination and improvisation, not to mention faith and grace! The companionship with the earth cannot be overplayed. Relationship with the earth has always been a hallmark of any feminine-based spirituality. The Desert Mothers recognized that their relationship with the raw desert was very intimate in both a beautiful and a terrifying way. Both of these components, sustenance and companionship, cycle back to the Goddess Mother. Christ (1997) reminds us that the Goddess image is not regulated to a delicate and venerable form. Ultra-feminizing the Goddess is fantasy. The Goddess is constructed, if you will, of a tough and hard core, like that of Pele, who spews rock and lava up out of her belly and builds land mass from that molten flow. As Homer (*Hymn to the Earth*, Public Domain) dared to barter future poetic recognition should the Mother honor his present life, he sang to her in his classic verse, "Mother of us all, oldest of all, hard, splendid as rock. Whatever there is of the land it is She who nourishes it."

Going "back to the earth" in seclusion and simplicity was a natural inclination for the ascetics. Certainly the Desert Mothers understood how the strength and demands of the harsh desert could strengthen sinew of body and spirit. It was from the earth they came and now back to the earth they went for spiritual rehabilitation. They harnessed the desert's hostility and the cloistered darkness by doing what many women do best: using their minds first and then using their hands in concert with what they intuitively discovered. They honed and relied on the most well-known components of ascetic life.

DESERT MOTHERS—MONASTIC MOTHERS

There is much entwinement between the Desert and Monastic Mothers. Most obvious is that they both chose seclusion. They separated geographically and behaviorally. The Desert Mothers withdrew into themselves a solitary breath that served as self-preservation, while the Monastic Mothers, still secluded but in larger community, began to breathe outwardly by using their toils and resources to serve in their communities.

Knowledge was a central component for the early Mothers. The Desert Mothers were perhaps more intuitive in their transference of knowledge in that their focus was not primarily on reading. We find that reading is central to the monastic life, however. In the desert, knowledge was transmitted one-on-one through Ammas, spiritual warriors of the desert. Securing one's Amma, or mother-teacher, was essential for the Desert Mothers. The Amma had acquired a solid understanding of the spiritual teachings and used her intuitive communication to educate her students. Swan (2001) notes that for the Desert Mothers it was "the kernel of the teaching that was important, not historical accuracy as we understand it today" (p. 18). With the Monastic Mothers there was a tremendous emphasis placed on reading—both discernment of the content and the advancement of instruction that came through their reading and acquisition of knowledge. While we don't have much directly written by the Monastic Mothers, nor are we in possession of their direct reports, historical commentary clearly illustrates the virtuous level of reading and knowledge of these women.

Because the Desert and Monastic Mothers were resistant to cultural expectation, the self-acceptance and independence of the ascetic mothers was quite evident. Because the Desert Mothers would not succumb to the social dictates of the fast developing and limiting Greco-Roman domain that infiltrated their spiritual community, they left their possessions and went to the barren desert. The relative new freedom that Christ taught had been widely advanced and highly enhanced through female followers. The communities in which they served were blooming with personal and social liberation that had been initiated by Jesus's remarkable equalizing of the sexes and granting of basic equality to all human beings.

When Constantine centralized Christianity in the fourth century, patriarchal dominance swiftly began to return, especially in the church. In this atmosphere, it was clear that not only would the spirit of the community/ service-based church be numbed, but women's freedom of leadership and personal direction would likewise be curtailed. With this impending and profound shift back into social female oppression, the ascetic Mothers retreated, not just for personal insight and meditation, but to avert forfeiture of spirituality as they knew and treasured it. So while there certainly was a personal and social initiation to asceticism, there was also that intuitive sense of an impending flaw in the system which dictated suffering by choice over suffering by oppression. Ryan (1998) suggests the Desert Mothers, driven by the Roman culture, were a "misguided attempt to control life, and thus a sure way to destroy the soul" (p. 26). In this sense, desert seclusion was simply spiritual self-preservation. It was indeed a deep spiritual inhalation that needed to last thought the oncoming centuries.

Living the Desert

Through clear writing and abundant stories, the spirit and breath of the Desert Mothers becomes tangible hundreds of years later through Swan's succinct presentation of Desert Spirituality (2001, pp. 20–31). The Desert Mothers were foremost about the "pursuit of abundant simplicity grounded in the possession of little—and the abundance of God's presence" (p. 21). Their detachment, notes Swan, was about cultivation of their truest selves. They were intimate and vulnerable within themselves and with their Ammas or spiritual mentors. Finally, they were incarnational: they trusted being full of God was being full of self. From this fullness they could give freely. This God-in-self experience was a very mature and integrated perception and no doubt was the deepest portion of their inward breath.

Anyone with a mindfulness approach to life or a monastic history will recognize that the practices of the ascetics were indeed simple and filled with intention. The ascetics sought solitude, yet were hospitable in relationships. Humility, suffering, and compassion were conceived as virtues of maturity rather than signs of weakness or self-assault. Prayer for all the ascetic Mothers was an endearing communiqué with their Maker but it also manifested action. Doherty (1985) says it well: "Thousands of books have been written on prayer. I don't suppose God minds the books, but I think he wants you and me to *be* the book. He wants us to *be* the word. He wants us to reflect his face" (pp. 7–8). Prayers, says Swan, were more of a yearning heart than a recitation. Recitation was reserved for daily psalms, songs of the soul that were communicated through bodily self-expression and were some of the deepest expressions of reverence. "Reverenced as a source of life, the word was seen as having a capacity to awaken deep sensitivity and to transmit life energy" (p. 28). With only the slightest guard, my personal projection can only imagine the freedom of dance and song that the Desert Mothers might have displayed as they lived out the psalms under the desert night skies.

The last two qualities or practices of these ascetic Mothers in the context of prayer are listening and, of course, silence. Listening, for the ascetic, was a practice in contemplation. It was a modality to avert judgment and distraction. Listening was just that: a practice of mindfully waiting, listening for hints from one's spirit. Silence, perhaps the most renowned practice, was the privilege to be fully present with the Divine—so much so that there could be no conflict between one's sprit and the spirit of the Divine. Swan cites a passage that most beautifully draws the picture:

> Drawn deeper into the desert, they are drawn deeper into solitude, deeper into themselves and at the same time deeper into community and deeper into God the ground of being, and thus closer to the ground of being within us, for the depth of being of each of us is as strange and alien, yet hauntingly as familiar, as the desert solitude. (Paphnutius, 2000, p. 10)

The secure, concrete literality of asceticism attracted hundreds of women through hundreds of years of desert and monastic life. Still today women and men of all interests seek a desert or monastic experience through either a vowed lifestyle or through retreats and daily meditation practices. Going apart, being alone, and finding one's inner spirit provides an honest, attainable, and fulfilling source of spiritual connection.

This quest for spiritual connection takes us back to the Goddess in a spirituality that is virginal in intent. The desert and monastic life was—and is intended to be—virginal in separating out from and abandoning external attachments and becoming one in spirit with God and God-in-self. It was a holy quest, to no longer be spoiled by strong emotions deemed to be negative, erupting out of physical, social, or relational needs. This depth of personal freedom and self-acceptance suggests that the ascetic Mothers consciously chose to follow an intuitive drive. It is in this intuition that we have the concrete melded with the abstract. Women did indeed displace their sexual drive in exchange for a full integration with the spirit. And yet, abstractly, and even allegorically, in becoming virginal, they inhaled a spiritual insemination that would be birthed generations later through social and gender equality.

Living the Monasteries

The transition from Desert Mothers to Monastic Mothers is really more about environment than time, since there is much overlap between them. The environments of these two ascetic clusters have great similarities in the ways they practiced their devotion and spiritual development. Many of the traits and activities that Swan attributed to the Desert Mothers hold fast for the Monastic Mothers. Their reflection went deep and sincere, and was as practical as well as intuitive. They graced their communities with enriched services to the poor and needy and blessed the ill and dying. They toiled on their property to supply for themselves and their communities as much as was possible. They relied on each other within their communities for spiritual communion and direction. They were as equally called out from the greater society via a personal and cultural passion to secure their thread of spirituality exercised in both private meditation and their service to their respective communities. The asceticism primarily evidenced in separation and isolation with the Desert Mothers, however, shifted to the asceticism of the Monastic Mothers where their spirituality was demonstrated more communally, both within their monastic communities and in society at large.

According to Ranft (2000), this broadening was based on freedom of choice in using personal resources. This great shift from a rather insular environment to a socially conscious life can be seen as a developmental, evolutionary, and maturing process which broadened the spiritual breath. Beginning with the overlap of the desert experience and monasteries in the earliest centuries, the feminine spirit deepened as the Monastic Mothers began to flow back out to a larger public life. As the Desert Mothers had taken a deep breath to survive in isolation, the Monastic Mothers began to move into select communities, breathing their personal resources toward a greater influence.

Schulenburg (1998) lends us a remarkable compilation of the historical environment of the *Mulieres Sanctae*, women saints. What is most featured in many of the histories of these saintly mothers can easily be considered an archetype of influence. In many of the stories recorded, the women who took the lead roles in these monastic communities were self-assigned or assigned to administrative roles because of their already elevated social status. Many women entered these monastic communities coming from wealth, a wealth that assisted the development of the monasteries and led to the leadership roles as abbess. Within the context of that social stratus, we find an increased opportunity that was seized upon by the women to use their means, or the means of their family, to create and maintain the sisterly environment. Then, within this environment, they coalesced their energies and transformed their segment of the world. If the Desert Mothers were intuitive, independent agents of the elements, the Monastic Mothers were conscious agents of the system. They breathed no deeper than the Desert Mothers, but in social context, they exhaled as administrators and social agents *par excellence.*

While coming to a monastery with financial means was helpful to some of these early women leaders, many of the actions and lifelong directives of these women came out of their independent thinking and subsequent skills of persuasion. These skills redirected many decisions regarding the downtrodden and enslaved. One short story, so indicative of this gift of persuasion through persistence, rests with St. Genovefa, patron of Paris (as read in Schulenburg, 1998, p. 75). Genovefa was known well and respected by the king for her social justice. The king, knowing Genovefa would try to dissuade him regarding his decision to execute a number of slaves, deliberated and decided to transport the slaves with him out of region. Subsequently, the king discovered that, following her passion for mercy, she had followed him and his army and whilst on the long road, she did indeed persuade him to spare the lives of the slaves.

The Monastic Mothers, living in community, maintained a great responsibility to each other as well as those outside their monastic walls. Delightful stories—some in fact, some in fable, and some collaborated across commentaries—reflect the extended breath of the Monastic Mothers. Stories of healing, stories of provision, stories of mediation in argument, and stories of jurisdiction in legalities abound. These stories, however, are not singular in plot. Multiple graces, gifts, and capacities are related toward any one of the Mothers. It isn't that one had one gift and another some other gift. Brigid of Kildare (fifth century), for example, is known to have given her chariot horses to carry the loads of passing pilgrims, exemplifying her extended breath toward those unknown to her and unaffiliated with her or her order. She also possessed in-depth knowledge of herbs and contemporary medicines and used her healing skills frequently. She is also said to have possessed great ability in administrating her society. These same virtues and gifts of compassion, wisdom, and logistics are noted similarly for many of the Mothers. Marcella (fourth century) was said to live quietly in her asceticism and in "holy tranquility" until a "tornado of heresy" blew things apart (Ranft, 2000, p. 59). When wind of "the new heresy" regarding Origen's (1973) *On First Principles* began to blow, she rose from her tranquility and stepped into the center stage to become the leader against the heresy. Ranft elaborates by quoting Jerome of her, "This much only will I say, that whatever in me was the fruit of long study and as such made by constant meditation a part of my nature, this she tasted, this she learned and made her own" (Jerome, letter 39, in NPNF, 6:49). Marcella was born to high status and lived thus until she was widowed. Then, after having warded off her suitors, not for want of financial security, but for her dedication to celibacy, she was ridiculed by high society. This societal rejection was no deterrent to her. She was eventually known to be a great tutor of great men.

There are many accounts of the knowledge base these women possessed. Numerous Monastic Mothers established libraries and advocated literacy. Hilda (middle 600s) is one of the better known in this category of library builders. She built a great library to which locals and nationals came to read and learn. Hilda is also recognized as the great mediator between rival religious traditions, moderating the debates at the Synod of Whitby in 664. It is said of Hilda that she counseled the meekest of the meek and the highest of royalty and that she continued to teach even upon her death bed.

The remarkable stories of social justice administered by the Monastic Mothers demonstrate how they expanded beyond a private monastic life with great energy. To maintain and revive this extended energy, they relied on their own sister community. The sisterhood of the monastic is self-descriptive. The friendship, kinship, or bonding within the community was intense. Schulenburg quotes from Gregory the Great and Isidore of Seville, "a friend is the *custos animi* or guardian of one's soul" (quote originating in McGuire, *Friendship and Community*, noted in Schulenburg, 1998, p. 308, n. 8). This definitive soul caring was a centrality in the monastic life. Unfortunately, much of the historical focus on midlevel monasticism has been on sexual concerns within and without the monastery. Holy men, so absorbed in self-righteous chastity, feared the female body (Schulenburg calls them "phobic holy men"). This basic lack of personal and social development sometimes presented a great absence of cross-sex friendship. The Monastic Mothers recognized the impracticality and even the silliness of this absolutism and disregarded it when they could.

The real focus of feminine connection in monastic life should be on the intensity of dependency the women had on each other for all manner of affection. Like the deep bonds the Desert Mothers had with their Ammas, the Monastic Mothers bonded with each other. Schulenburg notes how vital these "sororal" relationships were to the whole of that society and that they were viewed as a way to spiritually mature. The relationships between sister and sister as well as sister and Abbess were entwined emotionally, psychologically, spiritually, and physically. These women were both highly independent and fully interdependent. Caring for the physical as well as the spiritual needs of others was an extension of caring for their own physical and spiritual needs. This depth of care certainly served as a reciprocal succorance. Schulenburg (1998, pp. 357–358) relates one of the best examples of this *custos animi* as described between Leoba who shared a remarkable relationship with Hildegard, the wife of Charlemagne. Each being the other's soul guardian, when Queen Hildegard announced her impending death, Leoba declared her the "most precious half of my soul." Not surprisingly, Leoba died a few days after Hildegard.

This level of affection and affiliation was a primary characteristic of these women. As tender as was Leoba's affection with Hildegard, so was the affection displayed for Abbess Radegund of Poitiers upon her death. Radegund's 200 nuns mourned inconsolably, recognizing that all they had given up to serve under her leadership and tutelage was reflected in the great loss of her life: "We gave up our parents and friends and county and followed you" (Malone, 2001, p. 191).

The stories go on and on, each one a testament to bright intellectuals, compassionate nurses, independent social activists, and certainly women of deep and long nurtured spirit. These women are prime examples of how passion brought forth excellence in self-advancement as well as the process of social acceleration. Crude as it might be, these women were not just chanting bead-shifters; they were highly demonstrative, kick-ass women who recognized they had an opportunity to lighten the literal and spiritual dark ages in which they lived. Like the Desert Mothers, determining to hold fast to the Feminine Spiritual, they made significant choices that were both hardships and advancements. They tapped into their personal and collective passion and matured their excellence. They breathed long and hard and their breath shifted tides for generations that filter into our lives today.

CONCLUSION

There are numerous epochs in time when women have demonstrated the Feminine Spiritual. I reference these times as *Mother Movements*. Mother Movements are long periods in which collective passion has shaped society's direction. They are easy to identify because these feminine passions are secured in history as time-altering transitions. The *Renaissance Mothers* of the post enlightenment period, like Saint Catherine of Siena, Joan of Arc, and Teresa of Avila, are but a few examples of many. In recent history, the *Liberation Mothers* are most visible beginning with the suffragettes of the anti-slavery movement all the way up to our own bra-less mothers and sisters of the sixties. These are women who permanently carved out the canyons of freedom and equality. Seemingly unlikely candidates among the saints and liberators, there are the *Wilderness Mothers*, some of my own favorite "goddesses," like Helga Estby who walked across Victorian America to secure her homestead and Minna Hubbard who accompanied her husband on his expedition across Labrador, and when he died, she refused to turn back. She forged forward to map the vastness of this great wilderness province of Canada. These are examples of women who dared to take on Nature herself in demonstration of personal resolve, union with nature, and exploration for humanity. Today, we have the *Global Mothers*: young women and old women alike who have envisioned their passion and enacted it entrepreneurially by leading a global revolution of personal and ecological responsibility—women like Nina Simons, editor of one of the most profound books I have recently read, *Moonrise: The Power of Women Leading from the Heart* (2010). It is Simons's collection that best glorifies the passion of present-day women who are using their intellect, their spirit, and their hands to confidently and energetically cycle humanity back to the most basic premise of the Goddess: being one with the earth and all her peoples. They are demonstrating in concrete ways that self-preservation indeed comes from other-preservation. These women are breathing deep and steady.

It is impossible to address all of these magnificent feminine mother movements, current and past. Like the Desert and Monastic Mothers, they are all profound examples of personal passion that enlivened the world, testifying to the quantity and quality of the spiritual feminine breath. They all have breathed in and breathed out; they have given thanks; they have honored life, proving that, like breath, our passion must move us forward.

REFERENCES

Bolen, J. S. (1984). *Goddesses in every woman.* New York: Harper & Row.

Carr, A. (1986). On feminist spirituality. In J. W. Conn (Ed.), *Women's spirituality: Resources for Christian development* (pp. 49–58). New York: Paulist Press.

Christ, C. P. (1997). *Rebirth of the goddess.* New York: Routledge.

Doherty, C. (1985). *Soul of my soul: Reflections from a life of prayer.* Notre Dame, IN: Ave Maria Press.

Hillman, J. (1996). *The soul's code.* New York: Random House.

Jerome, Letter 39, in NPNF, 6:49.

Malone, M. T. (2001). *Women and Christianity. Volume 1: The first thousand years.* Maryknoll, NY: Orbis Books.

Origen, H. (1973). *On first principles.* Gloucester, MA: Peter Smith Publisher.

Paphnutius. (2000). *Histories of the monks of upper Egypt and the life of Onnophrius.* Translated by T. Vivian. Kalamazoo, MI: Cistercian Studies.

Ranft, P. (2000). *Women and spiritual equality in Christian tradition.* New York: St. Martin's Press.

Redmond, L. (1997). *When the drummers were women.* New York: Three Rivers Press.

Ryan, R. S. (1998). *The woman awake.* Prescott, AZ: Hohm Press.

Schulenburg, J. T. (1998). *Forgetful of their sex.* Chicago: The University of Chicago Press.

Shelley, P. (2015). Hymn to the earth. Retrieved on November 27, 2015, from: http://www.poemhunter.com/poem/homer-s-hymn-to-the-earth-mother-of-all/

Simons, N. (Ed.). (2010) *Moonrise: The power of women leading from the heart.* Rochester, VT: Park Street Press.

Swan, L. (2001). *The forgotten desert mothers.* New York: Paulist Press.

Walsch, N. D. (1995). *Conversations with God.* New York: G. P. Putnam's Sons.

Chapter 16

Feminism and the Pro-Life/ Pro-Choice Debate

Jennifer Elisa Veninga

In describing what she believes to be the false dichotomy between women and fetuses in the abortion debate, philosopher Bertha Alvarez Manninen writes, "All this serves to emphasize what should be the position on abortion from both the pro- and anti-choice perspective: the abortion question is hard" (2014, Manninen, p. 81). Such a statement appears self-evident, but in the current divisive public debate about abortion, the messiness and ambiguity surrounding both "pro-life" or "pro-choice" positions often go unacknowledged. Instead, one frequently hears rhetoric that assumes the answers to abortion-related questions are obvious and static. Yet the abortion question *is* hard. Of course this is why, since the passage of *Roe v. Wade*, abortion has been one of the most controversial points of conflict in state and national politics. "Apparently, *Roe* sits on a fault line, a fissure between right and left, traditional and modern, running through our national politics," write professors N. E. H. Hull and Peter Charles Hoffer (Hull & Hoffer, p. 7).

This chapter explores the "hard question" of abortion in relation to the two central themes of this book, feminism and religion. The goal of this section is to provide a brief historical and conceptual overview of the intersection of these three areas and to complicate assumptions that these relationships are static and straightforward. I will first provide a brief history of abortion in the U.S., and then examine both the pro-choice and pro-life positions in regard to feminism and religion. I conclude with suggestions by scholars about the possibilities of finding common ground between these polarized positions.

A BRIEF HISTORY OF ABORTION

The history of abortion begins long before the historic Supreme Court's passage of *Roe v. Wade* in 1973, which reversed laws established in the nineteenth century, decriminalizing abortion in a number of cases. Induced abortions, which intentionally cause a woman to end a pregnancy, have been practiced globally for thousands of years. For much of this time abortion has been regarded as a legal form of birth control, especially in contexts where infanticide was practiced, such as Egypt, Greece, and Rome. Some forms of abortion—such as the use of herbs and plants—were also used by women in ancient societies as a method to cleanse the reproductive system and cause menstruation to begin after it had stopped because of pregnancy. Some feminists have argued that abortion "was not a medical procedure at all, but a natural part of women's history, and when left to women, the procedure could be executed safely, cheaply, and easily" (Rudy, 1996, pp. 67–68).

Abortions continued to be legal and available in Europe and in the United States until the nineteenth century. In 1803, Britain passed "Lord Ellenborough's Act," which made abortion before "quickening" a crime. While difficult to prove, quickening referred to the point at which the mother could feel the fetus moving in the womb. A similar legal approach eventually came to the United States, and Connecticut became the first state to criminalize abortion in 1821. By 1900, all states had prohibited abortion from conception except when the mother's life was in danger, and an 1873 U.S. law (the Comstock Act) had outlawed information about or devices for contraception and abortion.

A number of Americans opposed the strict laws on abortion and birth control, however, and policies on contraception began to loosen in the 1930s and 1940s. Activist Margaret Sanger had founded the American Birth Control League in the 1920s, which became the Planned Parenthood Federation of America in 1942. Public opinion about abortion changed rapidly in the 1960s and many pushed for the repeal of nineteenth-century laws. In 1965, Planned Parenthood League of Connecticut won a Supreme Court case against the state's anti-contraception laws. *Griswold v. Connecticut* ruled that married couples could not be prohibited from using contraceptives because it interfered with their right to privacy under the

Fourteenth Amendment. By the early 1970s, a majority of Americans supported legalizing abortion.

The contemporary abortion debate begins with the Supreme Court decisions on two crucial cases in 1973, *Roe v. Wade* and *Doe v. Bolton*. The latter case, though lesser known, was significant in its challenge to Georgia's strict abortion laws. *Roe v. Wade* involved a case brought by Norma McCorvey ("Jane Roe"), who wished to obtain an abortion in Texas but was unable to because of state regulations. Decisions on both cases were announced together, with Justice Harry Blackmun writing the 7–2 decision in favor of both plaintiffs. Taken together, the rulings struck down previous restrictions on abortion, maintaining that: a) a woman has a right to abortion during the first trimester; b) a woman has a right to abortion during the second trimester, although the State can regulate abortion in the interest of the mother's health; and c) the State may regulate and even prohibit abortion in the interest of the mother's health during the third trimester. As will be seen, in reaction to these decisions and their responses, the contemporary American pro-life and pro-choice movements were born. In 2008, just over half of pregnancies among American women were unintended and about four in ten of them end in abortion (Finer & Zolna, 2014). In that same year, researchers determined that slightly more than one in five women will have an abortion (Jones & Kavanaugh, 2011). A broad cross-section of American women have abortions, with statistics indicating that 58 percent are in their 20s; 61 percent have one or more children; 69 percent are economically disadvantaged; and 73 percent report a religious affiliation (Jones & Kavanaugh, 2011).

PRO-CHOICE FEMINISM

Examining the history of abortion in the U.S. reminds us of the power of language to shape public debate. We are accustomed to hearing the buzzwords of abortion rhetoric in the public sphere; activists and lay people readily employ a host of terms that may appear to have universal meanings. Yet terms such as pro-life, pro-choice, fetus, person, baby, mother, rights and viability, are in fact polyvalent and dependent upon one's interpretive frame. Indeed, they are historically and contextually situated, a theme which will be a thread throughout this chapter. "The fact is, when foundational terms—particularly those associated with politically charged matters—have fluid and mutable meanings over time, their usage is easily manipulated or distorted and politicized," writes Rickie Solinger (Solinger, 1998, p. 2).

In this article, I have chosen to use the popular terms "pro-life" and "pro-choice," yet I emphasize that each "side" of the debate often finds the other's use of these terms problematic. Even among feminists who agree on the basic principles of what we usually call the "pro-choice" position, there are disagreements about the value of the term "choice." Rickie Solinger, for example, uses the term "abortion rights" rather than "choice." The latter terminology, she argues, reflects "the ultimate marketplace concept," which serves to justify the reality that many women do not have the financial means to purchase adequate reproductive services (Solinger, 1998, p. 9). In the same way, while most—though, as will be seen, not all—feminists adopt a pro-choice position, there is no absolute consensus on what this implies for religion, law, or politics.

Pro-choice feminists do, of course, agree that women should have the right to safe and legal abortions. President Bill Clinton's well-known call for abortion to be "safe, legal, and rare" is echoed by many pro-choice feminists who strongly uphold *Roe v. Wade* and at the same time argue that abortions should be infrequent. Some argue this point on the grounds that there are better and worse reasons to have an abortion, while others maintain that abortion wouldn't be necessary if all women had adequate access to education, health care, and community support. Ethicist Beverly Harrison echoes this position: "I believe most pro-choice proponents are aware that in the best of all worlds we would have the conditions for greater procreative choice, including safe and reliable means of contraception, which would preclude the necessity of frequent abortions" (Harrison, 1983, p. 18).

While pro-choice feminists support *Roe*'s decision to grant women far more access to reproductive services than they had had before, they regard the legal premises behind it—and the moral implications of them—in different ways. The Court ruled in favor of *Roe* based on two central concepts, privacy and personhood. While the Constitution does not explicitly mention a right to privacy, the majority maintained the Court had ruled in previous cases (including *Griswold v. Connecticut* mentioned above) that individuals are guaranteed a right to privacy in certain areas.

The Fourteenth Amendment, in particular, suggested to the Court a right to privacy that is "broad enough to encompass a woman's decision whether or not to terminate her pregnancy" (*Roe v. Wade*). Yet the Court also maintained that the right to privacy is not absolute and may be regulated by states in order to safeguard health, medical standards, and potential life. Pro-choice feminists have often noted that indeed abortion regulations do infringe upon the right to privacy, as the unique decision to abort is an extraordinarily intimate one that must ultimately be decided by the woman. Other feminists, however, have critiqued both the use of the right to privacy by the Court in *Roe* as well as the concept itself as it relates to abortion and reproductive rights.

Supreme Court Justice Ruth Bader Ginsburg has commented publicly on the problems with *Roe v. Wade*'s attention to privacy rather than equality and its subsequent impact on cases after *Roe*. In her dissenting opinion from a 2007 ruling in *Gonzales v. Carhart*, which upheld the "Partial

Abortion" ban of 2003, Justice Ginsburg wrote, "Legal challenges to undue restrictions on abortion procedures do not seek to vindicate some generalized notion of privacy; rather, they center on a woman's autonomy to determine her life's course, and thus to enjoy equal citizenship stature." Emphasizing gender equality and the right of both women and men to make decisions about their lives, Ginsburg and others would argue, supports the case for abortion rights much more than the concept of the right to privacy.

Another feminist criticism of the concept of privacy in this context is the way in which it ignores the public and social aspects of women's lives. While the decision ultimately may be the woman's, she is always situated in the context of family, community, and the larger public sphere. Some feminists point out that the concept of abortion as strictly a private decision reflects the problematic values and framework of political liberalism, which doesn't take into consideration our complex social realities. "From a moral point of view the idea that abortion is and should be a strictly 'private' matter does not deserve standing," Beverly Wildung Harrison (1983) writes. "It implies that childbearing is a purely individual concern, separable from our own and others' well-being, from all our interpersonal obligations, and from the common good" (p. 52).

Not only does this liberal concept of privacy ignore one's social reality, feminist theorists suggest, but it can actually serve to subordinate women in the domestic sphere. As Dorothy Roberts (1997) argues in her work about race and reproduction in the U.S., the liberal understanding of liberty "guards against government intrusion; it does not guarantee social justice" (p. 294). Liberty is preferred above equality and thus both gender and race oppression and injustice go unaddressed. Roberts notes the arguments of feminists who reject the privacy notion and point out that "the private realm of the family has long operated as a site of violence and male domination" (p. 296). Such an argument does not imply that abortion should be restricted, but rather, that singular appeals to privacy as the rationale for reproductive rights do not address the reality of women's lives and the choices they make.

As noted earlier, even the concept of "choice" is complicated by its intersectional relationship to gender, race, class, sexual identity, and sexual orientation. Some feminists have pointed out that while women officially have the choice of aborting (within the constraints of state law as mandated by *Roe*), not all women actually have this choice. The early feminist and pro-choice movements have been framed in terms of middle-class white women's lives. Dorothy Roberts describes the situation of many black women in the U.S., however, who may not have real reproductive options and choices. Illuminating racial and gender injustice in American history, Roberts examines the ways in which black women have been denied reproductive rights through prohibiting their access to services like abortion, as well as how reproductive regulations have been *imposed* on them. In distinction from white, middle-class women, the choices of black women—especially those who are poor—are limited. "Their reproductive freedom, for example, is limited not only by the denial of access to safe abortions, but also by the lack of resources necessary for a healthy pregnancy and parenting relationship. Their choices are limited not only by direct government interference in their decisions, but also by government's failure to facilitate them" (Roberts, 1997, p. 300).

In addition to the concept of privacy as it was understood in *Roe*, the question of whether the fetus is a "person" was a central concern in the Supreme Court case. Wade argued that the fetus was a "person" and should be guaranteed rights under the Fourteenth Amendment. The Court was not persuaded by this position, however, and countered that all mentions of "persons" in the Constitution apply only postnatally. Fetuses, therefore, do not have personhood and therefore cannot be guaranteed the right to life. As will be seen, it was the Court's decision to use the denial of prenatal personhood as a central rationale for ruling in favor of *Roe* that left an opening for the pro-life movement to lobby for personhood amendments in more than a dozen states since 2007, all of which could have invalidated the Court's 1973 decision. Following *Roe*, most pro-choice feminists argue that the fetus is *not* a person; fetal "life" is qualitatively different from postnatal life. As columnist Katha Pollitt writes in her 2014 book, *Pro: Reclaiming Abortion Rights*, the fertilized egg "has no brain, no blood, no head, organs, or limbs; it cannot think, feel, perceive, or communicate. It has no character traits or relationships and it occupies no social space. It is the size of the period at the end of this sentence. . . . If fertilized eggs are persons, God is remarkably careless about them" (p. 69).

Some feminists, whether they agree with *Roe*'s argument against fetal personhood or not, maintain that the Court should not have made the legality of abortion *dependent* upon the personhood argument. Bertha Alvarez Manninen, for example, argues that ultimately the logic of Roe fails because of its contingency on denying fetal personhood. Instead, she suggests that abortion rights should be defended on the grounds that restricting abortion access infringes on the *bodily autonomy* of pregnant women. Manninen bases her argument upon a well-known abortion rights argument put forth by philosopher Judith Jarvis Thompson in her 1971 article, "A Defense of Abortion." In the article, Thompson makes the case that women should have the right to abortion not because the fetus is a person (for the sake of the argument she actually grants that the fetus *is* a person), but rather because the woman cannot be compelled to gestate the fetus.

She poses an elaborate thought experiment in which we are to imagine that a famous violinist suffering from a blood disease has been plugged into our body for life-saving blood that we alone have to offer. Maintaining that while it might be a kind thing to do, we are under no obligation to remain connected to the violinist until he recovers; no one else's right to life should impose such an obligation upon another. In reference to Thompson's bodily integrity argument, Manninen poses the question of "whether one's prima facie right to bodily security is a right one loses in cases of unplanned pregnancy when one willingly engages in sexual intercourse" (Manninen, 2014, p. 55). Manninen answers "no," and that "the onus seems to fall on anti-choice advocates to argue that pregnancy is an exception to what seems to be a well-accepted rule about bodily integrity" (p. 55).

PRO-LIFE FEMINISM

As noted, almost immediately after the Supreme Court announced *Roe v. Wade*, anti-abortion groups came together to try to repeal the new legislation. It was in this context that the movement which describes itself as "pro-life" was born. Research in the late 1970s showed that many of those who became pro-life activists were "stunned" that the Court denied that fetuses were persons according to the Constitution (McBride, 2008, p. 20). The hierarchy of the Roman Catholic Church became active in mobilizing against abortion rights and shortly thereafter the "New Right" emerged as a powerful force bringing together evangelical denominations and the Republican Party. At the heart of the pro-life movement was, and is, the belief that abortion is tantamount to the murder of an innocent human being and most of those who identify with the traditional pro-life position argue that life begins with conception. Most, though certainly not all, of those affiliated with the pro-life movement identify as Christian. A 2012 Gallup Poll, for example, reported that 54% of Roman Catholics and 57% of Protestants describe themselves as pro-life (Saad, 2012).

Pro-life feminism arose within the broader pro-life movement in the 1970s, gaining momentum with the founding of Feminists for Life (FFL) in 1973. Still active today, FFL understands itself as "a renaissance of the original American feminism," which traces its roots to nineteenth-century first-wave feminists such as Susan B. Anthony and Elizabeth Cady Stanton. Drawing on comments made by the suffragists against abortion, they maintain that "Like Susan B. Anthony and other early American suffragists, today's pro-life feminists envision a better world in which no woman would be driven by desperation to abortion" (Feminists for Life). FFL argues that the availability of abortion demonstrates that society has not met the needs of women and has allowed men to sexually exploit them: "Women deserve better" is FFL's motto. Serrin Foster, the current president of FFL, describes the way in which the organization seeks to address the root causes of abortion: "We should start by addressing the needs of women—for family housing, child care, maternity coverage, for the ability to telecommute to school or work, to job-share, to make a living wage, and to find practical resources" (Foster, 2015, p. 17). Some pro-life feminists also maintain that women deserve better in terms of the impact of the abortion itself, which they argue deeply damages the woman's psychological and physical health.

Pro-life feminists have challenged the mainstream and pro-choice view of what it means to be a feminist. In 2010, former Alaska governor and presidential candidate Sarah Palin caused an outcry when she described herself as a feminist during a speech at a Susan B. Anthony List fundraiser, a pro-life organization that supports political candidates. Palin encouraged "a new revival of that original feminism of Susan B. Anthony," and told the crowd that "Together, we're showing young women that being pro-life is in keeping with the best traditions of the women's movement" (Lopez, 2010). Palin's remarks triggered debate regarding the longstanding question of "Who counts as a feminist?" Many pro-choice activists denounced Palin's remarks and challenged her feminist self-description. Feminist author and critic Jessica Valenti responded to Palin's comments in *The Washington Post*: "Palin's 'feminism' isn't just co-opting the language of the feminist movement, it's deliberately misrepresenting real feminism to distract from the fact that she supports policies that limit women's rights" (Valenti, 2010).

RELIGION, FEMINISM, AND ABORTION

Religion is both explicitly and implicitly at play in the American abortion debate. It is most explicit and recognizable in movements to restrict abortion access, from the criminalization of the practice in the nineteenth century through the development of the contemporary pro-life movement. While some pro-life activists (especially secular feminists) support their case against abortion with non-religious arguments, the crux of the case usually appeals to what most would describe as "religious" values and history. In the U.S., the majority of religious pro-life activists are affiliated with the Roman Catholic Church or an evangelical Protestant denomination. Typically, this pro-life position includes arguments that church teachings and/or biblical texts support the belief that life begins at conception and the fetus is a person. Because abortion ends a life created by God, it should be regarded as murder. For some pro-life supporters, this means that abortion should be prohibited with no exceptions. Others allow for exceptions in the case of rape or if the life of the mother is in danger.

The Catechism of the Catholic Church maintains that all human life is sacred because it is created by God, and that this life must be "protected absolutely from the moment of conception" (§2270). This section of the Catechism, which specifically addresses abortion, cites biblical passages including Jeremiah 1:5: "Before I formed you in the womb I knew you, before you were born I set you apart; I appointed you as a prophet to the nations." According to Church teaching, while the Bible doesn't explicitly mention abortion, its authors demonstrate such deep respect for prenatal life that the commandment not to kill should therefore include the embryo or fetus. *Gaudium et spes* (The Pastoral Constitution on the Church in the Modern World), a document issued during Second Vatican Council in 1965, iterates the Church's position on abortion: "For God, the Lord of life, has conferred on men the surpassing ministry of safeguarding life in a manner which is worthy of man. Therefore, from the moment of its conception life must be guarded with the greatest care while abortion and infanticide are unspeakable crimes" (§51). According to the Catechism, Church teaching has always reflected this belief: "Since the first century the Church has affirmed the moral evil of every procured abortion. This teaching has not changed and remains unchangeable" (§2270).

These positions are not, however, those adopted by all Catholics. A feminist pro-choice minority exists within the Roman Catholic Church which argues that the values and teachings of Catholicism actually support reproductive rights and the possibility for a woman to choose abortion. Some pro-choice Catholics point out that the Church has indeed changed its position on contraception and abortion over time. Catholics for Choice, an organization founded in 1973, states in its literature that "Although the Catholic hierarchy says that the prohibition on abortion is both 'unchanged' and 'unchangeable,' this does not comport with the actual history of abortion teaching, and dissent, within the church" (Catholics for Choice, 2011, p. 4).

Ethicist Christine Gudorf argues that there is "no clear and continuous tradition on abortion beginning in the early church," partly because it was not until the late nineteenth century that life was thought to begin at conception (Gudorf, 2003, p. 68). Until then, the Church's understanding on the matter was shaped by Thomas Aquinas, who adopted from Aristotle the idea that "ensoulment" of the fetus took place 40–80 days after conception (ensoulment of females took longer). As Gudorf notes, the pastoral position during this time was that life began at quickening. In the nineteenth century, the Church drew from scientific discoveries about the ovum and fertilization to argue that life begins at the moment of conception. Gudorf and others point out, however, that "this has led to some irreconcilable differences with later scientific discoveries, especially the discoveries that fertilization, and therefore conception, is an extended process, not a moment" (Gudorf, 2003, p. 69).

Some pro-choice Catholic feminists point to historical differences of opinion to suggest that there is room in the Roman Catholic Church for a diversity of opinions on abortion. Catholics for Choice disagrees with the dictates of the hierarchy, arguing that the "Catholic tradition supports a woman's moral and legal right to follow her conscience in matters of sexuality and reproductive health," and thus Catholics can rightfully believe that abortion can be a moral decision. Respecting the dignity of every person, the Church teaches, involves recognizing that humans are endowed by God with a moral conscience: "Deep within his conscience man discovers a law which he has not laid upon himself but which he must obey" (*Gaudium et spes* §16)

Just as Catholics for Choice emphasize that abortion can be a moral decision, other pro-choice feminists have also begun to emphasize the moral dimensions of abortion. Rather than cede all moral ground to those who oppose abortion, these feminists maintain that there is indeed a moral argument to be made *for* abortion rights. As is the case in other areas, there are a variety of ways that pro-choice feminists have understood the meaning of the morality of abortion. "The still widely held view that anti-abortion proponents have a monopoly on the moral factors in the abortion controversy remains not merely a substantive moral problem but a strategic one as well," writes Beverly Wildung Harrison (1983, p. 47). Attempting to counter analyses that fail to see the overlapping connections among politics, religion, and morality, Harrison argues that procreation and procreative choice are moral issues and that any morally sound society should value women's self-determination and decision-making. Maintaining that "feminism is fundamentally a moral claim," she presents aspects of feminist liberation theology and feminist spirituality which seek to interrogate patriarchal assumptions which privilege men over women (Harrison, 1983, p. 7).

These feminist theological frameworks challenge "Christian masculinist discussions of abortion," which "so often hinge on determining the one static moment when God 'acts' to create intrinsic or sacred value" (Harrison, 1983, p. 113). Feminist theologians, on the contrary, have drawn upon traditions such as process thought to demonstrate that the creation of life is not an act that begins at an easily discernible moment, but is rather a process of becoming. The question of the value of fetal life is thus one that "can be answered only be careful, moral reasoning" (p. 114). Furthermore, she argues, Christian theologies which stress the sanctity of human life too often forget that this value must include every "concrete, existent female person" (p. 185).

Ethicist Kathy Rudy has also suggested ways that the feminist case for abortion rights can be understood in moral and religious terms. Rudy maintains that neither the pro-choice nor the pro-life movement have given enough attention to the material conditions of women's lives and the ways in which these conditions—such as racial discrimination or economic inequality—affect whether and how women can make reproductive decisions. Seeking to find a way to transcend the polarization between pro-life and pro-choice positions, Rudy draws on feminist and Christian concepts to offer a new way of thinking about abortion. In addition to using the values of "justice" and "care," she suggests that Christians reclaim the concept of *casuistry* as a method of discerning the morality of abortion. Used in the early medieval and early modern Church to determine penance during confession, casuistry suggests that one takes decisions about a certain arena separately, case by case. Rather than judging them according to strict, universal rules, one can compare each case to other circumstances through analogies. In relation to abortion, then, one could ask, "Does abortion in a particular instance represent an act of caring? a murder? a freeing choice?" (Rudy, 1996, p. 116). Alongside Christian teachings and biblical texts, one can give fuller attention to the specific context of the woman making the decision. Attention to this context, Rudy argues, is central to feminism. She continues to suggest a theology that goes beyond the usual pro-life/pro-choice divide.

> As Christians, we need to move beyond the idea that abortion is always right or always wrong. Instead, we need to rely on the resources located in our theologies to articulate a world that transcends this debate and is more faithful to the Christian practices of welcoming the stranger and caring for each other in the community called church. (p. 113)

Bertha Alvarez Manninen, mentioned above, maintains a pro-choice position but also seeks to find common ground between traditional pro-life and pro-choice perspectives. As noted earlier, Manninen argues that the pro-choice case should be defended by appealing to bodily autonomy rather than the denial of fetal personhood. By doing so, one can support abortion rights yet simultaneously acknowledge that the embryo or fetus has worth and that aborting this life is an authentic loss. Furthermore, while this prenatal life has value, there are times when a woman's decision to abort is morally justified. "For most of the women," Manninen writes, "it was precisely their concern for the fetus and their high regard for the importance of parenting and motherhood, as well as their concern for others and for themselves, that led to their decision" (Manninen, 2014, p. 121). The common goal of both pro-life and pro-choice groups should be to create a society in which women who experience unintended pregnancies can, if they desire, give birth and raise their children. This would involve creating more extensive support and social services for women and their families.

Whether or not pro-life and pro-choice supporters can eventually find common ground and common goals remains to be seen. A brief exploration into the complexities of the relationship between feminism, religion, and abortion demonstrates that there are no simple answers and neither side of the debate is monolithic. Not only does this recognition of diversity remind us of the thickly textured nature of women's lives and experiences, but it also helps us to remember that the meaning of feminism itself is contextual and fluid. "Indeed, in the last decade, many of us have come to realize that no one thing called feminism accurately exists, that we no longer have 'feminism,' but 'feminisms,'" writes Kathy Rudy (p. 59). This intrinsic sense of plurality might indeed be what feminism is all about.

REFERENCES

Catholic Church. (1997). *Catechism of the Catholic Church: Revised in accordance with the official Latin text promulgated by Pope John Paul II*. Vatican City: Libreria Editrice Vaticana.

Catholics for Choice. (2011). *The truth about Catholics and abortion*. Washington, D.C.: Author.

Feminists for Life. Our Vision. http://www.feministsforlife.org/our-vision/

Finer, L., & Zolna, M. (2014). Shifts in intended and unintended pregnancies in the United States, 2001–2008. *American Journal of Public Health*, 104.S1, S43–S48.

Foster, S. (2015). The case against abortion: Recovering the pro-life roots of the women's movement. *America*, 14–18.

Gonzales v. Carhart. 550 U.S. 124. (2007)

Gudorf, C. (2003). Contraception and abortion in Roman Catholicism. In D. Maguire (Ed.), *Sacred rights: The case for contraception and abortion in world religions* (pp. 55–78). Oxford: Oxford University Press.

Harrison, B. (1983). *Our right to choose: Toward a new ethic of abortion*. Boston: Beacon Press.

Hull, N. E. H., & Hoffer, P. (2010). *Roe v. Wade: The abortion rights controversy in American history*. 2nd ed. Lawrence, KS: University Press of Kansas.

Jones, R., & Kavanaugh, M. (2011). Changes in abortion rates between 2000 and 2008 and lifetime incidence of abortion. *Obstetrics and Gynecology, 117*, 1358–1366.

Lopez, K. (2010). Sarah Palin: A feminist in the pro-life tradition. *National Review Online* (May 24, 2010). http://www.nationalreview.com/article/229811/sarah-palin-feminist-pro-life-tradition-kathryn-jean-lopez

McBride, D. (2008). *Abortion in the United States: A reference handbook*. Santa Barbara, CA: Praeger.

Manninen, B. (2014). *Pro-Life, pro-choice: Shared values in the abortion debate*. Nashville: Vanderbilt University Press, 2014.

Pollitt, K. (2014). *Pro: Reclaiming abortion rights*. New York: Picador.

Roberts, D. (1997). *Killing the black body: Race, reproduction, and the meaning of liberty*. New York: Pantheon.

Roe v. Wade. 410 U.S. 113. (1973)

Rudy, K. (1996). *Beyond pro-life and pro-choice: Moral diversity in the abortion debate*. Boston: Beacon Press.

Saad, L. (2012). In U.S., nonreligious, postgrads, are highly pro-choice. Gallup. (May 29, 2012). http://www.gallup.com/poll/154946/non-christian-postgrads-highly-pro-choice.aspx

Solinger, R. (Ed). (1998). *Abortion wars: A half century of struggle, 1950–2000.* Berkeley: University of California Press.

Thompson, J. (1971). A defense of abortion. *Philosophy & Public Affairs.* 1, 47–66.

Valenti, J. (2010, May 30). Opinion: The fake feminism of Sarah Palin. *The Washington Post.* http://www.washingtonpost.com/wp-dyn/content/article/2010/05/28/AR2010052802263.html?sid=ST2010062204464

Chapter 17

Historical Resonances of the Feminine in the Brazilian Christian Religions

Patricia Nobre

This chapter reflects on some aspects of woman's relations to Christian institutions in Brazil. It reflects on the models and patterns of being a woman. This includes upbringing, religious formation, and cultural values that shape feminine existence. The social and religious roles assigned to women are examined, and how women usually lose their voice in society. This chapter, therefore, is about political, religious, and ethical questions.

Such issues require an inquiry into how society images women, who holds the unconsciously assumed social power, and how women form their view of themselves. For example, how do a society's values structure the religious context which shapes images of women? It is imperative to review the implicit processes involved in religious values transmission to see how that process shapes images of women from generation to generation. This chapter looks at the ideological claims that form the society's values and affect the ways they motivate, for example, the "voluntary" servitude imposed on women in conformity to such ideological "truths," and the forms of freedom that are possible when the society's ideology is more reasonable and mature. I want especially to clarify the dizziness of doubt, the oppressive religious ideas and actions that dominate social values. I wish to reexamine the "truths" that have been historically developed about the feminine and internalized, embodied, and forged into women's identities and stereotyped in subjectively perceived self-images.

To think about what it means to be a woman is to remove the veils that, throughout history, have been specially woven among the games of power in theological, political, scientific, and capitalist interests. To think about the feminine point of view implies a dive into the structural formation of the power systems present since the formation of Brazil as we know it today. We must reflect on contemporary forms of domination, oppression, and the sophisticated forms of authority that determine one's identity in Brazil today. These all work silently to skew our values in a way that makes the feminine subordinate and turns the individual woman into an object. This turns into a way to colonize her body and life, naturalizing codes of conduct that are degrading and subversive. What then makes her recognizable as a woman in the society is her restricting herself to those behaviors that are said to be feminine, being merely subservient, and enhancing the lives of males by filling a role of servitude and aesthetic decoration or convenience for men.

What is it to be a woman? What does it mean? How does it look? What are the social places destined for women? What are the thoughts underlying the permissions and prohibitions regarding the female body? How do religious discourses influence her shape and freedom of function? What assumptions legislate the female body and her act of thinking about herself? How does this shape her soul? What are the expressions of unspoken claims echoed through religious discourse defining the feminine image? What are the historical threads, the echoed language, at the threshold moments of women's history in Brazil? How did Brazil's colonizers set the stage? What sacralized "truths" from those early days still echo in sacred and secular discourse on women's lifestyles? What forms of domination and feminine docile compliance persist? How does this shape the psyche and soul of nearly every woman, and shape her sense of God's presence?

These are some of the issues that touch the heart of women's relationships with God, always mediated by religious discourse. We start from the central thread in the history of feminine speech, initially covering the trail of theological discourse from the Middle Ages. Going forward, we speak about the secularization of this discourse, the ownership of the state, legal, and policy legislation about the body, and the forms of female body exposure. Next, we mention the passage of this languaged discourse into the hands of science, dealing with the female "nature." We next explore the capitalist discourse, which appropriates this feminine being within the economic sphere. Finally, we will look at the feminine Christian discourse in contemporary Brazil.

The image of the feminine was formulated by the way our history and theologies unfolded in Brazil. It is impossible to talk about the nature of women without unveiling the past. This has analytic implications, for the several power levels reflected in history and cultural development determine women's role and place in the world, and in her posture toward herself. The odyssey of this historical-cultural research reaches back beyond the standard historiography. Therefore, it would be unforgivable to sketch any kind of theoretical thinking about women without going deeply into that history.

THE BIRTH OF THE BRAZILIAN WOMAN IN BRAZIL: A BRIEF HISTORICAL CONTEXTUALIZATION

> No one is born a woman or becomes a woman. No biological, psychological, or economic destiny defines the path that the human female takes in society. It is the social group that produces this intermediate product between male and the castrated beings who qualify as female.
>
> Simone de Beauvoir, *The Second Sex*

Simone de Beauvoir has laid bare the central truth. We can now pull the thread that will reveal the constitution of the feminine and its relations to Christian theology and religion. Western civilization carries in her womb the seed of a culture's philosophical and theological *ethos*. Remembering that Western civilization was built upon the feminine, we may equip ourselves for asking the question as to what it means to be feminine. There are strongly present feminine thought structures in the constitution of the most significant forms of Western existence: its *modus vivendi*, its codes of conduct, and the social and religious liturgies allowed and imposed on the concept of the feminine—a carefully crafted and manipulated program about being female at the junction of power relations.

It is imperative that we move beyond these and seek to touch the real woman, escaping forms of domination and control and docile accommodation. This is what we are seeking—the language that escapes official discourse in Brazil. Diving into the historical labyrinths to ask the real question, we can confront non-canonized feminine knowledge. Here we find the dialectical tension between the concepts historically developed within the religious canons at the time they were being claimed by the spheres of power, on the one hand, and the absolute truths, the unquestionable word inscribed on the skin of a woman and in the female soul. In this direction, we appeal to the sense of *aletheia*—the search for truths that transcend oppressive control. *Aletheia* is subversive truth that, when unveiled, reveals the feminine in an authentic light.

Historically, we see the female circumscribed by coercion, the penalty of desire. She is rigorously limited in social actions. These limitations violate the truth and freedom of real women. The feminine has a religious and secular role in Brazilian society that is clearly designed, marked, and limited by non-females who have set the norms about being female. What about other truths: the mythic truths, the dull truths trapped in women's diaries stored in attics, the truths in literary and visual arts that reveal other feminine forms, other possible destinies?

In the history of women's representations in the West, we find the feminine image held in custody, alienated by the ecclesiastical heritage. There reigns today the medieval Christian theological discourse that is still the primary discourse at this time in Brazil. Words of this language come covered in the sacred overtones of God's voice. This sacred speech in the sacred spheres is strong and determinant for our meaning and values. From this form of "wisdom" echo practices, social and private conduct codes, laws, catechisms, and discourses that establish the settled "truths," the behavior codes that are encrypted in women's bodies. They are words that form a false femininity.

The Middle Ages sowed these thought-seeds and systematic practices that prevail in our time in Brazil. They focus especially on feminine representations and women's place in Christian religions. We researchers must keep a watchful eye always turned to the implications of these ideas, these terrain features designed to impose their physical marks and psychological distresses on real live women. A woman is forcefully driven by her sexual design and its well-defined purposes. Her body is normally well fitted for a specific destination, serving the noble task of childbearing, breastfeeding, and educating her children. This has been too easily turned in Brazil into fulfilling the needs of a master, caring for him as a servant, whether he is fatherly, a cherishing spouse, or an exploitive and abusive brute.

When we evoke the feminine discourse, we also evoke power issues, the power represented in control. The pleasures and the pathos expressed in feminine images are important to our identity. Too often, however, we experience in our culture the domination of the feminine mind and soul entrenched in the unconscious patterns of our society, reinforced by the language of medieval values. In any relationship, the scepter of power in the West is held by the Christian religion and Catholic theological indoctrination, reinforcing feminine-learned docility of spirit and behavior. Simone de Beauvoir (Klapisch-Zuber, 1990, p. 11) tells us that being "born as man or woman is not, in any society, a neutral biological datum, simple natural qualifications that remain inert." That this came to be differentiated as gender is the product of cultural development.

It is interesting to see how the expressions and record of women's achievements have been erased from history. When we look at this we can say that we are rummaging through the history of denial of women's existence. Here men are the ones who hold the word-power, the power of managing the social discourse, the language-power over women. The heads of this state of affairs in Brazil are the clergy, religion, church men. These men determine the writings, behavior, language, and social circulation. These men, who make up the senior circle of the religious *magisteria,* dictate what is possible and permissible for the laity. It is from this throne that the distorted truths defining the roles and place of women echo, whence the false knowledge about the biological and divine nature of women is transmitted. It is under this cloak of invisibility that women transit human existence, acting in various social spheres but always persecuted by catechisms and language oppression. The denial of her self-expression and self-definition is a silencing of the medieval and modern women's voices.

Authentic women's speech has been covered with the dust of the centuries and the corrosion of the years. To really listen to it we must excavate it from the longstanding silence. It is discourse that is haunted by numerous ghosts because worse than trying to silence the feminine voice was imprisoning her body into word strings, corrupting the pictures of her vision, and oppressing the dynamics of her desire, erasing them from conscious social memory. Erasing them from history! To the "medieval" women, ancient and modern, is accorded censorship; their word was denied by the clergy, parents, siblings, spouses, teachers. Oppression forced them to leave their writings in secret diaries, hidden in attics and barns. Their texts, clandestine literary productions, paintings, and profane speeches, were not given access to the memory and the records of the official tradition. However, that memory is echoed and continues to echo through myths and historical characters, covered by veils of fables and lost to martyrdom. The lords of language have forgotten or repressed the authentic meaning of "woman."

The discourse that sets the stage of life is emitted by the men of social regulation. In Brazil it is the clerics who are considered the consciousness principals and knowledge masters. From these minds images are drawn, deformed projections that are forcibly engraved into culture, history, and feminine flesh. In "A Cidade das Damas," Cristiana de Pisano writes, "In my madness, I got desperate that God had made me to be born in a female body." From her vertigo and inconstancy about herself, we can see that a woman's historical representation is conditioned by simple ideas. There is nothing complex about them; nonetheless, they are ideas impossible to weed out of woman's consciousness (p. 69). Pisano's outburst confirms the theologians' contempt, whose interpretation of the book of Genesis considered woman as a by-product, inferior to men. Pisano talks about the roots of the torment of medieval women and their modern counterparts. She lived with the complexities of her body and mind against the power of the authorities. The authorities of social mores require a female body to be aesthetically beautiful, seductive, and productive. Any resemblance of medieval to modern is not a coincidence. Ours is a social universe run essentially by males, figures to which women should be providers of work, beauty, and sexual play. In fact, the failure to comply with those rules can result in serious social penalties and damages to a woman and her family.

Given the scarcity that characterizes women's documented history and wholesome celebration of women's bodies, some works stand out as landmarks, like Pisano's narrative (1990). It describes the context of alienation of the female body from the social requirements in her historical moment, about 1400 CE, during the rise of the Renaissance. This reigning set of unconscious incongruities is not yet transcended or significantly altered in Brazil today. The order for the medieval woman is expressed in the aphorism of that day, "To the good and bad horse, the spur; to the good and the bad woman, a master and sometimes the stick" (Klapisch-Zuber, 1990, p. 27). This moralism, structured in religious pietism, expressed in deformed values by power sources, articulates an obsessive desire to subjugate women. This still is endorsed by religious ethics in Brazil today.

I had to "live with the words of those men whom a particular social organization and a very definite ideology had given the government of female bodies and souls" (Casagrande, 1990, p. 99). The historical memory of the feminine cry was restricted to shadow, expressed in virtually secret writing. In the historiography presented by Casagrande (1990), the male gaze is shaped by Christian theology, combined with medieval monarchy. This "look" indicates the social position occupied by men considered guardians and mentors of women. The male gaze becomes the filter through which the thought structures that form the feminine idealized images are fashioned. The woman becomes a captive slave of this look, the gaze from the Other to the Other. We can say that these resonances from this medieval theology, and the practices driven by its ideology, caused inflamed social and personal suffering throughout history: symbolic violence and mental anguish.

Within this body of hidden thoughts, discourses, and representations sprouted sayings, proverbs, aphorisms, and figures of speech expressing women's voices. These words are lost from the official discourse. From these words, however, we find the underground of the myths and echoes. Something important has escaped from beneath the monotheistic religious traditions of Judeo-Christian origin (Judaism, Christianity, and Islam). Those subversive words find their dwelling among the socially excluded, among the renegades, men and women considered inadequate to the prevailing system. In this wide margin of exiles, we are confronted with striking narratives, brave and subversive to the official order. This way, we unfold the Lilith myth, rescued by the Italian biblical scholar

Maria Soave Buscemi (1994), by tracking the historical traces left by Lilith's presence. Here is the representation of the incarnation of countless women speaking their word to authority and power. There is a tradition that Lilith may have been Adam's first wife. Lilith is the embodiment of subversive woman, subversive in the ways of love, in sexuality, in her powerful way of existing before God. The epitome of creation and Adam's companion! The myth presents Lilith as the worthy and faithful representative of the *old word memory*. Lilith is the one who awakens women's desires, veiled desire's memory that lurks in silent places but hopes, the history sleeping in silence's bed, in the dangerous desire to name aloud and openly the historical realities of demoted women and their symbols.

Buscemi (2005) says Lilith is the "dark and lunar desire of overcoming a patriarchal society, founded on the violent power against women, children, and nature." It is Lilith who throws into God's face the first vindicatory complaints about the subjugation of her body. Lilith, in her daring, questions the man's place, claims her sexual desire, the desire to ride her man during sex, unsubmissive to Adam. Lilith is the first to renounce her place in paradise. From the beginning she has questioned her position in creation, her place of equality with the other. In Lilith's myth there is suffering and crying. Lilith claims her right to be her own landlord, to function with autonomy. Exposing her pain, she says she wants to be mistress of her own fate, to possess a legitimate desire. Unsatisfied, she leaves Adam, God, and "paradise" to their own destiny. According to the myth, God calls her to return to paradise. Lilith tries to negotiate her place in heaven and before Adam. Despite Lilith's presence, desired and requested by both Adam and the deity, the place for Lilith is non-negotiable. Dissatisfied, Lilith refuses to return to paradise. On the irreducible position of Lilith, God shuts the doors of paradise to her. God looks at Adam and then, taking his rib and making it grow, raises another woman, Eve. Lilith was made from clay, as well as Adam, but Eve was born from Adam's rib, "and the bone which the Lord God had taken from the man he made into a woman, and took her to the man" (Gen. 2:23).

Passages like this were and still are raised as a divine legitimation for subjecting women to male authority, and worse conditions follow. In the next report, the text narrates the fall, from Eve's hands; in other words, the woman is associated with evil, a demonic power. Both Lilith and Eve stand against man and God in the myth.

THE TRANSFER OF POWER THROUGH THE WORD

In "Da Natureza Feminina," Thomasset (1990) argues that Christian theology loses its influence when biblical interpretation can no longer meet the social demand. As theology begins to lose its domain of power, the secular power—the state—fills the vacuum. Subtly the absolute power that medieval Christian theologians held was slowly transferred to secular power spheres. The state, united with the legal power, strongly influenced by theological discourse, progressively came to regulate the female body, mind, and spirit; determining woman's social functions, delimiting her space, reproduction and regulating womens' professions.

The legalization of this secular discourse about women continues to be elaborated by the speech of Christian theology, which, at this point, remains convenient to the demands of the secularism of the state. We agree with the work of Jacques Le Goff and Nicolas Truong (2011), *Uma História do Corpo na Idade Média*, when they say that no matter what the shift of attitudes about body and sexuality, speech produced during the medieval period left indelible marks upon discourse about the feminine that still affect thoughts and systematic acts in our time.

Advancing along the historical thread of the ages, we must note the influential medical-psychoanalytic writings and language about "feminine nature" elaborated during the nineteenth and early twentieth century. It is interesting that the presence of this medieval theological discourse still justifies medical, social, and psychological understandings about women. During the medieval period, knowledge of human anatomy and physiology was restricted to the religious collegiate, the clergy, and the university professors. The feminine in this discourse was portrayed as of frail and feeble nature, "as a disturbing force, as a body that escapes from the domain of the spirit, as a being governed by its organs, and in particular by its sexual organs" (Thomasset, 1990). In the modern era, the wisdom and understanding regarding feminine nature gained another master. Science began to determine the understanding about reproductive forms, the forms of the female body, and its normal behavior. From medical science rose gynecology, a special discipline dealing with women. This science was concerned with a new type of discourse about bodily functions, the female social role, and the reproductive function. In this bias women are still viewed in terms of their sexual role with well-defined purposes, the task of childbearing, breastfeeding, raising children, and tending the master, whether a compassionate father figure, a spouse, or a power figure. In whichever case, the model was warranted by social, religious, and state authority.

This discourse is sustained by the concept that feminine nature is deficient, incomplete, and fragile. It implies that women possess an impaired body, incomplete, unable to create authentically by themselves; a lack that is denounced as physical and mental weakness. "Anatomy, by indirection, confirmed the contempt of theologians, arguing from Genesis. They were naturally inclined to see the woman as a byproduct and therefore, inferior to man" (Thomasset, 1990, p. 69). An approximately similar bias is expressed in Arabic scientific discourse. It is laden with religious content.

Any Arabic representation of women and sexuality has a legacy of ancient science, transmitted by Arab scholars. At the end of the medieval period, new forms of alliances arose through theological discourse. Medical and legal dialogue started to be exchanged between the Muslims and the West about the rules of social conduct. These readily extended into daily life as new forces began to emerge for the control and manipulation of the female body (Foucault, 1985).

The power scepter shifted with consequences and developments for future transformations in human thought. "Truths" were put out by the authorities that legislated and colonized women. These power representations were designed in both obvious and subtle forms to control and dominate in ways common in the colonialization of South America. The conquerors who moored their ships on the Brazilian coast landed with their beliefs, ideologies, and European *modus vivendi*. South America sustained heavy blows against her humanity. Important works by Galeano (1978), Viveiros de Castro (2011), Sérgio Buarque de Holanda (1936), and many others of academic and social relevance have formed a vast historiographical and anthropological collection on religious, social, and cultural consequences of the impact of the Christian ideology of the Conquistadors. Our Brazilian eyes were hurt, the windows of our souls darkened, by the imposition of their absolute vision of God as masculine, divine, white, and the master of large estates.

Within this social indoctrination, Christianization was an arbitrary and cruel process. The dominant discourse was "We will save the New World from the devil's domain." The devil was the culturally different. The authoritarian religious discourse preached by Christian theology cared little or not at all about the cultural particularities of Amerindian and African societies. It simply interpreted them in terms of European society and legislated through violence—physical, psychological, and cultural—domination of the bodies and souls of our people who expressed another way to exist in the world. This encounter between the cultures has had shock resonances that still reverberate in Brazil: the similarities and differences, the dominion of one over the other. After our encounter with the stranger, the foreigner, the colonizer, none of our culture remained the same. Everything and everybody was affected.

The Brazilian nation's formation—and, more specifically, the concept of being a woman in Brazil—has its roots in this soil of multiform cultures. Of course, the way a woman relates to God is affected by this. For a long time woman remained under the social and spiritual regulation of religious power. The nuances are different in the modern world of Brazil, but the veil that covers the female being in relation to God and men remains the same. It remains under other garments, and in other areas. Subtle forms of control and domination are embedded in Christian tradition.

WOMEN'S DEMANDS UNDER CONTEMPORARY DOMINATION

"Be productive" is another imperative imposed on women. The contemporary woman "should" be a socially productive woman; that is, she has to meet the demands of capitalism, the demands of motherhood, the demands of salvation, and the sexual demands that are focused on her body. These demands include the sphere of desire. Women have to meet specific body aesthetics. They must fit into certain aesthetic types. The female body is in the capital market, as an object, and designed by the partner's or potential partner's look. She must meet these demands that customize the design of her image and of herself. A standardized body shape is required to ensure her place in the desirable circuit. Above all is the ceaseless struggle against the natural processes of aging. She must cultivate a denial of death.

The demands that fall on the female body show the centrality of several discussions—religious or secular. To Roiz (1992), "the body is the crucial place of one of the generating tensions of the Western dynamic" dialectical tensions, inevitable and insoluble conflicts between physical bodies, and religious, economic, political, aesthetic, and cultural interests present pathogenic demands. A discourse is imposed that makes all the natural female values unequal in relation to men. It would seem to be natural to this system, then, that the woman's body must be tamed, customized, designed, and manufactured to meet men's demands and society's standards: patriarchy at its worst.

Currently, women continue to be excluded from socially determined spaces for men, even as men are excluded from spaces considered feminine. Many women remain victims of dehumanizing systems absolutely governed by authoritarian and paternalistic leaders. Often when the leadership is female, the presence of these outdated standards is still clear. The old word finds fertile ground in the leader's way of thinking, advising, developing solutions, repeating the same compulsion. With so many demands that corrupt freedom in the human condition, the impossibility of a life free from distorted demands, unnecessary and cruel burdens, seems impossible. A call and a cry echoes from the ancestors of the dispossessed, now socially humiliated. The call has never been interrupted. The silent cry echoes uninterruptedly, generation after generation. It is an eternally prolonged crying, incarnated in rejected humanity by men's alienating habits, their social inadequacies. It is the cry of the voiceless child and of mature autonomy yearning for freedom. It is the embodied cry of the female figure and the unheard voice of female theology.

THE (IN)VISIBILITY OF WOMAN IN CHRISTIAN RELIGIONS

Women's experience with God was built within this historical context. The internalization of the masculine god left deep wounds on feminine function in religion and the secular world. However, there were historic gains of political, social, and theological significance in the rise of Liberation Theology in the 1950s and 1960s in Latin America. This movement arose as a critical and overwhelming spirit that fell upon fossilized systems that had produced and legitimated the longstanding social oppression. Liberation Theology tore back the veils that covered social and religious practices that violated women's lives. This allowed a murmur of feminist theology to rise between the 1960s and the 1980s. Christ's face was visible for a moment, so to speak. We could see Christ's face in the faces of the humiliated and excluded. Christ's face revealed the anguish of the social and ethnic groups historically dispossessed.

In the midst of this spirit of freedom, other voices were encouraged to shout for their human rights. Womanist theology called for new ways in which a woman could see her real self. Finally she could claim the right to present and represent herself free from the authoritarian powers constraining her. The Feminist Movement proposed political reconstruction, infiltration of the economic system, and the reinterpretation of concepts, principles, and policies. Feminist Theology was launched and continues to propel itself beyond the issues raised by Liberation Theology. The "female nation" began questioning its social and religious role, not only advocating on behalf of women, but joining with the strong voices of youth, children, marginalized ethnic groups, and trivialized men. Other ways of thinking began to emerge. The social roles of men and women started to enter more boldly into the public spheres. New thoughts arose about the Christian faith, Christian ethics was questioned, criticism was made of religious discourses that, over the centuries, sacralized systems that harmed humanity. New relational possibilities were being discovered. Gradually, the image of the masculine god, relentlessly designed by the classical theologians, was held to the fire of rigorous and honest criticism. This began opening the possibility of an intimate and personal relationship between God and woman. It was increasingly described as revealing the female face of God.

Liberation Theology and the Feminist and Womanist Theologies were rooted in the soul of the historically disregarded and exiled. It was sustained by the imperatives of Christian ethics of the highest order. It was inspired by the ethic of love expressed in the gospels. It was certified in the Pauline enjoinder, "In Christ there are no longer Jews or Greeks, male or female, slaves or free, for all are one in Christ, a new creation." The Womanist Theology of Brazil had a significant influence on the U.S. movement, fleeing the analysis based on gender, considering the concept of gender as merely a social construction. The notion of gender is regarded as a tool of the repression of women. It is used by the Womanist Movement to expose the injustices legitimized to devalue women. Gender provided a category by which the culture escaped confrontation with the fact that the problem of devaluing women was a human condition, not just a woman condition. The notion of gender made possible the centuries of denial of the real issue. This permitted both the brutal and subtle forms of violence: physical, emotional, psychological, political, cultural, and economic, committed against women. Finally, feminine theology seen from a woman-perspective opens the way to other senses, other semantics, other speech, able to foster freedom without exclusions.

Unfortunately, in our twenty-first–century Brazil, Feminist and Womanist Theologies have negligible influence on the religious and social environment. Theologians who set out to view things from the feminist point of view find no place to work in the academies, seminaries, seminars, journals, and research groups. Unfortunately, the historically sculpted contours about females retain their vibrancy. We see few women occupying important positions in Christian churches and in the social sphere. The struggle for visibility and legitimacy does not reach most women. The arena remains marked by oppressive systems and subtle control. Frequently women victims of domestic and social violation are slow to understand that they are victims, because of the great weight of coerced submission that reigns over them. Many abuses derive from this submission. Gender-based violence is still pervasive. Many religious women are advised by their churches to remain with the offending partners, submitting meekly to their whims. This is church-sanctioned femicide. It often kills the woman psycho-spiritually or physically. Women are taken as common goods, objects. Many have no voice until they are found murdered by their partners. Women, non-white persons, and gay persons are at the forefront of this kind of violation. If it is not officially legitimized, it is at least tolerated in the preconceptions of the social systems. Women often get harsher treatment than common criminals, thieves, violent pedophiles, murderers, and the like.

Socially, women in the workplace have a harsher journey than men through the devaluation of their work, the denial of autonomy over their own bodies, exposure to the dictatorship of aesthetic social standards, lack of public policies enhancing women's status, inaccessibility to certain options in society, and other violations. Violation of any kind is violence. It is regrettable to see official statistics of violence against women. Even these do not reveal the full breadth of the issue, all closely linked to masculine-entrenched parameters.

Women are endeavoring to negotiate these issues. Unfortunately, the historical constraints of gender, ethnicity, social class, and religion remain. God's name is strong and powerful, and under this name ideas and goods are bought and sold, values and subjective sentiments are fostered, social pathology is produced, psychological distress is inflicted, and women are devalued. In the name of God, a dishonorable human condition prevails. Counterproductive religious and social constraints are subtly or openly imposed upon women, and indirectly the back side of this deprives men and keeps them from living wholesome lives. It thus becomes an authentic woman's destiny to fight tenaciously for her public spaces, her imaginative ideas, her personal creative autonomy, her potentially productive authority, and her right to legitimize herself. She is left with the endless struggle of asserting her preferences, her place before the face of God, in God's world.

REFERENCES

de Beauvoir, S. (1980). *O segundo sexo: A experiência vivida.* Rio de Janeiro: Nova Fronteira.

de Beauvoir, S. (1986). *A velhice.* Rio de Janeiro: Nova Fronteira.

Buscemi, M. (1994). Lilith, a deusa do escuro. In Mandragora/Netmal. (Eds.), *O imaginário feminino da divindade.* São Paulo: UMESP—Curso de Pós-Graduação em Ciências da Religião.

Casagrande, C. (1990). A mulher sob custódia. In Duby, G., and Perrot, M. (Eds.), *História das mulheres no ocidente: A Idade Média.* Porto: Ed. Afrontamento.

Foucault, M. (1985). *História da sexualidade III: O cuidado de si.* Rio de Janeiro: Ed. Graal.

Galeano, E. (1978). *As veias abertas da América Latina.* 20th ed. Rio de Janeiro: Paz e Terra.

Holanda, Sergio Buarque de. ([1936] 1997). *Raizes do Brasil.* Luso Brazillian Books.

Klapisch-Zuber, C. (Ed.). (1990). *A history of women in the west.* Cambridge, MA: Belknap Press.

Le Goff, J., & Truong, N. (2011). *Uma história do corpo na Idade Média.* 3rd ed. Rio de Janeiro: Civilização Brasileira.

Roiz, J. (1992). *El experiment modern: politica y psicologia al final del siglo.* Madrid: Editorial Trotta.

Thomasset, C. (1990). Da natureza feminina. In G. Duby & M. Perrot (Eds.), *História das mulheres no Ocidente: A Idade Média* (pp. 65–69). Porto: Ed. Afrontamento,

Viveiros de Castro, E. (2011). *A inconstância da alma selvagem: outros ensaios de antropologia: Eduardo Viveiros de Castro.* São Paulo: Cosac Naify.

Chapter 18

Faith and Feminism: Resolving the Gender Issue through Mythology and Archetype

Deborah Brock

A PERSONAL INTRODUCTION

I am a psychologist. I am also a woman of faith. I have sought to integrate faith and psychology for the 35 years I have practiced psychotherapy, if not for most of my 60 years of life. Over my years of practice many people have sought my services specifically because I seek to integrate faith and psychology. As much as 50 percent of my clientele has been of conservative evangelical faith, and most of them women. For these faith-based clients it is important to trust one's deepest thoughts, fears, and hurts to a psychotherapist who values both psychology and faith. There is an interesting difference between evangelical women in their 20s and 30s and women who are in midlife. While many of the younger evangelical women affiliate with a broader social worldview, the older evangelical women come from a more traditional patriarchal culture and view. For these more traditional evangelical women, there is little to no separation between their faith and their social, psychological, and gender role perceptions. Their perceptions are predominantly based on what they have been taught largely by their male church leaders and male-dominated doctrine. Traditional evangelical teaching has come from a literal interpretation of the Bible as well as being patriarchal.

The presentation of evangelical women, especially mid-life women, has been from a faith perspective, and often from a perspective that seeks to incorporate life experiences that do not always seem to square with a literal interpretation of the Bible and with the patriarchy that has often followed in evangelical circles. Many of these women have come to me hoping to balance the occasional disparity between the doctrines they have been taught and their life experiences. It is always central that a therapist try to understand a client from her perspective, honoring her feelings, thoughts, experiences, and philosophical beliefs. Yet, at the same time a competent therapist must keep in mind that current life issues always relate to psychological factors that are related to other factors, such as early life history including traumata, unresolved intrapersonal conflicts, and unconscious factors. In other words, things are not always as they appear. "Faith issues" may not be matters singularly of faith.

Many, if not most, mid-life women present with "sexual issues," including preferred sexual expression, low libido, sexual abuse history, sexual identity, or gender identity concerns. Often these evangelical women have sought to understand these matters from a patriarchal or absolutist perspective. They have considered that these sexual issues are related to sin or some other doctrinal position. Having had many psychotherapeutic opportunities in this realm, I have come to believe the sexual and gender issues many evangelical women face exist because of the lack of a cultural appreciation for the androgyne archetype, or gender-balanced identification. Indeed, there may be a collective trauma in the form of neglect of a basic psychological need for association with the androgyne. In simplest terms, because of the patriarchal corral in which they are contained, many women of evangelical faith have not had access to the collective unconscious that feeds a basic human need for gender balance. Thus, I believe that a better terminology for the concerns women often have in their lives is that of *gender concerns* rather than sexual issues.

I have come to believe that gender concerns that women present are often a psycho-spiritual quest for the androgyne archetype. Furthermore, it is possible that only a clinical presentation of gender issues at large can provide these women an arena in which they can explore this psychosexual drive. An appreciation of the androgyne archetype may provide women a deeper understanding of themselves, the current life dilemmas that they experience, and ways to examine these dilemmas without repressing their own psychological structures. Understanding themselves within the context of the androgyne archetype might also relieve some of the clinical symptoms of depression and anxiety which generally accompany "sexual concerns."

Historically, it has not been possible for traditional evangelical women to examine these issues within their evangelical community. There are two basic tenets that prohibit such examination: The adherence to a male dominance rendering of the creation account and the doctrinal stance that all scripture must be interpreted literally. Given these two limits, it has been particularly challenging for evangelical women to consider their sexual orientation or gender identity as these questions may seem incongruent with a traditional interpretation of doctrine. Evangelical doctrine has simply not had room for a meaningful discussion, much less a personal examination of these matters, because they fall outside the two basic tenets of interpretation. For an evangelical woman to secretly consider an alternate sexual or even gender orientation is difficult enough even in the therapy room, but to openly challenge her expected orientation has been, until recently, anathema. Furthermore, if there has been some sexual experience associated with these concerns, there is often false guilt or shame associated with such activity. Thus, if a woman seeks to understand her sexual orientation and gender identity while remaining in a faith community, there is little in the way of support for such an endeavor.

It is noteworthy that the United States has dramatically changed in its understanding and appreciation of gender concerns, most specifically homosexuality. Two-thirds of the American population accepts gay marriage as equivalent to heterosexual marriage (Hinch, 2014). Furthermore, many young evangelicals now affirm homosexuality as an alternative form of sexual expression rather than something born of pathology or sin. There have, however, been two evangelical organizations that have been a generation or two ahead of the rest of America in understanding broader gender issues: Evangelicals Concerned and The Evangelical Network. Hinch confirms how the newer, younger generation of evangelicals is not only becoming more inclusive, not just in their acceptance, but many of them have themselves come out as gay. Hinch further reports that over this past decade the support for gay marriage has nearly doubled and that upwards of a quarter of the evangelical population support same-sex unions and many more evangelicals are now uncertain in their beliefs about homosexuality and related gender issues. And of equal significance within this same evangelical community, there is a growing momentum for more thoroughly examining the biblical narratives and directives toward all sexual matters, including a deeper understanding of biblical passages that have previously been used to foster an anti-gay mentality. Some have argued that this deeper re-examination of the Bible in light of cultural and historical data has assisted evangelicals to more carefully examine their own gender concerns.

Women in the evangelical community have traditionally had very little social exposure to a larger and enriched community that supports both sexual and gender examination. The Internet now provides access to a worldview that was simply not available 15 years ago. Previously, women in all religious groups only had access to "pulpit" and/or in-house taught doctrine maintained by their patriarchal denominations, which, of course, incorporated the two aforementioned limits: gender identification as found in the second creation story and the insistence on literal interpretation of scriptures. These two basic tenets have served as the primary limitations based upon which women have been denied access to a gender-balanced self-perception.

Now it is easy and enticing for women to see and hear what the rest of the world believes, and as a result to begin to experience seepage from that enticement to examine oneself, including one's gender concerns. We might say that the Internet has been a portal leading women to self-examination, tapping into the collective unconscious as represented in the androgyne archetype. Evangelical women can now explore the matter of sexual identity and other sexual matters in a way that simply did not exist in the previous centuries.

Religious doctrine and tenets have not generally encouraged self-examination for women, much less an understanding of more esoteric concepts revealed in mythology that contain important elements of the gender androgyne. Women now consider that they are more than "just female," "just Christian," or "just anything." Exploring the psycho-spiritual concepts of mythology, specifically the archetype of the androgyne, is a way evangelical women, and all women, can expand their sexual and gender consciousness as the recent openness toward sexual re-orientation occurs in their subculture. Expanding sexual and gender consciousness through an understanding of mythology includes deepening one's understanding of homosexuality, heterosexuality, transgenderism, and other gender and sexual issues that are important to all women. Such an examination can deepen a woman's spiritual awareness and bring her sense of spirituality to an active daily life. Tapping into a psycho-spiritual theme as provided by the androgyne archetype can provide an interface between faith and the natural instinct for a cosmic identification.

MYTHOLOGICAL ANCESTRY

Humanity has always sought a self-description. Psychologist Fritz Perls once said, "Awareness is curative" (1969) in reference to mental health impairment. Self-understanding and self-description have been sought for millennia and there have been numerous templates through which people and societies have sought to understand themselves. From some of earliest history, including primitive societies, mythology has assisted humanity in this personal and interpersonal identification. In addition to human identity, mythology has served as a template for the divine as well as the interaction between the divine and the human. Mythology is a casting stone, a psychological and spiritual mold from which we build our ideologies. Myth is, by definition, a perception of our existence that is rooted both before and beyond our physical existence.

The phenomenon of myth is significant in both a religious and psychological perspective predominantly because myths tell stories, and stories are intrinsically human. Without stories there would be no passage account of our religious heritage or our personal heritage. Such heritages are especially evident in the creation myths that are quite frequent in various religions. Creation myths, which obviously speak of origins, provide humankind an association to primordial connections, and they are intimately connected with our own physical origins. Leeming (1990) introduces his anthology by reminding us that we each have birth stories that suggest a celebration of individuality, something he calls "sacramental." Origin myths, suggests Leeming, "establish our reason for being, the source of our significance" (p. 16). Myths are the metaphors for awakening the conscious and ultimately the unconscious. Origin myths or stories provided ancient cultures a language for the unexplainable, including their own existence. Humans seek understanding, as well as meaning, of their existence, and origin myths provide these things. In this sense, origin myths are our cosmic birthday narratives, proving we exist as we are, as well as our historical connections.

The proliferation of these cosmic birthing stories spans all ages and cultures, most of which incorporate an androgynous theme. In the classic myth, made most familiar from Plato's *Symposium*, the prevailing theme is the human quest for preservation and fulfillment through self-identification. In this myth the original humans, perfectly round and fully androgynous, were so complete that the gods determined them a threat, and so sliced the round perfect entities into halves of feminine and masculine and hurled them into the distant galaxies. In this same myth the feminine and the masculine have sought to be reunited as a whole, and the search has been unending, i.e., finding somewhere in the universe that which is our long lost half-self so that we once again can be full and complete as an androgynous being. This Greek myth of human origin suggests that androgyne archetype mythology can serve as a bridge between our physical forms as they tie into our spiritual origins. It also implies that to be godlike, or of divine heritage, we must be both feminine and masculine.

Variations on the classic androgyne archetype shift from culture to culture and religion to religion, maintaining the prevalence of the divine within the human. Eastern religions, which are more broadly integrated into their larger cultural contexts, provide a rich and organic template of the true androgynous myth, and in most cases, always incorporate the divine within the androgyne. In Hinduism and Buddhism, for example, the androgynous spirit is a variation of sexual and spiritual transcendence. Several myths present Shiva as the great masculine and Shakti as the great feminine, often blending from independent genders to androgynous beings. The Chinese Yin and Yang (or Yin/Yang) is the classical symbol of the masculine and the feminine as it contrasts and unifies these two elements of the androgyne. Polynesian and Aboriginal deities often are represented as bisexual entities whose passion is manifest in both friendship and sexual love. African gods are embodied in both separate and androgynous form. Early South American cultures recognized gods who constituted a third gender, as do many Native American tribes that reference the third gender phenomena as "two spirits," often represented by shamans possessing a greater collective insight and healing capacity.

Christian and Judaic traditions, unlike the Eastern cultural religions, have less organic descriptions but do depict anomalies that might be interpreted as androgynous themes. Female mystics sometimes possessed the Stigmata, which could be seen as a physical representation of the male within the female. Some theologians have examined the enduring friendship between David and Jonathan as homosexual, which might further be considered to be androgynous. Likewise, the relationship between Ruth and Naomi could be seen as a kind of bisexual connection that might advocate an androgynous model.

As the philosophical mind of the Greeks evolved, so did the transition from myth to reason, with Plato providing the metaphysical understanding of the archetypal perspective. Tarnas (2009) described the Platonic formulation of archetypes as "absolute essences that transcend the empirical world yet give the world its form and meaning. They are timeless universals that serve as the fundamental reality informing every concrete particular" (p. 24). Tarnas continues to note that it was Plato's student, Aristotle, who took his teacher's insight further:

> Aristotle brought to the concept of universal forms a more empiricist approach, one supported by a rationalism whose spirit of logical analysis was secular rather than spiritual and epiphanic. In the Aristotelian perspective, the forms lost their numinosity but gained a new recognition of their dynamic and teleological character as concretely embodied in the empirical world and processes of life. For Aristotle, the universal forms primarily exist *in* things, not above or beyond them. (p. 24)

Tarnas then continues with a profound insight: "They (the universal forms or Plato's archetypes) not only give form and essential qualities to concrete particulars but also dynamically transmute them from within, from potentiality to actuality and maturity" (p. 24). I read this insight as a trinitarian perspective of evolution (potentiality to actuality and then to maturity). The author of our existence (Parent) is our potentiality. The incarnation of that origin (Progeny) manifests independence resulting in maturity (Spirit). This process can be equated to Jung's process of individuation. The Spirit is the reuniting of our existence with our origins, not as a return, but as a fulfillment of our potentiality. All potentiality flows from our origins, and we are actualized by independence and maturity as the result. Tarnas sums it up well: "For Aristotle, as for Plato, form is the principle by which something can be known, its essence recognized, and its universal character distinguished within its particular embodiment" (p. 25). The androgyne archetype is one form of embodiment that allows the fullness of creation to be known, be it on a subconscious level or for the more mature, on a conscious level.

Mythology, most specifically, archetypal forms, became a sustained debate in scholastic philosophy throughout the later Classical and Renaissance periods. Tarnas (2009) reports that the "locus of intelligible reality gradually shifted from the transcendent to the immanent, from the universal to the particular and ultimately from the divinely given archetypal Form (*eidos*) to the humanly constructed general name (*nomina*)" (p. 25). The author goes on to trace the resurgence of archetypal form following Kant's focus on the subjective, eventually leading to a major shift with twentieth-century depth psychology. This early psychology, of course, rests with Jung's archetypal psychology, which he later regarded as a collective unconscious projection as well as a larger construct of existence that integrates the physical world and the human psyche.

By the mid-twentieth century, Campbell (1949) popularized myth and recognized the archetype to be "the secret opening through which inexhaustible energies of the cosmos pour into human cultural manifestation." Campbell credited Jung and other psychoanalysts for conceptualizing the psychological significance of myths and began blending the profound with the ancient, thus reopening the door for society to rekindle ancient secrets and daily insights. More contemporary work by Sanford (1980), Hillman (1985), and many others built on the work done by Jung and his research predecessors, all constructing a socially accepted understanding of the intertwining between mythology and androgynous archetypes.

THE ANDROGYNE ARCHETYPE

Out of his study of mythology and dreams, and building on early century references, psychologist C. G. Jung built up his construct of the archetype serving as a conscious representation of our unconscious connection to the rest of creation. Jung recognized the archetype as an instinctual symbolic language long known across time and cultures but unspoken. Developing conscious connection to this instinct is an evolutional process fulfilling the primal drive for meaning. Jung suggested that while archetypes represent themselves in practical ways, they require emotion to gain numinosity and result in some consequence (C.G. Jung, 1964). Ageless truths found in pictures or symbols, as suggested by Jung, are remnants from the spirit of humanity that continue to link and unify humanity. While these symbols may indeed be symbolic, they provide a literal connection across time and culture. Archetypes in the broadest sense are imagined extensions of ourselves concretely linked to parts of ourselves in another time or space.

While Freud concretized neurosis simply as repressed sexual libido, Jung took a more rational view of human nature as limited and incomplete but naturally seeking evolution or maturity. For Jung, neurosis surfaced in a person when that person denied investment in his or her shadow part. It was only when a person examined one's shadow and integrated his or her archetype that maturity occurred and imbalance ceased. Jung's regard for humanity included the belief that anything short of confronting the irrational or abstract within the unconscious (the shadow) was a disservice and consequently limiting to the individual (Stevens, 1982). Jung's basic motive and understanding of human psychology, suggests Stevens, was based on the ever continuing need for finding fullness, wholeness, completeness, demonstrating that Jung's archetype was both a precondition of life and coexistent with life. Stevens defended Jung's conception that the manifestations of the archetype "not only reach upwards to the spiritual heights of religion, art, and metaphysics, but also down into the dark realms of organic and inorganic matter" (p. 29). It is a fundamental necessity to be able to both perceive need and comprehend its source that fed one of Jung's greatest contributions, the archetype. As Stevens points out, Jung himself was the first to admit "analytical psychology could never aspire to hand us a new system of beliefs to replace the old faiths that have disintegrated: what it provides is not beliefs, but rather practical insight into the nature of human experience, not a philosophy but techniques enabling individuals to achieve the perception of meaning" (p. 35). The androgyne archetype is what most preserves the reach of both the organic and inorganic nature of humanity. It reaches into the dark organics of primordial existence, as well as filling the common day-to-day roles of human capacity, rejoining Plato's perfect rounds by meeting the feminine and the masculine through the anima and animus, the projected gender aspects of each sex upon the other.

By clarifying the anima and animus as contrasexual projections, Jung provided a clear picture of what it means to possess the shadow gender within each of us. In all males, suggests Jung, is the innate feminine, as in all females resides an innate masculine that must be actualized through personal experience, bringing the unconscious to consciousness. Each individual must mature beyond the limitations of one's gender. The result of this integration is an androgynous balance, which is an access to the greater self. The anima and animus, suggested Emma Jung, C.G. Jung's daughter, are "rooted in the collective unconscious, thus forming a connecting link or bridge between the personal and the impersonal, the conscious and the unconscious" (E. Jung, 1957). She summarized the function of these two archetypes through example of the anima:

> In psychological terms we say that life's demands and the increasing development of consciousness destroy or mar the original wholeness of the child. For example, in the development of masculine ego-consciousness, the feminine side is left behind and so remains in a "natural state." The same thing happens in the differentiation of the psychological functions; the so called inferior function remains behind and, as a result, is undifferentiated and unconscious. Therefore, in the man it is usually connected with the likewise unconscious anima. Redemption is achieved by recognizing and integrating the unknown elements of the soul. (E. Jung, pp. 57–58)

The feminist movement, in search for guidance that would bring about gender equality, rediscovered, or at least brought back into consciousness, the androgynous theory and fostered a drive to demonstrate the validity of equality between the sexes in the physical sense and within gender identification in the symbolic sense. Alongside the feminists were numerous theists who rebounded with the goddess movements, as well as psychoanalysts who blended the drive for sexual rights with gender identification under an archetypal perspective.

Singer (1976), a Jungian analyst and feminist proponent, has presented an analytical examination of the androgynous concept as it applied to the societal current of feminism and the gay movement. Presenting androgyny as a "guiding principle for the new age," Singer highlights Jung's implication that bisexuality is not the same as androgyny, but rather an expression of a "natural but unconscious thrust towards androgyny" (p. 44). Androgyny, in contrast, is a conscious recognition of the feminine and masculine in each individual. While Jung's presentation of the anima and animus as the unconscious feminine and masculine was yet patriarchally biased, it provided a stage from which the feminist movement could clarify itself. By considering the feminine and the masculine as a whole, gender stereotypes, both conscious and unconscious, could be eliminated, thereby returning to a natural ego differentiation in which the complete self is in process toward psychological adaptation. Singer explored the consideration as to whether the androgyne was pathological or mythological in origin. She noted that any division of gender identification often settles in sexual issues wherein anomie is experienced as unnatural, a phenomenon that leads to unfulfilled relationships. Singer concluded, "the phenomenon of bisexuality, whether acted out or intuitively and privately sensed within one's own personality, was the avenue through which the more fundamental problem could be approached. That problem had to be, of course, the psychological realization of the essentially androgynous nature of each human personality" (p. 42).

EVANGELICAL LIMITS ON ACCEPTING MYTHOLOGY AND ANDROGYNOUS IDENTITY

While many world religions make association with mythology, conservative evangelical-based denominations do not. The general orientation and doctrine of evangelicals generally rely on the more literal and concrete aspects of life. This distinct tendency to focus on the concrete is augmented by the patriarchy that underlies evangelicalism. Personal identification from this perspective is developed not only through a literal orientation but also on the basis of patriarchal seclusion rather than on a collective sense of human existence.

The Evangelical community, being based on a patriarchal set of values, infers male superiority. Evangelical theology follows the "second creation story" of Genesis 2–3, in which woman was created as a secondary adjunct to the male. She was created as the "helper" for man and was the primary source of sin and evil by being seduced and then being the seducer of Adam. Evangelicals also base their gender doctrine on a singular Pauline statement in the New Testament where Paul speaks of female submissiveness to men, a statement that other scholars have examined as having more cultural than doctrinal implications.

The "first creation account," often referenced as the Priestly account, recorded in Genesis 1:26–27 reports that God created "Adam" (humankind) and gave *them*, an equated pair, God's likeness and image as well as shared rule over the world. The Yahwistic account found in Genesis 2–3 states that man was first created. In this account, Adam, the man, is first created but lonely, so all the animals were then created but they did not satisfy Adam. It was then that God drafted a rib of Adam and created Eve as his "help mate." Non-evangelical scholars have suggested that there is an implicit equality between male and female even in this second creation account in that woman was created out of the center of Adam, and hence his equal. While the Priestly account suggests a divine image infused within humanity, the Yahwistic account might suggest the superiority of the male as being created first and then woman being created solely to fill the need of the man, as a helper rather than an equal. It is the second account that evangelicals most affiliate with in that it presents, at least to them, a patriarchal set of values from which gender roles are assumed and to be followed.

Pagels (1988) reminds us that until Christianity became the officially declared religion of the Roman Empire, there was little quibble with the Genesis accounts of creation. Previous to Constantine's conversion and declaration of Christianity as the state religion, sexual interpretation and activity had relatively free license in both religious and secular circles. Once Christianity began to spread under the protection and direction of the Empire, so did the exacting beliefs on sexual practices and identification.

Yet within the Christian tradition, a divide began to swell between the Gnostics and the Orthodox. Gnostics criticized the Orthodox for being too literal, while the Orthodox claimed that the Gnostics were heretical. The Gnostics had projected interpretations shifting from "history with a moral" to "myth with meaning," which then implied a specific divinity within self (p. 64).

The major argument in the early centuries of Christianity had to do with freedom as discoursed from the Genesis accounts. The Gnostics interpreted freedom from a mythical or allegorical stance, while the Orthodox discussed freedom of will, a will that could lead individuals into sin. Thus, the Orthodox view of freedom led to the theological concept of original sin. The original dispute between these two theological camps was not so much about human equality between the sexes as it was staking blame for evil and sin in the world on Eve's choosing to disobey God and leading Adam into her fall. This gender blame was supported by the Tertullian reference, "You (female) are the devil's gateway, you are she who persuaded him whom the devil did not dare attack. . . . Do you not know that every one of you is an Eve? The sentence of God on your sex lives on in this age; the guilt, of necessity, lives on too" (Pagels, 1988, citing Tertullian, *De Cultu Feminarum* 1, 12). This blaming the woman for cessation of Eden's perfection has perpetuated the gender imbalance within the Church. Several New Testament references came to serve as directives for the evangelical communities' patriarchy, and have been interpreted according to the Greco-Roman patriarchal order of the early Christian church, reinforcing the stance of woman being in submission to man. Although many evangelical groups do not actively profess a literal inferiority of women, they continue to displace women within leadership roles and in a general attitude of being subject to men. This level of gender submission inhibits an independent examination of lifestyle and androgynous identification.

Interestingly, Singer also examined Genesis accounts of creation, suggesting Gnosticism as the collective shadow of early Christianity. Gnosticism, presenting all manner of androgynous reflections of the feminine onto the creation accounts, disrupted the "separation of the earthly and profane from the heavenly and sacred" as viewed by the Jewish and Christian systems (p. 127). Keep in mind that in Jungian thought the collective shadow is always the antagonist that eventually brings about maturity or unity but does so by challenging the complete ego personality or structure that is seemingly permanent. Singer suggested that Gnosticism provides an avenue of reflection on images and theories of the feminine components of creation that the orthodox religions prohibit.

From an evangelical perspective, any disruption of taking the Scriptures literally registers as a breach of doctrine. In this discussion, the evangelical orientation is not only disconnected to mythology at large but adverse to its followers, affiliating and incorporating mythological constructs into their spiritual lives. To consider *divine genetics* across gender is, for a large segment of evangelical religious, a falling into Gnosticism and away from "truth." This limitation denies any affiliation spiritually, psychologically, or interpersonally with an internal cross-gender identification, which is the heart of androgyny and gender equality and displays a lack of shadow (ala Jung) development.

The central message of any religion is important, and so it is with Christianity. The message of Christianity has been debated for 2,000 years from numerous theological perspectives and with different denominations focusing on diverse elements of Christ's message. Within the evangelical domain, the *kerygma,* or message, is taken to be literal, not mythological. Furthermore, evangelical exegesis of scripture is to find *the* (church or denominational) interpretation of a passage or message rather than *an* (individual) interpretation, much less anything mythological. This literal orientation has left little room for any kind of examination of possible archetypal identifications.

Bultmann (1961) examines the viability of the New Testament *kerygma* in modern times in absence of a mythological template. In debating the paradox of the mythological threads in the New Testament, he asks, "Does the New Testament embody a truth which is quite independent of its mythical setting?" (p. 3). He eventually argues that, indeed, the New Testament, the foundation of the evangelical community, risks oversimplification of the faith message by throwing out the mythology so entwined within the gospel. In presenting his debate, he defines the purpose of myth as an avenue through which humanity finds existential interpretation: "Myth is an expression of man's conviction that the origin and purpose of the world in which he lives are to be sought not within it but beyond it—that is, beyond the realm of known and tangible reality" (p. 10).

Evangelical negligence of entrance into the unknown and intangibility of myth as it relates to gender identification and preference has facilitated the recent fight of the gay movement and the transgender phenomenon. With the opening of the evangelical doors on equality for gay and straight persons has come the psychological permission to see gay, bi, and transgender issues as both an avenue for sexual direction and an archetypal expression. The primary archetype that the evangelical community has embraced has been "the likeness of Christ." While this is a viable archetype for some lifestyle issues and altruistic morality, it remains a masculine association within an all-male Trinity.

Davis (2004) argues that a mimetic hermeneutic, an objective search for "original meaning," compared to a subjective or transformative hermeneutic, represents the conservative orientation toward any biblical interpretation. Thus, all things biblical must be understood as factual in a literal sense, which functionally serves as a means of doctrinal control.

Evangelical theology and doctrine are encased in the belief of the absolute authority of the Bible, which itself is based on the view that it is inerrant in all manners, including gender references. This primary premise of biblical inerrancy bars any consideration of mythology as a means of understanding humanity and human origins. Christianity can only be witnessed as a union and identification with Christ in an objective way rather than in a subjective way. This objectifying of Christ and the kerygma can inhibit a larger application of the message that can occur when an individual sees the immense possibilities of interpretation through myth rather than singularly through an objective and literal understanding of Christ.

Within fundamental religions, including evangelical Christianity, mythology can cause disruption of doctrinal systems because of mythology's association both with pagan gods and the significance of matriarchal origins of religion. In evangelical denominations any allegiance other than to the male, objective, and literal Christ figure is considered non-Christian and heresy, as is any sway from the Yahwistic account of creation, where woman was created after man and hence "post-man" or "sub-man." Much of this rejection of mythology brews out of a position of inerrancy, that the scriptures are divinely inspired, literally true, and absolute.

Evangelical absolutism of current times reflects a similar reaction by the established church to the rise of Gnosticism, which sought to unify Christian tradition and philosophy (Tillich, 1967, p. 33). Tillich suggested that Gnosticism was the crucial internal threat to the early Christian Church as it attempted "to combine all the religious traditions which had lost their genuine roots, and to unite them in a system of half-philosophical, half-religious character" (pp. 33–34). Had Gnosticism won over the main Christian Church at that time, it would have prevented the rise and primacy of the absolutism that has existed in Christianity in some fashion for 20 centuries, and we now see in evangelicalism. Gnosticism suggested a less defined order of the Christian faith, and hence a less than unique order. The very cornerstone of Christianity is based on Jesus Christ as the incarnation of God. Yet as Tillich points out, the irony is that while the absolutism of evangelicalism denies a mythological understanding of the incarnation, it is, in fact, a mythological tenet. "Incarnation is one of the most ordinary events in Greek mythology and in all mythology. Gods come to earth; they take on animal, human, or plant form; they do certain things and then return to their divinity" (p. 32).

Having concrete and absolutist beliefs has always been attractive, especially when these beliefs are religious in kind. Johnson (2004) reflects on the quest of the concrete in religion, suggesting that some of the attractiveness of Fundamentalism (which bled over into Evangelicalism) is the assertion of having a direct connection to God with His (sic) absolute doctrinal rules. If God has spoken these words and given these exact rules, there can be no challenge to them. Johnson states, "Thus, in referring to

God as their partner and leader, Fundamentalists can follow God's directions without admitting to any self-interest. In so doing Fundamentalists can make themselves quite powerful while espousing an appearance of submission to God and humility to humankind" (p. 203). Both mythological and literal interpretations of the biblical narrative, such as an interpretation of the creation accounts, have a certain level of self-interest. Self-interest is not a non-biblical or anti-Jesus construct, even though evangelical profession espouses a certain self-denial and lack of self-interest.

CONCLUSION

As North American society continues to loosen its legal judgment on the varieties of human experience, we can expect that there will be a developing acceptance of these varieties. The evangelical will likely join the gay and heterosexual communities in this acceptance and find its voice. While the recent shift in the evangelical community is alarming for some, it is clearly liberating for others. While such cultural shifts of maturation do occur, they usually follow a pattern of radical demands, political battles, and subsequent social pendulum swings before the collective consciousness begins to accept what has been simmering in the collective unconscious for ages. Humanity does tend to eventually mature. It is only after this pendulum pattern weeds out and purifies consciousness that maturity genuinely begins. While this mainstay theological positional shift within the evangelical context is radical now, it will no doubt require a slow and arduous shift to maturity.

In that the evangelical community has largely been closed to anything with a mythological attachment, there has not been a cultural template for this community to examine a mythological search for a blended gender archetype. A rejection of anything mythological limits the ability to perceive beyond the literal and consequently denies what resides in the collective unconscious. The evangelical church has rejected mythological connections and in so doing has limited personal expansion of identification with the collective unconscious.

Being more open to a theory of mythology, more specifically the androgyne archetype, will facilitate a collective cultural and interpersonal maturity. Leeming (1990) reminds us that when we are broken, we return to our origins as reflected in the creation myths as they hold healing and order. Singer (1976) suggested that examining a broader view, specifically a monotheism that is androgynously based, is a viable route for Western religions looking for a healthier balance in philosophy, theology, and life at large. "Were God imaged as a pervasive Divine Essence containing the World Parents, the Two in the One" (p. 88), then a new culture-myth would come into being. Singer suggested that Christianity could benefit from an androgynous balance: "the motif of *loving* (union) would characterize the prevailing myth; instead of the more typically experienced motif of *strife* (separation), which produces so much of the degeneration and fragmentation we see all around us" (p. 88). Colegrave (1979) echoed Singer's passion for an integrated passage of the androgynous archetype by reiterating the necessity for both the masculine and feminine to create a satisfying fullness. This fullness, says Colegrave, is not limited to a literal form of conception but the conception of ideas as well. Hillman's (1985) insight that archetypes are metaphorically like gods, which require an ethereal access, reinforces Colegrave's notion that fullness must be both concrete as well as ideological. "An archetype is best comparable with a God. And gods, religions sometimes say, are less accessible to the senses and to the intellect than they are to the imaginative vision and emotion of the soul" (pp. xix–xx). By taking gender roles and identification out of the literal and into ideational, the evangelical church may be able to broaden its own psychological balance and deepen a sustainable archetype.

In assisting my more traditional evangelical clients, part of my responsibility is to provide resources, both conscious and unconscious, from which they can come to their own conclusions regarding the persons they are and choose to be. Without question, some of my clinical population is genuinely seeking a simple integration for sexual orientation, long buried by condemnation from their denominational bodies. And, thanks to social media and the other social pendulums, they can now examine, explore, consider, and even profess their sexual choices. For some, however, I think the matter is not about coming out of the closet but going deeper into the archetypal closet and finding long misplaced articles of connection to their primordial essence as androgynous beings.

There is evidence that gender bias and demand for literal interpretation of scriptural association has begun to stale. The long-term deprivation of access to the collective whole is lessening. Evangelical women who have historically been deprived of gender equality that would naturally lead to alternate sexual and gender identification are daring to explore their own orientation and choices. Furthermore, those who have been denied exposure to larger psychological and mythological understanding of life, including gender concerns, are tapping into a more wholistic psychological substrate: a creative, symbolic, and intuitive connection to their origin as androgynous beings, truly gender-full, as created by God.

The bottom line in all the cultural and religious presentation of the androgyne is, in simplest form, that humanity naturally seeks an internal balance. Intrinsic in that balance is the search for a primordial wholeness, an integration of the genders in either a physical or a spiritual perception within oneself. Using the archetype of the androgyne gives a voice to "I am all that I am and I am unbounded by gender." Tapping into this psycho-spiritual realm requires an interface that can be found through a review of the ageless archetype of the androgyne.

REFERENCES

Bultmann, R. (1961). *Kerygma and myth.* New York: Harper & Row.

Campbell, J. (1949). *The hero with a thousand faces.* New Jersey: Princeton University Press.

Colegrave, S. (1979). *Uniting heaven and earth.* Los Angeles: Jeremy P. Tarcher, Inc.

Davis, C. T. (2004). Seeds of violence in biblical interpretation. In J. H. Ellens (Ed.), *The destructive power of religion* (Vol. 1, pp. 35–53). Westport, CT: Praeger.

Hillman, J. (1985). *Anima: An anatomy of a personified notion.* Dallas: Spring Publications, Inc.

Hinch, J. (2014). *Evangelicals are changing their minds on gay marriage.* Retrieved on December 7, 2015, from http://www.politico.com/magazine/story/2014/07/evangelicals-gay-marriage-108608

Johnson, R. (2004). Psychoreligious roots of violence: The search for the concrete in a world of abstractions. In J. H. Ellens (Ed.), *The destructive power of religion* (Vol. 4, pp. 195–210). Westport, CT: Praeger.

Jung, C. G. (1959). *The archetypes and the collective unconscious.* New York: Bollingen Foundation Inc.

Jung, C. G. (1964). *Man and his symbols.* Garden City: Doubleday & Company Inc.

Jung, E. (1957). *Animus and anima.* New York: The Analytical Psychology Club.

Leeming, D. A. (1990). *The world of myth.* New York: Oxford University Press.

Pagels, E. (1988). *Adam, Eve, and the serpent.* New York: Vintage Books.

Perls, F. (1969). *Gestalt therapy verbatim.* Moab, UT: Real People Press.

Sanford, J. A. (1980). *The invisible partners.* New York: Paulist Press.

Singer, J. (1976). *Androgyny.* Garden City: Anchor Press/Doubleday.

Stevens, A. (1982). *Archetypes.* New York: Quill.

Tarnas, R. (2009). Archetypal principles. *The Journal of Archetypal Cosmology, 1*(1), 23–35.

Tillich, P. (1967). *A history of Christian thought.* New York: Simon & Schuster, Inc.

Chapter 19

Feminist, Womanist, and *Mujerista* Theologies in Conversation

Suzanne M. Coyle

The second wave of feminism crested during the 1960s and 1970s, deepening a conversation about women's roles in family and society that began with Elizabeth Cady Stanton and the suffragette movement. From abolition and the fight to vote, women steadily gained influence in familial and work relationships. From the secular to the sacred world, women sought to understand their identities.

Liberal mainline Christianity was the first domain of feminist-influenced thinking that birthed feminist theology. This feminist theology birth eventually impacted the evangelical world. It further extended to theology impacted by racial ethnicity and socioeconomic contexts.

In light of these developments, this essay will initially identify the principle tenets of feminist, womanist, and *Mujerista* theologies along with their methodologies. Then, exploration of similar and different methodologies to encourage conversation will be discussed. Finally, other emerging theologies focusing on women's identities will be briefly examined as well as future possibilities for conversation with all these theologies.

FEMINIST THEOLOGY

Many types of feminist theology are noted, such as liberal feminism, cultural feminism, radical feminism, or socialist feminism (Clifford, 2001). These different approaches to feminist theology have to do with theological and contextual foci. Identifying these delineating boundaries, however, I contend, is not as helpful for this discussion as initially identifying the commonalities of feminist theology.

The origin of feminist theology focuses on the emergence of the word "feminism" and its meanings. Feminism began in the 1960s and 1970s, along with both secular and theological reflections. Feminists "combine convictions about equal treatment with men with commitments to the special gifts of women" (Fulkerson, 2010, p. 209). Many men and women of varying worldviews could agree with this statement. However, as feminism and feminist theology pushes for sexual freedom, people divide sharply as to the moral and religious standards they have regarding sexual freedom and how that is defined (Fulkerson, 2010). Thus begins many divisions of feminist theology.

Two foundational approaches to feminist theology were initially articulated by Valerie Saiving and Mary Daly. Saiving identified two foci as critical to feminist theology. She argued that experience matters just as much as conceptual thinking in theological reflection (Fulkerson, 2010). For her, it is impossible to separate one's theological reflection from the personal experience a theologian has in real life. Her second focus lifted up concepts of sin as being integrally important to how theological reflection is practiced (Fulkerson, 2010). For instance, the traditional understanding of sin focuses on pride, which Saiving argues is attuned to the male experience. In contrast, female sin is focused more on passivity or not living up to one's full potential.

Mary Daly, a Roman Catholic theologian, approached feminist theology from the viewpoint of looking at the understood maleness of God through traditional theology (Fulkerson, 2010). Her further development of theology eventually understood Christianity to be a male-focused religion totally ignoring women's experience. This stance developed to her current position of having no hope for Christianity and developing instead a theology focused around goddess worship.

Her Catholic colleague, Rosemary Radford Ruether, while being critical of the male symbolism of Christianity, has worked to change the symbolism and metaphors of Christianity to make it more amenable to women's experience. While she has been concerned about the male image of God, she does not affirm "goddess" talk like her colleague Daly (Clifford, 2001). Her transformational approach paved the way for other feminist approaches such as the contribution of Protestantism in lifting up the role of women (Fulkerson, 2010).

As Protestantism began to wrestle with the inclusion of all women in the church, the impact of the Civil Rights Movement was felt. Feminist theology became limited to white women's activism. "Race, class, ethnicity, and sexual orientation have become key to its reading of gender and proliferation of constructive visions" for feminist theology (Fulkerson, 2010, p. 213). White women who might have advocated for their sisters of color often abandoned the struggle because of losing their own white privilege. Certainly, feminist theology was articulated by white women of education (Fulkerson, 2010). It can be argued that with a focus on the academic guild, concerns of everyday women could be overlooked.

At the same time, feminist theology became further divided along the boundaries of theological belief. The task of evangelical feminism, as represented by feminist theologians such as Letha Scanzoni and Virginia Mollenkott, was to "redeem" anti-women scriptural texts (Fulkerson, 2010). The focus of evangelical feminist theology begins with Scripture, whereas liberal feminist theology focuses initially on theological concepts and methodology. At the same time, it does share with other feminist theologies a hermeneutic of interpretation.

Ruether's desire for transformation of symbols is shared with Sallie McFague and Letty Russell. As "social liberationists," the purpose of feminist theology is to liberate women for full participation in society and the church (Fulkerson, 2010). This task of liberation in feminist theology focuses not only on liberation of women but the liberation of all people (Jones, 2000).

Despite these differences in feminist theology, a commonality of hermeneutical approaches exists. All feminist theology espouses a hermeneutic of suspicion to critically re-evaluate everything—especially traditional theology. This approach is in keeping with Ruether's initial naming of suspicion as a healthy approach for women. Further, a hermeneutic of proclamation lifts up the need for theology to name those values and ethics that are critical (Althaus-Reid & Isherwood, 2007). Through this hermeneutic, feminist theology takes an active role in the conversation of theology in engaging with common theological concepts such as sin and redemption through a feminist lens.

Finally, a hermeneutic of remembrance exists for feminist theology (Althaus-Reid & Isherwood, 2007). The feminist theologian needs to always connect what is current and corrective for women's experience with past traditions. Sometimes, traditional theology written historically in a distinctly male worldview can be reinterpreted with a feminist lens in surprisingly creative ways. This creative actualization can sometimes step outside the boundaries of traditional theology to lend new ways for women to understand their experiences in the light of faith (Althaus-Reid & Isherwood, 2007).

WOMANIST THEOLOGY

Womanist theology is a response to sexism in black theology and racism in feminist theology (Coleman, 2008). It attempts to straddle the divide between these two theologies while being true to the experience of African American women. In this approach, womanist theology examines "the social construction of black womanhood in relation to the African American community and religious concepts" (Coleman, 2008, p. 6).

The foundation of womanist theology differs from feminist theology. Womanist theology focuses on the meaning of faith in people's lives, not creeds. Jesus is the central figure, not theological constructions as in feminist theology (Clifford, 2001). Thus, it speaks beyond academic circles and is concerned about creating a theology accessible for African American women in everyday life (Mitchem, 2002, p. 12).

Feminist theologians have historically dealt with political and ideological constructs that do not address the need of African American women for "discourses and movement that embraces the spiritual and personal" (Floyd-Thomas, 2010, p. 39). In order to address this need, womanist theology aims for a sense of community, longing for justice, and a deep love of oneself (Floyd-Thomas, 2010). These goals stem from the days of the Civil Rights Movement when women's voices were largely disregarded and are a corrective to the male perspective of black theology.

Womanist theology focuses on both Scripture and feminist theories in its methodological claims (Floyd-Thomas, 2010). However, even more than these foci is the emphasis upon experience. In identifying what makes womanist theology womanist, Mitchem and Floyd-Thomas agree that womanist theology employs multidisciplinary methodologies, including such disciplines as political science, cultural anthropology, and social science, in addition to theology and biblical studies (Mitchem, 2002; Floyd-Thomas, 2010).

The importance of community life as expressed in the family and social activism of African American women further lays a foundation for theological reflection. Emilie Townes underscores this importance of family for womanist theology due to its importance to the African American community (Mitchem, 2002). African American families participate in the life of the community through an extended kinship system (Hines & Boyd-Franklin, 2005). This interconnectedness offers both pros and cons. On the positive side, when a positive change is effected, it moves throughout the whole community. On the negative side, oppression in any African American community embroils the whole community in pain and loss.

As womanist theologians are concerned with the whole African American community, it becomes important for womanist theology to engage in ethical and social analysis of oppression (Mitchem, 2002). Only by understanding the impact of racism over centuries can womanist theology really address the experience of African American women in the context of the entire African American community. It is indeed grounded in everyday living and is not "God talk but God walk" (Mitchem, 2002, p. 124).

In addressing racism, culture becomes an elevated focus in womanist theology. Through critical analysis of culture, womanists are better able to understand both the possibilities and barriers of African American women to connect with their faith. The central focus of faith is each woman's personal relationship with Jesus. And while Jesus is definitely viewed as a male in womanist theology, it is Jesus's humanness in understanding oppression that is at the core of His relationship with people of color; that is, His connection to their suffering and pain (Mitchem, 2002).

The maleness of Jesus does not obstruct the need for African American women through womanist theology to love themselves and lift up female images (Floyd-Thomas, 2010). Understanding Jesus as embodying human compassion enables a transformation of historical feminist theology to move from universalizing women's experience to focusing upon the personal and experiential (Mitchem, 2002). This radical subjectivity forms womanist theology around traditional communalism and redemptive self-love in a context of critical engagement (Floyd-Thomas, 2010).

Womanist theology's strengths lie in its awareness of both an academic and personal world for African American women. Its engagement with critical awareness of interdisciplinary approaches enriches the faith of women while holding in tension a concern for the whole African American community. Faith and theological reflection thus become engaged in the marketplace with a contextual emphasis on personal experience.

MUJERISTA OR LATINA THEOLOGY

Mujerista theology is defined by its pioneer theologian, Ada Maria Isasi-Diaz, as "a liberative praxis . . . mainly about moral agency" (Isasi-Diaz, 1993, p. 2). Through balancing systematic theology and ethics together in its approach, it seeks to always examine cultural values in the light of theological reflection. Further foci include the centrality of Hispanic ethnicity and social location, which determine the individual's position in society as being strongly influenced by socioeconomics and social status. The importance of the Spanish language for Latino/as is reflected as well in the term *mujerista* and the centrality of Hispanic ethnicity (Isasi-Diaz, 1993). The broader term of Latina theology is used to refer to *mujerista* theology.

Sources for Latina theology include: 1) experience, history, and cultural materials; 2) Hebrew and Christian scripture; and 3) tradition. From these sources, then, the theological task is to reflect critically on the experience of Christian faith for liberation. This liberation is from within and for the Latino/a community (Pineda-Madrid, 2010).

Solidarity, empowerment, anthropology, and encountering God are major themes in *mujerista* theology in its primary move toward liberation (Isasi-Diaz, 1996). It emphasizes economic oppression and male Latin machismo in their unique impact upon Latinas (Clifford, 2001). The image of the Babylonian exile is used by Isasi-Diaz to describe the North American experience of Latinas in terms of the immigration crisis. Thus, *mujerista* theology emphasizes liberation not as individuals but as a community.

As *mujerista* theology works toward liberation of community, understanding the development of internalized oppression is important (Pineda-Madrid, 2010). This analysis relies upon exploring the anthropology of culture in individual and community development. Theological reflection then becomes engaged with this social analysis to better understand both the social and theological implications of internalized oppression.

As such understanding is developed; Latina theologians believe that transformation of oppression in societal structures can occur (Pineda-Madrid, 2010). Theological reflection on the nature of hope both here in the present and in the future can contribute to this long process of societal change. Pioneer Latino theologians provide some continuity with Latina reflection on societal liberation as they both emphasize the call from God to have justice in this world and not just as a future hope.

Some differences in *mujerista* theology exist between Catholic and Protestant Latinas. Catholic theologians such as Isasi-Diaz emphasize Scripture less than do Protestant Latinas such as Maria Pilar Aquino and Daisy L. Machado. For Protestants, access to Scripture is paramount. Christ is emphasized less by Catholics than Protestants (Clifford, 2001). A further emphasis for Protestant Latinos is the involvement of women in the ordained clergy and increasing visibility of the role of women in the church. While the majority of Latino/as are Catholic, recent trends show an increase among Latinos to evangelical or Pentecostal Protestantism (Pew Research Institute, 2014). It would be interesting to discover what contributes to this shift in affiliation.

Both Catholic and Protestant Latinas share most emphases. The role of spirituality is critical in *mujerista* theology to both groups (Aquino, 2002; Isasi-Diaz, 1996). Salvation is understood as being here in this world through socioeconomic justice as well as in the next world (Pineda-Madrid, 2010). Salvation is equated with liberation and is not merely a reflection on action, but "action in and of itself" (Isasi-Diaz, 1996).

Mujerista theology shares with feminist theology a desire to reclaim traditionally male religious symbols with female imagery. However, it has more in common with womanist theology in its struggle to experience liberation from racism not only for women but for their own communities. Womanist and *mujerista* theologies both share concerns for social justice, and both demand socioeconomic justice for their communities. *Mujerista* theology differs from womanist theology in its critique on the capitalist neoliberal globalization that robs Latino/as of economic justice. Further, *mujerista* theology is faced with the current challenge of immigration injustice in North America.

Machado talks of the "unnamed woman"—she who is undocumented (Machado, 2002). Postcolonial/postmodern methodologies that explore essentialist philosophy that emphasizes only one definition for any concept is essential to *mujerista* theology. Latinas contend that identifying each person's story and identifying their preferred future may facilitate liberation.

EMERGING THEOLOGIES

Emerging feminist-related theologies include African women's theology, Asian American feminist theology, and queer theology. All these theologies share with feminist theology the desire to identify gender-limiting theology and transform such theology into inclusive theology. At the same time, unique differences exist, which shall now be discussed.

Mercy Amba Oduyoye can be credited with putting African women's theology in the forefront of theological discussion. It is based on the tradition of story in African culture, seeing itself as a narrative theology. The dialogue in this theology between African culture and biblical hermeneutics aims to discover a theology that addresses the dilemma of African women dealing with violence and gender oppression as well as the possibilities that the stories of the ancestors offer. It is a theology of relationships. The theological method reflects upon the narrating of story to analyze the various actors in the story and how they interact and view agency (Oduyoye, 2001). The household of family in African culture is the focus of African women's theology, as it seeks to transform oppressive gender narratives into inclusive relationships that benefit all.

Asian American feminist theology emerges from the Asian woman's experience of "having no name" in their Asian countries of origin. Immigration to the United States did not help the situation. Here in America, Asian women thought that by negating their own culture and becoming American, they would elevate their status. Instead, they lost all identity (Kim, 2010; Kim-Kort, 2012).

Asian American feminist theology seeks to correct this narrative. It is a contextual theology based on how cultural context impacts the Asian American woman. The great respect given to wisdom in Asian society is a starting place for this theology. Thus, this theology does not begin with the Bible or Christian doctrines but with the stories of women. Embedded in these stories are conflicting images of sexuality, "the other" implicit in Orientalism and the resultant marginalization (Kim, 2010).

The last emerging theology related to feminism is gay and lesbian theology or queer theology. Similar to theologies addressing racial oppression, queer theology seeks to transform the meaning of "queer" in such a way as to remove its negative connotation. It is a branch of liberation theology. The sources that inform queer theology are Scripture, seminal reports about LGBT issues, and publications that protect the LGBT movement (Shore-Goss, 2010).

METHODOLOGICAL CONSIDERATIONS

In consideration of the different methodologies of feminist-informed theologies, some commonalities do exist. Feminist, womanist, and *mujerista* theologies all advocate against essentialism (Jones, 2000). They do not believe that a narrowly defined description of words is ever possible. In order to develop, then, theologies of women's experiences, "localized thick descriptions" are needed (Jones, 2000, p. 39). Through an exposition of women's experiences, it becomes more possible to analyze the oppression of all women and thus determine ways to respond.

It is possible to conceptualize these three varieties of women's theologies in two camps. On one side—the "rock"—are those female theologians who build their theology on universal foundational concepts. Moving from this vantage point, they work primarily in Christian doctrine. Others on this side focus on psychoanalytic processes in developing a relational concept. Another approach explores a literary narrative/story that can be experienced differently by different women (Jones, 1997). This theological side offers some identifiable structures that can be used as conversation pieces by theologians of varying positions.

Those female theologians who stand on the other side—a "hard place"—emphasize experience that is not contained by solid theological constructions. They are, however, filled with grace and possibilities for creative endeavor. Aiding in this endeavor are cultural, anthropological, and poststructural thinking (Jones, 1997). Solid structures are not available with this side that can serve as readily identifiable conversation pieces. It does, however, offer the passion those theologies grown from human experiences offer.

FUTURE DIRECTIONS

What then is the future for feminist, womanist, and *mujerista* theologies? How do the emerging theologies connect or not connect? As one reflects upon the development of women's theologies, or gender-focused theologies, observations emerge. The primary considerations of these theologies is a focus on one's gender and one's racial ethnicity. It is difficult to separate the two.

A promising development are women's process-relational theologies which seek to connect process thought in a relational context (Coleman,

2011; Russell, 2011). Women from varying perspectives are engaging in critically re-examining process theology as a welcoming context in which to explore women's concerns relationally. While the "rock" and the "hard place" of theologies have different approaches, they both strongly believe that the outcome of women's theologies needs to be relationally rich if change is to occur for women and men.

Women's process-relational theologies have the promise of being sensitive to experience while offering a flexible structure in process theology. By inviting conversation between these aspects, these theologies have the grace and toughness that is needed to situate relationality in theological context.

This conversation fits well with Schneider's contention that the person of the theologian is what impacts theology (Schneider, 1998). What is further needed is attention to power as well as the agency of power. If women's theologies of all perspectives are to offer critical change, then female theologians need to re-fashion power into a construct that offers possibilities for compassion and empowerment.

REFERENCES

Althaus-Reid, M., & Isherwood, L. (2007). *Controversies in feminist theology*. London: SCM Press.

Aquino, M. P. (2002). Latina feminist theology: Central features. In M. Aquino, D. Machado, & J. Rodriguez (Eds.), *A reader in Latina feminist theology: Religion and justice* (pp. 133–160). Austin, TX: University of Texas Press.

Clifford, A. M. (2001). *Introducing feminist theology*. Maryknoll, NY: Orbis Books.

Coleman, M.A. (2011). Introduction to process theology. In M. Coleman, N. Howell, & H. Russell (Eds.), *Creating women's theology: A movement engaging process thought* (pp. 12–19). Eugene, OR: Pickwick Publications.

Coleman, M.A. (2008). *Making a way out of no way: A womanist theology*. Minneapolis: Fortress Press.

Floyd-Thomas, S. M. (2010). Womanist theology. In S. Floyd-Thomas & A. Pinn (Eds.), *Liberation theologies in the United States: An introduction* (pp. 37–60). New York: New York University Press.

Fulkerson, M. M. (2010). Feminist theology. In S. Floyd-Thomas & A. Pinn (Eds.), *Liberation theologies in the United States: An introduction* (pp. 209–226). New York: New York University Press.

Hines, L. B., & Boyd-Franklin, N. (2005). African American families. In M. McGoldrick, J. Giordano, & N. Garcia-Preto (Eds.), *Ethnicity and family therapy*, 3rd ed. (pp. 87–100). New York: The Guilford Press.

Isasi-Diaz, A. M. (1993). *En la lucha—In the struggle: A Hispanic women's liberation theology*. Minneapolis: Augsburg Fortress Publishers.

Isasi-Diaz, A. M. (1996). *Mujerista theology: A theology for the twenty-first century*. Maryknoll, NY: Orbis Books.

Jones, S. (2000). *Feminist theory and Christian theology: Cartographies of grace*. Minneapolis: Fortress Press.

Jones, S. (1997). Women's experience between a rock and a hard place: Feminist, womanist, and *Mujerista* theologies in North America. In R. Chopp & S. Daveney (Eds.), *Horizons in feminist theology: Identity, tradition, and norms* (pp. 33–55). Minneapolis: Augsburg Fortress.

Kim, G. J. (2010). Asian American feminist theology. In S. Floyd-Thomas & A. Pinn (Eds.), *Liberation theologies in the United States: An introduction* (pp. 131–148). New York: New York University Press.

Kim-Kort, M. (2012). *Making paper cranes: Toward an Asian American feminist theology*. St. Louis: Chalice Press.

Machado, D. L. (2002). The unnamed woman: Justice, feminist, and the undocumented woman. In M. Aquino, D. Machado, & J. Rodriguez (Eds.), *A reader in Latina feminist theology: Religion and justice* (pp. 161–176). Austin, TX: University of Texas Press.

Mitchem, S. Y. (2002). *Introducing womanist theology*. Maryknoll, NY: Orbis Books.

Oduyoye, M. A. (2001). *Introducing African women's theology*. Cleveland, OH: Pilgrim Press.

Pew Research Center. (2014, May 7). The shifting religious identity of Latinos in the United States. Retrieved from http://www.pewforum.org/2014/05/07/the-shifting-religious-identity-of-latinos-in-the-united-states/

Pineda-Madrid, N. (2010). Latina theology. In S. Floyd-Thomas & A. Pinn (Eds.), *Liberation theologies in the United States: An introduction* (pp. 61–85). New York: New York University Press.

Russell, H. T. (2011). Introduction to feminist theology. In M. Coleman, N. Howell, & H. Russell (Eds.), *Creating women's theology: A movement engaging process thought* (pp. 3–11). Eugene, OR: Pickwick Publications.

Schneider, L. C. (1998). *Re-imagining the divine: Confronting the backlash against feminist theology*. Cleveland, OH: The Pilgrim Press.

Shore-Goss, R. E. (2010). Gay and lesbian theologies. In S. Floyd-Thomas & A. Pinn (Eds.), *Liberation theologies in the United States: An introduction* (pp. 181–208). New York: New York University Press.

Chapter 20

Confucianism and Feminism

Mary Wittbold

For many and sometimes complex reasons, and in societies everywhere, female roles have traditionally been subordinated to male roles. Until relatively recently it was the males who led the tribes, ruled the kingdoms, and were the authority figures in the families. A major contributor to this male-centric environment has been society's patriarchal orientation. From the earliest of civilizations until today, civilized society has been arranged along patriarchal lines.

The early patriarchal arrangements involved "dialectical processes, which means that they were mutually interactive, mutually reinforcing processes" (Lerner, 1987). In that sense, it would seem that the patriarchal arrangement was intentional. That it intended for men and women to interact through prescribed roles implied a mutual responsibility for sustaining the culture. Patriarchy does not mean that the men agree to do all the work or bear the responsibility for all the work. It does not necessarily mean that a man's work is more important than a woman's, though that is what the resulting interpretation has come to imply and reflect—that men carry the responsibility and authority in society, which by proxy of interpretation subordinates the woman's role to the man's. In hindsight we can clearly see how this interpretation has fostered the "historical defeat of the female sex" (Engels, 1909).

When taken together, the above quotes presuppose that either the premise of the mutually consented to patriarchal arrangement was flawed to begin with or that something (or a combination of things) happened along the way to distort the original intent, which led to the creation of the inequity we perceive today. Either way, what may have originally been only a slight and hardly noticeable imbalance long ago eventually created a major distortion in the surrounding cultural environment as the gender gaps reflected in the environment grew more and more proportionately out of sync with cultural reality. The feminist movement is a response to this distortion in the cultural perspective.

The feminist movement has made great strides. Historically speaking, however, this progress has been made over a relatively short period of time. The patriarchal arrangement has been in place since the dawning of civilization, and is the only arrangement that civilized society has ever known. The feminist movement, at least as an organized movement, has only been around for the last couple of hundred years, barely enough time to even register a historical context that might reflect in the current worldview that it is shaping. More time is needed before we can expect the progress to reflect in the whole population.

It takes a lot of time and effort to "get ahead" professionally, years of learning and experience to establish, run, and grow a business, or to climb the corporate ladder. It will take more years still before these changes are registered in the entire population and proportionately reflected in the rankings.

The female stereotype has been cemented into place over such a long period of time that stubborn vestiges of cultural expectation are still clinging to it. The contemporary worldview is starting to reflect a more hopeful picture for women but does not yet reflect equal reality. It is important to note that feminism does not attempt to subordinate men's roles to women's roles but rather to promote choice. In theory, this should grant a wider range of latitude for women and men alike to choose between home and career.

Chinese women lag even further behind women in the West with respect to equal rights, and Confucianism is often seen as a barrier. Perhaps it should rightfully shoulder some of the blame. There is no question that it is a rigidly patriarchal philosophy. But it would be careless to reject Confucianism entirely out of hand without first reflecting on why this is so, or perhaps why it is still so. Any attempt to sort this out should attempt to distinguish between what Confucianism is capable of expressing versus how it has been interpreted and applied through a predominantly male lens. The worldview that fostered Confucianism some two and a half millennia ago is the one it was originally intended to serve. The worldview that fostered the feminist movement reflected a different reality and is still recent in cultural memory.

Confucianism is ripe with timeless and universal themes. To blame it for repressing women in China is to risk jumping to a conclusion based on a picture that may have been distorted by non-Confucian influences over time and deny a fair assessment of its flexibility and ability to adapt to a changed cultural environment. To measure how and why Confucianism might be influencing the current expression of gender equality in China, we have to trace it back to the context of its original intention.

Confucius was born and lived during a particularly turbulent time in Chinese history when the political system was collapsing. The situation motivated Confucius and many other scholars to come up with solutions to stop the bleeding and restore cultural stability. It was a time of striking cultural contrasts, of political decline germinating a thriving intellectual, philosophical, and artistic community. On the one hand, the weakened political system was quickly devolving into widespread anarchy. On the other, political leaders were desperately seeking viable solutions to shore up the government's crumbling foundations. These contrasting fronts created the perfect storm of opportunity that launched the Confucian solution that answered the need for cultural sustainability and stabilization. It fulfilled that original objective and, like patriarchy, continued as a dominant influence.

The more deeply rooted a cultural tradition becomes, the further it grows beyond the limits of its original intent. It grows beyond answering to the needs of the community and begins to weave its way into the fabric of the cultural environment itself as a self-sustaining institutional perspective.

Institutional perspectives may continue to sustain their communities, but rather than existing to sustain the community, they now exist to sustain themselves. They become answers unto themselves, less flexible and more fixed in place. Whether this is good or bad depends not only on the institution itself but also on how far the community perspective has deviated from the institutional perspective over time. Confucianism and patriarchy are not unique in this way. Any long-held cultural tradition can become an institutionally fixed perspective, including a religious tradition. If the fixed institutional perspective falls out of balance with the needs of the community, fewer can agree on what a balanced world should look like.

The burden falls back onto the community to sort this out and find ways to recalibrate the institutional perspective to the requirements of the citizenry. This is what Confucius attempted to do and what the feminist movement attempts to do—to bring about adjustments to align the fixed cultural tradition with the current cultural reality.

IS CONFUCIANISM A RELIGION?

There is often a cloud of confusion surrounding the question of whether Confucianism is a religion. Most scholars agree it is not—technically—yet people assume otherwise. Similarities in the way they behave might help illuminate why this is so. For example, the Abrahamic traditions of Judaism, Christianity, and Islam are, like Confucianism, philosophical systems of thought. They carry a prescribed moral code or ethical standard that originated within a specific community to sustain that community and eventually grew beyond the confines of the initial communities to became self-sustaining traditions. What Confucianism omits from the religious side of the equation is the sacred, or spiritually sustaining, factor—it does not expressly deny the sacred, it simply doesn't address it. In the same way, the feminist response doesn't expressly deny men's rights; it simply doesn't address the problem at hand in those terms. What Confucianism does specifically address is a prescribed standard for social and political behavior, a factor that most religious systems omit or only *imply.* Where religion is concerned with experience of the sacred or spiritual world, Confucianism is concerned with experience in the secular world.

These traditions also employ the use of symbols that serve to help make difficult or complex concepts more readily understood by conveying meaning that a community can recognize and will relate to. For example, a religious symbol might convey the concept of a divine deity. The symbol might borrow on an earthly element to deliver sacred meaning in a way that the earth-bound community can relate to. The subjective nature of the symbol enhances understanding and underscores the relevancy to the community of the message being delivered. Ancient indigenous communities that lived immersed in nature found sacred symbolism in nature. They personified the sacred by taking elements they recognized and could relate to and infusing them with supernatural qualities to convey symbolic meaning. Making the sacred personally meaningful helped the community to understand life. Thousands of years later, if the community has shifted from a natural to an urban orientation, these symbols once borrowed from nature will have lost their relevance, and unless they have been updated to reflect the new worldview, they will no longer convey the meaning they once had.

This could be a contributing factor to what the feminist movement perceives in the cultural environment today. An obvious example is the endowing of the sacred, in this case a divine deity, with *male* qualities. This can be seen as a once relevant way of conveying a sacred concept that became fixed in the cultural psyche over time. Unfortunately, this has also served to perpetuate male dominance in society. If it has lost some of its relevance, society is loath to tinker with the "sacred." Anything sacred is considered untouchable. If the community can't touch it, then it can't recalibrate the perception it conveys to an updated and more inclusive worldview.

When the invisible supernatural force was imbued with masculine characteristics, it was also shorn of some of its universal quality. It is this abbreviated version that has become institutionally fixed in tradition as a self-perpetuating, hands-off, masculine energy. This less than universal concept persists despite our changing worldview and carries with it the potential for further distorting the surrounding cultural environment by continuing to perpetuate a patriarchal God-like arrangement that has lost, or is losing, relevance to half the population. What has been lost, first in the translation (personification) and then in the fixation on the personification, is the universal scope of the concept and the potential for meaning that it is capable of delivering to an *entire* community.

It is possible that Confucianism has followed along a similar path, and that its precepts are capable of being more universally applied than the fixed institutional perspective is capable of delivering. The question becomes, what is it that needs to be recalibrated: Confucianism or the cultural assumptions that have been hardened into place around it?

Confucianism developed out of an ancient worldview. Feminism is still developing as a relatively recent phenomenon. There is no question that Confucius did clearly spell out that the woman's role was subordinate to the man's and that this became a self-perpetuating notion. But to pin society's inequities on Confucianism is to deny its potential to convey meaning that the entire community can still find relevance in today. Despite their fixed institutional perspectives, Confucianism and the Abrahamic traditions have endured for many a good reason and justifiable cause. From the feminist perspective, we owe it to ourselves to reexamine Confucianism and consider whether its institutionally fixed perspective can be recalibrated to conform to an updated reality. If we unwind history back to the time when Confucianism conveyed the positive life-changing message it was intentionally designed to deliver, we might also be able to recognize its inclusive potential.

CONFUCIANISM

China is one of the oldest continuous cultures in the world. Until recently (early in the twentieth century), it was ruled by an imperial system. This imperial rule was held by family dynasties in which the entire succession of dynastic rule was descended from the same family line. Dynastic succession followed along patrilineal lines, with rulership passing from father to eldest son.

China's historical timeline is divided into dynastic eras, named after the families of the respective ruling dynasties. These historical eras vary in length, from as little as a couple of decades to several centuries. Each dynastic era put its own unique fingerprint on the surrounding cultural landscape to influence the political, religious, economic, and artistic expressions during the time of its reign. The last dynasty to rule over China was the Qing Dynasty, which ended in 1911.

Confucius was born during the era of the Zhou Dynasty (also commonly referred to as the Chou Dynasty). The Zhou Dynasty lasted from approximately 1046 until 256 BCE, its 790-year reign distinguishing it as the longest lasting of all the dynastic eras. The Zhou Dynasty ushered China into the Iron Age and a cultural transition from a tribal culture to a land-based feudal culture and economy.

The Zhou rulers had relied on a series of alliances to overthrow the preceding dynasty. For payback, and as a necessary means to hold control after the victory, the initial Zhou ruler divided the conquered territory into individual states, that were actually like fiefdoms that were for the most part parceled out along extended family lines. Those extended families that ruled over their individual states answered to the central governmental authority, which prearranged a rigid hierarchical order intended ultimately to induce fealty to the authority of the central Zhou authority. A troublesome side effect of this arrangement from the start, however, was that it also served to dilute the power of the central authority and set the stage for further draining of that power.

The history of the Zhou Dynasty is divided into two time periods. Before 770 BCE it is known as the Western Zhou Dynasty. This period was marked by peace and harmony. After 770 BCE it is known as the Eastern Zhou Dynasty. This period was marked by the centralization of local powers (states) and an escalation of conflict that led to the eventual breakdown of the super-state that had until then been the stabilizing factor. This later Eastern period is further subdivided into two time stages: the Spring and Autumn period (770–476 BCE), during which Confucius was born and lived, followed by the Warring States period (475–221 BCE), which marks the bloody conclusion of the Zhou era.

At the beginning of the Spring and Autumn period, there existed a hundred or more feudal states. As time marched on, these individual fiefdoms grew and thrived in their own right. Extended families grew comfortable in their rulership roles and, as their economies flourished, began to take matters of authority into their own hands, which further eroded the stability of the central power base. When the local states began to realize that the central authority had weakened to the point that they could no longer depend on it for the support and protection that it had once provided, the local states began to squabble amongst themselves. Wars randomly broke out between them, and the instigators ceased adhering to the customary rules of engagement. As a result, tens of thousands were slaughtered and maimed in a brutal and humiliating fashion. As the level of anarchy increased, the local authorities found it more and more necessary to centralize. Larger states then began to invade their smaller neighbors and to annex them under the umbrella of their authority. These increasing instances of power division are what eventually broke the back of the central authority.

The long, gradual erosion of the Zhou Dynasty's governing authority—and resultant structural deterioration of the feudal system that began during the Spring and Autumn period—is a centuries-long shift during which none of the centralized states was powerful enough until the end of the Warring States period (in 221 BCE) to claim victory over all and establish a new dynastic order. By the end of the Spring and Autumn period (which marks the beginning of the Warring States period), the initial 100+ states had been consolidated into seven larger states. These seven states would "duke it out" until the end of the Warring States period, when one would finally triumph over the rest to mark the end of an era.

Confucius was born in 551 BCE, about three-quarters of the way through the Spring and Autumn period. The Spring and Autumn period is named after the Spring and Autumn Annals, a written chronological record of all significant events that occurred in the state of Lu from 722 to 479 BCE. It is thought to be the first chronological record of its kind ever recorded in China.

The Spring and Autumn Annals became one of the significant core texts now associated with Confucianism. Its significance is threefold. First, the events occurred and were recorded in Confucius's native state of Lu. Second, Confucius is thought to have been responsible for the record keeping during a portion of the time, and he is also credited with preserving them. Third, he is believed to have graced them with a subtle editor's touch, which he turned to his philosophical advantage by making subtle hints that underscored the political instability, insinuated blame, and hinted at a means to rectify the situation.

His editorial revisions to the Autumn Annals included innuendos, such as that certain of the recorded destructive natural phenomena be interpreted as a warning to the ruler that his unworthy actions may have triggered such an unfortunate reality. These subtle "suggestions" took hold over time and began to shape Chinese political thinking and cultural norms. At the same time that the social front was breaking down, a window of opportunity was opening on another front for men like Confucius who was a member of a growing class of citizens known as the *Shi*, or gentleman class. Thanks to the disordered state of the government, the men of this class were being enlisted to help find solutions to shore up the leaking foundations of the system.

Confucius's father was a low-ranking military officer. He was not wealthy but he did claim a remote blood tie to the Shang family, who had ruled over the previous dynasty, which provided him a minor claim to the ruling class. He was well into his sixties by the time Confucius was born.

His first wife had given him nine daughters, but no son to carry down the family name. So he took another woman as concubine or wife, we're not sure, who did succeed in giving him a son. However, that son was born lame and, apparently, did not constitute a suitable heir. Confucius was the product of yet a third union, between his father and another much younger woman. Theirs was an "illicit union." It is uncertain what qualified it as such. It may have been the age difference. Various sources put Confucius's mother somewhere between her mid-teens to early twenties at the time of his birth, while his father was in his early sixties—a far from customary difference in marital age. Or it may be that Confucius's father and mother had never married, which would have meant that Confucius's mother had been his father's concubine. All we know for sure is that their relationship did not conform to the marriage ritual (*Li*) and was therefore an "illicit union" (*yehe*).

Confucius was three years old when his father died. Because of the illicit nature of his parents' union, he did not inherit his father's social status. After his father's death Confucius's mother left the father's family and moved Confucius and his lame stepbrother to another city to live among the members of her family clan. This may have been an act of her own volition or it may have been because the father's family shunned her after his death. In any event, life after his father's death was much harder for Confucius and his mother. They received meager support from her relatives, for they were commoners and had little to offer. Confucius did many of the house chores until he became old enough to find odd jobs that would help support them.

Though they were impoverished, sources are unanimous that Confucius had a loving mother. Her father (his grandfather) is thought to have been a local scholar who had tutored Confucius's mother while she was growing up—even though the practice of tutoring girls was not customary at that time. This instruction from her father would equip her with the skills to tutor Confucius later on, which she did in their home until he was old enough to attend school. She prepared him well and took care to nurture his personal interests. One of these interests was cultural ritual. She encouraged him to practice the rituals and specifically encouraged him to thoroughly familiarize himself with the rituals and rites of the Zhou court, which instilled in him the notion that he might someday land a professional opportunity to instruct the court. Ritual is an important component in Confucianism. For Confucius, ritual conveyed deep meaning, just as Abrahamic rituals—such as grace before meals, kneeling while praying, and the singing of hymns—do today.

At the same time that she tutored Confucius, his mother tutored other students in her home too, as a means to support her family. Confucius was well primed for further education by the time he reached school age. His mother sent him to the best school available to him. There is no indication that he was a spectacular student but he was an enthusiastic learner and became well versed in arithmetic, poetry, classical literature (the Chinese Classics), history, and, of course, rites and rituals.

Confucius, who had enjoyed a close and loving relationship with a single mother, was understandably grieved when she died at a relatively young age (he was in his early twenties). Though it is unclear whether his father had ever actually married his mother, Confucius insisted on burying her next to him. He had never been told where his father was buried and made the effort to search out the location of his father's grave. He insisted on showing his mother the proper respect by adhering to all the customary funeral rites and rituals of the day. He spent his employment proceeds on a proper burial (next to his father) and adhered to the traditional three-year mourning period. By these acts, we can assume that it wouldn't have mattered to him that she was "just a female."

The paying of respect to one's ancestors was already an ingrained tradition in the ancient Chinese culture of Confucius's day. Confucius would raise this theme to another level by introducing the practice of "filial piety," or obedience, respect, and veneration for one's parents, and all elders for that matter, regardless of whether their social position was above or below one's own. Filial piety became one of the prime virtues in Confucianism, and the one Confucius placed above all others. He regarded filial piety as the cornerstone from which all other virtues flow.

"Learning without thought is labor lost. Thought without learning is perilous."

Confucius was a member of the *shi*, or gentleman class. The *shi* class ranked below the aristocracy and above the commoners. The *shi* class was ascending during Confucius's lifetime because as states centralized power, they installed new governments, which gave rise to numerous governmental positions needing to be filled along with the necessity to establish new policies and procedures. Because of the urgency of these demands, social positions were now being filled on the basis of ability rather than heredity. Members of the *shi* class, who were most often scholars, court officials, and teachers, were the most likely candidates to fill these positions that mandated creative new ways to approach intellectual and philosophical solutions to society's problems.

This created a fertile ground for the expression of new and different ways of thinking about the world. Thoughts and ideas were encouraged and flowed freely. This flourishing of intellectual and philosophical ideas inspired many new schools of thought during this time and gave rise to a historic phenomenon that is today considered to have been the golden age of Chinese philosophy and is known as the Hundred Schools of Thought.

The Hundred Schools of Thought that produced Confucianism also produced several other philosophical traditions that would go on to have a powerful influence on Chinese culture for years to come. Taoism and Legalism are two other examples of philosophical schools of thought that were seeded during this time and went on to become established in Chinese thought. Many of the classical texts, which are closely associated with Confucianism and would influence Chinese thought for the next two and a half millennia, were also written during this time.

"Study the past if you would define the future."

Those who filled the new governmental positions were charged first with developing local administrative, military, and political procedures and then with traveling around to neighboring states to exchange ideas and promote their own agendas. Confucius, who looked to traditions that had worked in the past for inspiration, developed his new school of thought around the concept of personal character and virtue. Character and virtue would serve to impose a sense of moral responsibility on the ruling classes and instill an ethic of respect that flowed both ways, up and down the hierarchical ladder of relationships. He aspired to work in government and ascend to an influential enough position to promote his ideals for social behavior and civil decorum. He did manage to secure a few (some sources say several) minor government appointments, but he never ascended to the position of authority he desired, quite likely because he was known to be strongly opinionated.

He met his objective of promoting his ideals by establishing a private school. He then patterned the itinerant habits of the *shi* government scholars. He became an itinerant teacher to find people to listen to his ideas. His students became his disciples and together they eventually gained a substantial following.

Confucius recognized that education played a crucial part in personal development. He became one of the first (if not the first) private Chinese citizens to establish a private school (schools had been traditionally run under the auspices of the government). Confucius's school touted education as a foundational component of personal and moral development. He felt strongly that this was the correct path to shoring up the crumbling foundations of society.

The Confucian concept, an ethical-social-political system of thought, did not gain traction in Chinese thinking until after his death. Later, however, it proved one of the most enduring schools of thought and, of all the schools founded during the golden age, the one that would have the most lasting impact on Chinese society.

Confucius's founding philosophical maxim, *Study the past if you would divine the future,* worked brilliantly to shore up another transition that was happening in conjunction with the breakup of the old order: the transition of Chinese culture from a primary (primitive) to a secondary (civilized) society. Religious studies scholar Houston Smith, author of *The Illustrated World's Religions,* writes, "In times of transition, an effective program must meet two conditions. It must be continuous with the past, for only by tying in what people are familiar with does it stand a chance of being accepted. At the same time, the answer must take clear-eyed account of developments that render the old answer unworkable" (Smith, 1994).

A primary society functions close to nature, and holds a communal perspective. The traditions of a primary society are rooted in inherited tribal instinct, and are a product of what has been determined through generations of trial and error to best sustain the group. Because these traditions are fundamental to the survival of the tribe, they are never questioned; they are the glue that holds the seams of a primary society together. In a primary society, the sustaining of the group supersedes in importance the survival of the individual. A primary society "has no power to modify human nature" (Li, 2010). The hunter-gatherer communities of ancient indigenous cultures whose tribes lived semi-nomadic lifestyles to follow the hunting and gathering seasons are an example of a primary society.

Fiefdoms and states do not normally conform to the conditions of a primary society. However, the ancient Chinese feudalistic states of ancient China did: "Ancient Mediterranean civilizations did not meet those [primary] conditions while Chinese civilization did. The ancient Chinese formed a superstate to function as police to keep peace among local powers, and this relatively peaceful environment allowed the Chinese people to still live in primary societies until the Warring States Period" (476–221 BCE) (Li, 2010). The ancient Chinese Feudal system *overseen by a superstate* had kept China stable. But now, thanks to the widespread centralization of local power, the system was rapidly deteriorating and losing its instinctual footing.

A secondary society is a man-made construct. It functions according to a prescribed value system. Traditions are established to modify human nature for the purpose of supporting the value system. The glue that holds a secondary society together is thus subjective or value based, rather than nature based. Social and institutional hierarchies are created within secondary societies as a means to stabilize them, as well as to guard against outside threats to their survival. Group consciousness begins to give way to self-consciousness as the individual identity emerges apart from the group.

To meet the conditions of a primary society, the ancient Chinese culture of Confucius's time would have been dependent on inherited (which is the same as saying unconscious) tradition, convention, and group expectations. Confucius lived near the end of an era, when the primary society was in crisis but the secondary society had yet to replace it. The cultural symptoms of the time suggest the secondary society had already begun to take seed in Confucius's lifetime. The culture had probably entered into a quasi-primary state, where some secondary components were already in the process of transitioning into new cultural norms. The notion of a cultural commitment to "individual *class* rights" or "quality of life for all hierarchical *classes*" came out of the increased instances of state centralization, and further suggests that the cultural shift to a new identity and consciousness was already underway.

A new cultural order would require new mechanisms (traditions) to defend against the conflict and anarchy arising from the centralized states taking matters into their own hands, and to protect against future threats to the system. The primary society had functioned closer to the level of nature, where the hierarchical arrangement (overseen by a superstate) would have operated on the principle of "survival of the fittest." More value would have been placed on the strongest and the fittest, in this case, those members who inherited the richest and most powerful rankings who would have been charged as the protectors and enforcers of the group.

With the emergence of centralization and individualism, while society was still held in the grip of a primary mentality, Confucius recognized a need to protect the lowest, and therefore weakest, members of the hierarchical order. The commoners were in danger of getting trampled underfoot. In the primary society, the mandate to preserve the interests of the entire group is what held the rulers in check. At the top of the hierarchy, their role mandated that they protect the rights of the entire group. This required them to be sensitive to public opinion. Therefore, they were accustomed to bowing before the needs of the group. Rulers held value (power) in this role; as individuals they were expendable. Their survival depended on the sustenance of the group.

Such was the cultural environment during Confucius's lifetime. The potential for complete annihilation of society was both dire and near. It was a threat that could no longer be ignored and it fueled a pervasive sense of urgency. Confucius engaged himself in the most pressing challenge of the day: figuring out how to restore order. He yearned to bring back the traditions of the earlier tranquil years of the Dynasty that we refer to today as the Western Zhou.

The original founders of the Zhou Dynasty were his idols. Those early years over which they ruled became his template, or ideal, for a perfect society. According to Smith, the way he did this was to appeal to the classic texts: "He appealed to the classics as establishing the guidelines for his platform. Yet all the while he was interpreting, modifying, and reformulating. Unknown to his people, and largely to himself we may assume, he was effecting a momentous reorientation by shifting tradition from unconscious to conscious status. . . . It was a powerful routine, perhaps the only one by which distinctively human values ever permeate large groups" (Smith, 1994). This was timely with respect to meeting the conditions Houston Smith identifies as necessary for a transition to a secondary society, which is to be *continuous with the past* and to have continuity with past proven traditions that have stabilized society.

He breathed new relevance into an old system by assigning a *conscious* solution to an obvious problem. The solution retained some elements of the previous cultural structure, namely, the rigid hierarchical order that flowed from the top down demanded unquestioned respect for authority—a power that had heretofore been based solely on birthright.

The revised rules of hierarchy centered around relationship obligations. Confucius defined five core relationships assigned to superior/subordinate status. They were ruler–subject, father–son, husband–wife, elder brother–younger brother, and friend–friend, in which (except for the last of these) the former held the higher station and latter the lower station in the hierarchical succession. The former had a responsibility to ensure the care and protection of the latter, while the latter was bound by duty and respect for the higher station. He then outlined five virtues that bound these relationship roles to an ethic of responsibility: To be able under all circumstances to practice five things: gravity, generosity of soul, sincerity, earnestness, and kindness. In this way he introduced a "law of relationships" that was to be enforced by a fundamental ethic of behavior rather than by a civil law of enforcement because Confucius believed that the perfect society must be predicated on trust rather than threat or reward. Perfection could not be attained unless the citizens took responsibility for fulfilling their roles regardless of whether they were rewarded for doing so or not. Where the needs of the group had previously held the rulers in check, their survival would now depend on the condition of their "superior personhood." This new relationship order advocated for the rights of the commoners by assigning them a prescribed role in society.

"Let the ruler be a ruler and the subject a subject."

Here Confucius ushered in another important new element and requisite condition of secondary society: self-awareness. He took the conscious rules of relationship that were bound to the five virtues a step further by stressing the importance of education. Self-awareness was to be cultivated through higher learning. This step, which ultimately reinforced the element of conscious adherence to tradition, would serve to ensure stability in the early stages of the transition to the new secondary order and would safeguard its systemic health going forward. Confucius did more than just emphasize the importance of education; he also provided a model for learning. Rather than just lecture to his students, he adhered to the Socratic method of teaching them how to think, by asking questions that encouraged critical thought and working things through for themselves, thus guiding them through the steps of a democratic learning process. He believed that true understanding and personal development flowed from careful study and personal reflection. This teaching style is one of the hallmarks of Confucius's legacy.

FEMINISM

The history of the feminist movement can be broken down into three waves. The first wave began in the Western world as a response to women's suffrage (right to vote). The suffrage movement did not begin to gain any real traction until the late nineteenth century when, in 1893, New Zealand granted voting rights to female property owners over the age of thirty, and in 1894, when South Australia granted females the rights to vote and stand for parliamentary office. Women's suffrage was legally recognized by a few states in North America from as early as 1869. In 1878 a bill was introduced to establish a national women's right to vote but it was not finally approved until decades later, after the First World War, during which a serious shortage of able-bodied men had required women to fill many of the traditional male roles. This afforded them a practical opportunity to prove what they were capable of doing. The ratification of the 19th Amendment to the U.S. Constitution in 1920 marks the end of the first wave.

The second wave of the feminist movement began in the mid-1960s and lasted through the late 1970s. This wave, known as the Women's Liberation Movement, formed in the wake of the publication of several books that hit a nerve by calling attention to the pervasive stereotyping of female roles. These publications, one of which was *The Second Sex* by Simone de Beauvoir, argued that to presume that a woman's place was in the home was to presume that women could only find fulfillment through homemaking and child-rearing, and suggested this had devolved into a convenient excuse for society to discriminate against them.

This idea created the backlash response known as the women's liberation movement, which advanced education and career opportunities and the legal elimination of discrimination in the workplace, and saw the Equal Rights Amendment to the United States Constitution passed in 1972.

The third wave began in the early 1990s and is known as Neo-Feminism. This wave formed partly as a backlash to the second wave, or women's liberation movement, which was perceived by many to have focused too exclusively on upper-middle-class white women and excluded other ethnicities and nationalities, religious affiliations, as well as issues of sexual preference, reproductive rights, and so on. Feminist theory became more diverse in scope and branched into additional areas to address a variety of issues. These branches fall under headings such as liberal, social, cultural, and radical feminism, with subheadings such as sexist feminism, black feminism, separatist feminism, eco-feminism, Christian feminism, and many more. Feminism is now so diverse as to foster disagreement between feminist factions.

Another movement that has developed in tandem with feminist theory from its earliest inception is feminist ethics, though the term was not used until the late 1970s or early 1980s. Feminism recognized early on that most traditional ethical schools were based solely on men's moral experiences and overlooked the female perspective, an omission that feminism believes devalues women's moral experience.

FEMINISM AND CONFUCIANISM

Feminism is evolving into a philosophical ideal that has cultural, political, and ethical ramifications as a response to perceived unfairness or cultural imbalance. Like Confucianism, feminism formed around an effort to recalibrate an established order that was no longer working by actually proposing a solution. Confucius may have eventually got around to feminist rights had he lived long enough or hadn't had to start lower down the ladder of Maslow's hierarchy of needs. The threat to society that feminism perceives is relevant to half the existing population, and likely significantly more when you factor in those men who are unhappily stereotyped into choices other than what they would prefer. Hopefully, the feminist philosophy will continue to be able to strive for equal rights and equal choices for all genders without creating a negative stereotype around any women or men who choose to stay within the boundaries feminism has so successfully started to break down.

As mentioned above, the feminist movement first surfaced in the Western world. Western society as we know it was cultivated after the Middle Ages, first in Europe and then spreading to America, Australia, New Zealand, and eventually to other parts of the world. As a relatively recent construct, the Western worldview has only ever borne the conditions of a secondary society. However, Western society itself derives from Western civilization, a diverse heritage that hails back to the days of ancient Greece and Rome, which themselves were built on the backs of even earlier cultures such as Mesopotamia and ancient Egypt.

The common thread that weaves through all phases of civilization is our patriarchal foundation. The civilized worldview can continue to progress positively for all members of society only if the issues confronting it are held in view of a conscious self-aware community lens. Stereotypes that esteem one population over another do not represent conscious awareness of community needs. Rather, these indicate self-perpetuating institutional precepts that have wormed their way into the unconscious levels of the establishment, or established tradition. Because some aspects of the patriarchal orientation are holdovers from nearly the dawning of civilization itself and are fixed in the institutional mentality, the distortion they have created has a tangible negative effect on more than half of the population. If the strengths of a patriarchal system and a matriarchal system could be united, and their weaknesses weeded out, the prevailing conditions could be perceived through conscious community awareness and further cultivated toward inclusivity.

For example, one of patriarchy's strengths is that it encourages a more rational individualistic forward-driving orientation. To this we owe the scientific and technological advances that have been made over the past several centuries. One of its weaknesses is that this has come at the expense of the environment. One of matriarchy's strengths is that it encourages a more group nurturing, intuitive orientation. In an exclusive matriarchal arrangement, this would protect the environment but that would come at the expense of the individual. If both perspectives can be combined to work together through their strengths, this will reduce threats such as environmental pollution and individual rights and lead to a more harmonious and self-sustaining environment for all concerned.

Just as most religions have strengths and weakness, still it is safe to say that they intend good outcomes, not bad ones. In theory they should be able to coexist with one another and comfortably conform to the pockets of society they are intended to serve. Where we get into trouble is how we approach a "proper" balance when asserting a limited perspective or subjective value judgment. In the same vein, in theory at least, if their weaknesses are culled and their strengths combined, Confucianism and feminism should be able not only to coexist but also to amplify a positive cultural outcome.

Though Confucianism reinforces the notion of a hierarchy of dominant and subordinate relationships, what Confucius intended was not to change the arrangement but to modify it by making relationship roles dependent on reciprocity. That women were subordinated to their husbands and their world did not range to outside of home management and caring for the children is a holdover from an ancient worldview that has persisted throughout much of Asian culture and the Western world to this day. The best answer to the problem of his day "smacks" of prejudice in view of today's far more egalitarian and "politically correct" worldview. The same can be applied to Christianity and other faiths, which need to be refreshed from time to time to remain relevant in contemporary expressions. If, instead, those terms intended for a worldview that is no longer relevant today are taken literally, or out of context, they become fixed in rigid fanaticism. They lose their timeless quality and universal appeal to compassion, ritual, and duty.

Over time Confucianism has gone in and out of favor in China. With the rise of communism there early in the twentieth century, Confucianism was at first condemned by Chairman Mao because it represented the very gentry he wished to abolish. Later on the communist party changed direction but only to spin the message to their favor by highlighting the aspects of imperial conditioning that highlighted hierarchy, obedience, and respect for authority—taken out of context. There is a renewed resurgence in its popularity today, both in scholarship and throughout the general population. The middle classes in particular still read the *Analects* and value education as a means to personal development. Perhaps in a way this back and forth has kept Confucianism in the conscious discussion and perhaps for that reason it will stand a chance to find renewed relevance in modern Chinese culture.

The continuity of a lengthy history allows us to step into the realm of a higher perspective, where we can rise above all the twists and turns and manipulations and begin to appreciate its timeless quality and intuit the quality and flow of its universality. At the end of the day Confucianism is about harmony and balance. Confucius's influence carried beyond the culture of his time to inspire many of the thinkers who followed him. His contribution to the Eastern world is very much similar to what Socrates contributed to the Western world.

Today China is a different place. It is beginning to resemble the West more in that it has become a leading economic power and enjoys one of the richest economies in the world. The Chinese have even surpassed the United States as buyers of the most luxury goods and they are starting to see the same problems observed in America, where the most wealth (and wealth is a form of power) is held by a few. It seems as if the more things change, the more they stay the same.

Again, Confucius recognized the cultural need for balance and harmony. Whether the governments of Eastern or Western nations recognize the need (or are willing) to rebalance social, political, and economic policies toward that end is another matter. Most governments do seem to try—but they too can represent fixed institutional perspectives. Confucianism, like so many religions, has long since vacated its role as community advocate and been kicked up to the level of bureaucracy. It still serves, in its own way, perhaps the best it can as an institution, but down at the community level one gets the nagging sense that it is capable of serving so much more. Perhaps there is good reason why most established governments and religions operate at the institutional level. The problem is that the original missions of the institution become separated from the consciousness of the community. The community and the institution begin to fight against each other rather than for each other toward a mutual goal. The irony is that we may ultimately all have the same goals but something gets lost in transmission when the message is kicked back and forth over that line. Confucian principles continue to percolate through contemporary life in China, in family, social, and business relationships, and the importance of education and personal development.

Confucianism and feminism should be able to survive time and coexist to remain relevant to society. In the case of Confucianism, the original objective was to shore up society with a value system based on virtue and right behavior, and not only did it meet that objective, but many of its foundational principles have remained intact. Whether that is a good thing or a bad thing depends on who is interpreting the good and the bad. In the case of feminism, the original objective was to establish women's right to vote. This objective has been met and feminism has grown and spread to include equal rights for women of all cultures throughout all areas of society. In some ways, its foundational principles are still being developed. It has only been around for about one-and-a-quarter centuries. Compared to Confucianism, the history of feminism is barely out of its infancy. Hopefully, it will continue to conform to the needs of the society it originally intended to serve and, when that objective has been met, grow to serve the population at large.

REFERENCES

Engels, F. (1902). *The origin of the family, private property, and the state.* Hottingen-Zurich.

Lerner, G. (1987). *The Creation of patriarchy*. Retrieved on September 2, 2015, from http://w3.salemstate.edu/~hbenne/pdfs/patriarchy_creation.pdf

Li, Y. (2010). *The ancient Chinese super state of primary societies: Taoist philosophy for the 21st century.* Bloomington, IN: Authorhouse.

Smith, H. (1994). *The illustrated world's religions.* New York: HarperOne.

Chapter 21

Men Are Not Yang and Women Are Not Yin: Gender Construction in the *Tao Te Ching* and the *I Ching*

Maija Jespersen

It is hard to know what to expect from gender roles in this day and age. Many old patterns are being contested or are already on their way out the door, but what should replace them? LGBT studies have identified more than two genders—more than *three* genders. Caitlyn Jenner—former Olympic athlete Bruce Jenner—is on TV and in the news as America's first openly transsexual public figure. It makes me wonder, what makes one a woman? Or a man? What do those terms even *mean?*

An ancient philosophy and religion can come to our rescue in facing this modern problem. The balancing of yin and yang that is so central to Taoism contains insights about the universe that can help us not just answer, but reframe, the question in a new way.

The yin/yang symbol central to Taoism is a circle made up of two interlocking paisley shapes, one white and the other black. It is meant to indicate motion. As the white, active, paisley shape reaches its widest part, the skinny tail of the dark, receptive force starts and begins to grow. As the dark yin reaches its own widest part, the sliver of white yang commences.

In this way, they form a perpetual cycle, combining to form *ch'i*, the breath of the universe (Hinton, 2015, p. 125).

Yin, or the receptive, is associated with the feminine gender, and the yang or active force is associated with the male, both popularly and in many places in Chinese philosophy. It does not contradict Western ideas of gender, wherein women are seen as more intuitive, thinking in expansive, lateral processes instead of linear ones, and more emotionally in tune with others—all qualities of the receptive yin. Some feminists have embraced these as inherent qualities of women, and formulated paths to gender equality that involve revaluing "women's ways" of doing things.

A closer look at Taoist philosophy, though, suggests that it is a misreading to assign yin to women and yang to men. There is a principle of perpetual transformation in Taoism that prevents a fixed assignment of yin or yang to either gender. This would seem to worsen our gender identity problems, but ironically, applying ancient understanding to the modern question can help us construct new gender identities in ways that are more expansive for everyone involved.

TAOISM

According to Chinese legend, Taoism was founded by Lao Tzu, the Keeper of the Archives in the late Chou dynasty (1122–255 BCE). He was essentially the court librarian, and as such one of the most educated people around. After serving for most of his life in the corrupt and violent government, he finally couldn't stand it anymore and in 516 BCE, he left the court as an old man to wander in the western hills. The city gate keeper, knowing a great treasure was about to vanish, asked—or begged, or ordered, depending on the story—the old man to write something of what he had learned before he passed. So Lao Tzu wrote down the five thousand characters that we now know as the *Tao Te Ching* and left them as his toll to escape the folly of worldly life. Other great sages have expanded the body of literature that now makes up Taoism, but the *Tao Te Ching* is its foundational statement.

It is entirely possible, and even quite a bit more likely, that these sayings were collected over several hundred years in the late Chou dynasty (Hinton, 2015, p. 12). "Lao Tzu," after all, is not a name, but more of a title, "Old Master"—or, because ancient Chinese did not have clear plurals, "Old Masters" (Wilson, 2010, p. xxvi). The late Chou was a tumultuous, warring period politically. The dynasty had originally supplanted the preceding Shang dynasty by claiming that the "mandate of heaven," the divine power bestowed upon the emperor and his descendants, could change if the emperor did not live up to his duties. But by later in the dynasty they were paying a high price for that maneuver, as upstart nobles and self-declared princes in various parts of the kingdom declared they now had the mandate of heaven. Rulers—not just the imperial court, but the upstart nobles as well—started to look for well-educated advisors, generating for the first time an independent intellectual class (Hinton, 2015, p. 17). This went on for a couple of centuries, so there were plenty of old masters around. The great Chinese historian Ssu-ma Ch'ien mentions both Taoism and the book on Tao (way) and Te (virtue), near the beginning of the first century BCE, and it is from this reference that the collection gets its current name, the *Tao Te Ching* (Wilson, 2010, pp. xxvi–xxvii).

The "T" in Tao and Te is actually a "D" sound, so the title of the book sounds like "Dao De Ching." *De* is a common word in several European languages, meaning "of." I knew that "Tao" meant "way," and for years I thought the book meant "the way of Ching." What is this mysterious Ching?, I wondered. Later I encountered the *I Ching*, and there it was again! "This Ching must be so important," I thought. It turns out *ching* just means "book." That was literally the least important word in the title.

Tao is a difficult term to define, and translators are always grasping for concepts in other languages that will convey it fully. One such translator describes the dilemma.

> One of the first to ask about its meaning was a prince from eastern India who, wishing to read the book, requested a number of translators to explain it to him . . . One of them linked *Tao* to the term *marga*, meaning a track, path, or way by which one arrives at enlightenment. To him, it was clear that the path is the cause that leads us to the result, the enlightened mind (Sanskrit: *bodhi*). The other translation team declared that just the opposite was true. They interpreted *Tao* as *bodhi*: knowledge, understanding, or pure wisdom. In this way, the Tao does not cause or lead to enlightenment; it is enlightenment itself.
>
> In Western languages, the first Latin translator (name unknown) interpreted the word as "ratio," derived from the word for "reason." Later, more sophisticated terms like *natura naturans*—nature, naturing—were employed to indicate that the Tao was an ongoing process, not one complete as in the sense of *natura naturata*. In English, words as dissimilar as "nature," the "highest good," or the "Path" or "Way" are common attempts to convey a sense of the word. (Wilson, 2010, p. xxxiv)

It is confusing because it is both a means and an end—things that are separate in the West. It is both nature and reason—things we think of as even more separate. These things can coexist without contradiction for Taoists because they see the universe as constantly changing, and reason (whatever reason the Latin translator was trying to get at) as part of original human nature (Hinton, 2015, p. 25). For Westerners who want things to stay still, and see reason as a process developed in the European Enlightenment by which we subdue our animalistic nature, though, the combinations do not make sense. But leaving that aside, we can describe Tao as the cosmic order (Smith, 2015, p. 17), elucidated in the *Tao Te Ching*, containing the secrets of the nature of the world, the living in harmony with, which constitutes enlightenment.

So it *is* a path, but it's not *just* a path. It's the path to itself.

Central to the idea of following the path is the concept of, well, *following*. Not forcing things, but allowing things to unfold each according to their own inner nature. This unfolding of inner nature is called *zi ran* (sometimes spelled *tzu jan*), meaning, "self-so" or "of-itself" (Hinton, 2015, p. 21). Interfering with *zi ran*, whether by trying to impose order on things, trying to dictate what they should be, or any other kind of manipulation, is going against the Tao. Getting out of the way of Tao, on the other hand, by acting naturally instead of with forethought and intention, is referred to as *wu wei*, or "acting without acting" (Hinton, 2015, p. 124). Verse 55 dictates this clearly:

> To enhance your life is called *tempting fate*,
> and to control ch'i with the mind is called *violence*.
> (Hinton, 2015, p. 93)

One should just follow one's innate nature, because one's nature was dictated by heaven's command; therefore, following it is falling in line with the will of heaven. This inner nature, or natural inner virtue, is the meaning of the other word in the title, *Te*. Taoism is about cultivating and being true to your own Te. This can be taken to all kinds of extremes. Freely wandering around without a care in the world—like Lao Tzu intended to do after he passed through the gates—is a perfectly Taoist thing to do.

Water is the perfect image for all of this flowing and following, and is a central image in Taoism. This yielding does not result in dissipation, as one might expect, but in increased power.

> 66. Oceans and rivers become emperors of the hundred valleys
> because they stay so perfectly below them.
> This alone makes them emperors of the hundred valleys.
> So, wanting to rule over the people
> a sage speaks from below them,
> and wanting to lead the people
> he follows along behind them. (Hinton, 2015, p. 105)

This following, yielding behavior is described as female in verse 61.

> In its stillness, female lies perpetually low,
> and there perpetually conquers male. (Hinton, 2015, p. 99)

Already in both descriptions of yin behavior we have an element of its opposite, power. Laughlin and Wong (1999) challenge the association of the Tao with feminine, claiming that it wrongly ignores the central need of Taoism to balance yin and yang which renders them inseparable (p. 162). The fundamentally co-occurring nature of yin and yang will be explored further below as it appears in the Doctrine of Perpetual Change and in the *I Ching*.

INCLUSION OF WOMEN

Laughlin and Wong (1999) discuss how Taoism both describes women as more yin in some ways, and in other ways as similar and equal to men. Part of Taoism focuses on changing the patterns of your internal fluids in order to increase your longevity; as such, men and women have different training for their different physiologies. In addition, women's more yin disposition gives them different strengths and weaknesses: they are better at sitting still, but more prone to idle gossip. But this yin disposition—perhaps more accurately describable as an inclination—was not significant enough to prevent women from participating fully in Taoism and holding all the positions men did: teachers, heads of monasteries, and even "immortals," the most highly adept sages (Laughlin & Wong, 1999, p. 152). After initial training, the different beginning practices of men and women merged into the same practice, and women and men were treated without discrimination (Laughlin & Wong, 1999, p. 158).

The fact that since its inception, women have participated in rigorous training, held the same positions and titles, and received the same instruction as men indicates that they were considered with a large measure of equality within Taoism. The merging of the training program of male and female adepts suggests their essential natures are the same. These factors point to the yin and yang inclinations of the two genders as more surface differences than essential characteristics. And, indeed, this is what we would expect, because another essential feature of yin and yang is that they are always turning into each other.

To explore this, we need to look at the ancient Chinese way of viewing the world, which had already been well established hundreds of years before Lao Tzu got his job as Imperial Archivist. Wilson (2010) calls this cosmology a kind of Oriental "Perennial Philosophy," making reference to Aldous Huxley's book of that name about universal mystical trends (p. xlii). It was universal in ancient China in much the same way the framework of the scientific method is universal today. Lao Tzu (whoever he was or they were) would certainly have been familiar with it (Wilson, 2010, p. xxxviii), and would have assumed that his readers were familiar with it as well. Still, "Perennial Philosophy" is not very descriptive, so since there is no official title, we refer to it here as the "Doctrine of Perpetual Change."

DOCTRINE OF PERPETUAL CHANGE

Based on ancient Chinese cosmology, *Ch'i* is the basic energy of the universe. Primal chi divides into yin and yang, which then divide into the five elements, which then divide into "the ten thousand things" (meaning all of the multiple things existing in the universe) which emerge and vanish in perpetual cycles (Wilson, 2010, p. xlii). An important feature of *chi* is that it is in constant motion as the universal breath (Hinton, 2015, p. 125). The Taoists were not wrong; the universe *is* in constant motion. In modern physics, that motion is the basis of Adrian Bejan's theory of Constructal Law, which explains the seemingly spontaneous development of complex designs in nature. It is a mistake, he posits, to try to consider the designs as the discrete properties of objects. It makes more sense to consider the whole system as a giant flow state: physical design happens in response to the constant need of energy to move through the system. That is why patterns recur in nature, and the branching of lung tissue looks so much like the branching of a river delta: the same design optimizes flow in both cases (Bejan & Zane, 2012).

This constant motion of the universe has a very important consequence for yin and yang: they cannot stay still. They can get more and more divided and extreme for a while, but at some point *they have to turn into each other*. Another feature of the ancient Chinese universe is that yin always turns to yang, and vice versa.

To expand these ideas, we will turn to the *I Ching*, which pre-dated the *Tao Te Ching* by somewhere between 500 and 3,000 years, and which is pivotal to the Doctrine of Perpetual Change. The *I Ching* gives structure and context to the *Tao Te Ching*, which is otherwise abstract enough to leave it open to widely divergent translations. By looking at how yin and yang function in the *I Ching*, we can grasp the background ideas Lao Tzu would have assumed his readers understood, and get a clearer picture of what he meant.

I CHING

The *I Ching* is one of the oldest and most influential books in Chinese history. It has wielded a central influence on all facets of Chinese culture, including religion, philosophy, and art, from its prehistoric inception into the 20th century (Smith, 2015, p. 1). *I* means "change," and the book is essentially an analysis of how things change, based on the observed cycles of nature and humankind. Divining the future was a major pastime in ancient China and the *I Ching* was a divinatory tool.

According to Chinese legend, the first element of the philosophy was created around 3000 BCE by China's first great sage, Fu Hsi (Sung, 1969, p. ix). This was a time when sages sat around contemplating nature as a serious pastime. Fu Hsi took the basic duality of yang and yin, represented by a solid line or two dashes respectively, and arranged those lines in trigrams to represent eight large natural elements like mountains and thunder. Those then combine into 64 hexagrams, representing states along a cyclical process of change. The first historically verifiable figure associated with the *I Ching* is King Wen, founder of the Chou Dynasty in 1143 BCE. He explained each complete hexagram (Sung, 1969, p. 1). His son, the Duke of Chou, explained each changing line in each hexagram. The hexagrams, the changing lines, and their explanations together constitute the original text of the *I Ching*. Many commentators, beginning with Confucius, have sought to brave its intricacies by adding their own explanations, and the puzzle has by no means lost its fascination, despite being 3,000 years old; a new English translation was published just this year.

Supplicants threw yarrow stalks (now people use three coins, throwing them six times) to construct the hexagram. There was a twist, though; some combinations of yarrow stalks or of heads and tails meant the line was changing into its opposite, which carried special, more specific instructions. For example, hexagram 33, Mountain, carries a connotation of stillness and instructions about the importance of stopping, which can be read as general advice about the situation. The first changing line says, "Stop at the feet and there is no fault," meaning if one stops at the very beginning, before harm is done, there is no loss. Line three, however, warns of trying to stop while others around you can't or won't, thereby creating internal contradiction and problems, as in, "Stopping the waist breaks the spine." These are very different readings, even though they are within the same hexagram. One predicts the supplicant will prevent the entire problem by nipping it in the bud, whereas the other predicts difficulty and chaos (Cleary, 2003, pp. 331–335).

After tossing the coins and reading the first hexagram, the changing lines are transformed into their opposites to form a new hexagram, indicating where things are headed. To follow our example, changing the first line of Mountain gives you hexagram 22, Adornment, foretelling cultural events and meetings. If one threw the Mountain hexagram with the first line as a changing line, the whole forecast would be something needs to be stopped, you will stop it in time, and because you did, you will find social advantage. Changing the third line of Mountain instead, however, gives you hexagram 23, Stripping Away, which predicts petty people tearing down the cultural achievements of great people (Cleary, 2003, pp. 122–129). *That* whole reading would be something needs to be stopped, but you will cause a fundamental rupture by trying to stop it, and there will be negative social consequences. The hexagrams are listed in numbered order, but because of the changing lines system, any hexagram can change into any other, which makes it a very versatile divinatory tool.

The changing lines system should also serve to clarify just how central the concept of yin and yang constantly changing into their opposites is to the whole concept of yin and yang. Not only are they changing into each other, but the height of yin contains the beginning of yang, and vice versa—just like in the symbol. This, too, can be seen from the action of the changing lines in the *I Ching*. With coins, it is not a combination of heads (yang) and tails (yin) that makes up a changing line; the combinations of yin and yang are considered stable. We might think that *all* heads or *all* tails would be considered solidly yang or solidly yin, but the opposite is true. All heads represents the height of yang, which by definition has already started changing into yin.

So how could it be possible to assign one human gender an energy quality that by definition is constantly changing into its opposite? It would not make sense to attempt to have one without the other, as is suggested by the formulation, "yang is the male, yin is the female," unless you ignored their constantly moving nature and tendency to reverse.

Even the fluidity called for in Taoism is at first described as yin, but also has a yang aspect. Although it is externally yielding, it contains a central firmness. This externally yielding/internally firm character is reflected in the trigram for water, which consists of a central yang line surrounded by two yin lines. Water meets obstacles in a yielding manner, but it is also one of the strongest movers and shapers in nature, as described in verse 78 of the *Tao Te Ching*:

> Nothing in all beneath heaven is so soft and weak as water.
> And yet, for conquering the hard and strong,
> nothing succeeds like water.
> And nothing can change it:
> weak overcoming strong,
> soft overcoming hard. (Hinton, 2015, p. 117)

The Tao itself is yielding like water on the outside, but internally is the foundational force in the universe, without which nothing happens. A practitioner of Taoism embodies this principle by being outwardly flexible in dealing with people and external situations, but inwardly firm in commitment to truth and principles. These are just a few of the many ways in which yin and yang always occur in balanced forces, never individually, and never in fixed ways.

The question remains, how did yin became associated with the female and yang with the male at all? It happened along two paths. On one hand, later commentators added the gender assignments to what was a multifaceted, nature-oriented system (Pearson, 2011, p. 19). On the other hand, the *I Ching* makes use of patriarchal gender constructions of the day to describe situations in terms that would be widely understood, but mentions of social norms are mistakenly read as support of those norms—as if I told you to go right at the oak tree, and you went home and told everyone I love oak trees.

To understand the first issue, it is necessary to look at the tradition of writing commentaries on the *I Ching*. The hexagrams are perhaps suggestive, but are just stacks of lines. The explanations are cryptic and short, and often use nature metaphors that leave us guessing. For example, the explanation for hexagram 64, Unsettled, reads, "The unsettled succeed. A young fox, crossing [the stream] boldly, gets its tail wet. Nothing is gained" (Cleary, 2011, p. 397). What does that mean? It is clearly a very specific event in nature, totally different from geese flying into the sunset, or water flowing into a series of deeper and deeper chasms, both of which occur in other places in the book. But that is the only clear thing about it. What is it warning against or advising us to do?

Enter the tradition of commentaries. Part of the appeal of trying to re-translate the *I Ching* is the chance to add your own ideas about what it means, including whatever information the supplicant needs in order to interpret the advice. Confucius was the first known sage to do this, and his writing—or at least, something as close as it is possible to get across the several major linguistic changes that happened in the interim, including a national forced unification in the Han dynasty—is included in Sung's (1969) translation of the *I Ching*. Besides explaining the explanations, Confucius integrated some of them into more general statements of truth; those latter statements became appendices.

It is here, in Confucius's appendix, that we find elaboration of the active and receptive principles. The first hexagram, Heaven (or, The Creative, or Firmness Symbolizing Heaven) is all yang lines, and is the fullest expression of yang in the *I Ching*. King Wen writes of it, "*Khien* represents what is great and originating, penetrating, advantageous, and firm" (Sung, 1969, p. 1). Confucius adds,

> In its (individual) stillness it is self-absorbed; when exerting its motive power it goes straight forward; and thus it is that its productive action is on a grand scale. (Sung, 1969, p. 282)

The second hexagram, *Khwan*, is all yin lines, the fullest expression of yin in the *I Ching*, and about it King Wen writes,

> *Khwan* represents what is great and originating, penetrating, advantageous, correct, and having the firmness of a mare. When the superior man (here intended) has to make any movement, if he take the initiative, he will go astray. (Sung, 1969, p. 15)

Confucius adds,

> In its (individual) stillness, it is self-collected and capacious; when exerting its motive power, it develops its resources, and thus its productive action is on a wide scale. (Sung, 1969, p. 282)

So far yin and yang each have an active mode and a still mode, they are both great and originating, and they are both penetrating, all as originally set down by King Wen. That they should each have an active mode makes sense, since they are both major forces in the universe.

It is in Confucius's appendix, though, which was written some 600 years after King Wen's commentary, that we read, "The attributes expressed by *Khien* constitute the male; those expressed by *Khwan* constitute the female" (Sung, 1969, p. 272).

In considering the significance of Confucius adding gender, it is important to realize that Confucianism is all about the proper ordering of relationships in society. If everyone acts according to the duties and responsibilities of their roles, Confucianism asserts, then the world turns smoothly and peace is maintained. But ancient China was a hierarchical society in which women were generally subservient to males. Of the five major Confucian relationships pivotal to the ordering of society, women are mentioned in only one: husband and wife, and in this relationship the wife takes a subservient role to the husband's leadership. It sounds a bit like the *Khwan* hexagram, or expression of yin—but only if you simplified yin to just following, and forget the originating, penetrating aspect. Assigning the gender of female to the force of the universe credited with following would both add the weight of a massive cultural force to his new system of theories, and encourage women to stay in their place.

But it is reductive and inaccurate. If yin and yang were adequate to describe multi-faceted things like human genders, Fu Hsi and King Wen could have just stayed with the two lines. They would not have had to elaborate the hexagrams in order to be able to describe the complicated dynamics of the ten thousand things. And it should be remembered that Confucius's desire for everyone to stay in his or her roles was the utter opposite of wu wei and Taoism. The Confucian assignment of gender should be understood as a later addition to the yin/yang dynamic/perennial philosophy so central to Taoism, and an attempt to steer it into, or at least show that it supports, a more fixed system of order.

Pearson (2011) identifies how the assignation of gender to yin and yang was infused into the text by 250 BCE, the approximate time of the earliest complete existing commentary by Wang Bi.

> Wang Bi wrote his commentary based on the assumption that the paired concepts of *yin* and *yang* were gendered and existed at the

> time the *Book of Changes* was created, and that these concepts are expressed throughout the book, so that every solid line in the hexagrams represented *yang* and every broken line *yin*. He assumed that *yang* represented strength, goodness, and masculinity, and that *yin* was associated with physical and moral weakness and with women. Later scholars followed his reasoning. (Pearson, 2011, p. 18)

Thus, a text that originally only mentioned yin once, referring to a nest of cranes in a way that implies shelter (Pearson, 2011, p. 20) but which is otherwise rich in complex natural imagery, becomes reduced back into an over-dichotomized framework that obscures much of its real meaning (Pearson, 2011, pp. 22–23).

A second gendering of yin and yang happened with the confusion of description with advocacy. The *I Ching* sometimes refers to patriarchal situations in ancient China to describe situations accurately. Hexagram 44 is a perfect example of this: in Sung's 1969 translation, it is called *Kwei Mei*, "Marriage of a Younger Sister." It initially sounds like a happy omen because it mentions marriage, but it is actually a very negative portent, clearly stating that action will be evil and in no way advantageous, because heaven and earth are in the wrong relationship (Sung, 1969, p. 227). This is because, according to ancient Chinese custom, the older sister was supposed to marry first, before the younger sister. The implication here is that the younger sister is marrying out of turn, which bodes ill. The sister, though, is just a stand-in to illustrate the concept of things happening in the wrong order.

Many translators either tone down or obfuscate the patriarchal language because it seems offensive and no longer applicable. Cleary (2003), for example, titles hexagram 44, "Meeting," and translates the explanation as, "Meeting. The woman is strong. Do not marry the woman" (p. 272). Here, he has ditched the expectation that women should marry in a particular order, and changed it to the idea that because man and woman need balance in a relationship, it is not good to marry a woman who is too strong (p. 272). However, the original hexagram is about proper order, not about women, any more than hexagram 64 above was actually about foxes.

Besides, although there was a gender hierarchy in ancient China, it was neither uniform nor universal; it coexisted with hierarchies of birth and status. As a result, some women had lots of power. Some were leaders alongside males; some women were independent queens; as such, many women would have themselves consulted the *I Ching* (Pearson, 2011, p. 32). The inclusion of references to very patriarchal situations was a kind of shorthand description, the way someone today might refer to Nazis or the Holocaust in order to describe a genocidal situation. Everyone knows what it means, yet nobody confuses the reference for a statement of how things should be.

In sum, a desire for social orderliness that was the complete opposite of Taoism and incompatible with the Doctrine of Change crept into the philosophy, and took the form of ascribing a female gender to the yin polarity and a male gender to the yang. This was a later addition, incompatible with the basic tenants of both Taoism and the Doctrine of Change. Assigning the genders of female to the receptive and male to the creative is completely contradictory to an accurate grasp of yin and yang.

Recognizing that yin and yang are constantly changing into each other, and are inseparable because they contain each other's root, is not at all the same as lumping everything together and stirring it up into undifferentiated sameness. Some feminists in the later 20th century focused on trying to erase the differences between women and men, but thank goodness feminism has since abandoned that impossible task. The challenge for the Western mind is how to acknowledge that differences exist, without pigeonholing people into those differences.

The Western love of stasis is at fault. We love to pin things down, the nature of the genders being one of them, so it is no surprise that we took to an explanation of men as yang and women as yin. And we like things to be definable, not to be constantly morphing into their opposites. Unfortunately, Taoism rejects the simplistic separation of yang and yin, and instead tells us, in verse 39, to realize that both operate perpetually together:

> Heaven realized primal unity
> and so came to clarity.
> Earth realized primal unity
> and so came to tranquility.
> Gods realized primal unity
> and so came to spirit.
> Valleys realized primal unity
> and so came to fullness.
> The ten thousand things realized primal unity
> and so came to life. (Hinton, 2015, p. 76)

This may initially seem like not much of an answer to people looking for lasting answers, but it is actually useful. Taoism tells us that by asking questions like, "what are men?" and "what are women?" and expecting answers that don't change, we are barking up the wrong tree. In creating new gender roles, we should be asking questions more accurate to the nature of the universe—questions like, "who are you and I right now?"

REFERENCES

Bejan, A., & Zane, J. P. (2012). *Design in nature: How the constructal law governs evolution in biology, physics, technology, and social organization.* New York, NY: Anchor Books.

Cleary, T. (2003). *I Ching: The book of change.* Boston, MA: Shambala.

Hinton, D. (2015). *Tao Te Ching: A new translation.* Berkeley, CA: Counterpoint.

Laughlin, K., & Wong, E. (1999). Feminism and/in Taoism. In A. Sharma & K. Young (Eds.), *Feminism and world religions.* Albany, NY: State University of New York Press.

Pearson, M. J. (2011). *The original I Ching: An authentic translation of the Book of Changes.* North Clarendon, VT: Tuttle.

Smith, R. J. (2015). *The I Ching: A biography.* Princeton, NJ: Princeton University Press.

Sung, Z. D. (1969). *The text of Yi King (and its appendixes): Chinese original with English translation.* New York, NY: Paragon Book Reprint Corp.

Wilson, W. S. (2010). *Tao Te Ching: An all-new translation.* Boston, MA: Shambala.

Chapter 22

American Muslim Women and Faith-Inspired Activism

Asma Uddin and Firdaus Arastu

The population of Muslims in the United States is a mosaic, with diverse ethnicities, national origin, and sects. African Americans make up thirty-five percent of American Muslims, while White, Asian, and other ethnicities make up twenty-eight and eighteen percent respectively (Gallup, 2009). A majority of Muslims in America are Sunni, but there are also minorities of Shiite and Sufi Muslims (McCloud, 2003). In addition, the American Muslim community is among the most affluent in America, and Muslim women are the second most highly educated female religious group in the United States (Gallup, 2009).

The American Muslim community enjoys constitutional protection for the free exercise of religion. Since the terrorist attacks of 9/11, however, the Muslim community has faced an onslaught of social hostility, much of it based on stereotypes of women's rights in Islam. Many texts published during the post-9/11 climate claim that Muslim women endure violence at the hands of Muslim men (Razack, 2008). This claim is used as an overarching statement about Muslim women around the globe, rather than about some women in some communities. Muslim women are often portrayed as oppressed by Islam. A cartoon by the *Philadelphia Inquirer* editorial cartoonist Tony Auth represents the common stereotype. The cartoon portrays Muslim women clad head to toe in a Pashtun-style *burqa*, subservient to and oppressed by Muslim men.

Like most political cartoons and broad comedy, though, this cartoon uses stereotypes to quickly make a political or social point, without regard to the intricacies or diversity of the issue it is commenting on (TeachMideast, n.d.). Not all Muslim women wear burqas or headscarves, many do not even consider it religiously obligatory, and contrary to common misrepresentation, they actively participate in their families and societies. The difficulties some Muslim women face in their lives "are not connected specifically to religion and are problems that are shared with other women worldwide," such as poverty, lack of education, cultural restriction, war, or domestic or social problems (Mahmoud, n.d.). Muslim women, in fact, do participate in discussions of politics, education, and social issues, though the "degree of their political participation varies from country to country. In some, like Saudi Arabia, women's participation is largely informal; in others, like Turkey, Bangladesh, Indonesia, and Pakistan, Muslim women have been elected as the country's leader" (Mahmoud, n.d.).

Muslim women in America have worked for the government and nonprofit sectors to advocate for civil and constitutional rights. Women like Dalia Mogahed and Farah Pandith have led faith-based initiatives at the White House and State Department, respectively; there are Muslim women and civil rights leaders like Zahra Billoo, Linda Sarsour, and Remziya Suleyman, and heads of Muslim organizations, like Maha Elgenaidi and Ingrid Mattson. American Muslim women are also published authors, influential academics at various universities, and top-performing athletes. These examples directly counter the common portrayal of Muslim women as oppressed and submissive (Islamic Networks Group, n.d.).

These stories of accomplishments are increasingly coming to the fore because Muslim women are speaking up. They are actively sharing their personal experiences and opinions on various issues in books and online web magazines. Fawzia Afzal Khan's book, *Shattering the Stereotypes: Muslim Women Speak Out* (2004), provides a comprehensive collection of "academic and non-academic pieces written by Muslim women in the United States and addresses the most controversial questions surrounding Muslim women" during the post-9/11 era (Ghavamshahidi, 2006). Using an anthology of personal narratives, Khan shows how Muslim women respond to wars, social injustice, terrorism, and the misrepresentation of Islam. One section of her book explains how Muslim women are encouraging journalists to educate people about Islam and promote relationships between Muslims and non-Muslims. Saleemah Abdul Ghafur's book, *Living Islam Out Loud: American Muslim Women Speak Out* (2005), follows a similar approach, narrating the diverse experiences and perspectives of several first-generation American Muslim women, and the way they have negotiated their strong faith with their lived realities. Maria Ebrahimji, a former CNN producer, and Zahra Suratwala co-edited a series of books of first-person essays titled *I Speak for Myself*. The first volume in the series, *American Women on Being Muslim* (2011), was composed of short essays by forty American Muslim women. In these essays, the authors reflect on some of their deepest spiritual struggles and discuss their ambitions, family expectations, and cultural traditions.

Online web magazines provide a platform for American Muslim women to voice their opinions on their role in society, their identity, their patriotism, and their womanhood. The co-author of this chapter, Asma Uddin, founded altMuslimah.com in March 2009 to foster intra- and intercommunity dialogue on a wide range of gender-related issues. The pieces published at altMuslimah cover both analysis and personal stories (altMuslimah, n.d.). Whereas altMuslimah's readership largely consists of 25–35-year-old American Muslim women, a separate initiative, MuslimGirl.net, founded by Amani Al-Khatahtbeh, helps empower voices and cultivate leadership among a younger generation of Muslim girls (MuslimGirl.net, n.d.).

WOMEN'S VOICES ONLINE

altMuslimah.com

Founder and editor-in-chief (and co-author of this chapter) Asma Uddin created altMuslimah ("altM") over six years ago in response to the need for innovation in the media portrayal of gender in Islam. The magazine was the first of its kind to focus wholly on the issue of gender; it has given Muslim women a space to *speak for themselves* on a wide range of gender issues rather than permitting mainstream media to speak for them. Growing up in America and inquisitive about her faith, Uddin realized that, often, discussions of Islam and Muslims in the media come to rest on issues of gender, and Western media in particular focuses on stories of Muslim women as oppressed. Media accounts typically depict Islam as a backward religion on gender inequality, and an overly simplistic discourse has developed which entirely fails to capture the diversity, vibrancy, and beauty of the lived Muslim experience. Islam is seen as outside modern feminism, its values fundamentally contrary to modern societies. altM seeks to change that perception, and has made major strides toward that goal.

Uddin launched altM to showcase how Islam guides, informs, and empowers women to be drivers of a free and virtuous society. She envisioned a platform that would do this, and in doing so rebut the negative mainstream depiction of Islam and gender issues and redefine modern feminism to include the experiences and views of Muslim women (Hodgetts, 2011).

The overarching goal of the online magazine is twofold. First, it hopes to engender greater gender equality in the Muslim community. Secondly, with respect to the relationship between Muslims and non-Muslims, altM aims to "affect the conversation on gender-in-Islam so that it is more nuanced, thoughtful, and attuned to the realities on the ground" (Hodgetts, 2011). Contrary to the frequently biased and one-sided narrative presented by the media, altM moves beyond identity politics to create real change; its discussions surrounding Islam and Muslims reflect the subtle yet complex and diverse perspectives of Muslims themselves. Submissions made to altM have consistently and accurately identified crucial issues within Muslim communities ahead of other publications while being inclusive of perspectives that are relevant to both women and men (Hodgetts, 2011).

altM also invites Islamic scholars to contribute feature pieces for the magazine and is currently working on a partnership with Imams Online (altMuslimah, 2015). The magazine's impact in academic circles and on public discourse has not gone unnoticed. altM receives numerous invitations from prestigious universities (for example, it has co-organized several conferences at Princeton University), think tanks (among them, The Brookings Institution and The Council on Foreign Relations), the mainstream media (*The Washington Post*, *The New York Times*, *The Huffington Post*) and international partners (U.S. Embassy in Bosnia, U.S. Department of State, etc.) to speak at various forums and partner on gender-related programming (altMuslimah, 2014; Uddin & Tarin, 2013; altMuslimah, 2013).

The magazine's effort to successfully initiate and facilitate discussion has also been recognized by several leading American media professionals. With several million views a month from across the globe, altM has had a tangible social impact. Paul Brandeis Raushenbush (a former dean at Princeton University and now religion editor at *The Huffington Post*), Sally Quinn (*The Washington Post*'s On Faith editor), and Georgetown University's renowned Islamic Studies scholar, Dr. John Esposito, have praised altM as a much-needed resource on gender-in-Islam (altMuslimah, n.d.). The global popularity is in part due to altM's history of covering topics that are usually not discussed in Muslim communities. The ongoing discussions on widely held and taboo topics have created an online culture of openness and mutual respect.

altM has not only created a website to showcase its original content, it has also focused on training young people of faith, and particularly Muslim women, to engage in digital media. In doing so, altM has hosted conferences, symposia, and mentoring events; has been invited to lead media trainings in Bosnia-Herzegovina, Montenegro, and Kosovo; and has spoken to academic and civil rights organizations in Egypt, Jordan,

Morocco, and Indonesia (altMuslimah, 2013). altM wants to train a new generation of Muslims to write, speak, and engage with mainstream media.

altM has also been a leader in creating interfaith dialogues around gender. Ms. Uddin and the altM team decided to replicate the success of altMuslimah across different faith communities. Soon after launching altM, Ms. Uddin created a non-profit organization called altVentures Media, Inc. Under the banner of altVentures, Ms. Uddin partnered with Catholic women interested in exploring gender and faith-related issues and launched altCatholicah in 2010. In 2014, altV launched the multi-faith site, *altFem Magazine*. altFem's launch event was widely attended by leaders in the media, faith, and academic communities interested in these issues, and the event was covered in depth by *The Washington Post* (Uddin & Tarin, 2013).

In all these efforts, altM has placed Muslim women at the forefront of leading media platforms on faith and gender.

MuslimGirl.net

Amani Al-Khatahtbeh is founder and editor-in-chief of MuslimGirl.net. She began the website as a blog when she was a teenager and frustrated by "all the negative and flagrant misconceptions" she consistently heard about Islam on the news, on television programs, and from her own peers (Haute Hijab, 2013). She initially started blogging as an afterschool hobby to provide a more accurate portrayal of how Islam interacts with and responds to current lifestyles. Her blog posts sought to rebut the often misunderstood and incorrect depiction of Islam as obsolete and irrelevant to modern times. Since its inception, MuslimGirl.net has grown to include a team of passionate bloggers from around the world, each of whom share Amani's vision in developing a space for young Muslim women to be able to talk about real issues they face on a daily basis. This space for conversations and commentary is continuing to "aid women from varying religious and backgrounds to connect, learn more about each other, and eliminate stereotypes" (Haute Hijab, 2013).

The blog is aimed at "eliminating stereotypes surrounding Islam and promoting the place of Muslim women in Western societies" (Al-Khatahtbeh, n.d.). Amani's "ambition for building bridges across different religious and cultural communities has been recognized in a New Jersey state resolution honoring the top community service pioneers in the state" (Al-Khatahtbeh, n.d.). Following the success of the blog, the first collegiate chapter of MuslimGirl was founded at Rutgers University in 2011. The chapter creates a space for Muslim women on campus by hosting events to raise awareness about issues impacting Muslims. The Rutgers chapter is now one of many that have been formed all over the state, with the "mission of promoting interfaith dialogues through the spirit of sisterhood" (Haute Hijab, 2013). Together with the online publication, these student-led chapters train minority students to communicate their opinions on the nation's politics and policies (Al-Khatahtbeh, 2014).

MuslimGirl.net also offers students internships with the magazine to further its mission of empowering women, facilitating interfaith relationship building, and eradicating stereotypes surrounding Muslims and Islam. These internships are designed to develop leadership skills and give students the "experience of developing an online publication aimed at social change" (MuslimGirl.net, n.d.). To further promote this effort, MuslimGirl.net has launched a program called Clique. Clique is an international society of members seeking to revolutionize the way Islam is portrayed to the world. Clique members are innovators and entrepreneurs who find new ways to exemplify the "ideals and principles of being a modern Muslim woman" (MuslimGirl.net, n.d.). The women in Clique are fighting stereotypes and changing the way Muslims have previously been perceived. MuslimGirl.net, its chapters, and Clique are wielding the mic and taking back the narrative. They are speaking up for themselves, and standing up against long-held stereotypes (MuslimGirl.net, n.d.).

INTERSECTIONALITY AND CIVIL RIGHTS ACTIVISM

The current generation of American Muslim civil rights activists are advocating for a range of civil rights and human rights issues impacting communities within the United States and abroad. They utilize an array of tactics, drawing on new forms, such as social media, while continuing to engage in traditional forms of protest, including demonstrations, direct action, grassroots community building, and boycott/divestment, among others. While activists Ramah Kudaimi and Margari Aziza Hill focus on particular issues, they also emphasize the need to advocate for overlapping causes and for collaboration across communities and issues to fight for the shared goal of liberation.

Ramah Kudaimi

For Ramah Kudaimi, her work as an activist is rooted in her identity as an Arab American and informed by values of justice and equality in Islam. Kudaimi's work focuses on United States government policies targeting Muslims domestically and internationally. She organizes around foreign policy advocacy in Palestine and Syria. As an Arab American, Kudaimi has family ties to the Middle East, so the turmoil in the region connected to American foreign policy decisions strikes close to home. In the aftermath of September 11th, a number of American Muslim organizations and institutions allowed themselves to be co-opted to support the War on

Terror. Kudaimi is interested in how the American Muslim community is organizing and pushing back against these policies.

Kudaimi draws on her background in journalism and conflict resolution for her work as a national organizer for the U.S. Campaign to End Israeli Occupation, a national coalition formed in 2011 of more than 400 groups working to change U.S. policy toward Palestine and Israel to support human rights, international law, and equality. Her work is guided by the importance of working in solidarity with Palestinian activists, working locally to affect global change, and using a rights-based approach to call for justice, equality, and an end to the occupation. Kudaimi coordinates and supports campaigns in the Boycott, Divestment, and Sanctions (BDS) movement, which has become mainstream and successfully increased pressure on Israel by targeting the actors who exploit and profit from the occupation (Palestine Center, 2014). Before joining the U.S. Campaign, Kudaimi worked as a grassroots organizer for CODEPINK, a women-led anti-war and social justice organization working to end U.S. militarism. She often provides commentary and analysis on independent news and media outlets about Palestine and Syria.

Kudaimi was a prominent figure in organizing the boycott against the annual White House *iftar* (evening meal the last night of Ramadan) in 2014, which illustrates the issues around which she passionately advocates and organizes. While boycotts have occurred in previous years, the 2014 boycott focused on U.S. policies which infringed on the human and civil rights of Muslims in the United States and abroad, particularly the NSA spying on American Muslim leaders and the United States's endorsement of Israeli airstrikes on the Gaza strip that began in early July (Greenwald & Hussain, 2014). The boycott also included other policies by the Obama administration affecting Muslims, such as the administration's drone policy, the failure to close Guantanamo Bay, and the disproportionate surveillance of Muslims (Siddiqui, 2014; OnIslam.net, 2014).

Kudaimi draws inspiration from the people who are impacted by and mounting resistance against systems of oppression. These forms of resistance are sometimes through simply existing and refusing to submit. She finds strength from Palestinians who are steadfast against Israel's constant efforts to displace them from their land and from the families of people struggling to free their relatives from prison who are persecuted by the U.S. government for their activism. In 2009, Kudaimi spent a year working at the Arab American Action Network in Chicago, an experience that solidified her desire to spend her life "making the world a better place" (Kudaimi, 2015). The associate director of the Arab American Action Network, Rasmea Odeh, a 67-year-old Palestinian American activist and torture survivor, became a role model and inspiration for Kudaimi. Odeh was a beloved and highly respected leader who championed the idea of empowering one's local community and equipping them with "the tools to transform their lives" (Kudaimi, 2015). Odeh was convicted of immigration fraud in November 2014 for not disclosing she had been unjustly imprisoned in 1969 by an Israeli military court (Murphy, 2015). Along with other supporters around the country, Kudaimi mobilized support for Odeh by raising money for her legal defense.

Kudaimi's work to combat oppression is grounded in her faith in Islam and a strong belief in justice, which is a necessary prerequisite for peace. She references the Islamic duty to enjoin what is good and forbid what is evil: "Muslims are taught that God put us on the Earth to do good, that when we see injustice we should speak out against it even if it [is] being committed by our own brother" (personal communication with R. Kudaimi, August 1, 2015). Kudaimi also believes strongly in connecting the local to the global and building alliances across different communities to establish justice and achieve peace. Soon after the bombing of Gaza, which began in July 2014, the community of Ferguson was rocked by the shooting of Michael Brown. From the use of tear gas and militaristic presence to the issues of racism and settler-colonialism, the parallels between the situations in the United States (as highlighted by Ferguson) and in Palestine were clear for Kudaimi and other activists (Reinl, 2015; Marcelin, 2014; Palestine Center, 2014). Kudaimi expressed her solidarity with the Black Lives Matter movement and organized a "Palestine to Ferguson" group to attend the demonstrations in Ferguson. As she explained, promoting Palestinian liberation is "part of a greater movement to liberate all oppressed people" and it is necessary to build coalitions with other communities in systems of oppression to accomplish this shared goal of liberation (Palestine Center, 2014).

Margari Hill

Margari Aziza Hill is the co-founder and programming director of Muslim Anti-Racism Collaborative (MuslimARC). Hill converted to Islam at the age of eighteen and her activism and research are born out of her experiences as a Black American Muslim woman (Khan-Ibarra, 2014). She writes regularly on the intersectionality of religion, race, and gender on her blog. MuslimARC addresses and challenges racism in American Muslim communities by drawing on a range of influences, including the Islamic sciences, grassroots activism, and human rights law (MuslimARC, n.d.). MuslimARC has organized online panels and viral Twitter campaigns and conversations to discuss racial identity and anti-Blackness in the Muslim community. Its first hashtag conversation, #BeingBlackandBeingMuslim, saw more than 7,000 tweets posted within 24 hours (Adil & Palmer, 2014). Hill believes that "by amplifying voices, building bridges, and challenging racism . . . we can build a stronger community that is more true to the egalitarian ideals we are taught in Islam" (Khan-Ibarra, 2014).

For Hill, conducting anti-racism work is deeply connected to her faith. She draws on Prophetic tradition, Quranic verses, and Islamic principles to form the foundation of her anti-racism work. She specifically cites Quranic verses 9:71 and 49:13 affirming the equality of humanity and Muslims as a basis for her conviction, yet cautions that racism cannot be solved just by referencing the Quran. Fighting racism "is a lifelong process and commitment to transformative practices that uproot racism from within ourselves and addressing racism in our society"; it is not just "something that is read in a book," but grappled with and confronted whenever it appears (Hill, 2015). Hill argues that confronting racism requires "soul work," a term borrowed from the Unitarian community, who define anti-racism as a "theological and spiritual issue" (Hill, 2015).

Hill was motivated to become an activist out of frustration with the reality of racism in Muslim communities and to create a better world for her daughter (Caplowe, 2015; Khan-Ibarra, 2014). She calls out Muslims who pay lip service to the idea of the equality of all Muslims regardless of race and depict our community as multicultural and diverse, yet remain prejudiced and racist in their interactions (Hill, 2015).

Like Kudaimi, Hill stresses the importance of collaboration in social justice activism. American Muslims' ability to address Islamophobia is undermined by the divisions in our community and particularly by the marginalization of Black Muslims. Hill reframes what it means to be an ally with the Islamic concept of *wali*, which "comes from the word *al-Wilayah*, meaning the willingness to take responsibility, manage, to be the authority, or administer something" (Hill, 2014). This confers a greater responsibility, sincerity, and spirituality to the role (Hill, 2014).

WOMEN AND THE MOSQUE

Mosques are an integral part of any Muslim community. Throughout Islamic history, mosques have been the center of the Muslim community as "a place of prayer, meditation, religious instruction, political discussion and a school" (Waardenburg, 1965). Since mosques serve a multifaceted role in the Muslim community, it is essential that Muslim women feel as welcomed in mosques as men do. However, this is not the case in many mosques. Mosques in most Western Muslim communities have inadequate spaces for women, and those that do, often keep these spaces locked or reserved for men who may come late for congregational prayers (Makki, 2012).

In recent years, American Muslim women have developed initiatives to encourage Muslim women to take leadership roles in mosques. They are promoting much-needed change in the American Muslim community, specifically with respect to how women are treated in mosques. In an effort to create awareness about unsatisfactory mosque experiences, activist

Hind Makki started a Tumblr blog called *Side Entrance* to share pictures of women's prayer areas (Makki, 2012). M. Hasna Manavi and Sana Muttalib founded a complementary space of worship exclusively for women in January 2015 (Audi, 2015). American Muslims, like Maryam Eskandari, have also begun revolutionizing the conventional design of mosques. Eskandari's goal is to build mosques with environmentally sustainable materials and with new designs to better facilitate the needs of the American Muslim community. Her designs are focused on facilitating interfaith activities and providing equal spaces of worship for men and women (Rydhan, 2011).

Hind Makki

The Side Entrance project began in 2012 to showcase pictures of mosques from all over the world (Rydhan, 2011). Makki intended to juxtapose worship spaces available to men and women (Makki, n.d.). She acknowledges that while there are several mosques that boast "incredible space for female congregants . . . there are many more with inadequate or bad space for women" (Makki, n.d.). Muslim women often find that they are either barred from entering or that the spaces provided to them are insufficient (Makki, n.d.).

Makki believes that the frustration and inconveniences women experience are not due to financial restriction, but due to "lack of awareness on the part of male decision makers about the experiences of women in mosques" (Makki, 2012). Prominent organizational and religious leaders are just now beginning to address this widespread problem. A report published by the Islamic Society of North America (ISNA) and the Hartford Institute for Religion Research identifies problems women face in North American mosques and provides pragmatic solutions to the American Muslim community. According to the report, women make up a mere eighteen percent, on average, of the congregation during Friday prayers. Only fourteen percent of mosques score the highest mark, "excellent," for women-friendliness. Mosques that allow a more flexible interpretation of Quran and Sunnah, in addition to those that actively participate in interfaith and community service activities, tend to be friendlier (Sayeed, Al-Adawiya, & Bagby, 2013).

Makki helps educate others about the inequality in worship spaces available to women. She also provides practical steps mosques can adopt to make women feel more welcome and comfortable. For example, Makki featured Dudu Kücükgöl's essay, which noted the following: women and men should each have their own main entrances, with equal sized, separate, and sufficient spaces. The goal overall: mosques should be physically and socially reconceptualized so that women feel not just that they can come to the mosque, but also that they are a vital part of it (Kücükgöl,

2015). Although women could simply create a mosque for themselves in response to the problems they face at mosques, Makki insists that working with the male community leaders is the better way to ensure that mosques remain equally welcoming to men, women, and children. That requires that women's spaces be designed with "the same care and attention to comfort and beauty as men's spaces" (Makki, 2012).

M. Hasna Maznavi and Sana Muttalib

Taking a different approach than Makki, M. Hasna Maznavi and Sana Muttalib started the Women's Mosque of America. Women's mosques are not unprecedented in Islamic history. In fact, women's mosques currently exist in China, Syria, India, Egypt, Palestine, and even in ultraconservative societies like Sudan (Maznavi, 2015). Maznavi and Muttalib inaugurated America's very own all-female mosque in January 2015, in Los Angeles, California (Street, 2015). They contend that, although women are increasingly serving as board members for their local mosques, and mosques are becoming friendlier toward women, there is persistent "relegation of Muslim women to basements, balconies, and other less desirable spaces" and this inspired the founding of the Women's Mosque of America (Sayeed, Al-Adawiya, & Bagby, 2013; Street, 2015).

Maznavi explains that it had been her childhood dream to build an all-female mosque. The Women's Mosque of America began as a team effort by Muslim women and men. The founders intend for the mosque to "celebrate and respect" the diversity of opinion within the Muslim community by being inclusive of all Muslims, regardless of "sect, cultural background, school of thought, or level of practice" (Street, 2015). Both Maznavi and Muttalib feel that the Women's Mosque can play a pivotal role in strengthening the Muslim community by allowing Muslim women greater access to Islamic knowledge, encouraging female participation in existing mosques, and fostering leadership and scholarship within and without the Muslim community. This will be made possible by the mosque's comfortable learning environment for women, which will enable them to explore active leadership roles (Blumberg, 2015). The mosque does not intend to alienate Muslim women from the community at large (Street, 2015). Moreover, certain events and classes that the Women's Mosque plans to hold will be open to men and women of all faiths (Tan, 2015).

Maryam Eskandari

While Makki, Maznavi, and Muttalib have been informing and changing the experience American Muslim women encounter upon entering mosques, Maryam Eskandari, on the other hand, is challenging the mosque's very physical structure. According to Eskandari, mosques all across the United States have imported not only culture, but also architecture. She believes that the architecture of the mosque impacts the functionality of the mosque and the facilities it can provide. Architecture needs to reflect the cultural needs of people, especially when it regards mosques. She advocates that American Muslims need to develop a deeper interest in art and architecture of mosques as apolitical forms of expression. As American Muslims strive to create their own unique cultural identity, spaces of worship should reflect elements of that identity (Rydhan, 2011).

Mosques in the United States can also be redesigned so that they more accurately represent and emphasize Islamic values. For example, mosques can be built with sustainable materials and can be streamlined to remove the cost-ineffective domes and minarets. Since American Muslim mosques are increasingly participating in community services and interfaith activities, much of the mosques' interior design needs to be specialized, so that internal spaces can be easily used for interfaith programs and service projects, such as soup kitchens (Rydhan, 2011).

Eskandari also emphasizes designs that reflect gender equality. She looks to the design of the Holy Mosque in Mecca as a model of gender inclusivity. "The Ka'ba and the surrounding mosque are the sites of revelation, a powerful symbol of parity of race, gender, and ethnicity, and express equality between women and men gathered together for prayer in a shared space" (MIIM Designs, n.d.). Eskandari has had two exhibitions in efforts to research and explore gender issues in architecture: Sacred Spaces and Women's Spaces in American Mosques (MIIM Designs, n.d.). She founded MIIM Designs to provide inspiring designs for American mosques and help people create a place of worship while fulfilling the contemporary needs of the American Muslim community.

DOMESTIC AND SEXUAL VIOLENCE

Domestic and sexual violence among American Muslims is an issue that is just beginning to be recognized and addressed publicly. For comparison, the broader American community only recognized it as a serious issue about 50 years ago. Until recently, discussing domestic violence was taboo in many Muslim communities. Many Muslims perceive the term itself as foreign, since it is not used in Islamic literature and they associate it with Western feminism. As such, they believe it to be irrelevant or inapplicable to Muslims. "In many Muslim communities, responses to addressing domestic violence include denial that it actually occurs in Muslim homes and an unwillingness to 'air dirty laundry' in an international climate that already stereotypes and discriminates against Muslims" (Alkhateeb & Abugideiri, 2007).

Darakshan Raja

Darakshan Raja is a Pakistani-American community organizer and researcher. She received her master's degree in forensic psychology with a concentration in victimology from John Jay College of Criminal Justice. Raja is a passionate and knowledgeable activist "hop[ing] to bridge the gap between grassroots advocacy and policy organizations in order to strengthen the social justice movement," and build a world rooted in justice and equity (Washington Peace Center, n.d.).

Her activism sits at the intersection of state and gender-based violence, where she leads efforts to reform the criminal justice system and strengthen institutional responses to survivors of sexual assault and domestic violence. Raja has experience as a Sexual Assault Response Team advocate in the Bronx and was a Vera Institute of Justice Fellow, where she examined gaps in service provision for survivors who had cases within the Integrated Domestic Violence courts in New York City. Raja worked as a research associate in the Justice Policy Center at the Urban Institute conducting a range of criminal justice evaluations for federal and state government agencies, including a national evaluation on the reauthorization of the Violence Against Women Act (VAWA) and an evaluation of the effectiveness of an intervention by the Texas Juvenile Justice Department against sexual violence in state juvenile detention facilities. Raja is an advisor for a study funded by the Department of Justice which will examine the intersection of forced marriage and domestic and sexual violence within South Asian communities (Falling Walls Initiative, n.d.). She co-authored "Voices from the Frontline: Addressing Forced Marriage in the United States," documenting responses to survivors of forced marriage, and "Breaking the Silence," a report for Safe Nation Collaborative on the barriers victims of crime in the Muslim community face in reporting crimes and seeking services (Sri & Raja, 2013; Safe Nation Collaborative, 2013).

While she continues her activism on domestic violence, she has expanded her work on state violence as a program manager and Hella Hergz Organizing Fellow at the Washington Peace Center. There, she supports local grassroots movements in Washington, D.C., providing resources, support, and training to organizers. She has been conducting solidarity organizing with the Black Lives Matter movement and organizing events that unpack anti-Black racism within White communities and South Asian, Arab, and non-Black Muslim communities in Washington. Her other projects have focused on gang violence prevention, human trafficking, and elder abuse. She also spent time organizing on ending the War on Terror.

The issues that Raja advocates for are deeply personal. They are connected to experiences she lived or witnessed growing up in Pakistan and in the Bronx. As a Pakistani Muslim immigrant woman in the United

States, she was impacted and oppressed by such systems of violence. Raja shares that becoming an activist was the only way for her to survive, reclaim power, and attain justice in a world structured to prevent her from succeeding (personal communication with D. Raja, September 1, 2015).

A key component of Raja's faith and identity as a Muslim is standing against injustice and working toward building a more equitable world. She views her work fighting injustice and serving her community as a form of practicing Islam. This involves "being active in one's community, engaged in social justice issues, and speaking truth to power" (personal communication with D. Raja, September 1, 2015). Even embracing and being open about one's Muslim identity is a powerful form of resistance and liberation. Raja draws inspiration from other Muslim women who have worked tirelessly to advance Muslim women's liberation. Her mother, in particular, exemplified to her what it meant to be a revolutionary and enabled her to be the activist she is (personal communication with D. Raja, September 1, 2015).

To counter the marginalization and violence she witnessed being committed against Muslim women, Raja founded the Muslim American Women's Policy Forum, an organizing space that prioritizes investment in the leadership of Muslim women. Its goal is to dismantle systems of state violence and gender-based violence through political education and empowerment of local communities (Muslim American Women's Policy Forum, n.d.).

Asma Hanif

Raja's work dismantling state-supported policies that perpetuate gender-based violence complements the grassroots work conducted by Asma Hanif, who tackles domestic violence one person at a time. Hanif's work sits at the intersection of community and gender-based violence, with a focus on rehabilitating and strengthening the capacity of survivors. Hanif founded and runs Muslimat Al-Nisaa, a shelter for Muslim women, including those who are survivors of domestic violence, which provides holistic assistance that is religiously tolerant and culturally sensitive. Hanif trained as a nurse and has spent most of her life serving those who are marginalized and most in need. When her brother contracted HIV and was ostracized by the rest of the family, she took him in and cared for him until he died in the early 1990s (Samuels, 2013).

Muslimat Al-Nisaa began as a non-profit organization in 1987 to provide social services to American Muslim women and their children. The organization is now composed of the shelter and a free clinic, Al-Nissa Holistic Health Center, which provides services to women who are homeless, uninsured, and/or survivors of domestic violence. The shelter was established in 2005 when Hanif converted a house in Baltimore. For the last ten years, she has provided a physical, emotional, and spiritual safe haven to Muslim women for Muslim women, many of them immigrants.

The shelter provides housing, occupational, medical, and educational (HOME) services to help the women become self-sufficient (Ruiz, 2013).

Muslim women who become homeless, particularly immigrants and/or those who are survivors of domestic violence, are especially vulnerable as they often have nowhere to go; their families refuse to help and there are few community resources (Tarabay, 2010). Those who are sent to shelters serving the general population face challenges to their faith and are thrust into an environment that clashes with their practice of Islam (Spinner, 2007). Shelters run by people of other faiths often try to convert Muslim women out of Islam and blame the domestic violence on Islam. Hanif points out this problem: "My biggest problem was that if you send a Muslim woman to be counseled in a shelter that's run by Christians, then what the people say is the reason why you're being beat is because of that religion. We do not want Islam to be the focal point of domestic violence" (Tarabay, 2010).

The Muslimat Al-Nisaa shelter, separate from the clinic, is exclusively for Muslim women. Hanif lives at the shelter so that she is better able to support the women, and maintains an environment that is healthy, supportive, and in accordance with Islam: "When a person is a victim of domestic violence, sometimes the only thing that they have to hold onto is their belief in God. And so we try to make sure that they have that, and that they're with other individuals that are feeling the same thing" (Ruiz, 2013). The women there are able to live and practice what they believe "without judgment, criticism, or fear of retaliation" (Ibrahim, 2012).

Hanif was first inspired to become an advance practice nurse by her grandmother, who worked tirelessly as a "maid slave" for a physician in the South and died from stomach cancer (The Melissa Harris-Perry Show, 2013). Her mother encouraged her to pursue nursing, a profession in which she felt race would not be an issue that would prevent her daughter from succeeding (Samuels, 2013). Hanif converted to Islam during her college years at Howard University and witnessed the discrimination that many Muslim women patients experience while she completed her hospital training. Since one does not "know who it is that God has sent on your path to help," Hanif is motivated to help whomever she can, following the legacy of her grandmother (Ruiz, 2013). For Hanif, her work at the shelter is a calling and she is compelled by her accountability to God. She says she would not be able to answer God on the Day of Judgment if she denied help to someone who was in need: "I'm afraid that on the Day of Judgment, God will say to me, 'One of my servants came to you and you turned them away'" (Ruiz, 2013).

ART AS PROTEST

Artist activists combine their creativity with their spirituality to draw attention to social issues. Zareena Grewal and Alia Sharrief use storytelling forms that elevate the voices and struggles of the people to address issues impacting the American Muslim community. Grewal relies on ethnography and film, while Alia Sharrief uses hip-hop. Both forms allow people to speak for themselves. Hip-hop in particular is an art form for "victims of an oppressed system"; it "began as the voice of the underdog, the voice of the ones whose story is never told, of those who are spoken about but not spoken to" (Blumberg, 2015).

Zareena Grewal

Zareena Grewal is a historical anthropologist and documentary filmmaker who uses her ethnographic research to deeply examine what it means to be an American Muslim and the ways in which American Muslims are often treated as an Other in the United States. She is an Assistant Professor of American Studies and Religious Studies at Yale University. Her research is intersectional, focusing on "race, gender, religion, nationalism, and transnationalism across a wide spectrum of American Muslim communities" (Yale University Department of American Studies, n.d.). Grewal is the author of the ethnography, *Islam Is a Foreign Country: American Muslims and the Global Crisis of Authority* (2013). In it, Grewal "follows the journeys of American Muslim youth who travel in global, underground Islamic networks . . . in search of a home for themselves and their tradition." The book is the product of ten years of research and emerged from her experiences growing up in a diverse Muslim community in Detroit, Michigan (Khan, 2014).

Grewal directed and produced *By the Dawn's Early Light: Chris Jackson's Journey to Islam* (2004), a film about the story of Mahmoud Abdul Rauf (formerly Chris Jackson) and the controversy that ensued when he refused to stand for the national anthem as a form of protest against oppression. The documentary explores a number of themes, including the nature of dissent in a democracy, racialization of Islam, and the scrutiny and discrimination American Muslims faced in the United States following September 11, 2001. Grewal was interested in Rauf's story as an example of the American Dream, which connected to her own parents' experience as Pakistani immigrants to the United States, and his moment of dissension that called into question his identity as an American (Grewal, 2013). Grewal uses this historic moment as a lens to examine identity politics and "representations of Islam and African American political consciousness" in the United States (Leeming, n.d.). The symbolic complexity of his stance reveals the intersectionality present in American Muslim communities; his views were "consistent with the political orientation of many African American Muslims, [but] perplexed many immigrants Muslims who know little of the long history of American dissent" (Leeming, n.d.).

The film acquired new meaning in the post-9/11 era, in which "the culture of patriotism" changed and dissent against the United States government, a right enshrined in our Constitution, came to be viewed as un-American and a "patriotic betrayal" (Grewal, 2013). Grewal's film challenges the notion that Islam is incompatible with democracy and the West, particularly since condemning internal dissent, a democratic value, blurs the line between the United States as a democracy and oppressive regimes in the Middle East (Grewal, 2013).

Alia Sharrief

Independent hip-hop artist Alia Sharrief is spreading a message of social consciousness and faith through her art. Sharrief has performed in California, New York City, and in Sri Lanka. Her unique style represents the confluence of her identities as a Black Muslim woman and, like Grewal's documentary, challenges the notion that being American and being Muslim are incompatible.

As an independent artist, Sharrief has greater control over her work and her brand. She writes her own lyrics and controls the production of her music videos. This control allows her to maintain her modesty, which is important to Sharrief, as she wears and performs in *hijab*. She finds inspiration in her faith and in the Prophetic tradition. Sharrief hopes to spread Islam through her art; she calls this "Hiphop Dawah" (Khan-Ibarra, 2014). Her lyrics explore "helping people, protesting, speaking up for humanity, having dignity, and self-respect" (Khan-Ibarra, 2014). She released her debut album, *Mental Cycles and Mood Swings*, in 2012 and is working on a new album, *Back On My Deen*, which she hopes will elevate "the listener's understanding of Hiphop and Islam to another level" (Khan-Ibarra, 2014). The album will address current issues affecting Black Americans (Sharrief, 2014).

Sharrief is the founder of The Hijabi Chronicles, a collective of female Muslim artists from spoken word and hip-hop. She founded the group to show that "Muslim women belong in hip-hop" (AJ+, 2015). Hip-hop has been a predominantly male space and it carries a stigma in Muslim communities, particularly for Muslim women to perform on stage wearing *hijab* (Erbentraut, 2015). She stakes a claim in the space for herself and other Muslim women, as they are talented and knowledgeable: "we have soul and we have something to say" (AJ+, 2015). The group is a supportive and empowering environment for Muslim female hip-hop artists to share their experiences and fight against the stereotypes of women in hip-hop as objectified and "submissive" (AJ+, 2015).

CONCLUSION

To understand the strength of their struggles, it is important to note the steep challenges and barriers Muslim women activists face in their work, from both Muslims and non-Muslims. These include Islamophobia, sexism, patriarchy, xenophobia, and racism—forces that have a compounded effect because of the intersectional identities of Muslim women. They also have to struggle against the White savior complex and the myth that Muslim women are oppressed by Islam and therefore must be saved. As these stories show, Islam is a source of guidance and strength for these Muslim women activists.

Muslim women from around the world have "a rich history of fighting for their rights, creating positive social change, and uplifting their communities through service and advocacy, education and media, health and social services, philanthropy and spiritual growth" (Women's Islamic Initiative in Spirituality and Equality, n.d.). American Muslim women in the United States are a part of this global community of activists who are creating real change in their society. The women featured in this chapter exemplify Islamic feminisms. They are empowered women who all draw inspiration and strength from their identity as Muslims and their faith in Islam, citing Islamic principles and Prophetic tradition among the values that guide their work. By virtue of their activism and their lived experiences, these Muslim women subvert the idea that Islam is incompatible with gender equality and social justice.

REFERENCES

Abdul-Ghafur, S. (Ed.). (2005). *Living Islam out loud: American Muslim women speak*. Boston: Beacon Press.

Adil, S., & Palmer, S. (2014, March 12). MuslimARC launches Twitter campaign against racism. *The Chicago Monitor*. http://chicagomonitor.com/2014/03/muslimarc-launches-twitter-campaigns-against-racism/

AJ+. (2015, May 18). Hip-Hop Hijabis: Spitting rhymes about being Muslim and female. https://www.youtube.com/watch?v=paw52O8IRJM

Al-Khatahtbeh, A. (2014, February 11). An inside look at the fight for freedom of speech in college newspapers. *The Huffington Post*. http://www.huffingtonpost.com/amani-alkhatahtbeh/the-fight-for-freedom-of-speech_b_4761906.html

Al-Khatahtbeh, A. (2015, April 29). How to draw Muhammad (a lesson plan for Pam Geller). *The Huffington Post*. http://www.huffingtonpost.com/amani-alkhatahtbeh/millennial-muslim-women-w_b_7160638.html

Al-Khatahtbeh, A. (n.d.). Amani Al-Khatahtbeh. http://www.huffingtonpost.com/amani-alkhatahtbeh/

Alkhateeb, M. B., & Abugideiri, S. E. (2007). Introduction. In M. B. Alkhateeb & S. E. Abugideiri (Eds.), *Change from within: Diverse perspectives on domestic violence in Muslim communities*. Great Falls, VA: Peaceful Families Project. http://www.peacefulfamilies.org/CFWIntro.pdf

altMuslimah. (2013, April 30). Asma Uddin to lead working group at U.S. Islamic World Forum in Doha, Qatar. http://www.altmuslimah.com/2013/04/asma_uddin_to_lead_working_group_at_u-s-_islamic_world_forum_in_doha_qatar/

altMuslimah. (2013, September 4). Asma Uddin to lead media training in Sarajevo, Bosnia. altMuslimah. http://www.altmuslimah.com/2013/09/asma_uddin_to_lead_media_training_in_sarajevo_bosnia/

altMuslimah. (2014, November 11). Asma Uddin speaks at University of Oklahoma. http://www.altmuslimah.com/2014/11/asma-uddin-to-speak-at-university-of-oklahoma/

altMuslimah. (2015, March 15) Princeton & altM's Panel on literary arts, spirituality, and representation. http://www.altmuslimah.com/2015/03/princeton-altms-panel-on-literary-arts-spirituality-and-representation/

altMuslimah. (n.d.). Mission. http://www.altmuslimah.com/about-us/mission/

altMuslimah. (n.d.). Testimonials. http://www.altmuslimah.com/about-us/testimonials/

Audi, T. (2015, January 30). Feeling unwelcome at mosques, 2 women start their own in L.A. *The Wall Street Journal*. http://www.wsj.com/articles/muslim-women-to-launch-their-own-mosque-1422639983

Blumberg, A. (2015, January 30). Women's mosque opens in L.A. with a vision for the future of Muslim-American leadership. *The Huffington Post*. http://www.huffingtonpost.com/2015/01/30/womens-mosque-los-angeles_n_6572388.html

Blumberg, A. (2015, March 19). Poetic Pilgrimage is the Muslim women's rap duo the world needs right now. *The Huffington Post*. http://www.huffingtonpost.com/2015/03/18/poetic-pilgrimage-rap_n_6877936.html

Caplowe, C. (Interviewer), Nemani, A., Huerta, E., Espinoza, R., Hill, M. A., & Keesey, B. (Interviewees). (2015, July 15). The GOOD dinnertime conversation: On the true meaning of failure. GOOD. http://magazine.good.is/features/issue-34-good-dinnertime-conversation-failure

Ebrahimji, M., & Suratwala, Z. (Eds.). (2011). *I speak for myself: American women on being Muslim*. Ashland, OR: White Cloud Press.

Erbentraut, J. (2015, May 19). Muslim women's hip-hop collective confronts stereotypes and breaks up the boys' club. *The Huffington Post*. http://www.huffingtonpost.com/2015/05/19/hijabi-chronicles-muslim-hip-hop_n_7317106.html

Falling Walls Initiative. (n.d.). Our Team. https://fallingwallsinitiative.wordpress.com/our-team/

Gallup. (2009). Muslim Americans: A national portrait. http://www.themosqueinmorgantown.com/pdfs/GallupAmericanMuslimReport.pdf

Ghavamshahidi, Z. (2006). Shattering the stereotypes: Muslim women speak out. *Journal of Middle East Women's Studies*, *2*(3), 112–113.

Greenwald, G., & Hussain, M. (2014, July 9). Meet the Muslim-American leaders the FBI and NSA have been spying on. *The Intercept*. https://theintercept.com/2014/07/09/under-surveillance/

Grewal, Z. (2013, October). ABC News In the Mix interview (2005) with filmmaker Zareena Grewal. https://www.youtube.com/watch?v=rdr4vKdXTHo

Grewal, Z. (2013). *Islam is a foreign country: American Muslims and the global crisis of authority*. New York: New York University Press.

Haute Hijab. (2013, May 19). Hijabi of the month May—Amani Al-Khatahtbeh. Haute Hijab blog. http://www.hautehijab.com/blogs/hijab-fashion/7910687-hijabi-of-the-month-may-amani-al-khatahtbeh

Hill, M. A. (2014, December 1). Being a good ally. Muslim Anti-Racism Collaborative. http://www.muslimarc.org/being-a-good-ally/

Hill, M. A. (2015, April 4). Anti-racism works: Rad talks. http://radtalks.com/antiracism/

Hodgetts, C. (2011, September 5). Interview with Asma Uddin, founder of AltMuslimah. Gender across borders. http://www.genderacrossborders.com/2011/09/05/interview-with-asma-uddin-founder-of-altmuslimah/

Ibrahim, A. (2012, September 7). Positively Muslim in the west: Sister Asma Hanif. MuslimMatters.org. http://muslimmatters.org/2012/09/07/positively-muslim-in-the-west-sister-asma-hanif/

Islamic Networks Group (ING). (n.d.). Muslim women beyond the stereotypes. https://www.ing.org/muslim-women-youth/#

Khan, F. (2014, May 10). Islam is a foreign country. Audio file of Zareena Grewal's lecture at Elmhurst College in April 2014. http://communitybuilderscouncil.com/?p=119%E2%80%8B

Khan, F. A. (2004). *Shattering the stereotypes: Muslim women speak out*. Olive Branch Press.

Khan-Ibarra, S. (2014, April 19). Margari Hill. Muslimah Montage. http://muslimahmontage.com/margari-hill/

Khan-Ibarra, S. (2014, August 17). Alia Sharrief—Youth Muslimah. Muslimah montage. http://muslimahmontage.com/alia-sharrief-youth-muslimah/

Kücükgöl, D. (2015, August 7). How a mosque can welcome women. Patheos. http://www.patheos.com/blogs/hindtrospectives/2015/08/how-a-mosque-can-welcome-women/

Kudaimi, R. (2015, March 11). Rasmea Odeh should be honored, not imprisoned. The Arab American news. http://www.arabamericannews.com/news/news/id_10173/Rasmea-Odeh-should-be-honored,-not-imprisoned.html

Leeming, M. (n.d.). Review of the film *By the dawn's early light: Chris Jackson's journey to Islam*. http://faculty.vassar.edu/maleeming/Files/204/Links/ChrisJackson.htm

Mahmoud, F. (n.d.). Hijab: Religious or cultural? Islamic Research Foundation International, Inc. http://www.irfi.org/articles/articles_951_1000/hijab_religious_or_cultural.htm

Makki, H. (2012, July 27). Where's my space to pray in this mosque? Patheos. http://www.patheos.com/blogs/altmuslim/2012/07/wheres-my-space-to-pray-in-this-mosque/

Makki, H. (n.d.). Project Origins. Side entrance. http://sideentrance.tumblr.com/about

Marcelin, M. F. (2014, August 18). Linking violence in solidarity: Ferguson, Gaza, and the US state. Jadaliyya. http://www.jadaliyya.com/pages/index/18935/linking-violence-in-solidarity_ferguson-gaza-and-t

Maznavi, M. (2015, May 20). 9 things you should know about the Women's Mosque of America—and Muslim women in general. *The Huffington Post.* http://www.huffingtonpost.com/m-hasna-maznavi/9-things-you-should-know-about-the-womens_b_7339582.html

McCloud, A. B. (2003). Islam in America: The mosaic. In Y. Y. Haddad, J. I. Smith, & J. L. Esposito (Eds.), *Religion and immigration: Christian, Jewish, and Muslim experiences in the United States* (pp. 159–174). Walnut Creek, CA: AltaMira Press.

MIIM Designs. (n.d.). Sacred Space. http://www.miimdesigns.com/women-in-american-mosques/

MIIM Designs. (n.d.). Women's spaces in American mosques. http://www.miimdesigns.com/women-in-american-mosques/

Murphy, M. C. (2015, June 11). Rasmea Odeh seeks reversal of immigration fraud conviction. The Electronic Intifada. https://electronicintifada.net/blogs/maureen-clare-murphy/rasmea-odeh-seeks-reversal-immigration-fraud-conviction

Muslim American Women's Policy Forum. (n.d.). About. http://mawpf.org/2014/11/08/about/

Muslim Anti-Racism Collaborative (MuslimARC). (n.d.). http://www.muslimarc.org/about/

MuslimGirl.net. (n.d.). About. http://muslimgirl.net/about/

MuslimGirl.net. (n.d.). The Clique. http://muslimgirl.net/clique/

New York University Press. (n.d.). Summary of *Islam is a foreign country: American Muslims and the global crisis of authority.* http://nyupress.org/books/9781479800568/

OnIslam.net. (2014, July 15). US Muslims snub Obama's iftar over Gaza. OnIslam.net. http://www.onislam.net/english/news/americas/475015-obama-hosts-ramadan-iftar-defends-israel.html

The Palestine Center. (2014, November 14). Video file of The 2014 Palestine Center Conference Panel II. http://www.ustream.tv/recorded/55411840

Razack, S. (2008). *Casting out: The eviction of Muslims from western law and politics.* Toronto: University of Toronto Press.

Reinl, J. (2015, August 18). Gaza and Ferguson: Can two struggles unite? Middle East Eye. http://www.middleeasteye.net/in-depth/features/gaza-and-ferguson-can-two-struggles-unite-457420998

Ruiz, L. (2013, March 30). Meet Asma Hanif, nurse to Muslim women in need. MSNBC. http://www.msnbc.com/melissa-harris-perry/meet-asma-hanif-nurse-muslim-women-nee

Rydhan, I. (2011, June 30). Sacred space: Islamic architecture. 2.0. ILLUME Magazine. http://www.illumemag.com/zine/articleDetail.php?Sacred-Space-Islamic-Architecture-20-13727

Safe Nation Collaborative. (2013). *Breaking the silence: Addressing crime victimization in the Muslim community*. Washington, D.C.: Darakshan Raja. http://www.safenationcollaborative.com/wp-content/uploads/Breaking-the-Silence.pdf

Samuels, R. (2013, April 19). Asma Hanif, founder of Muslim women's shelter, finds herself in need of care. *The Washington Post*. http://www.washingtonpost.com/local/asma-hanif-founder-of-muslim-womens-shelter-finds-herself-in-need-of-care/2013/04/19/63973ace-a086-11e2-be47-b44febada3a8_story.html

Sayeed, S., Al-Adawiya, A., & Bagby, I. (2013, March). *The American mosque 2011: Women and the American mosque*. http://www.hartfordinstitute.org/The-American-Mosque-Report-3.pdf

Sharrief, A. (2014, October 30). Biography. Alia Sharrief. http://www.aliasharrief.com/biography/

Siddiqui, S. (2014, July 14). Muslims call for boycott of White House iftar over Gaza conflict. *The Huffington Post*. http://www.huffingtonpost.com/2014/07/14/white-house-muslims_n_5585851.html

Spinner, J. (2007, December 29). Muslim women who become homeless have limited options. *The Washington Post*. http://www.washingtonpost.com/wp-dyn/content/article/2007/12/28/AR2007122802493.html

Sri, V., & Raja, D. (2013). Voices from the frontline: Addressing forced marriage within the United States. Gangashakti. http://carrcenter.hks.harvard.edu/files/carrcenter/files/vidyasri_voicesfromthefrontline.pdf

Street, N. (2015, February 3). First all-female mosque opens in Los Angeles. *Al Jazeera America*. http://america.aljazeera.com/articles/2015/2/3/first-all-female-mosque-opens-in-los-angeles.html

Tan, A. (2015, February 4). Why Muslim woman started 1st all-female mosque in the US. *ABC News*. http://abcnews.go.com/US/1st-female-mosque-opens-us/story?id=28725435

Tarabay, J. (2010, January 1). Muslim Women's Shelter provides refuge, support. NPR. http://www.npr.org/templates/story/story.php?storyId=120752667

TeachMideast. Stereotypes of Arabs, Middle Easterners, and Muslims. http://www.mepc.org/teachmideast

The Melissa Harris-Perry Show. (2013, April 1). Transcript of The Melissa Harris-Perry Show for Saturday, March 30th, 2013. NBC. http://www.nbcnews.com/id/51393436/ns/msnbc/t/melissa-harris-perry-show-saturday-march-th/

Uddin, A., & Tarin, H. (2013, November 5). Rethinking the "red line": The intersection of free speech, religious freedom, and social change. The Brookings Institution. http://www.brookings.edu/~/media/Research/Files/Papers/2013/11/us%20islamic%20world%20forum%20publications/Free%20Speech_English_Web.pdf

Waardenburg, J. (1965). Some institutional aspects of Muslim higher learning. *NVMEN, 12,* 96–138.

Washington Peace Center. (n.d.). Who we are. http://www.washingtonpeacecenter.org/whoweare_new

Women's Islamic Initiative in Spirituality and Equality (WISE). (n.d.). Activism. http://www.wisemuslimwomen.org/activism/

Yale University Department of American Studies. (n.d.). Zareena Grewal. http://americanstudies.yale.edu/people/zareena-grewal

Chapter 23

Special Women in the Holy Quran

Sayyed Mohsen Fatemi

The Holy Quran highlights the role of women in the transcendental process of human beings' perfection and elucidates their idiosyncrasies in multiple chapters. The wife of Ibrahim the Prophet (salavatollah alayh) is one of the exemplar women who has spoken with angels and received the blessings and promises of the angels. God Almighty bestowed upon Ibrahim (salavatollah alayh) the promise of a sagacious and patient son when Ibrahim was an aged man. The blessing was also announced to his wife.

The angels told Ibrahim, "We give you glad tidings of a forbearing son" (Chapter Safat, verse 101). Ibrahim (salavatollah alayh) stated: "Do you give me glad tidings in spite of the fact that old age has overtaken me? Of what then do you give me glad tidings?" (Chapter Al-Hijr, verse 54).

This was not out of disbelief but it was out of surprise since old age had overtaken him. So what were the glad tidings? The angels stated, "We have, indeed, given thee glad tidings in truth; be not therefore one of those who despair" (Chapter Al-Hijr, verse 55). This suggests that the angels' promise and their glad tidings resounded with truth. The word *Ba* in the

Arabic verse of Belhaq indicates that the words uttered by the angels were not in vain.

Then Ibrahim (salavatollah alayh) inquired, "And who can despair of the mercy of his Lord except those who go astray?" (Chapter Al-Hijr, verse 56).

This corroborates that not only a prophet but also a believer would never feel despair. Despondency and despair suggest lack of faith in the ability of God to solve a problem, and thus no true believer can ever feel despair.

In the Holy Quran, the same issue has been discussed with respect to the wife of Ibrahim (salavatollah alayh).

She said, "Oh, Woe is me! Shall I bear a child when I am an old woman, and this my husband is an old man? This is indeed a strange thing!" They said, "Dost thou wonder at Allah's decree? The mercy of Allah and His blessings are upon you, O, people of the House. Surely, He is Praiseworthy and Glorious" (Chapter Hud, verses 72–73).

The Holy Quran has specified numerous verses that concern fighting against oppression and tyrannical powers. In delineating the fight against despotism and tyranny, women bring about a special and remarkable presence. The Holy Quran cites three women who played a significant role in saving Moses the Prophet (salavatollah alayh) and in his education. Moses's upbringing has been credited to his mother, his sister, and the wife of Pharaoh. These three women waged a political campaign against the tyrannical regime at the time and jeopardized their lives to maintain the life of Moses.

The mother of Moses (salavatollah alayh) cast her son, according to Divine instructions, into the water in the sea, "And we instructed the mother of Moses, 'Suckle him; and when thou fearest for him, then cast him into the river and fear not, nor grieve; for We shall restore him to thee, and shall make him *one of the Messengers*'" (Chapter Al-Qasas, verse 7).

She then told Moses's sister, "Follow him" (Chapter Al-Qasas, verse 11). The wife of Pharaoh said, "Kill him not, haply he will be useful to us or we may adopt him as a son" (Chapter Al-Qasas, verse 9).

All three of these women facilitated the process of Moses's upbringing and they provided him with support to ultimately wipe out the tyranny of the Pharaoh.

All these tasks required bravery, perseverance, and initiative. These women put their lives in great risk to help Moses (salavatollah alayh).

The wife of Pharaoh has been exemplified as a brave woman with great virtues: "And Allah sets forth for those who believe the example of the wife of Pharaoh when she said, 'My Lord! Build for me a house with Thee in the Garden; and deliver me from Pharaoh and his work, and deliver me from the wrongdoers'" (Chapter Al-Tahrim, verse 11).

Here the Holy Quran is not just presenting the wife of Pharaoh as a moral example for decent and virtuous women but is also holding her up as a model for Islamic society in general, both men and women, to follow her example. God did not present her as merely an example for women but also for everyone in the society. She was living in a house where egoism and despotism were prevalent and she chose to be a believer in the same house.

Among her conspicuous virtues, the Holy Quran points to her worshipping and her prayers as salient features which give her special manifestation. She appealed to God Almighty, "Build for me a house with Thee in the Garden." She asked to be in the presence of God in the Garden. She was not merely asking for the Garden. In the practice of the daughter of Prophet Mohammad (Sallallah alayhe va alehee va sallam), Hazrate Zahra (Salamollah alayha), one may notice also that she was asking for God first and foremost.

In the prayer of the wife of Pharaoh, one can also see that she was asking for a dissociation from not only the oppressor—namely, Pharaoh—but also from any act of oppression. One can be emancipated from the oppression of the oppressor and yet undertake an act of oppression himself/herself. You may see the depth of the meaning here in disconnecting not only from the realm of the tyrant but also from the domain of any wrongdoing. A woman with such a profound depth of understanding needs to be set forth not only as the epitome for women but also for Islamic society as a whole, both men and women.

Harzarat Maryam (Salamollah alayha) also stands at the apex of Quranic descriptions of exemplar women and as the epitome of a human being. She is presented as the exemplar for the believers, whether men or women.

We also have the example of Mary, the daughter of 'Imran, who guarded her chastity, so "We breathed into him of Our spirit—and she fulfilled *in her person* the words of her Lord and His books and was one of the obedient" (Chapter Al-Tahrim, verse 12).

Mary or Hazrate Maryam (Salavatollah alayha) acquired such a lofty and glorious status due to her virtues, piety, decency, purity, and spiritual soul that God describes her in the following manner: "she fulfilled *in her person* the words of her Lord and His books and was one of the obedient" (Chapter Al-Tahrim, verse 12).

The abovementioned examples may indicate that in the Islamic school of thought, men are not merely the exemplar for men and women are not solely the exemplar for women. The exemplar human being serves as the epitome and exemplar for all human beings and does not belong to male or female.

In discussing the upbringing of Hazrate Maryam (Salavatollah alayha), the Holy Quran says that "whenever Zachariah visited her in the chamber, he found provisions with her. He said, 'O Mary, whence hast thou this?' She replied, 'It is from Allah. Surely, Allah gives to whomsoever He pleases without measure'" (Chapter Al-Imran, verse 37).

In discussing the glorious and lofty status of Hazrate Maryam (salavatollah alayha), the Holy Quran states, "And remember when the angels said, 'O Mary, Allah has chosen thee and purified thee and chosen thee above the women of all peoples, O Mary, be obedient to thy Lord and prostrate thyself and worship God alone with those who worship'" (Chapter Al Imran, verses 42–43).

The Holy Quran also indicates that the angels said, "O Mary, Allah gives thee glad tidings of a word from Him; his name *shall be* the Messiah, Jesus, son of Mary, honored in this world and in the next, and of those who are granted *nearness to God*" (Chapter Al-Imran, verse 45).

Mary has been exemplified as the woman who victoriously substantiated evidence of her purity, faith, and obedience. The Holy Quran highlights her role as a demonstration of faith in the face of trials and challenges. She is set forth for both men and women who seek to abide by an exemplar in the path of perfection and transcendental sublimity.

The Holy Quran frequently describes Mary or Hazrate Maryam (Salavtollah alayha) by virtue of attributes such as truthfulness, purity, and sublimity and in the same status as the righteous.

These examples and evidence suggest that in the Islamic school of thought, both men and women are fully entitled to proceed with their perfection and their elevation. It is for them alone to prove in practice their degree of success and failure.

The Holy Quran also describes the presence of Hazrate Zahra (Salamollah alayah), the daughter of Prophet Mohammad (Salaloh alayhe va alehee va salaam), as an immense source of graciousness. "Surely, We have given thee an abundance *of good*" (Chapter Alkausar, verse 2).

Studying the life of Hazrate Zahra (Salamollah alayah) in different personal, social, cultural, and political scenes would demonstrate how she embodied some of the elevated features of a perfect human being. Her presence is not only presented as an exemplar for women, but numerous traditions (Hadiths) and words from the Prophet Mohammad (Salaloh alayhe va alehee va salaam) and the Infallible Imams of Shiites (Salavatollah alayhem ajmaeen) testify to her life as the epitome of virtues, purity, leadership, perfection, decency, grace, wisdom, and compassion for all human beings.

According to the Islamic school of thought, no superiority is attributed to men, and women are not inferior in any way to men. The criterion for human elevation does not lie in possessions or what a person owns. Wealth, power, even knowledge should not serve as the template for human superiority. The only feature that may facilitate the process of betterment lies in *Taqva* and Taqva transpires through a disconnectedness from egoism, egotism, selfishness, greed, solipsism, exploitation of others, and a connectedness to faith, obedience to divine values, devotion, compassion, kindness, mercy, magnanimity, grace, honesty, and faithfulness.

Values derived from social Darwinism prescribe different forms of superiority, material indulgence, and egoism. Deep down in social Darwinism, there is no room for the endorsement of soul, and thus souls perish both in theory and action when one practically abides by carnal desires and their ontological limitation.

In the Islamic school of thought, ontological limitation is rejected and human beings can incessantly strive for their existential expansion though a rigorous practical awareness of purifying their souls. Women and men can both equally participate in the undertaking of their soul enhancement through establishing the pearl of great price in their lives. Imam Ali (Salavatollah allayh) states that "ignorance is the root of all vice" (Alhayat, Chapter 1, p. 96).

Imam Reza (Salavatollah allayh) explains that "He/she who deceives or uses any falseness in his/her treatment of other Muslims does not belong to us" (Oyoone Reza book, Chapter 2, p. 29). This applies to all types of activities from economic to political facets of life.

In another Hadith, the holy Prophet of Islam (Salaloh alayhe va alehee va salaam) states that anyone who believes in God and the hereafter does not bring persecution or trouble to his/her neighbor (Osoole Kafi, Chapter 2, p. 667).

These teachings are addressed to both men and women and they both need to contribute to developing a healthy society where the interpersonal and intrapersonal aspects of life are improved through the implementation of divine values.

REFERENCES

Babeveyh, M. A. (1984). *Oyoone Akhabar AReza (Alayhessalam)*. Edited by M. H. A'alami. Beirut: Moassese Ala'lami Lelmatbooat.

Hakimi, M. R., Hakimi, M., & Hakimi, A. (2010). *Alhayat*. Qom: Daleele MaPublication.

The Holy Quran. Translated by Abdullah Yusuf Ali. Mt. Holly, NJ: Islamic Educational Services.

Kulayi, M. Y. (1983). *Alkafee*. Tehran: Darol Ketabe Islamieh.

Chapter 24

Feminism and the Future of Religion

J. Harold Ellens

Feminism is a 5,000-year-old problem. Lately it has been renewed as a constructive movement in culture and religion. Feminism has now become a worldwide issue. World culture is maturing as a consequence: maturing in values, rights, justice, freedom, and equality. That is a good thing, long overdue. How will this new achievement influence the future of religion? Religion has been uniformly and aggressively patriarchal for 5,000 years. Can the Feminism Movement radically change that?

Under Benedict XVI, the Roman Catholic Church reasserted its patriarchal policy by officially closing seminary education to women by restraining those seminaries from training anyone in the MDiv programs except male priest candidates and by putting out the authoritative regulation that there would be no female priesthood in the church. This rolled back significantly the spirit of the Vatican II conciliar perspective and the movement toward married priests and women priests that many of us saw at work there. Moreover, this set aside the expression of the popes that immediately followed John XXIII, under whose aegis the Second Vatican Council was mounted.

Fortunately, the sounds made recently by Pope Francis are more congenial to reducing the patriarchal authoritarianism of the Roman Catholic Church, to the great relief of both Catholic and Protestant Christians. That may suggest that the Feminism Movement has had some impact even upon the psychology of the bastions of exclusive male authoritarianism and power. It is long overdue and remains to be seen whether the softening tone can be maintained and progress toward women's rights can grow in such a contrary tradition as that of the Roman Catholic Church.

However, Roman Catholicism is not alone in religious institutions that are slow to accord a full range of prerogatives to women. Protestantism in general has been both slow and behaviorally inept in considering women to be fully and completely human and of equal capability, opportunity, and trust as men. Baptists, who do not wish to be categorized as Protestants, generally are slower than the Presbyterians, Episcopalians, and Methodists in granting women the full rights of the office of ministry and priesthood.

What the future may be for this growth and change toward a more congenial disposition toward women's prerogatives of equality remains to be seen. We have reason to hope, however, that the indications of progress that we have seen in the recent decade may be sustained and, indeed, flourish as we move forward. History is marked by frequent and massive setbacks, however, in the flow of the imperative progression that decency and good sense would dictate. Nonetheless, the Feminist Movement seems to have achieved a sturdy wave of tidal flow that has begun to carry most of the obstacles with it, and it does not give any evidence of the force of that tide lessening or faltering in the long future.

The movement has grown from the first generation of angry and hostile women, to the second generation of a more considered and thoughtful corps of protagonists, to a third generation of women who are powerful, able, and visionary in their own right, without needing to be masculinized in order to hold up their end of the stick, so to speak. The first and second generation seemed to be mostly about power. The third generation seems to be more about a full-fledged intention to achieve all the sound self-realization of truly self-actualized womanhood.

This does not exclude on the part of modern women the expectation that such a posture makes room for, avowedly wishes for and wants to count on, true maturity and self-actualization on the part of men. If women are given the room and freedom to be full-fledged women, then men can be and need to be full-fledged men. Real men are not condescending, exploitative, or negatively dependent upon women as compliant underlings. Real men are sufficiently self-confident and self-actualized to be resourceful and independent agents of their own interests and needs so that they can choose interdependence with women who are equally self-confident and self-actualized, thus bringing the full weight of their whole vitality and wisdom to the interaction or relationship.

However, the question we are asking may not be only or primarily about whether the women's movement will succeed in the long run. The future of feminism in religion is an important question and one that ranges far beyond the Roman Catholic Church, far beyond all the forms of Christianity, and far beyond the range of world religions. The real question or a major part of the issue may be the enigma of the future of religion. Today the community of those whose creed seems to be No Religion but True Spirituality is growing faster than any religion within or beyond Christendom. "I am not Religious but Spiritual," they are saying. Moreover, some of the elements of that community are not merely shaped by the gross dumbness of pooled mutual ignorance. Some are authentic truth seekers who mean what their slogan says.

What is the future of religion? Let us start with Christianity, as we have above. Douglas John Hall, premier theologian of Canada, has written a fine little book entitled *The End of Christendom and the Future of Christianity* (Hall, 2002). He argues that the status of religion throughout the church today is quite different from what the churches realize or generally think it is. Many denominations believe that the church that Constantine sanctioned as the queen of the empire in 325 CE is still the church of today in the experience of the church leaders and laity, as well as in the experience of the church by the world. Neither the church's image of its important presence in society as the source of the divine word, nor society's image of the church's irrelevant presence in society as a vestigial organ of social structure, is accurate.

The Imperial Church, says Hall, has not existed since the rise of the Enlightenment in the 18th century. Not even in the pseudo-imperial presence of the Roman Catholic Church can one find the authentic Imperial Church any more. It died with the death of blind faith and unquestioned dogma. He asserts that the only ones who have not realized its death are the churches themselves. It is his judgment that the institutions of our world no longer listen to the church's claims or preachments as a source of wisdom that shapes their decisions and behavior. The church has merely been talking to itself for the last three centuries and society does not hear its voice anymore, much less take its message seriously. The Not Religious but Spiritual movement is the greatest illustration of what happens when the constituency of the church finally catches on that the authority of the church is dead and its power and authority is a false posture.

Hall does not think that this means that the church as community is dead. He thinks the death of the Imperial Church does raise two questions. Does the church have a future as community and as institution; and in what manner must the church function if it is to have a usable future? He answers the first question by speaking to the last question.

Hall thinks that the church must get completely out of the posture of power and authority. It is no longer the queen of the empire. It acquires no power and authority from the political system and must stop acting like it is a player in the game of power and authority. It must return to the posture it held before it became the Imperial Church. When it became the Imperial Church, it became the Oppressor Church. The prior posture of the Primitive Church or the Early Christian Church of the first three centuries was that of a servant church and a witnessing church. The Romans observed, "Take notice of how they love one another."

For the church to restore its true mission and become the authentic church again, it needs to replace its authoritative posture with the posture of simply standing calmly for the authentic Christian truth-claims. To do that it must figure out what those claims are when the corrosion of historic dogma and mythology is set aside. It must forego its pretensions to having a power voice that is heard and taken seriously by society and replace it with the simple speech of witness to what works spiritually. Such a church is a servant church in the sense that it is in service to the world, like medical institutions are in service to the world, and social services are in service to the world.

The church that is always tentative about its dogma and assured about its witness can become a servant church. That church has a role in society to live into society's struggle with society's own difficulties, speaking from the inside of them to society, instead of standing over against society on the outside, so to speak, and preaching to the organism of the human community. Some churches have already found this posture, I think, but not all have found their focus on the real issues. Some of them have, for example, missed the issue of women's rights and prerogatives—of the full appreciation of the true nature of what real authentic and self-actualizing women are like and are all about.

However, if the church can become what Hall urges, it is a foregone conclusion that it will see the urgency of the maturing movement of Feminism in Religion. The two movements, that of the church being the church and women being free and self-realizing women, go forward hand in glove, so to speak. These movements are corollaries and not in opposition. The church will refocus on spirituality instead of religion, and religion will again arise authentically out of spiritually motivated worship behaviors and social action that works and counts (Ellens, 2007).

What about world religions in general? Is there a future for them and is the role of authentic feminism going to be a part of that? The field is, of course, one of very mixed issues. There is a great variety in the roles of women in the history of world religions and it has been very negative in many of them for the last 5,000 years. This volume on *Feminism and Religion* tells that story in informative and challenging ways. I need not rehearse it here. This text represents a wide range of religions and religious practices. In general, it brings the state of affairs of feminism in religion up to date. What, therefore, of the future?

The prospects of the future of the women's movement in religious institutions and religious practices in the religions of the world are very similar to the state of affairs in Christianity. That is, the degree to which a religion shifts its focus from traditions of prescribed religious behavior to the dynamics of living spirituality, to that extent it makes itself amicable to the radical shift toward valuing women appropriately. I have a church musician friend who was married half a year when his wife was diagnosed with terminal cancer. During the long ordeal of treatment and the slow gains which stabilized the cancer and then progressively eroded it so that her life is now hopeful again, he joined the suffering with her and served her needs in close and tender care. I asked him what kind of help he felt reaching them in their ordeal. He replied that the church as an institution, and religion as prescribed behavior, has no ability to meet people at the point of their pain. He said that what mediated some solace to him was Bach's B-Minor Mass and the music he composed himself. He said that these came to him as reflections of the faith and ministry of Bach, who suffered his own pain, the real human pain of a guy suffering crucifixion, and the community of spiritual friends that those stimuli brought with them to his and his wife's pain.

Then I asked myself what pain oppressed women as members of the church, deprived of their full self-realization within that community for the last 17 centuries, must have suffered and how they endured the ordeal with no succor provided by their religious institutions and their religious liturgies—only that, I judge, which they derived from their personal spirituality.

Now, project that across the world of religious institutions of every kind and prescribed religious behavior of every kind, and you have a pattern of oppression. The routine experience must have been relieved only by the personal spirituality that women were able to generate themselves. This would have come to them in spite of the religions of the world. It must have been engendered mainly by the fellowship of their own community of women and men congenial to it. It is no wonder that women were so important to the early church, so prominent in creating and leading its fellowship, so closely allied to Jesus himself, and so quick to see his point and respond to his spirit. No wonder that when, with Constantine, the church was changed into a power institution, women were eliminated from is priesthood and leadership.

In almost all the religions of the world, the pattern has been the same. Prescribed behavior in worship and work brings with it some kind of orthodoxy and oppression. With that the nurturant spirit is jeopardized and the universal divine spirit is repressed. Where the pervasive divine spirit is repressed, women are easily victimized in all religious traditions, by the spirit of patriarchal power (Ellens, 2009). Authentic spirituality is the only hope for the future of religion and of feminism in religion.

REFERENCES

Ellens, J. H. (2007). *Understanding religious experience: What the Bible says about spirituality.* Westport, CT: Praeger.

Ellens, J. H. (2009). *The healing power of spirituality: How faith helps humans thrive.* Westport, CT: Praeger.

Hall, D. (2002). *The end of Christendom and the future of Christianity.* Eugene, OR: Wipf and Stock.

About the Editors and Contributors

Michele A. Paludi, Ph.D., is the series editor for Women's Psychology and for Women and Careers in Management for Praeger. She is the author/ editor of 35 college textbooks, and more than 160 scholarly articles and conference presentations on sexual harassment, campus violence, psychology of women, gender, and discrimination. Her book, *Ivory Power: Sexual Harassment on Campus* (1990, SUNY Press), received the 1992 Myers Center Award for Outstanding Book on Human Rights in the United States. Dr. Paludi served as Chair of the U.S. Department of Education's Subpanel on the Prevention of Violence, Sexual Harassment, and Alcohol and Other Drug Problems in Higher Education. She was one of six scholars in the United States to be selected for this subpanel. She also was a consultant to and a member of former New York State Governor Mario Cuomo's Task Force on Sexual Harassment. Dr. Paludi serves as an expert witness for court proceedings and administrative hearings on sexual harassment. She has had extensive experience in conducting training programs and investigations of sexual harassment and other Equal Employment Opportunity (EEO) issues for businesses and educational institutions. In addition, Dr. Paludi has held faculty positions at Franklin & Marshall College, Kent State University, Hunter College, Union College, and Union Graduate College, where she directs the human resource management certificate program. She is on the faculty in the School of Management at Union Graduate College. She is also in Human Resources and leadership at Excelsior College.

J. Harold Ellens is a retired university Professor of Philosophy and Psychology, retired Presbyterian Theologian and Pastor, retired U.S. Army Chaplain (Colonel), Executive Director Emeritus of the Christian Association for Psychological Studies, Founding Editor and Editor in Chief Emeritus of the *Journal of Psychology and Christianity*, and Founder and Chairman Emeritus of the Section on Psychological Hermeneutics of Bible Themes and Texts in the International Society for Biblical Studies. He has published extensively in the interface of psychology and religion/spirituality. His recent publications include *The Destructive Power of Religion* (4 vols., 2004), *Psychology and the Bible* (4 vols., with Wayne Rollins, 2004), *God's Word for Our World: A Festschrift for Professor Simon John De Vries* (2 vols., 2004), *Sex in the Bible* (2006), *Text and Community: A Festschrift Commemorating Professor Bruce M. Metzger* (2 vols., 2007), *Radical Grace: How Belief in a Benevolent God Benefits Our Health* (2007), *Understanding Religious Experience: What the Bible Says about Spirituality* (2007), *Miracles: God, Science, and Psychology in the Paranormal* (3 vols., 2008), *Sex in the Bible* (2007), *The Spirituality of Sex* (2009), *Probing the Frontiers of Biblical Studies: A Festschrift in Honor of Professor David J. A. Clines* (with John T. Greene, 2009), *The Son of Man in The Gospel of John* (2010), *The Healing Power of Spirituality: How Faith Helps Humans Thrive* (3 vols., 2010), *Honest Faith for Our Time: Truth Telling about the Bible, the Creed, and the Church* (2010), *Light from the Other Side: The Paranormal as Friend and Familiar* (2010), *Explaining Evil* (3 vols., 2011), *Psychological Hermeneutics of Biblical Themes and Texts: A Festschrift in Honor of Wayne G. Rollins* (2012), *A Dangerous Report: Challenging Sermons for Advent and Easter* (2012), *God's Radical Grace: Challenging Sermons for Ordinary Time(s)* (2013), *By Grace Alone: Forgiveness for Everyone, for Everything, for Evermore* (2013), *Heaven, Hell, and Afterlife: Eternity in Judaism, Christianity, and Islam* (3 vols., 2013), *Winning Revolutions: The Psychology of Successful Revolts for Freedom, Fairness, and Rights* (3 vols., 2013), *Seeking the Sacred with Psychoactive Substances: Chemical Paths to Spirituality and to God* (2014), and *The Psychedelic Policy Quagmire: Health, Law, Freedom, and Society*.

He has authored, coauthored, or edited 274 published volumes, 178 professional journal articles, and 205 review articles. He is currently teaching at the Ecumenical Theological Seminary. He is a psychotherapist in private practice.

CONTRIBUTORS

Firdaus Arastu is Assistant Editor at *altMuslimah*, where she writes on gender, faith, and cultural identity. She was a staff writer for *Winnovating*, profiling women innovators around the world. Her work has been published in *Al Jazeera English, The Huffington Post*, and *The Tribune, India*.

Arastu provided research assistance for the chapter "American Muslims, American Islam, and the American Constitutional Heritage" in *Religious Freedom in America: Constitutional Roots and Contemporary Challenges* (2015). She received her bachelor's degree in Anthropology and Psychology from Syracuse University.

Adrien J. Bledstein leads adult Bible study in congregations and is a published independent scholar in the Bible compared to ancient Near Eastern literature. Trained as a reading specialist to increase a person's level of reading comprehension, critical thinking, and writing, she conducted a private practice for individuals, including graduate students and professional people. Publications on the Bible include: "Was Eve Cursed? (or did a woman write Genesis?)," "Binder, Trickster, Heel, and Hairy-man: Rereading Genesis 27 as a Trickster Tale Told by a Woman," "Tamar and the 'Coat of Many Colors,'" "Is Judges a Woman's Satire of Men Who Play God?," and "Female Companionships: If the Book of Ruth Were Written by a Woman . . . ." Challenged with a respiratory disorder, Adrien turned to invention and became a businesswoman. Some of her publications are available at http://icanbreathe.com/designer.htm.

Kamila Blessing is an ordained Episcopal priest of over 30 years and holds a Ph.D. in New Testament and Christian Origins from Duke University (1996). She also holds previous credentials in Systems Science, focusing upon the health of communication among members of families, organizations, and religious groups, across time and geography, as well as across the table. Her first work in this area received national attention, winning the Doctoral Forum Award of the American Society for Information Science (1976). She has consulted for Fortune 500 and other companies, the U.S. Navy, and numerous churches and denominations. Her current research concerns the use of family systems to interpret the Bible. Blessing's research poses to the church a compelling question: do we really know the most radically inclusive leader in the history of religion—Jesus? Blessing is the author of several books, including *Families of the Bible: A New Perspective* (ABC-CLIO, 2010).

Deborah Brock, B.A., B.S., M.A., Ph.D., is a psychotherapist with foci on women, trauma resolution, and integrated multifaceted psychotherapy. Her private practice is in the Madison, Wisconsin, area. She also maintains a long-distance practice in California, where she is a registered psychologist. She has published on narcissism and gender issues, and she has presented numerous papers and workshops on psychological issues including psychological–theological integration. She is currently working on a book dealing with the necessity and value of sadness in life.

Anna Byrne is a student of the Living School at the Center for Action and Contemplation in New Mexico. Previously, she taught youth with mental health challenges. She is a hospice volunteer and enjoys meditating, gardening, and writing. She lives in Ontario, Canada, with her husband Andrew.

Linda Chiang is a Professor of Education at Azusa Pacific University in California. She is a recipient of Dean's Accomplished Scholar, and the Outstanding Researcher of the School of Education at Azusa Pacific University. Her research interests include culture and learning styles, cross-cultural communication, and teaching pedagogies. Her academic publications include books, articles, and chapters in two books and are published in Chinese or English. Her works include: *Multicultural Education* (2000), *Positive Psychology: Implications for Life, Work and Education* (2008, 2010), and *Globalization and Confucianism in Chinese Societies* (Greenwood, 2002), co-authored with Joseph Tamney. Her research has focused on various ethnic groups and education such as education for Muslim women, Tibetan education, and interethnic children's education. She is active in various professional associations and presents papers at national and international conferences routinely. Currently she is writing a column entitled "Perfect Schools in an Imperfect World," published in the *Teacher Educator Monthly* journal in Taiwan.

Suzanne M. Coyle is Associate Professor of Pastoral Theology and Marriage and Family Therapy at Christian Theological Seminary in Indianapolis, where she directs the Counseling Center and the program in marriage and family therapy. She received her M.Div. and Ph.D. from Princeton Theological Seminary. Coyle also has a Postgraduate Diploma in Narrative Therapy and Community Work from the Dulwich Centre in South Australia. In 2014–2015, she was named a Tutu Fellow of the Desmond Tutu Center for Peace, Reconciliation, and Global Justice for her work in using collective narrative practice with marginalized persons to tell their stories of resilience.

Paula A. Drewek is a retired Professor of Humanities and Religious Studies at Macomb Community College in Warren, Michigan. She taught courses in arts and ideas and comparative religion for 39 years. After retirement she served as Coordinator of Macomb's Multicultural and International Initiatives Program. Her Ph.D. in the Sociology of Religion at the University of Ottawa was a cross-cultural study of two communities of Baha'is—in Canada and India—using a psycho-social model of human development. Since her retirement in 2007 she has devoted her time to numerous interfaith activities in the Detroit metro area. These include WISDOM president, the Scholar Colloquy, the Worldviews Seminar

Planning committee at U of M–Dearborn, Warren-area interfaith activities with ICRJ, and participant in the Detroit Region Harvard Pluralism Project. She has been a Baha'i respondent on the television show *Interfaith Odyssey* since its beginning in 2001. Paula also sings in the Metropolitan Detroit Chorale and has joined several Baha'i choirs for special performances in the United States and Europe. In Summer 2005, she spent a month in China on a Fulbright GPA grant studying religions in China, and has visited India six times serving Baha'i development activities at the Barli Institute for Rural Women.

Sayyed Mohsen Fatemi (Ph.D., University of British Columbia, 2003; Post-doctorate, Harvard University, 2009–2013) did his postdoctoral studies in the Department of Psychology at Harvard University in areas of social, clinical, health, and cross-cultural psychology with a focus on mindfulness. He is an Associate and a lecturer at Harvard University and works in areas of social and cross-cultural psychology. He is a frequently published author and poet with numerous conference presentations. He teaches in the Department of Psychology at Harvard University. In addition to Harvard, he has also taught at the University of Massachusetts in Boston, Boston Graduate School of Psychoanalysis, the University of Toronto, Western Washington University, and the University of British Columbia. Fatemi's present areas of research focus on the psychological implications of mindfulness for negotiations, media, cultural understanding and communication, creativity and leadership, persuasive and influencing skills, and clinical and counseling psychology. He has been the keynote speaker of a number of international conferences and, as a licensed and registered psychologist, works on the implication of mindfulness for stress management, anxiety management, panic attacks, interpersonal problems, and personality disorders. He is also a popular guest of multiple television and radio programs and has consulted and coached corporate managers and executives on the application of mindfulness to enhance a broad array of vital business skills. His work includes the development of mindful intercultural understanding, negotiation, communication, conflict resolution, influencing, team building, presentation skills, creative decision making, and crisis management. In addition, Dr. Fatemi has done studies on Islamic philosophy, Islamic mysticism, and Islamic jurisprudence in the presence of a number of renowned scholars of Islam.

Kathy L. Gaca, Ph.D., is Associate Professor of Classics at Vanderbilt University. Her research explores how sexual norms rooted in antiquity inform current concerns of social injustice and violence against women and girls. She is the author of *The Making of Fornication: Eros, Ethics, and Political Reform in Greek Philosophy and Early Christianity* (2003, winner of the

CAMWS 2006 Outstanding Publication Award) and of numerous articles, including "Martial Rape, Pulsating Fear, and the Sexual Maltreatment of Girls (*paides*), Virgins (*parthenoi*), and Women (*gynaikes*) in Antiquity," *American Journal of Philology* 135 (2014). She is currently at work on her second book, *Sexual Warfare against Girls and Women: Ancient Society, Modern Witness, Overpowering Injustice,* and has published "Girls, Women, and the Significance of Sexual Violence in Ancient Warfare" in *Sexual Violence in Conflict Zones: From the Ancient World to the Era of Human Rights,* edited by Elizabeth Heineman (2011). She received her Ph.D. in Classics at the University of Toronto and held the Hannah Seeger Davis Postdoctoral Fellowship in Hellenic Studies at Princeton University.

Jeanine M. Galusha-Glasscock is a doctoral candidate in the Clinical Psychology program at the University of Texas Southwestern. She is a 2010 graduate of the University of Texas at Tyler where she earned a B.S. in psychology and a 2013 graduate of the University of Texas at Tyler where she earned an M.S. in Clinical Psychology. Her academic and research goals include completing her doctorate and continuing research in the field of neuropsychology. She is also an alumni member of the Honor Society of Phi Kappa Phi and Alpha Chi National Honor Society.

Silvia Geruza Fernandez Rodrigues is an ordained minister at Bethesda Church of São Paulo. She earned her B.A. in English, American, Portuguese, and Brazilian literatures at the Federal University of Ceará. She also is a psychologist. She trained post-graduation in systemic family and couple therapy at the Pontifice University of São Paulo, specializing in community therapy. She holds a master's degree in Religious Science from the Methodist University of São Paulo. She also holds a master's degree in Christian Leadership from the South American College of Londrina. She is the author of five books in Portuguese, including *Romantic Love: Does It Exist?; History from Its Myth and Post Modern Conceptions* and *Another Gender of Church—Can Women Be Ordained?*

Virginia Ingram (Ph.D. candidate) lectures in literacy and academic language at Murdoch University in Perth, Australia. She has numerous publications, including the book, *Grace: Free, Costly, or Cheap?* Her most recent publication is *Satires of Love or Hate: Jonah to Charlie Hebdo*, published in the investigative newspaper, *The Italian Insider.* Virginia is also a regular presenter at theological conferences. Her areas of interest are literary studies, psychological hermeneutics, and topical theology.

Maija Jespersen is a writer and artist living in Philadelphia. Her area of interest is peace studies, with a focus on normative violence. Her previous publications include "Creativity and Positive Peace: Moving Past Conceptual Antagonism," and "Gandhi's Nonviolent Sources of Power."

Paula K. Lundberg-Love is a Professor of Psychology at the University of Texas at Tyler (UTT), where she teaches psychopharmacology, behavioral neuroscience, physiological psychology, sexual victimization, and family violence. Dr. Lundberg-Love is also a licensed professional counselor at Tyler Counseling and Assessment Center, where she provides therapeutic services for victims of sexual assault, child sexual abuse, and domestic violence. Her research interests have focused on the treatment of women with histories of incestuous abuse. She is the author of nearly 200 publications and presentations and is co-editor of *Violence and Sexual Abuse at Home: Current Issues in Spousal Battering and Child Maltreatment; Intimate Violence against Women: When Spouses, Partners, or Lovers Attack;* and *Women and Mental Disorders.*

Patricia Nobre is a theologian and psychologist in Brazil. She holds a master's degree in Social Psychology and Religion. She is a research member of LATESFIPE—Laboratory of Social Theory, Philosophy, and Psychoanalysis at the University of São Paulo. She is a published essayist. She is currently employed as a professional psychological social worker in the Facilities for Senior Care at Universidade São Marcos in São Paulo. She is the proud mother of two children, very talented professionals, who seem ready to follow in her footsteps.

Divyaben Patel is a clinical neuropsychology graduate student at the University of Texas at Tyler. Currently, she is a research assistant in the Social Emotions and Motivation Laboratory. Her future academic interests are to pursue her doctoral degree in Neuropsychology.

Ilona Rashkow, who holds a Ph.D. in Comparative Literature, is Professor Emerita at the State University of New York at Stony Brook, and teaches regularly at New York University. Among her book publications are *Taboo or Not Taboo: The Hebrew Bible and Human Sexuality; The Phallacy of Genesis: A Feminist-Psychoanalytic Approach; Upon the Dark Places: Sexism and Anti-Semitism in English Renaissance Biblical Translation;* and numerous academic journal articles. She presents papers routinely at national and international academic conferences and has been the Visiting Aaron Aronoff Chair in Judaic Studies at the University of Alabama as well as a Visiting Research Scholar at the Jewish Theological Seminary.

Katherine Anne E. Scott has worked in numerous research and academic settings and is currently focusing on expanding her clinical testing and interpretive skills in the hospital setting. Her primary research interests lie in memory performance and cognitive dysfunction in relation to Traumatic Brain Injury, Mild Cognitive Impairment, Alzheimer's Disease and other dementias, and the rates of deterioration associated with the aforementioned disorders. She is also interested in the neurophysiological underpinnings of Post-Traumatic Stress Disorder (PTSD), and the consolidation and retrieval of memory related to traumatic experiences. Katherine Anne holds a bachelor's degree in psychology and a master's degree in clinical psychology with a specialization in neuropsychology.

Maria Stoyadinova holds an M.A. with Honors in International Relations from the Johns Hopkins University School of Advanced International Studies, with specializations in International Law and International Economics. She obtained her B.A. in Economics and Diplomacy and World Affairs from Occidental College. She has translated medical and sociology texts for several non-profit organizations through the online forum Translations for Progress and has published for the *Washington Post* online blog PostGlobal. She has also worked at Amnesty International and the World Bank and is currently working as an economic consultant.

Asma Uddin, in addition to being a constitutional lawyer, is the Founder and Editor-in-Chief of AltMuslimah.com, a web magazine dedicated to issues on gender and Islam. Her work at AltMuslimah has earned the praise of many, including Dr. Robert George of Princeton University, who has said, "On matters of sexual morality, marriage, and family in Islam, particularly in the American context, I recommend the writings of two exceptionally gifted young Muslim women writers: Suzy Ismail and Asma Uddin." The *Huffington Post*'s Senior Religion Editor, Paul Brandeis Raushenbush, noted, "AltMuslimah.com is important because it gives a specific platform to the intersections between gender, belief, and well-being in Islam—all with superior levels of intellect and writing. The internet would be the poorer without AltMuslimah as a destination and font of knowledge for seekers of all religious backgrounds." Asma speaks and publishes widely on issues of gender and faith, and national and international religious freedom.

Jennifer Elisa Veninga is Assistant Professor of Religious and Theological Studies at St. Edward's University in Austin, Texas. She holds an M.T.S. degree from Harvard Divinity School (2002) and a Ph.D. from the Graduate Theological Union (2011). Her research and teaching interests include Søren Kierkegaard and existentialism, Scandinavian religion and politics, Islam and the West, and feminist and queer theologies. The author of *Secularism, Theology, and Islam: The Danish Social Imaginary and the Cartoon Crisis of 2005–2006* (2014), she is currently researching the intersections of theology and trauma studies with a focus on the 2011 tragedy in Norway perpetrated by Anders Behring Breivik.

Mary Wittbold holds a B.A. in English. She has done graduate work in health sciences, psychology, and creative writing. She worked in professional sales, was a firefighter/EMT, and has been a volunteer in her community. She is now a scholar with interests in the interface of psychology and religion. She lives in Farmington Hills, Michigan, with her husband Karl. They have two grown children.

Index

Abortion, xxii–xxiii, 249–260; brief history of, 250–251; feminism and, 256–260; morality of, 258–259; rape and, xxii–xxiii; religion and, 256–260; Roman Catholic Church and, 255–256
Absalom, 76–79, 83–87, 91–92
Adelman, O., 216
Adler, Rachel, 208
Agleadas, 192
Akita, Lailah Gifty, xxvii
Al-Khatahtbeh, Amani, 337, 339
Ali, Imam, 99–101
All India Women's Conference, 113
altMuslimah (altM), 337–339
Ambrosio, 64–65
American Birth Control League, 250
American Psychological Association, xxiv
American Women on Being Muslim, 337
Amnon, 75, 77–85, 87, 91–92, 189
Anabasis, 177
Ancestral grounds, 222–224
Ancrene Riwle, 48
Angirasmriti, xxi–xxii
Anthony, Susan B., 255
Aquinas, Thomas, 66, 257
Aquino, Maria Pilar, 298
Arab American Action Network, 341
Arastu, Firdaus, 335–352
Aristotle, 283
Ascetic Mothers, 238–239; Ammas, 240–241; the call apart, 238–239; Desert Mothers, 238–246; desert spirituality, 241; identifiable traits of, 238; living in the desert, 241–243; living in the monasteries, 243–246; Monastic Mothers, 238–246
Ashtoreth, 34
Associative implicit memory, 5, 13–14; sexism and, 7
Atwood, Margaret, xxiii
Augustine, xx, 64–66
Australia, 316–317
Auth, Tony, 336

Back on My Deen, 351
Baden, Joel, 77, 85
Baha'i: characteristics of theology, 158–159; Divine Essence, 159, 163; God's Messengers

(Manifestations), 158–159, 163–164; *Kitabi-Iqan*, 160–161; Maid of Heaven, 160, 166–168; Mother Word, 162–163; mystical feminine in, 157–169; mysticism and the use of metaphors, 159–161; Progressive Revelation, 163; Scriptures, 157; Signs of God, 159; Tablet of Carmel, 164; Word of God, 162–163
Baha'u'llah, 163–168
Balch, D., 131
Balkan Wars, 178–179, 188, 196–197
Baring, A., 24
Bathsheba, 77–78, 83–85, 87, 92
Beecher, Henry Ward, xxiii
Bejan, Adrian, 326
Ben Hannah, Phineas, 133
Benedict XVI, 365
Bharata Mahila Parishad (Ladies Social Conference), 113
Bible: authorship, 75–92; daughters in, 43; faith and feminism, 3–14; feminism and, 3–14, 39–55, 68–70; gender-inclusion and, 9; God's gender, 45; God's names, 45, 88–89; God's tests, 89–90; golden rule, 4–5; harmful material in, 9, 12–13; Hebrew, 39–55, 75–92; patriarchy in, 3–5, 10, 43–44; rape in, 75–92, 173–197; sexism in, 6, 42–43, 63; social ordering in, 5; women of, 75–92
The Bible and Women: An Encyclopedia of Exegesis and Cultural History, 41
The Bible with Sources Revealed, 76
Billoo, Zahra, 336
Birch, Bruce, 40
Bison of le Tuc d'Audoubert, 21
Blackmun, Harry, 251
Bledstein, Adrien J., 75–92
Blessing, Kamila, 129–141
Bodes, Mabel, 126
Bodgidharma, 118
Bodhisattva, 230–231
The Book of J, 76
The Book of Special Grace, 62
Bosnian War, 174, 178–179
Brazil: birth of the Brazilian woman in, 265–269; historical resonances of the feminine in, 263–275; Presbyterian Church in, 71
Brigid of Kildare, 244
Brock, Deborah, 235–247, 277–292
bucharania, 31–32
Buddha: Guatama, 118–119, 121–122; Shakyamuni, 119
Buddha Dharma Education Association, 127
BuddhaNet, 127
Buddhism, xxi; Eight Chief Rules, 122; enlightenment and gender, 125; female status in sacred books, 119–120; feminism in, 117–127; Four Noble Truths, 122, 223; gender equity in, 120–123; Hinayana, 123; history of, 118–119; love, 124; Mahayana, 119–120; meditation, 123, 227; motherhood and, 123; Religious Order of Nuns, 122, 223; sacrifice, 125; sutras, 119, 121, 126; views towards women, xxi; Zen, 118, 123–125; Zen women and Buddhist practices, 123–125
Bulgaria, 143–145
Burial rituals, 21–22
Buscemi, Maria Soave, 269
By the Dawn's Early Light: Chris Jackson's Journey to Islam, 350–351
Byrne, Anna, 221–232

A Call to Action: Women, Religion, Violence and Power, xxv
Cantor, Aviva, 208
Carr, Anne, 64
Carroll, M., xxvi
Carter, Jimmy, xxv
Cashford, J., 24
Catherine of Siena, 246
Catholics for Choice, 258
Cato, 67
Chapin, L., xxiii–xxiv
Chaplin, Vsevolod, 153
Chaves, M., 70
Chiang, Linda, 117–127

China, xxi; ancient, 26–27; communism, 318–319; historical timeline, 307–308; feminism in, 303–320; Lahu, 26–27; Qing Dynasty, 308; Zhou Dynasty, 308–309, 314, 322–323, 327
Chopsticks Only Work in Pairs, 26
Christ, Jesus, 223; death, 139–140, 223; mother, 137–139; relationship with women and, xxv–xxvii, 61–63, 132–140; resurrection, 62, 133, 223; teachings vs. organization of religions, xxv–xxvii
Christianity: church record with women, 63–68, 265–269; Evangelical limits on accepting mythology and androgynous identity, 286–290; Evangelical women, 277–280; feminist movement and woman's ordination, 70–72; Fundamentalism, 289–290; gender equality and, 70–71; Gnostics, 287–288; invisibility of women in, 272–275; Medieval, 267–271; Methodism, 71; Orthodox, 287; transfer of power through the word, 269–271; women's history in religious literature, 61–63
Chrysostomos, Archimandrite, 146–147
Church of the Latter Day Saints, xxiv–xxv
Civil Rights Movement 295
Clearchus, 190–191
Cleary, T., 331
Clines, David, 7
Clinton Bill, 252
Clinton, Hillary, xxii–xxv
Cohen, Debra Nussbaum, 216
Collyridians, xxvii
Communism, 318–319
Comstock Act, 250
Confucianism: definition of, 307–308; feminism and, 303–320; philosophical basis, 312–313; principles, 311–316; religion and, 306–307; rules of hierarchy, 315; self-awareness and, 315–316
Confucius, 121, 329–330; education, 310–311; father, 309–310; grandfather, 310; mother, 310
Constantine, 241, 286
Corinthians, xxvi, 12, 63, 65
Coyle, Suzanne, M., 293–301
Crete, 19, 35
Culver, Robert, 63–64

Davis, C.T., 288
Dakhini, 224–225
Daly, Mary, 14, 294
Darius, 184
David, 75–78, 80, 82, 85–87, 89, 92
Davids, Caroline Rhys, 126
D'Ávila, Teresa, 62, 68, 224–226, 230, 246
De Beauvoir, Simone, xix, 69
De Castro, Viveiros, 271
De Hackeborn, Matilde, 62
De La Cruz, Juana Inêz, 62
De Magdeburg, Mechthild, 62, 228
De Pisano, Cristiana, 267–268
Deborah, 76
Ded, Lal, 109–110
Deuteronomy, 185, 189–190, 195
Deutsche Welle, 153
Dimitrov, Christo, 196–197
Dinah, 77–78, 81, 83, 92, 189
Doe v. Boltom, 251
Dogen, Eihei, 124
Domestic violence, 274; church attendance and, 11–12; Protestantism and, 11–12; Russia and, 153–154
Drewek, Paula A., 157–169
Dyads, 24–27, 32–34

Eastern Orthodox Church, 143–153
Ebrahimji, Maria, 337
Egalitarianism: arguments regarding, 18–20; feminist, 17–36; Neolithic, 19–20; prehistoric, 17–36
Eilberg, Amy, 210
Eisler, R., 19–20

Elgenaida, Maha, 336
The End of Christendom and the Future of Christianity, 367
Ellens, J. Harold, 10–11, 129, 365–369
Equal Rights Amendment, xxiv, 316
Eskandri, Maryam, 345–346
Esposito, John, 338
Estby, Helga, 247
Esther, 76
Evangelical Network, 279
Evangelicals Concerned, 279
Exodus, 6, 88–89
Exum, Cheryl, 7, 40

Faith, 3–14, 277–292
Fatemi, Sayyed Mohsen, 95–101, 359–363
Femicide, 274
Femineity, 129–141; definition of, 130
Feminism: basic background information on, 206–207; faith and, 3–14, 277–292; first wave, 207, 316; future of religion and, 365–369; history of, 316–317; Judaism and, 207–217; pro-choice, 251–255; pro-life, 255–256; second wave, 207, 211–212, 293, 316; third wave, 207, 316–317
Feminist biblical hermeneutics/criticism, 3, 6–7, 10–11, 13; Adam and Eve and, 47–54, 59, 106, 269; gender and, 42, 44–45; historical development, 40–42; patriarchy and, 43–44; sexuality and, 42; various approaches to, 42–47; women and, 68–70
Feminist.com, xxvii
Feminists for Life (FFL), 255–256
Feminist Theology, 273–274, 293–301
Ferguson, B., 28
Figure with a Phallic Neck and Breasts, 32–34
Fine, Cordelia, 5
Fiorina, Carly, xxiii
Fiorenza, Elisabeth Schüssler, 10, 40–41, 72
The Flowing Light of the Godhead, 62
Floyd-Thomas, S. M., 296
Fonda, Jane, xxvii
Foster, Serrin, 255
Fowler, James, xx
Francis, 366
Freud, Sigmund, 284
Friendship and Community, 245
Friedan, Betty, 207
Friedman, Richard E., 76
Fu Hsi, 326–327, 330

Gaca, Kathy L., 173–197
Galeano, E., 271
Galusha-Glasscock, Jeanine M., 103–114
Gandhi, Mahatma, 110–111, 114
Gautauma, Siddhartha, 118, 223; birth, 118; childhood, 118–119; marriage, 119
Genesis, 130, 286; Adam and Eve, 39, 41, 47–54, 63–64; Cain, 86–87, 91; creation of Eve, 50–52; curse on women, 53–54; eating of the fruit, 52–53; feminist reading, 49–50; Lilith, 268–269; pre-feminist reading, 47–49; the punishment, 53–54; sexism in, 43, 47–48
Genovefa, 244
Gertrude the Great, 62
Gestalt therapy, 237
Ghafur, Abdul, 336–337
Gimbutas, Marija, 19, 28, 35
Ginsberg, Ruth Bader, 252–253
Gleanings from the Writings of Baha'u'llah, 167
Global Mothers, 247
Gods (non-Abrahamic): Centaurs, 31; Dyaus, 104–105; Dying God of Vegetation, 31; Guardian of Wild Nature/Master of Animals, 31, 35; partner gods, 30–32; Phallic God or Snake, 31; Siva, 109; Vegetation God, 32, 35; Year God, 30
Goddesses: Aditi, 105; Chandrika, 108; Death goddess, 30; Durga, 108–109, 114; Goddess of

regeneration, 30; Grain/ Vegetation Goddess, 31; Hindu, 103–114; history of, 34–35; Kannaki, 111; Lakshmi, 108; Mistress of Animals and Plants, 30; Mother, 235–247; Near East, 34; Nirrti, 105; Prajnaparamita, 120; Pregnant Goddess/Fertility Goddess, 30; Pregnant Vegetation Goddess, 30, 34–35; prehistoric, 17–36; Prithvi, 104–105; Puranas, 108–109; Rahda, 108; Ratri, 105; Rig Veda, 104–105; Saraswati, 105; Shakti, 109, 114; Usas, 104, 114; Vac, 105
Gonzales v. Carhart, 252–253
The Gospel of Mary, 7–8; male values in, 7–8; patriarchy in, 8
Gospel of John, 129–141; femineity in, 132–140; Haggadah, 140; interpretation of womanliness in, 130–132; Jesus in, 132–140; Martha in, 135–137; Mary Magdalene in, 135–137; Nicodemus in, 133–135; Peter in, 135–137; Samaritan woman in, 133–135; Thomas in, 135
Greenberg, Blu, 208
Gregory the Great, 245
Grewal, Zareena, 349–351
Griswold v. Connecticut, 250–251
Gudorf, Christine, 257
Guhu, 225

Hall, Douglas John, 367–368
Halpern, Caruch, 85
The Handmaid's Tale, xxiii
Hanif, Asma, 348–349
Harrison, Beverly Wildung, 252–253, 258
Hatcher, John, 160
Haughton, R., 63
Hebrew Institute of Riverdale, 213
Henkin, Chana, 210
Hentsch, A. A., 49
Hera, 27
Herodotus, 179
Hidden Book in the Bible, 76
The Hijabi Chronicles, 351
Hilda, 245
Hildegard, 246
Hill, Margari, 342–343
Hillel, 206
Hillman, J., 237
Hinduism: bhakti movement, 109–110, 114; female gurus, 112–113; female icons in folk and regional, 111; feminism in, 103–114; gender issues in, 105–106; Mahabharata, 106–107, 114; Manusmriti, 106, 112; origins of, 103–104; portrayal of women in the great Hindu epics, 106–107; reinterpretation of ancient scriptures, 110–111; Rig Veda, 104–106; *sati*, 106, 110; Shakti, 111–112; status in the Epic period, 107; Upanishads, 109–110; Vedic period, 105–106
Hoffer, Peter Charles, 249
Homer, 174, 176–177, 179, 240
Honer, Isaline Blew, 126
Hosea, 6, 50
Hubbard, Minna, 247
Huldah, 76
Hull, N. E. H., 249
Human Rights Watch, 150–151
Hunt, Mary, xxviii
Hurwitz, Sara, 213
Hyman, Paula, 208, 216
Hymn to the Earth, 240

I Ching, 324–332; Adornment hexagram, 327; gender construction in, 328–329; Heaven hexagram, 329; *Khwan*, 329; *Kwei Mei*, 331; Meeting hexagram, 331; Mountain hexagram, 327; Stripping Away hexagram, 327
I Speak For Myself, 337
Idaho Chooses Life, xxii–xxiii
Iliad, 174, 176–177, 179–180, 186–187
India: child brides, xxi–xxii; Hinduism, 103–113; Indian Renaissance, 106; modern times and feminist roles in, 113–114

Ingram, Virginia, 3–14
International Conference on Feminism and Orthodoxy, 212
Isadore of Seville, 245
Isasi–Diaz, Ada Maria, 297–298
Islam: art as protest, 349–351; domestic and sexual violence, 346–349; faith-inspired action, 335–352; gender issues and, 71, 95–101, 335–352; intersectionality and civil rights activism, 340–343; special women in the Holy Quran, 359–363; stereotypes, 335–336, 346, 351; voice's voices online, 337–340; women and the mosque, 343–346
Islam is a Foreign Country: American Muslims and the Global Crisis of Authority, 350

Javad, Imam, 100
Jenner, Caitlyn, 321
Jesperson, Maija, 321–332
Jespersen, Maija, 17–36
The Jewish Catalog, 208
Jewish Orthodox Feminist Alliance (JOFA), 212
Jewish Women's Center of Pittsburgh, 216
Jezebel, 76
Joan of Arc, 246
John XXIII, 365
Johnson, R., 289–290
Johnson, Sonia, xxiv–xxv
Joseph, 77–78, 80, 82–83, 91–92
Journal of Baha'i Studies, 158
Judaism, xx–xxi, xxvi; American feminism's influence on Jewish rituals, 213–217; basic background information on, 205–206; Biblical period, 206; circumcision, 214; feminism and, 205–218; gender discrimination, 208; Haredim, 210–211; Hebrew Scriptures, 75–92; impact of feminism on, 208–217; impact on feminism, 207–208; languages, 206; Lilith, 268–269; Modern Orthodox, 211–213; Mosaic, 206; negative experiences, 208; non-Orthodox American, 209–210; Orthodox, 210; post-19th century, 206; Rabbinic, 206, 209; traditions, 206, 215–216; *Yoatzot Halacha*, 210
Judith, 193–194
Julian of Norwich, 224, 228–229
Jung, C. G., 283, 284
Jung, Emma, 284–285

Kalama, Alara, 119
Kalmanofsky, Amy, 40–41
Kelly, Megyn, xxiv
Kemp, Margery, 224–225
Kerouac, Jack, 125
Khan, Fawzia Afzal, 336
Kishwar, Madhu, 106, 113
Kostyuchenko, Elena, 153
Kudaimi, Ramah, 340–342

Lahu, 26–27, 35; childbirth among, 26; creation myth, 27; gender equality, 26–27; religion, 27, 32
Lao Tzu, 322, 324–325
Last Supper, xxvii
Laughlin, K., 325
Le Goff, Jacques, 270
Leeming, D. A., 281, 290
Lemaire, Rita, 60
Lerner, Anne Lapidus, 208
Leroi-Gourhan, A., 21, 24, 34
Liberation Mothers, 246–247
Liberation Theology, 2736
Lilith magazine, 208
The Living Book, 225–229
Living Islam Out Loud: American Muslim Women Speak Out, 336–337
Lost Goddesses of Early Greece, 17
Louhelen Baha'i School, 157
Lundberg-Love, Paula K., 103–114
Lycophron, 189

Machado, Daisy L., 298–299
Magdalene, Mary, 132–133, 135–137, 139, 223

Magnus, Albertus, xx
Makers conference, xix
Mahabharata, 106–107, 114
Makki, Hind, 344–345
Malleus Maleficarum, 48, 66–68
Mandelstam, Nadezhda, xxii
Manninen, Bertha Alvarez, 249, 254–255, 259
Manu, 106
Manusmriti, 106
Marcella, 245
Marinites, xxvii
Mary, 17, 137–139, 361–362; cults, xxvi–xxvii; virginity, 66
Masnavi, M. Hasna, 345
Mattson, Ingrid, 336
McCorvey, Norma, 251
McFague, Sallie, 295
Menstruation: before marriage, xxi–xxii; derogatory language regarding, xxiv
Mental Cycles and Mood Swings, 351
The Messenger of Divine Love, 62
Metzger, Bruce, 9
Miscall, Peter, 45
Mirabai, 110–111
Miriam's Well: Rituals for Jewish Women Around the Year, 216
Mitchem, S. Y., 296
Mogahed, Dalia, 336
Mollenkott, Virginia, 295
Moonrise: The power of women leading from the heart, 247
Moses, 88, 185, 360
Mother Movements, 246–247
Ms. Magazine, xxviii
Muhammad, 96, 223
Mujerista theologies, 293–301
Muslim American Women's Policy Forum, 348
Muslim Anti-Racism Collaborative (MuslimARC), 342
Muslimat Al-Nisaa, 348–349
MuslimGirl.net, 337, 339–340
Muttalib, Sana, 345
Myers, Carol, 44
Mythological: ancestry, 280–283; androgyne archetype, 283–285; birth stories, 281; evangelical limits on accepting, 286–290; human origin, 281–282
Mysticism, 222–223, 229; contemporary, 231–232

Naidu, Sarojini, 114
Nallatankal (The Good Younger Sister), 112
Nast, Thomas, xxiii
Nathan, 76–77, 82, 84
National Council of Women in India (NCWI), 113
Neolithic age, 27–34; art, 18–21, 25; bucharania, 31–32; dyadic imagery, 32–34; female imagery, 29, 31; gender egalitarianism, 26–29, 34; male imagery, 30–32, 35; religion, 29; settlements, 28; technology, 28; writing, 29
Neu, Diann, xxviii
New Zealand, 316–317
Nishmat, 210
Nobre, Patricia, 263–275

Odeh, Rasmea, 341–342
Oduyoye, Mercy Amba, 299
Olney, Richard, 237
On First Principles, 245
On Women and Judaism, 208
Order of Discalced Nuns, 225
Origen, H., 245
Orthodox Christian Information Center website, 146
Osiek, C., 131
Our Inner Lives, xxvii–xxviii

Pagels, 286
Pakistan, 103–104
Palin, Sarah, 256
Paludi, Michele, xix–xxviii
Pamela, 61
Pandith, Farah, 336
Parvey, C., xxvi–xxvii
Patel, Divyaben, 103–114
Patterson, O., 180
Paul, xxvi, 12, 62, 132–133, 286
Pausanias, 192

Pearson, M. J., 33
Perls, Fritz, 280
Persian and Peloponnesian Wars, 178, 184
Peter, xxvii
Pew Research Center, 205
Philadelphia Inquirer, 336
Philip II, 178
Piscopia, Elena Lucrezia Cornaro, 62
Planned Parenthood Federation of America, 250
Plascow, Judith, 214
Plato, 283
Pogrebin, Letty Cottin, 207
Politics, sexism in, xxii–xxv
Pollitt, Katha, 254
Power dynamics, 17–18
Prajnaparamita of 100,000 Lines, 119
The Prajnaparamita Sutra, 119
Pravoslavie.bg, 147
Pravoslavieto.com, 148
Prejean, Helen, 230
Priesand, Sally, 210
Pro: Reclaiming Abortion Rightsi, 254
Pro-life/pro-choice debate, 249–260
Psalms, 77, 84
Purpose of Physical Reality, 160
Pussy Riot, 151
Putin, Vladimir, 150–152

Quinn, Sally, 338
Quran: *Ba*, 359–360; Hazrate Maryam, 360–362; special women in, 359–363; women in, 95–101, 359–363

Rabia of Basra, 224, 227
Radegund of Poitiers, 246
Raja, Darakshan, 347–348
Ranft, P., 243
Rape: Benjamites of Israel, 184; gang, lethal, 183–184, 195; martial, 173–197; procreation through, 181–183; religion and, 173–197; spear-conquest marriage, 189–190; war captives, 176–177, 180–181
Rashkow, Ilona, 39–55, 205–216
Rauf, Mahmoud Abdul, 350–351
Raushenbush, Paul Brandeis, 338
Reconstructionist Rabbinical College, 210
Religion: Christ's teachings vs. organization of, xxv–xxvii; sexism in, xx; subjugation of women and, xxii–xxv
Renaissance Mothers, 246
Reproductive rights, xxii–xxiv, 249–260; race and, 253–254
Review of Biblical Literature, 41–42
Richardson, Samuel, 61
Rig Veda, 104; goddesses in, 104–105
Ringe, Sharon H., 40
Ripley, David, xxii–xxiii
Roberts, Dorothy, 253–254
Rodriguez, Silvia Gureza Fernandez, 59–72
Roe v. Wade, 250–252, 253
Roman Catholic Church, 255–260, 365–367
Roy, Ram Mohan, 106, 110–111, 114
Rubio, Marco, xxiii
Rudy, Kathy, 258–260
Ruether, Rosemary Radford, 294
Rufinus, 67
Russell, Letty, 295
Russia, 145–153; Olympic Games, 151; violence against women in, 151–153; women's rights in, 145–153
Russian Orthodox Church, 148, 151–153
Rutgers University, 339–340
Rwanda, 183, 190
Ryan, R. S., 238–239

Saiving, Valerie, 294
Sakenfeld, Katharine Doob, 40
Samuel, 75, 77–85, 87
Sanger, Margaret, 250
Sarsour, Linda, 336
Sasso, Sandy Eisenberg, 210
Saudi Arabia, xxi
The Scandal of the Male Bible, 7
Scanzoni, Letha, 295
Schneider, Susan Weidman, 208

Schneider, L. C., 301
Schneiders, Sandra, 129
Schulenburg, J. T., 244–246
Scott, Katherine Anne E., 103–114
The Second Sex, 69–70
Second Vatican Council, 257, 365
Self-perception, 10, 13
Seneca Falls Convention, 207
Seneca Falls Declaration, 207
Sex, Politics, and Putin: Political Legitimacy in Russia, 152
Setta, S., xxvi–xxvii
Sexual purity, 61, 66; Christianity and, 66–67; Hinduism and, 112
Shanshan Du, 26
Sharrief, Alia, 349, 351
Shattering the Stereotypes: Muslim Women Speak Out, 336
Shechem, 77–78, 81–82, 92, 189
Shunkai/Suzu, 124
Side Entrance Project, 344
Simons, Nina, 247
Singer, J., 285, 287, 290–291
Slavery, 180–181
Smith, Houston, 314–315
Society of Biblical Literature, 40–41, 45
Solomon, 76–77, 96
Song of Songs, 46, 75, 86–87
Southern Baptist Convention, xxv
Sperling, Valerie, 152
Spirituality, 221–232; feminine, 235–247; passion and, 237
Ssu-ma Ch'ien, 323
Stanton, Elizabeth Cady, 4–6, 13, 39, 42–43, 207, 255, 293
Steinem, Gloria, xix–xx, xxv, 207
Stereotype priming, 13
Stowe, Harriet Beecher, xxiii
Stoyadinova, Maria, 143–153
Suffragette movement, 4, 6
Sukhasiddhi, 224
Sulyman, Remziya, 336
Sung, Z. D., 331
Suratwala, Zahra, 337
Susan B. Anthony List, 256
Swan, L., 241–243
Swindler, L., xxvi
Synod of Whitby, 245

Tablets of Baha'u'llah, 163–164, 168–169
"The Tale of King Udayana of Valsa," xxi
Talmud, 206
Tamar, 75–92; Court Historian, 77–78; early life, 76–77; *HaSopheret*, 84–86; later life, 86–87; rape, 75, 78–84, 189; reading through the eyes of, 91–92; themes of the "master" storyteller, 87–90; writings about YHWH, 89–90
Tao Te Ching, 321–332
Taoism, 321–332; *Ch'i*, 326; Doctrine of Perpetual Change, 325–326, 332; founding, 322; inclusion of women, 325; Perennial Philosophy, 325; yielding behavior, 324–325
Tarnas, R., 283
Taussig, Hal, 40
Thomasset, C., 269
Thompson, Judith Jarvis, 254–255
Thurston, B., 131
Tikkun Olam, 207
Tillich, P., 289
Torah, 214–215, 217
Tracey, Steven, 11
Trible, Phyllis, 5–7, 40, 86
Trogus, Pompeius, 178
Trump, Donald, xxiv
Truong, Nicolas, 270
Tutsi, 183, 190

Uddin, Asma, 335–352, 337
Uma História do Corpo na Idade Média, 270
United Nation's International Women's Day, 127
University of Padua, 62
University of Pennsylvania, 77
Upanishads, 109–110
Upper Paleolithic age, 20–25; dyads, 24–27; imagery in, 22–23; objects, 22–25

Valenti, Jessica, 256
Valerius, 67
Vasistha, Yogi, xxi
Veninga, Jennifer Elisa, 249–260
Venus figurines, 18–19, 23–24
Venus of Brassimpouy, 24
Venus of Willendorf, 18, 23
Verbermacher, Hannah Rachel, 225
Virupa, 224
Villaneuva, Karen, 125

Wallström, Margaret, xxii–xxv
Walsch, N. D., 237
Wang Bi, 330–331
War on Terror, 341
Ward, Mary, 62
Warfare, 173–197
Washington Post, 256
Weems, Renita J., 40
Weil, Simone, 180, 225
Weis, Avi, 213
Wilderness Mothers, 247
Witches, 66–68
Wittbold, Mary, 303–320
Womanist Theology, 273–274, 293–301; impact of racism on, 296–297
Women in the Church, xx
Women in the Orthodox Church, 146
Women's Alliance for Theology, Ethics, and Ritual (WATER), xxviii
The Women's Bible, 4, 39
Woodhull, Victoria, xxiii
Word Buddhism, 127
Written So That You May Believe, 129
Wong, E., 325

Xenophon, 177, 180
Xuel-Sha, 27

Yang, xxi, 321–332
Yeshiva University, 211
Yeshivat Maharat, 213
Yin, xxi, 321–332
Yugoslavia, 177–178
Young, Serenity, xix

Zen Flesh, Zen Bones, 124
Zeus, 27, 191
Zipporah, 88